PRECIOUS METAL

PRECIOUS METAL

DECIBEL Presents
the Stories Behind
25 Extreme Metal Masterpieces

Edited by

ALBERT MUDRIAN

DA CAPO PRESS
A Member of the Perseus Books Group

Designed by Jeff Williams
Set in 11 point Adobe Caslon by the Perseus Books Group

Library of Congress Cataloging-in-Publication Data

Precious metal : Decibel magazine presents the oral histories of 25 extreme metal essentials / edited by Albert Mudrian.
   p. cm.
  Includes index.
  ISBN 978-0-306-81806-6 (alk. paper)
  1. Extreme metal (Music)—History and criticism. 2. Death metal (Music)—History and criticism. 3. Heavy metal (Music)—History and criticism. 4. Rock musicians—Interviews. I. Mudrian, Albert, 1975– II. Decibel (Philadelphia, Pa.)
  ML3534.P73 2009
  781.66--dc22

                2009007835

Published by Da Capo Press
A Member of the Perseus Books Group
www.dacapopress.com

Da Capo Press books are available at special discounts for bulk purchases in the U.S. by corporations, institutions, and other organizations. For more information, please contact the Special Markets Department at the Perseus Books Group, 2300 Chestnut Street, Suite 200, Philadelphia, PA 19103, or call (800) 810-4145, ext. 5000, or e-mail special.markets@perseusbooks.com.

10 9 8 7 6 5 4 3 2 1

FOR JENNIFER AND GROB OF SONIC RELIEF PROMOTIONS

CONTENTS

ACKNOWLEDGMENTS

Decibel's Managing Editor Andrew Bonazelli, who tirelessly edited each Hall of Fame in this anthology *at least* five goddamn times. Senior Editor Patty Moran, who's also copyedited more of these stories than she likely cares to remember. *Decibel* Publisher Alex Mulcahy, who still doesn't understand why there's no Hall of Fame on Sepultura's *Arise* album. Gordon Conrad, who waits in vain for a Judge Hall of Fame. *Decibel* Art Director Jamie Leary, who would still rather listen to *You Fail Me* instead of *Jane Doe*. *Decibel* designers Bruno Guerreiro and Jon Loudon, who've somehow made 6,000-word features look awesome—even over seven-page spreads in the magazine. Mark Evans, who remains cautiously optimistic about the possibility of a Fudge Tunnel Hall of Fame. Scott Hungarter and Lucas Hardison, who are secretly bummed that both Katatonia and Mastodon didn't make the cut for this volume of the book. J. Bennett, who has written half of these Hall of Fame pieces and turned in less than 10 percent of them under word count. Michaelangelo Matos, who has been talking peoples' ears off about us for years. Ben Schafer, who was smart enough to listen. Nick Green, who is still waiting for Refused, Suicidal Tendencies and Rage Against the Machine to return a few emails. Adem Tepedelen, who has obviously been metal longer than any of us. Kory Grow, who is still splicing that Bill Steer interview tape back together. Matt Widener, who owns the corresponding t-shirts for half of these Hall of Fame records. Kevin Stewart-Panko, who owns the other half. Scott Koerber, who'd rather bridge a scene if he could. Chris Dick, who is currently working on a Moog-less mix of *Tales from the Thousand Lakes*. The *dB* online forum, which has created over a dozen unique threads dedicated to just the Hall of Fame. And all the band members who agreed to be interviewed for these pieces—we literally couldn't have done it without you. Everyone mentioned here rules. Thank you.

INTRODUCTION

"What's gonna be the next Hall of Fame album?" As *Decibel*'s Editor in Chief, that's the question I'm asked more than any other by our readers. "What the fuck were you thinking running a cover story on Trivium?" is probably the second-most-asked (though it's clearly the most often posed by Jeff Walker of Carcass).

I conceived the Hall of Fame as a nice excuse for us to revisit our favorite records in the magazine. I'm a pretty nostalgic guy (um, I actually *collect* CD long-boxes) and still regularly spin dozens of LPs that I worshipped in high school. So, the success of the Hall of Fame series suggests that there are actually plenty more dorks just like me who can't really "grow out" of certain albums.

If you don't already know the *dB* HOF deal, it goes a little something like this: Take a classic extreme metal record (as determined by our staff) released at least five years ago, track down and interview *every* band member who played on it, and present them questions exclusively about the writing, recording, touring and overall impact of said album. Sounds easy enough, right? I even often wondered why other publications never pursued similar features until I discovered first-hand what a complete bitch it is to assemble every month. Whether it's tracking down old, long-forgotten-about metal bones or convincing bands to talk at length about past records universally considered more relevant than their current release, it's always a unique challenge to make every Hall of Fame installment a reality.

In fact, I could write another book about all of the HOFs that *didn't* happen. For starters, there's the piece on Faith No More's *Angel Dust*, where we convinced everyone except pumpkin-farming former guitarist Jim Martin to participate. Or the story on Helmet's *Meantime* record—a perpetual source of discontent for *dB* Managing Editor Andrew Bonazelli—that was scrapped after it was revealed that ex-drummer John Stanier made some midnight blood pact with guitarist Peter Mengede and bassist Henry Bogdan to never speak of their time in Helmet again. Henry Rollins won't do a Black Flag one (but Greg Ginn is *totally* available!). Neurosis have refused to partake in HOF stories for *Souls at Zero*, *Enemy of the Sun*, *Through Silver in Blood* and *Times of Grace* (but they're always *really* nice about it when they shoot us down). And features on records from the first Danzig LP (guess who isn't into talking for that one?) to Bolt Thrower's *Realm of Chaos* (I honestly think this is due to sheer laziness disguised as "punk as fuck" attitude on the band's part) have been aborted prior to their completion. So, the next time you wonder, "Why isn't such-and-such record in the Hall of Fame?" just remember, there's an excellent chance we *tried* to get it together.

The "interview *every* band member who played on it" rule—which is strictly enforced—raises another obstacle. As they say, dead men tell no tales, which sadly precludes the likes of *Master of Puppets*, *Vulgar Display of Power*, *Scream Bloody Gore* and several other indisputable metallic classics from induction in the Hall. But—let's be honest—without Cliff, Dimebag or Chuck to weigh in, they would be incomplete portraits at best.

However, the following 160,000 or so words are all about those that *did* make it. As of January 2009, we've inducted 50 records into the *dB* Hall of Fame, so whittling those down to our 25 favorites contained in *Precious Metal* was no small task. Editing and expanding each piece—in some cases, nearly doubling their original running lengths—was perhaps an even greater challenge. So, after five years of countless cold calls, innumerable bounced emails and literally hundreds of hours spent transcribing interview tapes, we bring you this *definitive* collection of untold stories from these genre-defining landmarks. Now go get your dork on.

ALBERT MUDRIAN
Editor in Chief, *Decibel* Magazine
January 2009

CHAPTER 1

HOLY HELL

THE MAKING OF BLACK SABBATH'S *HEAVEN AND HELL*

by Adem Tepedelen

Release Date: 1980
Label: Warner Bros.
Summary: Metal godfathers reborn
Induction Date: September 2008/Issue #47

A s far as Hall of Fame inductees go, the making of Black Sabbath's ninth album, and first with former Rainbow vocalist Ronnie James Dio, easily ranks as one of the most drama-filled. Though the title *Heaven and Hell* was lifted from one of the record's more epic songs, it also accurately sums up the highs and lows the band experienced while making it.

The original Sabbath foursome—vocalist Ozzy Osbourne, bassist Terry "Geezer" Butler, drummer Bill Ward and guitarist Tony Iommi—nearly snuffed the band's already diminishing career in the fall of 1978 with the horrendous, and ironically titled, *Never Say Die* album. Osbourne, who had already left the band once prior to recording *Never Say Die*, was in bad shape and when it came time to do a follow-up in 1979, he simply wasn't up to the task. The band, living together in a house in Bel Air, CA, reluctantly fired their longtime friend and hired Dio.

In retrospect, Dio's hiring seems like a stroke of genius—his melodic, powerful voice and mystical lyrics were a perfect match for Iommi's crushing riffs. Yet, at the time, the change in frontmen would also help further splinter the remaining original trio as they struggled to come to terms with continuing Black Sabbath without Ozzy. One member would leave shortly after Dio was hired and another was so incapacitated by drugs and alcohol he has no memory of recording the album.

Once *Heaven and Hell* dropped in the spring of 1980, however, the "new" Black Sabbath—more melodic, more dynamic, yet still decidedly heavy—was embraced by a younger generation of metal fans who had little knowledge of the band's Ozzy-led past. The plodding dinosaur Sabbath had become in the late '70s was reinvented as a modern metallic juggernaut on Dio's Sabbath debut, still one of the most beloved and influential albums in their entire catalogue. Though he went on to record two other studio and one live album with the band (*Mob Rules*, *Dehumanizer* and *Live Evil*, respectively, which, along with *Heaven and Hell*, have been remastered for *The Rules of Hell* box set on Rhino), Dio's first effort, sparkling with a newfound chemistry and creativity, is clearly that incarnation of Sabbath's finest.

PART I: EXIT OZZY, ENTER DIO

The original Black Sabbath lineup has its last hurrah in a Bel Air mansion and the three remaining original members welcome an American into the fold.

What were the circumstances of Ozzy's departure and was there any question at the time that you'd carry on as Black Sabbath without him?

Tony Iommi: It got to the stage where we were all living in a house in Beverly Hills to write [a new] album with Ozzy. And it just really wasn't happening at all. Ozzy wasn't in a fine state at that time and, to be honest, we weren't too far behind him. We were coming up with the music, but Ozzy just couldn't put his head around getting into doing anything on it. I used to deal with the record company at that time and they'd be asking me, "How's the album going?" and I'd say, "Oh, fine." But it wasn't. Nothing was coming up. Riffs were coming up, but there weren't a lot of vocals on it. So, basically it came to the crunch where we decided that we either had to break up or replace Ozzy.

Bill Ward: There were conversations about getting a new vocalist. On one of the walks I had with Tony, I can remember talking about such things. In one sense I felt extremely uncomfortable, and in another sense I thought that this was the right thing to do. The bottom line was that we weren't getting a lot of work done at all. And I'm not putting that all on Ozzy, either.

Geezer Butler: None of us were happy about Ozzy going. It destroyed me for a bit. We were all unhappy about it. We all grew up together. The whole thing was really hard to do, to part company. It had been coming for four years before that, but none of us could face it. When we finally faced it, we knew that that particular era of Sabbath had to come to an end and Ozzy had to get himself together.

How did Ronnie enter the picture?

Iommi: I met Ronnie at a do that I was at and we talked. I got in touch with him and told him what was happening and asked if he was interested in coming up and having a go with us. Which is more or less what he did. He came over to the house and we did one song with [Ronnie] and knew that this was the way we wanted to go.

Butler: We just thought, let's give Sabbath one last go. We owed Warner Bros. one more album. At that particular moment, we'd been working on a song called "Children of the Sea," though it wasn't actually called that at the time, so we played that to him and he came out with a great vocal straight away.

Ronnie James Dio: I met them at the house that they were using to rehearse in and I purely went up to say hello and get to know them. I had no thoughts whatsoever of being in the band. As far as I knew, Ozzy was still in the band. During the conversation, Tony asked me if I'd like to see the studio they were doing their things in. He, Geezer and Bill picked up their instruments and started to play [what became] "Children of the Sea" and I liked it very much. Tony asked me if I could do anything with it. I said, "Give me a few minutes, I think I can knock something out." We pretty well wrote the song that quickly. I think that's when Tony decided he wanted to make some music with me.

At the time, how well did you know each other's music?

Iommi: I really loved Ronnie's voice when I first heard it with Rainbow. I was well aware of what he'd done before.

Butler: I may have a heard a [bit] of it, but I didn't have any of the albums. I think I'd heard one track, or something.

Ward: The two songs I'd heard by Ronnie, one was called "Love Is All (Butterfly Ball)," which is a bit of a pop song, but I thought Ronnie's voice sounded very nice. And then I'd heard "Stargazer," with Rainbow, and I thought Ronnie had done an unbelievably good piece of work. I love the song.

Dio: Of course I knew the singles [Black Sabbath] had—"Paranoid," "Iron Man," "War Pigs"—all these songs got played on the radio stations I was listening to. So I knew of the music, but I hadn't rushed out and bought the albums and listened to Sabbath. It was a little bit foreign at the time for me. I think maybe because the music I was making certainly wasn't that heavy. And I was involved perhaps in a lot more melodic writing, too.

Ronnie, did they ever play you any demo/studio recordings of versions they may have rehearsed with Ozzy?

Dio: I think a lot of the ideas they had were things that they had instrumentally put down as backing tracks. How many of them Ozzy did, I have no idea. I'm assuming none of them and that's probably why Tony was a bit dissatisfied. I'm sure that some of those things were ideas they'd had, but didn't come to fruition during the writing process [with Ozzy]. But of them, the only one that I'm definitely sure of is "Children of the Sea," because it's the first thing I heard and I know it was something that they had been working on. From there everything seemed like it was starting from scratch.

Butler: We'd had about five or six ideas already done that Ozzy hadn't bothered to sing on. And as soon as we played them to Ronnie, he was able to come out with ideas straight away for them. It was just exactly what we were missing—somebody with enthusiasm. He was really into what we were doing and just felt like part of the band.

Since Ronnie's voice and style are so distinctive, was there ever consideration as to how he would fit in with Black Sabbath?

Butler: Well, we didn't even [initially] think about it being called Black Sabbath. Personally, I was hoping that we would come out with a total change from then on, because we'd always said if any one of the original [members] leaves, we'd change the name of the band. And I was all for changing the name of the band. Ronnie didn't care one way or the other. But we owed Warner Bros. an album and Warner Bros. convinced us to do a Black Sabbath album.

Iommi: What we did originally was deal with what we had in front of us: making a really good album. Because if we didn't do that, we weren't going to be doing anything. So, that was our major thing, to do the album. We thought we'd deal with the rest when it comes. Ronnie's such a totally different singer to Ozzy, of course, which was good in a lot of ways. I'd looked to find somebody with a different approach and a different voice. I think it was good to go with somebody different. And, of course, it was good for us for writing the music because it gave us somewhere else to go.

Dio: When you have to replace someone who's been some kind of an icon, it can be very difficult. But knowing that Ozzy and I were completely different people, completely different artists, there was never, in my case, any [pressure] to be what he was or make this band anything other than what it became.

Ronnie, did you at the time consider the scrutiny you'd face when the album was ultimately released and you went out on tour?

Dio: It wasn't like that for me; it never has been. It's like, "Here's a challenge, let's have a go at this." So, we just began songs and I wasn't overwhelmed or overawed by any of that at all. It's just not in my nature. For a start, I'd just gotten done playing with one of the greatest guitarists and musicians [Ritchie Blackmore] I'd ever known. Rainbow was huge, especially in Europe. I thought I was coming from a very good place.

When you began writing together in Bel Air, how involved was everyone in the process?

Iommi: We had a studio put onto the side of the house, in what was originally the garage, where we had all the gear set up. Inside the house we had a small set-up in one of the rooms, with little amps, and we used to sit in there with Ronnie and play fairly quietly with a little kit of drums. And we'd sort of jam around. We had a few ideas of riffs to play Ronnie from the off and that's what we'd do. We'd play something and he'd sort of chip in and we'd build the song from around that. Like "Heaven and Hell," that sort of came from nothing—just sitting in the house jamming along.

Dio: When the decision was made that Ozzy was not going to be in the band and I was, a few days after that, Geezer went back to England. So the writing process became myself and Tony, with Bill. Bill did have a few musical ideas, but Tony and I were certainly going in a different direction than Bill had been before.

Ward: I felt like I had less to do in the band as a helper, or as a lyricist, or wherever I could help—not only with drums. I tried to be helpful wherever I could. But Ronnie was very strong in the sense that when he got together with Tony, they were able to write very well together.

Butler: At first I was quite involved. We both were, me and Bill. Well, the whole band was, because we carried on the way we had always written. We jammed around, came up with some stuff and then we'd carried on with that idea. About three or four songs into it, I had some traumatic personal problems back in England and, on top of all the change with Ozzy [leaving], I had to get out of there to clear my mind. So I went back to England for a few months.

Did the new writing arrangement provide a spark of inspiration, because **Heaven and Hell** *saw Sabbath go off in a whole new direction?*

Iommi: Oh, absolutely. It opened me up more, because it pushed me more. It gave me a lot more opportunity to try different things because of the different way that Ronnie works with his vocals and also the way the writing had changed. Where with Ozzy we'd write a riff and Ozzy would sing the riff—like "Iron Man," where he'd sing the sounds that I'm playing—but Ronnie's approach was different. He wouldn't sing so much over the riff; he would sing in separate places.

Dio: I always wanted to make music that was so incredibly heavy with a lot of melody in it. And what better place could you find to do that in than [a band] with Tony and Geezer and Bill? Especially with Tony, whose riffs are sometimes scary. [In Sabbath] you get this giant block of sound coming at you and space to do what you have to do. For me, it was the perfect scenario, absolutely perfect.

Did the addition of a vocalist who wrote all his own lyrics alter the chemistry of the band?

Butler: It was definitely a relief for me when Ronnie came in and could write lyrics because I was sick of writing lyrics at the time. And it was good to have expanded by bringing in keyboard player [Geoff Nicholls], as well, from the very start of writing. That sort of gave an extra dimension. It freed a lot of space up for me as a bass player.

Dio: It was always understood right from the get-go that I would write the lyrics. Geezer said, "Thank god you've got to do this now." I think he was just so absolutely relieved that that was a chore that he didn't have to deal with anymore.

Ronnie's lyrics were a marked change from previous albums. Was that ever a concern with any of the original members?

Dio: I was never questioned about what I was going to write or what I did write. *I* questioned more than they. Sometimes I would say, "That's a bit jolly, isn't it?" But no, there was never a problem on that album, not one question at all.

Butler: No, not at all. He took [the lyrics] more in the fantasy theme, but the song "Heaven and Hell" was still very Sabbath. It wasn't about falling in love or going down to the disco, or anything like that. It stayed on that same sort of mystical theme. I was more political, and he stayed away from politics. I always liked listening to Ronnie's lyrics. They were so different than what I could do.

Ward: Ronnie was a new energy that came into the picture. He came to the band with a very strong energy. He's very direct. He knows what he likes to put together, which is very good. He's very confident in that sense. I saw that whatever [Sabbath was], I saw [us] kind of moving away [from that] a bit. For me, there were some lyrics that were absolutely brilliant, and there were some lyrics that [I was] kind of like, "Oh, I can't believe I'm participating in that." That's been a focal point for me throughout the years. I've always had a little bit of a red flag with some of the lyrical content that Ronnie uses. And I'm only saying that in the context of when I'm playing with him. It's not a put-down on Ronnie.

Was there a conscious effort, or perhaps even subconscious, to make Sabbath Mk II a different beast to differentiate it from the Ozzy era?

Iommi: I think it becomes different because you bring somebody in with a different voice and a different look. Everything was different about Ronnie. It pushed us into a different look and sound altogether.

PART II: AND THEN THERE WERE TWO . . .

Butler departs to sort out his personal problems, leaving only two original Sabbath members, Ward and Iommi. Guitarist/keyboardist and fellow Brit, Geoff Nicholls of Quartz (a NWOBHM band Iommi had produced) is brought in and the band continues writing.

How did Geoff Nicholls, who became the band's longtime keyboardist, get involved during the making of the album?

Iommi: [After Geezer left] we needed someone to come and play bass, but we didn't want anybody coming in that we [didn't] know, because it wasn't a permanent situation bass-wise. We just wanted someone that would understand that and come in and just jam along with us.

Dio: Well, I think there's a couple of things probably. I'm sure a lot of this was really traumatic for Tony, as his life had been turned upside down. He was starting over in a new band without a manager. It was a really volatile time for him. He was in L.A. and he needed some companionship as well. Someone who he was comfortable with, familiar with, who was also a musician, who might even be able to come and play a bit—play parts when Tony was soloing. Geoff was a really good guitar player, too—so much like Tony it was unbelievable. It really helped Tony a lot, and Geoff had a lot of ideas and he was very positive to the whole project, which made the rest of us feel positive as well.

Ward: Geoff Nicholls was very much a bonus, and very much a prominent part of *Heaven and Hell*. I don't know whether he's gotten any credit yet, but the guy needs to be credited. He was very much a big part at that point. He was there in the initial writing of the song "Heaven and Hell."

So, did Geoff Nicholls play bass until Geezer came back?

Iommi: Actually we had somebody Ronnie played with before in Rainbow, [Craig Gruber]. He came in and played bass for a while and Geoff went on to play keyboards.

Dio: I had suggested [Craig] and he was in L.A. He came up and started to play with us. He obviously wasn't Geezer, but he was a great bass player, so we decided we would use him for what we were going to do.

Did you have all the songs pretty well arranged and finished before going to Criteria Studio in Miami?

Iommi: We were still writing in Miami. "Die Young" came up in Miami and one or two others. It was an ongoing thing. When we moved from L.A. to Miami, we moved into a house and did the same thing [as in the Bel Air house] basically.

Dio: The [songs] were pretty well set by the time we got down there. I think we wrote a couple of tracks, or perhaps just one. But most of the things were [ready].

Why bring in producer Martin Birch after recent Sabbath albums had been self-produced?

Iommi: Ronnie had worked with Martin before and I thought it would be good to have somebody else to come in that [we] could work with. And it was a big relief for me, too, as with Geezer and the lyrics. I used to have to sit there to the death doing the producing side of it. I had no option; I was sort of pushed in the deep end. But once Martin came in, I could relieve myself a bit [of that responsibility] and sort of think about what I'm playing, instead of thinking about the other side as well.

Dio: I think it was actually Tony's suggestion to call Martin. He just asked me, "What was Martin Birch like?" and I started going off on Martin. He's a brilliant engineer, a great guy—the kind of person I knew they would love. But I wanted to make sure that I handled this all with kid gloves, because once you start bringing in all your own people, no matter how much you believe in them, it makes it look like you're trying to take control, and god knows I've been accused of that enough times.

What kind of producer was Martin? Was he hands-on with everything and very heavily involved?

Iommi: Oh no. It would have been fairly difficult to come in and try to control this lot. [*Laughs*] At the same time, he could suggest stuff. It was like having another mind on it. We'd done all the arrangement side of it and I don't remember him getting involved with that at all. He was more involved with the technical side and pushing you a bit: "Do another solo, or do this or do that." It all seemed to flow very well. We all got on well and any ideas or advice, we welcomed. If he did have a suggestion, we would try it.

Dio: Martin is a brilliant engineer. That's what he does. He's not stupid musically, but he's also smart enough to know that when it's working, you don't fix it. And it was working. You don't tell people who have done this so well for so long how to change something that they've been busting their asses on. It just doesn't work with this band.

Butler: Well, it was great to be able to sit in with somebody apart from the band and work on my sounds. Before that, we used to bore each other, all sitting in the studio waiting for each one of us to get our sounds and everything. So it was great to work with just one other person and not having like three or four people suggesting doing this and doing that.

Ward: I can just remember him laughing. I can't remember anything else. This is where my part in this interview gets real rocky. I really was a real mess.

PART III: THE DAMAGE DONE

Already dealing with alcoholism and drug addiction, Bill Ward loses his mother during the making of *Heaven and Hell*, further continuing his descent. He continues on, but alcohol-induced blackouts virtually erase his memory of this time.

What were your recollections of how Bill performed in the studio?

Iommi: I think on *Heaven and Hell*, Bill was OK. Yes, he did have problems with drugs and alcohol, but I think playing-wise he was fine. He used to have his moments, of course, like any alcoholic, I suppose. But I thought he held it all together well.

Dio: Well, Bill was Bill. Bill has always been Bill, sober or not sober. He's always been a really special person. He's one of the sweetest guys on earth, such a caring person, big heart. He was always that. He had some problems with doing too many illicit things, so that's the only Bill that I ever knew until [about] 10 years ago when I saw him again and realized that he was clean and sober. [During the recording] he was conscientious, he played really well on the album. When it came time to play, he didn't mess around.

Butler: Ronnie was probably the straightest one, but we were all heavily into various substances at the time. Bill had the worst drinking problem. He used to do a lot of drink and drugs, but at least he could still function. He'd still be capable of playing his drums. So we didn't give it that much notice, I suppose. It was just Bill; he'd been like that for years.

Ward: I don't think I did a very good job. It's not bad. Looking back and listening, there are a lot of areas where my energy did not function. I listen back to the sound and I know that I could have opened up my drums much wider and gotten better sounds, like I do now. I have to give all the credit to Tony, and my loyalty and respect to the man. Just his strength kept me going. There were a lot of times when he would give me the nod, you know, the famous nod, because there was a lot of times when I was just in blackouts. I didn't know that I'd played on certain things. When I eventually got sobered up, which was three years later, I listened to *Heaven and Hell*, and, to this day, I cannot remember doing some of the songs. I can't remember what studio it was. I can't remember playing it at all. I have no memory.

At the time did you get the sense that Bill was unhappy with the direction or personnel?

Dio: I didn't. I really, really didn't get any idea about that. I don't think he ever broached the subject. You know, he and Ozzy were very, very close and I'm sure [Ozzy being gone] was somewhat of a problem for him. It was a band that the four had created and suddenly there was an interloper in there. Luckily we got along very, very well. I can understand any feelings that he would have had that way, but he never broached them to me. He may have to Geezer or Tony, but never to me.

Iommi: Not at the time, no. [Ozzy's departure] hit us all, because Ozzy was the only singer we'd had and it's not something you're all eager to get rid of. We all felt bad about it. We really didn't have any choice. We couldn't have carried on as the way it was—even Ozzy would admit that. Bill half-accepted that and I think later he thought about it, and I think he went through some different stages in his life as far as not liking the way it was going. But, at first, he certainly did.

Ward: I really, really missed [Ozzy] and I didn't know how much I missed him at the time. I had a mixture [of emotions]; it was both heaven and hell, really. I had a lot of mixed feelings, but I felt very transient myself. With Sabbath—the original band—I felt like that was my home, that's where I belonged, that's where I lived. And there was a change going on and I still felt very transient with it. I was trying to get used to everything. I didn't realize that my addiction to alcohol and drugs was ripping me away from myself, let alone from the band. I didn't even realize what was going on until much later, to be honest with you.

How much recording did the band do in Miami when Geezer was away?
Iommi: I can't remember. We did a fair bit there, quite a bit there.
Dio: Everything was done in Miami except for "Neon Knights."

Was Craig Gruber still playing bass then?
Dio: We started recording with Craig, and then, when Geezer came back, he put a whole different slant on those songs. It became something totally different, in such a positive, good way. When [Geezer] played the parts, they came so much more alive.

What was involved in getting Geezer back?
Iommi: You just have to let people sort out their personal problems. He had to sort them out himself and he needed the time to do that. When he was ready to come back, we had a phone call—I called him—and we got him back, which I was very glad about. We didn't see carrying on too much without him. We knew he'd be back at some point.
Dio: Tony asked me what I thought and I said, "Absolutely, I think it's very, very smart if we're still going to be Black Sabbath. Obviously we'll be a whole lot stronger with three-fourths of the band still intact."
Butler: Tony and I kept in touch and I'd gotten myself sorted out and I said, "If you want me back, then I'll come back." Everybody wanted me back, so I came back over. They'd already recorded quite a bit of the songs in Miami and I just came in and completely redid all the bass on them.

Geezer, what were your impressions of hearing Heaven and Hell in the studio upon your return?
Butler: It was incredible. I loved it. It was the first time I'd ever heard a Sabbath album with fresh ears. As soon as I heard [the songs], I knew exactly what to do with them.

PART IV: BLACK SABBATH: THE NEXT GENERATION

Before the album is completed, the band attempts to return to England for "tax purposes," only to find that they have returned too soon. They quickly leave the country and decamp to the Channel Islands, where "Neon Knights" is written, and shortly thereafter recorded at Studio Ferber in Paris. *Heaven and Hell* is then mixed by Birch and the band in London at Town House Studios.

After it was mixed, but before it was released, was there any trepidation as to how the album would be received by longtime Sabbath fans?

Ward: I definitely know I had that fear. I didn't know which way it was gonna turn. I didn't know that it was a good album. I was concerned a little bit about the soft edge on it, coming from some of the vocals, some of the lyrics. I was just wondering how it might be received.

Iommi: I felt pretty confident with it, because I thought what we were doing was great and I just really hoped that the fans were going to stick by me. There's always gonna be somebody who's not going to like it as much. You're gonna lose some and you're gonna gain some, which is what happened. We gained a lot more people that ordinarily wouldn't have listened to us in the past.

Dio: We knew that it was a good album, but there was some trepidation: What are [people] going to think about it being Black Sabbath without Ozzy? Like any artist who has just delivered a baby and has to chuck it out on the street and let it grow up really quickly, we were certainly concerned about what was going to happen to it.

What song or songs that you recorded for **Heaven and Hell** *did you really feel distinguished this version of Sabbath from the Ozzy era?*

Iommi: I thought "Heaven and Hell" itself was great. I like "Neon Knights"—a lot of them on that album.

Dio: "Heaven and Hell" without a doubt. That's the bulwark of that album and it's the title for a reason. That album is just packed with so many good songs. "Children of the Sea" is a great example of what people wanted to hear from that band at that point. "Lady Evil," another one. "Die Young," a great, great song that went in so many different directions. They're all wonderful, but certainly those four stand out.

Ward: I loved "Heaven and Hell." [It] was and still is a classic metal song. I thought that song was absolutely brilliant. I love that song.

The song "Heaven and Hell" feels iconic because it's the title track and because it seems so particular to this lineup.

Iommi: Exactly, yeah. We would never have done it with Ozzy. It would have been a terribly different approach. It wouldn't have worked like that. It was written as it was for those members. None of those songs would have worked with Ozzy.

Dio: It's a big epic kind of song—something that you didn't hear from Sabbath before—with a lot of melody in it and a lot of wonderful choral and orchestral changes inside of it. I think right away that divorced us from what had come before.

Ronnie has been quoted as saying that this is his favorite of all the albums he's played on—how does it rate with you?

Iommi: Yeah, I think it's a great album. It's difficult for me to say if this is the best album or some other [Sabbath] album is the best. I think it's a great album, I think *Mob Rules* is a great album as well.

Dio: It was the entire process. It took such a long time to get from writing "Children of the Sea" to fulfilling that ambition by releasing the album and having it be as good as it was, despite all the pitfalls. To me that will always be why this album was the best one for me. The songs to me are second nature; they're great songs. If they weren't, we wouldn't be talking about this album.

Were you aware that **Heaven and Hell** *was the first Sabbath album for a new generation of metal fans?*

Dio: So many people of that generation have said, "That's the Black Sabbath that I grew up with." I think it was just at a very good, fortunate time. That album was released when a new generation of fans were coming along [who] embraced [it] for the good album that it was and didn't make any judgments about it, like, "Where's Ozzy?"

Iommi: Oh, absolutely. 90 percent of the bands out there mentioned that it was the first Sabbath album they got into. It certainly got people like David Grohl and Nirvana into those albums.

Butler: None of us knew that at the time, but today so many people have come up to us and said that they love the *Heaven and Hell* album and that era of Sabbath. It's amazing.

Ward: One of the things I never realized about it until I started talking to guys in some of the newer bands like In Flames, is that they actually used *Heaven and Hell* as a sounding board, a jumping off place. They don't really mention the years of Sabbath before that. But they certainly mention *Heaven and Hell* as being the early stuff that they listened to, and how influential it was in their music.

RAINBOW CONNECTION

Q&A with bassist Craig Gruber

Had Geezer Butler not opted to rejoin Black Sabbath in the middle of recording *Heaven and Hell*, Craig Gruber, a longtime friend and bandmate of Dio from his Elf and Rainbow days, would have been his replacement. We offered Gruber, who now crafts custom-made basses for his company Infinite Metal Werkz, the chance to share his brief experience in the band during the making of *Heaven and Hell*.

—Adem Tepedelen

How did you find out Sabbath needed a bassist?

Craig Gruber: Ronnie had called me about it. At that point I wasn't really enthused about it, because [Black Sabbath] hadn't done well in a long time.

How did they audition you?

Gruber: We met and spent a day together at the [Bel Air] house. They had a studio set up in the garage, but we played in the house with the smaller [set-up]. They showed me a couple of songs and then we went out to the garage with the full gear and had a full blow. It was awesome. We locked right in. It felt right.

Did they at that point ask you to join?

Gruber: Tony was the first one to come forward and ask me to join the band based on how quickly I learned the music. I was a studio musician at the time, so you could show me something and I would play it right back to you. Tony and Ronnie offered me the position in the band as the bassist, and then we worked out a financial arrangement. I was paid from like the second week on. I was on a salary.

How far along were they in the writing process?

Gruber: When I came into the picture, I think there were about five songs already written. The first song they showed me was "Wishing Well" and the second song they showed me was "Children of the Sea" and we worked those up pretty fast.

How much recording did you do before Geezer returned?

Gruber: Tony, Bill and I went in and laid down the rhythm tracks. We had them really well rehearsed and we worked very, very well together. We were in there for two weeks, that I remember, and literally had five or six tracks down that we were gonna keep. Then we took a week off and I think that's when Geezer had gotten back in contact with the band. I didn't think he was going to be gone forever. I had no intention of staying with Black Sabbath forever; that was always Geezer's position. I didn't look at it like [I was] Geezer's replacement. Anyway, we had a meeting and there was a discussion that Geezer may be interested in coming back. And then the recording stopped. They said, "There's no sense going forward with the recording if Geezer's going to come back."

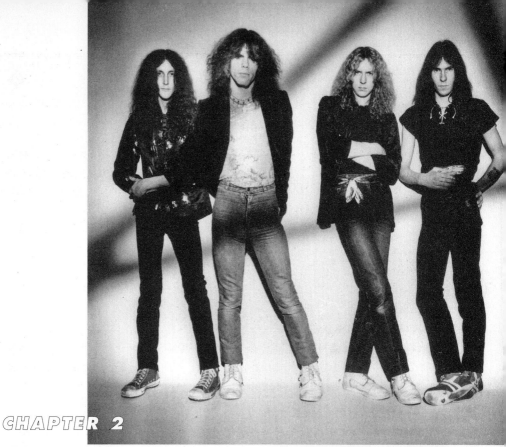

CHAPTER 2

A RARE GEM

THE MAKING OF DIAMOND HEAD'S *LIGHTNING TO THE NATIONS*

by Adem Tepedelen

Release Date: 1980
Label: Happy Face
Summary: A NWOBHM/proto-thrash cornerstone
Induction Date: December 2007/Issue #33

I t's a stretch to call Diamond Head's 1980 debut, *Lightning to the Nations*, "extreme" metal. In their era, the über-influential New Wave of British Heavy Metal, Diamond Head—four teenage mates from Stourbridge, England—were well-respected practitioners of a burgeoning new form of metal that was brash, raw and relatively fast. But extreme? Hardly. Diamond Head are being inducted as much for their ultimate impact and influence as the quality of

Lightning, a self-released effort which featured a meager original vinyl pressing of just 2,000 copies.

If metal's Book of Genesis begins with the creation of Black Sabbath, who then begat (and still continue to) many other influential and important bands, Diamond Head—admitted Sabbath disciples themselves—begat a couple of bands, Metallica and Megadeth, that eventually became two of the major players in metal's New Testament: the extreme era. And since it has been well established that *Decibel* won't enshrine any of the first three Metallica albums in the Hall of Fame because bassist Cliff Burton isn't alive to participate in the discussion, the importance of Diamond Head's *Lightning to the Nations*—four of its seven songs having been recorded by Metallica—to the extreme metal pantheon becomes that much more crucial.

Further adding to the mystique of this nearly 30-year-old album is the fact that, despite the hype that surrounded the band when *Lightning* was released—they were being touted by the U.K. press as the next Led Zeppelin before they even had a record deal—Diamond Head ultimately sold very few records and were plagued by bad luck and ineffective management. In 1980, what seemed like the promising debut of an ambitious young band that was destined for great things ultimately turned out to be their most consistent and solid effort. Two subsequent major label releases on MCA—*Borrowed Time* and *Canterbury*, both now out of print—were scattered and probably overly ambitious, and by 1984, the original foursome of guitarist Brian Tatler, vocalist Sean Harris, bassist Colin Kimberley and drummer Duncan Scott had split up.

Lightning to the Nations, originally recorded in one week as simply a demo to get a record deal, however, remains the band's finest moment and an essential proto-thrash classic.

People look back at the NWOBHM and connect the dots between all the bands that came from the U.K. during the late '70s and early '80s, but did you feel at the time like something special was happening?

Brian Tatler: I did think something special was happening. There were a lot of young bands around our age—19, 20, 21. I can remember when Def Leppard were on the front cover of *Sounds*. Once they got noticed and signed, that really gave us a kick start. We already thought we were good, but once another young band like Def Leppard got signed it gave us an even bigger boost. Growing up watching the gods like Led Zeppelin and Deep Purple, you kind of aspire to be like them, but you almost think, "I'll never be that good and play to 100,000 people and have an album at the top of the charts." But once Def Leppard got signed, it was almost like a light bulb went on and we thought that we could take [it] the whole way.

Duncan Scott: There were a lot of kids forming bands at that time, getting up there and giving it their all. I always kind of wondered what I was doing in Diamond Head. But I figured, if I can do this, any kid on the street can get up there and do [it].

Colin Kimberley: There was definitely a feeling of a movement. We'd had three or four years of punk rock and new wave in the late '70s, and there was sort of a resurgence of bands like us who had grown up listening to metal, and we were sort of influenced by punk to an extent. But we still wanted to play heavy metal. There were a lot of bands coming up of the same age as us, doing the same thing. Perhaps it was manufactured by the music press, who like to create the idea that there's a scene happening, but, yeah, we felt there was a movement at the time.

Sean Harris: We followed Def Leppard and Saxon early on and bought all the Samson, Witchfynde and Angelwitch singles. We'd get a hold of one and give it a listen. But although we felt a scene happening, I suppose, it was like part of the post-punk revolution going on. We thought we were more in the tradition of Sabbath, Priest, Zeppelin and Purple. We thought we were just a rock band. We did relate to what was going on, but we didn't see ourselves as part of it.

Were there bands from that era you looked up to at all?

Tatler: I don't think we were particularly inspired musically by the other bands from the NWOBHM. We were maybe looking to bands like Sabbath, Judas Priest, AC/DC.

Kimberley: The already established bands from the '70s—Sabbath, Zeppelin, Deep Purple—that influenced us. Also more contemporary bands [at the time] like AC/DC, Judas Priest and UFO. We were big on all those at the time.

What was happening musically in the area where you lived?

Tatler: There were other bands around our age that have all disappeared long ago. Witchfinder General were one of our main rivals. There was also Zeitgeist, Split Image, Effigy—we'd go check them out. We'd stand at the front with our arms folded and see if they've got any good riffs. Stourbridge did have probably half a dozen bands, but Diamond Head made it the biggest. We were the only band that signed to a major label and played odeons and things like that.

How old were you when **Lightning** *was recorded?*

Tatler: 19.

Scott: 19. We were just four kids that got together and said, "Let's form a band." And to actually come up with an album like that . . .

Kimberley: I was 20. The oldest at the time. I turned 20 in November 1979 and we recorded the album in March 1980.

Harris: 19. We didn't know shit.

The songs on Lightning seem very well developed and complex for such a young band.

Tatler: We didn't have a rule book for how to write a song. We just kind of went on instinct. We decided that if we wanted to have a song that's nine minutes long like "Sucking My Love," then nobody's going to say—we didn't have a manager at that point—"You can't do that" or "You can't put that on a single." We'd just do these songs that felt right to us, and it didn't matter if they had five verses or they changed time signatures or there was a little bit in the middle that was really tricky to play. We just kind of did what felt right. We were trying to do something new. There also did seem to be a race to be the fastest around that time. I can remember when I first heard "Exciter" by Judas Priest and thought, "Wow, that's fast," and we wrote "Helpless" not long after that. We thought we should write something as fast as ["Exciter"] or even faster if possible. We definitely wanted to write something that was the fastest.

Kimberley: Sean and Brian wrote all the songs, and originally our songs would be one guitar riff all the way through the song. We sort of realized that we needed to be a little bit more interesting than that. And I think we've probably taken the influence of Black Sabbath more than anybody. We also listened to bands like Rush as well, who were pretty complex. We just found [writing longer songs] interesting. Why just do a two-minute song, when you can do a seven-minute song with lots of changes in it? We didn't have the musicianship or skills of a Rush or Led Zeppelin, so we sort of did it in our own crude way and, I suppose, came up with something that was original.

Harris: It was just what felt right at the time. The songs sort of followed the lyrics a lot of the time and I was usually dreaming, [*laughs*] so the song would sort of have to dream and evolve and weave. Which is what they did. They took a long time [to write], some of them.

How much recording had the band done before you recorded Lightning?

Harris: We'd done demo tapes at little four-track demo facility in Kidderminster.

Tatler: We always did a lot of home recording. We did stuff in my bedroom, from pretty much when we started, with a cassette recorder. But in 1979 we went and did a proper demo at the four-track studio at a place in Kidderminster. That was like five pound an hour and we managed to record five songs in five hours, and we thought that was pretty efficient. We did that twice. We already had "Am I Evil?," "Shoot Out the Lights," "The Prince" and "Helpless," and probably did demo versions of those songs before anyone was actually interested in us. We probably paid for that ourselves. We were making demos and constantly trying to record songs and learn the art. I was as interested in learning how to write songs as much as anything else. We didn't understand what production meant, but we knew we liked good songs and we had some great bands to influence us, so we wanted to be great if we could.

You'd already put out a couple of self-released singles in '79 and '80, so what was the impetus at this point to record an album? How did that come about?

Harris: I think it was originally to try and get an album deal. It was suggested to our manager at the time, Reg Fellows [who passed away at the age of 62 in 2005], by my mother, Linda, who was his secretary. Being a businessman, I think he thought, best to just do it ourselves. He either knew of, or had been in contact with, Muff Murphy, who was the owner of the Old Smithy Studio in Worcester. We'd done a few demos at that point, a few different things. And I think he just thought that they didn't pay off really.

Tatler: They thought if we recorded [a] whole album, then [Reg] could go to the labels and say, "Here's the album, do you want to sign the band?"

Kimberley: I think we thought that if the recording was good enough, a label may release it as it was. It would save the label from having to fork out loads of money for us to record an album. As it happens, it didn't really work out like that.

Who paid for the recording?

Kimberley: Reg put up all the money for that. I have no idea how much it must have cost.

Tatler: For some reason, the sum of 4,000 pounds has been bandied about a couple of times over the years.

After having previously just done demos in a small four-track facility, what was your impression of the 24-track Old Smithy?

Tatler: It was pretty impressive. It had big monitors that made everything sound fantastic. It was the first time I'd heard stereo guitars. I'd do the track and [engineer Paul Robins] would say, "Now do another track exactly the same." When I heard it back panned left and right, I thought it sounded fantastic. I'd never heard anything like it in my life. So, that was the way forward for me.

Scott: I just found myself in this claustrophobic drum booth that was a bit like a big phone booth. I could just about get the kit in. You didn't want to breathe too deeply because it seemed to be airtight and it was carpeted wall to wall. There was a little window to look out. I just remember it as being claustrophobic and scary, but I think at that time I was happy just to get the tracks down. It was a very strange situation to be in because my mum and dad always said that I had to get a proper job and to find myself in a studio actually recording an album was quite scary. There's so much of it that I listen to now and go, "Oh, I'd never play that like that now." I've always thought that things could have been played better on my part.

Kimberley: It was our first time in what I would say was a real recording studio, a decent-quality studio. It was exciting and certainly intimidating. You get to hear what you *really* sound like. There's no chance to bluff your way through.

Harris: I wasn't intimidated by anything in those days. Not really. It was just really exciting. I didn't feel any fear. It was just an opportunity to strut your stuff.

Were the songs pretty well rehearsed?

Harris: Oh yeah. We didn't have to write anything [in the studio]. The only thing we wrote was the backing for the solo in "Am I Evil?" We rehearsed all the time. Our manager had a factory and before that, Colin's dad had a factory and we used to just go there every time. On the weekends we'd go to Colin's dad's factory and then, when Reg got involved, we'd go three nights a week. Because the songs kept having to be fine-tuned all the time and rearranged.

Scott: I think the rehearsals paid off. For however twee or unacceptable or whatever we are considered in certain places, we were well rehearsed. It's easier when you go in to record your first album because you've been doing those numbers for so long—you have years to rehearse and 18 months on the road. So, you get into the studio and you know what you're doing.

You were recording fairly complex and longer-than-average songs. Did this require multiple takes?

Tatler: Most of the stuff was done pretty much live. We didn't require very many retakes. The drums, bass and guitar went down at the same time and I think we double-tracked the guitar and Sean would do the vocal. Even some of Sean's vocals were done in one take. We didn't spend a long time laboring over details.

Kimberley: There weren't a lot of takes. We only had a week to do it. So it was pretty much just a case of going there and laying it down as quickly as we could.

Sean played rhythm guitar onstage in the early days. Did he also play on the album?

Tatler: I don't remember. He used to play the intro to "Am I Evil?" [live] and then I would play the lead. On the album, I may have played both parts just for ease. It was always recognized that I was a better player, so he always left it up to me, I think.

Kimberley: I don't think so. At the time he played guitar onstage a little bit, but my instinct is to say no, he didn't play anything. He's a pretty decent guitar player now, but at the time I don't think he really played much.

Harris: We laid it down together. I used to play guitar in them days on all the early stuff. Brian probably overdubbed some of the stuff, but I'd be playing on "Am I Evil?" and "The Prince" and "Lightning to the Nations." It was only later on that I dropped the guitar when I wanted to run around and be a rock star.

Did you only record the songs that ended up on the album, or were there leftovers?

Tatler: We just recorded those seven songs. There was nothing extra. We had written a lot of songs and it seemed to me that those seven songs were the best that we'd done up to that point.

So you recorded and mixed all seven songs in a week?

Kimberley: We actually went back and recorded "It's Electric" again. I can't remember if we recorded it [the first time] and didn't like it, so we went back and did it again, or if we didn't have time [in the first session]. But I seem to remember that we went back a couple of weeks later for one or two days. I think the production on it sounds a little bit different.

Your former manager Reg is listed as the producer on the reissues of Lightning. *Was he actually involved with the recording?*

Kimberley: He was a businessman, so he'd be running his business during the day and then coming down in the evenings, or whenever he could get time. He certainly wasn't involved musically.

How involved was the engineer, Paul Robins, in the production?

Tatler: He would get the drum sound and mix it and stuff like that. I don't remember him being that creative.

Kimberley: He was a very laid-back guy and I don't think he was particularly into heavy metal. Some of the time I can definitely recall him sitting back and reading the newspaper while we were playing. In all fairness to him, we didn't really know what we were doing in the studio. He probably added more to it than we remember. He did come up with suggestions and ideas.

"Am I Evil?" is the song from this album that most people know, thanks in no small part to Metallica's version. What are your recollections of writing and recording it?

Tatler: That song's got fabulous dynamics. Something I've realized over the years—it's very hard to write songs with dynamics like that. Even now I don't really know how to do it. It's just something that came naturally at the time. It's just something that occurred back then and we managed to record it. Somebody once said to me, "What you ought to do is write another 10 'Am I Evil?'s." And I thought, that's easy for you to say. I simply can't rewrite "Am I Evil?" You can take it apart and put it back together, but it's what it is and you've just got to leave it be. There's magic occasionally in the air. And the bit in the solo when I finally worked out the finger-tapping bit and how the track moved underneath it, going from A to F to A-sharp to F-sharp and back to B, was [written] in the studio. Probably with Paul Robins' help, if I remember correctly. I was probably still messing with that solo right up until we recorded the actual track. I was so proud of that solo, and I still am. I play it exactly the same now as I did then.

Scott: Brian came up with the [main] riff; at the same time I was sitting at home listening to some Black Sabbath, and I noticed the way that Bill Ward played a riff back to front and then switched it back into time and then turned it back to front again. We kind of put those two things together. I think it's just by chance that my idea and Brian's worked together like that. And what a gift, getting Metallica to pick up on that.

Kimberley: It's one of the few tracks I specifically remember recording. The bass was slightly out of tune when we first recorded it, so I needed to redo it. I distinctly remember sitting in the control room with the bass plugged into the mixing desk, and I played it all the way through in one take, which was quite a feat, I thought.

Harris: It's such a benchmark. I still think for what it is, there ain't many songs better. The lyric is amazingly demonic, isn't it? It's probably a bit like the "Stairway to Heaven" thing. Somebody on your shoulder telling you what to write.

Was "Am I Evil?" written in one session or did it evolve?

Kimberley: I can think of various different versions that we did, even after the album had been released. We probably even changed it slightly then.

Harris: It [originally] had a different introduction and different parts. It wasn't really until the lyric was done that it took real shape. It took about a year before we put the "Mars" intro on there. We had this awful intro for a while. It was really bad. We were sort of peddling that for six months until we realized how shit it was.

Tatler: I don't know why I thought of [using Gustav Holst's "Mars" as an intro]. I just thought it would make a great start. It's dramatic. It draws you in.

Did Sean write all of the lyrics? There seems to be a difference between songs that are more fantasy-based, like "Am I Evil?," and those that have more typical rock 'n' roll subject matter.

Tatler: He did write all the lyrics. "It's Electric" is the oldest song on the album. That was maybe where he was at in his head at that time, maybe '78 or something. Some of the early songs, he was thinking about being a rock star and being onstage. A lot of the lyrics seem to be about that. And then later songs like "Lightning to the Nations," he started to discover sci-fi, at the end of '79.

Harris: Yeah, I wrote the lyrics. It was about arriving, you know. Being something, hopefully something sparkling, something new. The fantasy aspect was just sort of trying to reach beyond. I used to like Ronnie James Dio's fantasy lyrics, thought they were quite cool. And Milton, stuff like that. It's the two sides of me, I suppose, battling it out for supremacy! [*Laughs*]

Did it this "demo album," once it was finished, then get shopped around to labels?

Harris: As far as I'm aware, yes. But for some reason, we had lukewarm receptions to it. I don't think they got it. When we spoke to people, they always seemed to want to make us something that we weren't. There was always somebody that seemed to want to meddle.

Tatler: [Our management] just made some acetates to take around to record labels, but nobody was biting. Nobody was particularly interested. They didn't see the potential in it.

Kimberley: Possibly it wasn't being presented to the [labels] in a professional way. In a way that they wanted to be approached. Partly they maybe just didn't get it. With hindsight, it's easy to look back and say, "Yeah, it's a classic album," but at the time it was just another New Wave of British Heavy Metal album. Some new band was coming out with a new album every week. But record companies weren't in tune with what was going on in the grassroots heavy metal scene. It wasn't a scene that was that popular with the music business. A lot of this was sort of dealt with by management, so we didn't have direct dealings with the labels. Certainly [management] would be saying such-and-such a label is interested, or we've heard so-and-so is interested, but it never seemed to lead to anything. It was very frustrating. I can't put my finger on what the problem was, whether we were too amateurish or not good enough, or they didn't like the music. It baffles me to this day, really.

So, without any serious interest from a major label, you just decided to self-release it?

Tatler: Because we were gigging a lot, it was decided that we'd press a thousand copies and sell them at gigs and through mail order. There was an ad in

Sounds that ran for four weeks. [Our mail order] was run out of Sean's house. Lars Ulrich ordered one. That's how he got his.

Was it common to self-release an album on your own label at the time?

Tatler: We'd just had punk rock, which was kind of "do it yourself, back to basics," but it wasn't common for [NWOBHM] bands to do their own album. A lot of bands did their own singles. I don't know why we did it; I think it was just because we had the opportunity to. It probably wasn't going to cost much. There was no artwork or anything to pay for. Just press a thousand copies, sell them at gigs and Bob's your uncle. We sold all of the first thousand and then printed another thousand, this time with a printed label on, so it actually identified the songs.

Kimberley: There were other bands that were releasing stuff on their own labels. Mainly singles, more than albums. This is something that came from the punk rock movement. Suddenly you didn't have to have a major label to go out and record a single or an album and have it pressed yourself and promote it yourself. This was very much the "do it yourself" attitude. Get off your ass and do it, rather than wait for some record label to do it for you. It was definitely the attitude at the time.

The fact that it had absolutely no info on the plain white sleeve—just the band's signatures—probably added to the mystique.

Harris: I agree. We didn't intend to do that. It was a budget thing. The fans were allowed to interpret it. It was open to interpretation—like a book without a cover. I think that worked toward the mystique.

Kimberley: I think that's true. But if it hadn't been for Metallica, it might have disappeared into obscurity. Nobody might ever have heard of it, apart from the people who were there at the time.

How quickly did you sell through the first pressing of a thousand?

Tatler: Not long, I don't think. Maybe a few months. Something like that.

What was the critical reaction at the time?

Harris: That was great. Paul Suter's review [in *Sounds*] was pretty good. And the public loved it. We were sort of a bit overawed by it; we didn't realize what we had. Because we were ambitious, we were always looking ahead instead of looking behind. We'd lit the fuse and it was burning.

Tatler: I can only remember *Sounds* reviewing it. It was a pretty good review as a whole. We sent one off to Geoff Barton [at *Sounds*] and he loved it, especially "Am I Evil?" On the whole, it was very well received. The fans thought it was great. We thought it was great. We just had trouble convincing the record labels to sign us. I think there was a couple of labels interested, but they wanted to make changes and they wanted to do a single deal or two singles. We didn't want to do singles. We wanted to be like Zeppelin and not do singles and just be a big album band. We were sort of forced into doing singles. It never really felt natural.

Kimberley: We always got very positive press, actually. There were a few writers that latched onto us. It always frustrated us, in that respect, that it took us so long to get a record deal.

Scott: I was the member of the band that, when the criticisms came out, was always getting the barracking. There was a time when I was sort of labeled the weakest link. Which I can understand listening back. I accept their criticism. I just wasn't a studio drummer. I liked it out there live, giving it hell and delivering the goods.

When you started getting the Led Zeppelin comparisons at the time, did that put extra pressure on the band?

Harris: It wasn't good. It seemed for some reason that we were being hyped. It didn't feel too good at the time. People always wanted to typecast you, even back then.

Tatler: Unfortunately, we didn't live up to that expectation. That's a bit of a high yardstick, isn't it? We were flattered that journalists thought that highly of us, but I couldn't see [the comparisons] myself. We might have been good, but I didn't think we were going to eclipse Led Zeppelin's legacy.

Explain the situation with Woolfe Records, who released Lightning in Germany. *Was this authorized by the band?*

Kimberley: I think that came out in 1980 or '81, pretty much contemporary with the original release. It did have a cover, with a really cheap photograph of a map on fire. That was certainly one of the first versions of the album that came out.

Tatler: As far as I know, our manager just sent the tape off to this guy in Germany who ran Woolfe Records. And we never saw them again. They just disappeared. And, according to Reg, he never received any royalties or statements or anything. It was a bit of a strange move, if you asked me.

Who first started referring to this record in a plain white sleeve as Lightning to the Nations?

Tatler: I think it was originally known as *Lightning to the Nations*, but it was also known as the *White Album*, as well, because it was just in a white cardboard sleeve. I think on the second pressing it said *Lightning to the Nations*.

Kimberley: If it was picked up by a label and released properly, it was going to be called *Lightning to the Nations*. That was always the intention. And then afterwards it got referred to either as *Lightning to the Nations* or the *White Label Album*. I tend to refer to it as the "demo album" a lot, as well, because it was a demo album. That's what it was meant to be: a demo for the record companies.

Harris: I think the title came about when Reg had interest from Woolfe Records. He did this dodgy deal, one of many dodgy deals. They sort of needed a title for it. I think *Lightning to the Nations* sort of summed up what it was about. It was about arriving like a bolt out of the blue. I think that's how it got the title.

Why has Lightning *been so sporadically in and out of print and in so many different configurations?*

Tatler: I don't know really. If Diamond Head had been properly managed and not dropped by MCA, it could have stayed in circulation. Or it could have been licensed properly. Once Reg was [no longer managing Diamond Head], it was probably his decision to recoup some of the money he initially put into the band. So he was just doing any deal he could and it ended up on small labels like FM Revolver, Metal Blade. Any deal he could get around the world, it seemed like he would do a version of that album, with maybe a different title. It's come out as *Am I Evil?*, *To Heaven From Hell*, *Behold the Beginning*, all with different covers. It wasn't our property, so we couldn't look after it and give it the care that a band deserves. It was just licensed to whomever wanted it. We used to go around [to Reg] and say, "We want that album." But he would say, "Well, I paid for it, it's mine." And once you look into copyright law, it says that if you pay for the recording, you own it. It seemed weird that we'd done all the work and wrote the songs and recorded it, but because he paid for it, he owned. But that's the way of the world.

Kimberley: I don't feel too happy about it. It's been very exploitative. Lots of little record labels that I've never heard of are releasing the album almost on a continual basis. We've never been consulted about it and I think it's a great shame. There's one or two that were done a little better than others—with sleeve notes and stuff—but I generally feel pretty pissed off about it. It's pretty sad, really, when you think that there are other people making money off of it that had nothing to do and weren't there at the time, who don't respect it or anything. It sours it all a little bit.

Harris: It was who owns the rights. There was some sort of thing going on with Woolfe Records, who says he's got the rights. Between him and Reg, they'd conjured up all these different ways of exploiting it. And, of course, other people have seen the loopholes and exploited it as well. We weren't very good at our business in the early days. It's been a shame, because it's taken the shine off it.

Behold the Beginning *[Metal Blade, 1987] was one of the first reissues of* **Lightning,** *and it was critically hammered for its altered sound. What happened with that?*

Kimberley: I think Brian worked on that remixing it. I can't remember how different the mixes are, to be honest. When these things come out, even if I'm given one, I tend to not listen to them.

Tatler: Because Reg had sent off the quarter-inch masters to Woolfe Records and never got them back, it was decided that we would remix the 24-track album at the Old Smithy and put it out as *Behold the Beginning.* So, I went along to try and keep my eye on it. But it kind of got messed around with, rather than trying to make it exactly the same as the original. It was almost like we were trying to make it better than the original. So a few little things were done to it. And it does to me sound a bit naff. In a way, I wish we hadn't done that, because the tapes did come back eventually. Lars Ulrich tracked them down. He got someone at Phonogram Records in Germany to knock on the guy's door and get the tapes off him, and they eventually found their way back to me. I've got the tapes now. The original survived and it's still in existence. It's just that back then in 1985, Reg thought that the tapes had been lost forever and that it would be a good idea to remix the originals—soup them up a bit. But, of course, people don't want that. It would be like remixing the first Metallica album. It wouldn't be right, would it?

Have you been happy at all with any of the reissues?

Harris: They've all been messed with. I'm not quite sure what I'm listening to these days.

Are you ever consulted with the new versions?

Kimberley: No. It's just a case of whoever's got the tapes. I never know if it's the ex-manager who's got the tapes simply relicensing them. Who does it? I have no idea. Who makes the money from it? I don't know.

Is it strange that an album that initially had such a limited release has ultimately had such a huge impact?

Harris: You stop thinking about it as the "demo album" and you start thinking of it as a precursor to something else. And you get to realize that it was what it was. A fuse had been lit. Over time you learn to appreciate what you were doing. The sheer raw energy, enthusiasm—it was just on fire.

Kimberley: We didn't realize at the time that if we'd have churned out albums similar to this one that it would have been a great thing. Thrash metal didn't exist at the time and we didn't feel that we'd created a new sort of style of heavy metal; it was just sort of the best album we could do at the time. [Later] we just wanted to do what we thought of as being better albums. We kind of moved away from [*Lightning*]. Many of the songs on the album we stopped doing live because we were sort of bored with them. It's only with hindsight that it's been regarded as a classic album. We look back on it with an understanding of how influential it was, but it's weird being influential on other bands without having sold millions of copies of the record. It's very surreal.

The story goes that a young Lars Ulrich—pre Metallica—was so impressed with the copy of **Lightning** *he ordered from you that he flew to England to hang out with the band in 1981. What did you think of him at the time?*

Harris: We thought he was a weirdo, of course. [*Laughs*] But he was nice enough. He got on with us all. He stayed here for a week at the foot of my bed, playing "It's Electric" every night, keeping us up. It was that sort of thing that made us realize that maybe we had done something a little bit extraordinary.

When were you first aware that he was in a band that was heavily influenced by Diamond Head?

Harris: I don't remember anything much until he sent us a copy of the "Creeping Death" single. He used to keep us informed by sending us stuff. I did have a word with his management once when they wanted to cover the songs. They had to get permission to do the lyrics and stuff.

Tatler: He sent me the "Creeping Death" EP in '84, but it was only on Music for Nations Records and I presumed at the time that they were still quite a small band. They were part of the thrash movement. I probably still looked down on them and thought, "They're coming along, they've made a record; I'm flattered that they covered one of our songs." But the penny hadn't dropped that they were gonna conquer the world.

Kimberley: I remember seeing Brian after I'd left Diamond Head in maybe 1983 or '84 and he said, "Hey, do you remember Lars Ulrich, who came over? He's in a band and they've recorded 'Am I Evil?'" When Lars came over and stayed with Brian and Sean and came to a few gigs, I never remember him mentioning that he played drums or was in a band.

What did you think of their version of "Am I Evil?"?

Harris: I thought it seemed quite different than what we were doing. I always thought our version was better. It seemed like they were taking what we were doing and inventing something new from it.

Kimberley: I thought it was pretty cool. It was quite flattering. I heard stories secondhand that much of their set in the early days consisted of Diamond Head songs. It's weird to think of a band in California playing these songs that we'd been playing to an audience that didn't know who Diamond Head was, but just got off on the songs because they were good songs. It's quite nice, really.

When you first heard their originals, did you hear your influence? What specifically did you hear that you thought they got from Diamond Head?

Harris: I can hear it on the albums. It shows in the arrangements. They go under the skin of what we did. There's a lot of it in there. There's even a bit of me in there at times. They just kind of turned some of our riffs upside down, stuff like that.

Tatler: I think bits of it were obvious. "Seek and Destroy" was a little bit like "Dead Reckoning" or "Sucking My Love." But it didn't annoy me or anything. I knew they were influenced by Diamond Head, so I presumed they might sound a little bit like us. But James was such a different singer than Sean that they didn't really sound that much like us anyway, because they didn't have that kind of vocal. It was much more aggressive and angry, and less melodic. They sounded tight and powerful, but they seemed to lack the melody that we had at that stage.

Scott: I'm very, very flattered that [Lars has] said that I was his favorite drummer. When he came over and visited, he used to come to the rehearsals and songwriting sessions and that. So I think that's perhaps where our songwriting style rubbed off on him.

Kimberley: I don't think we can take all the credit for who Metallica are. Probably my favorite Metallica track is "Master of Puppets" and I've always thought of that as their "Am I Evil?" to an extent. I don't know if anyone else would think that, but I sort of feel an influence there. If I see early photographs of Metallica, they almost even look like Diamond Head with their Flying V guitars and the hairstyles. Apart from the fact that they've covered so many songs, the influence is undeniable.

*After **Garage Inc.** came out in 1998 with the four Diamond Head covers, that must have been pretty amazing.*

Scott: I was flattered. It was very complimentary. It was quite a tribute to have a band of that size actually covering our numbers. It was very strange. One minute he was this little guy from America taking up all of my legroom in the back of the car on a way to a gig, and then, years later, he's a multi-millionaire. Metallica has been very much a life-support system for Diamond Head. They've kept Diamond Head in the press for all those years Diamond Head was gone.

Harris: They couldn't have paid us a bigger compliment. They got it and they were carrying on and giving us the legacy that we deserved. I thought that was amazing. They were giants by then. It was good to be remembered in the right way.

Does it bother you, though, that a lot of younger metal fans simply know you as the band that influenced Metallica?

Tatler: We influenced them and you can't get away from that. We didn't sell that many records in our day, whereas they have. We're always going to be tied in as an influence on Metallica. You never see a write-up on Diamond Head without Metallica being mentioned; it's the hook line. You can't get away from it.

Kimberley: If it hadn't been for Metallica, and Megadeth to a lesser extent after them, we wouldn't be having this conversation. We would have just been another band that was around 20-odd years ago who disappeared, and that would be the end of it. I think it's cool that [*Lightning*] is still remembered. If nothing else, we have the satisfaction of knowing we did something that's lasted and people still enjoy. I'd rather it was remembered in some way than being buried and forgotten.

CHAPTER 3

PROCREATION OF THE WICKED

THE MAKING OF CELTIC FROST'S *MORBID TALES*

by J. Bennett

Release Date: 1984
Label: Metal Blade
Summary: Black/death metal genre touchstone
Induction Date: February 2007/Issue #28

O f all the classic albums inducted into *Decibel*'s Hall of Fame thus far, none has had a greater influence on the death metal and black metal that succeeded it than Celtic Frost's *Morbid Tales*. Recorded and mixed in a single week in October 1984 at Caet Studio in West Berlin, Germany, during the waning years of the Cold War, the album was the work of vocalist/guitarist Tom Gabriel Fischer (a.k.a. Tom G. Warrior), bassist Martin Eric Stricker (a.k.a. Martin Eric Ain) and session drummer Stephen Priestly, all three of whom had done time in the Swiss proto-black/death outfit Hellhammer. Within days of Hellhammer's self-induced demise, Warrior and Ain formed Celtic Frost and immediately plotted the musical and aesthetic trajectory for the fledgling band's first three albums. Produced by Horst Müller (who had also engineered Hellhammer's *Apocalyptic Raids* EP), Frost's debut featured such merciless classics as "Procreation (of the Wicked)" (later covered by both Sepultura and Enslaved), "Into the Crypts of Rays" (later covered by Marduk, the song detailed the sordid exploits of serial child murderer/rapist Gilles de Rais, who also fought alongside Joan of Arc in the Hundred Years' War), and "Nocturnal Fear" (a Lovecraftian night-terror later covered by Dimmu Borgir, the song's lyrics were perhaps influential on the likes of future Swedish goth-mongers Tiamat and Morbid Angel guitarist George Emmanuel III). With the Celtic Frost power-axis of Warrior and Ain reunited and storming stages with a combination of new and vintage extremities, we figure it's about fucking time we gave *Morbid Tales* some props.

How did you make the transition from Hellhammer to Celtic Frost?

Martin Ain: When Hellhammer started out, it was pretty much a local project with people who had just started to play their instruments. It wasn't a real band with skilled musicians. When I joined for the *Satanic Rites* demo, I was 15, and the lineup was always changing. It's not like we were known for our skilled musicianship or accomplished songwriting, but we were working hard. We were working like five days a week on our music, rehearsing our asses off to get to a point where we could master our instruments and get out of them what we wanted to. When we did the *Apocalyptic Raids* album, we realized that we were sort of stuck with the abysmal name we had made for ourselves as musicians with the first couple demos. This was very much in the tape-trading days, when thrash metal became popular through tape-trading, which was an underground thing. We realized that if we wanted to be taken seriously, it would probably be helpful if we used a different name, because a lot of people were like, "Oh, it's Hellhammer—they can't play." We wanted to disassociate ourselves from that.

The other reason was that the black metal scene was rising at that time with Venom's *Welcome to Hell* and *Black Metal*, and there were a lot of die-hard fanatics jumping on the bandwagon who didn't have a clue about Satanism, but they were completely dedicated. They were you know, "totally evil," so that was something that bothered us. And other bands that were using the term "Satan" or had evil-sounding album titles because that's what was selling at the time, like Mötley Crüe's *Shout at the Devil*, for example. They were about as Satanic as Stryper was Christian. It just seemed like an American showbiz thing to us. So we disbanded Hellhammer and formed Celtic Frost.

Stephen Priestly: It couldn't go any further with Hellhammer, music-wise. To be honest, none of us could really play an instrument. [*Laughs*] That's the truth.

Martin and I had a band before called Schizo, and we didn't have any instruments at all. We were just like a poser band, looking as hard and as aggressive as possible. We made pictures before we could even play instruments. I only started playing drums about a year before we recorded *Morbid Tales*. On "Into the Crypts of Rays," I had the double-bass thing, and I worked my ass off to be able to do that. As you can hear at the end, I have some problems at the end with the timing, and that's just because I couldn't play at all back then. Even Tom, he had a wah-wah pedal, and that was the way he made his guitar solos. We couldn't really play— it was more about the image. I was 17, just a kid, and back then, I was more into music like Journey and Boston and stuff like that—even though I liked Venom and all this New Wave of British Heavy Metal stuff a lot. And as you can hear on the record, it was definitely influenced by bands like Venom and Cirith Ungol. Tom went to London and came back with some records, some of that British heavy metal stuff, including the very first Def Leppard seven-inch and the very first Venom single—and said he wanted to do something like that, but even heavier. He wanted it to be the most brutal stuff people had ever heard. When he played me the first demos from Celtic Frost, I was blown away, so we made the first songs, like "Into the Crypts of Rays" and stuff like that. The amazing thing was that Martin and Tom had the vision for the first three records already in their minds. They knew exactly what they wanted to do, and to be honest, I was just a drummer—even on the record sleeve, it says "session drummer." I couldn't do anything to put myself into it, because it was their vision.

Tom Warrior: To this day, people say that Celtic Frost was just Hellhammer renamed, but this is not true. Every detail about Celtic Frost was different. Martin and I were so shocked at how the Hellhammer EP came out and, given our ambitions to become better musicians, we knew there was a lack of quality in the vehicle called Hellhammer. The night we formed Celtic Frost, we approached everything differently than the band Hellhammer had done, and we set out to form a new band in accordance with these targets we had set. So it was much more complex than two guys just changing the band name. We really wanted to form a different band. Hellhammer was all about extremity; Celtic Frost only had extremity as a basis. Our ambitions had outrun Hellhammer—we wanted to be able to do whatever came into our minds. We wrote down all the things we hated about Hellhammer and changed everything around.

The approach of Hellhammer and early Celtic Frost was similar to that of punk rock. Were you listening to much punk music at the time?
Warrior: I loathed those bands, to be quite honest. There was only a very small group of punk bands that I had respect for at the time—for example, Discharge, which to me, was a revolution, much like Venom. When I heard the first

two Discharge records, I was blown away. I was just starting to play an instrument and I had no idea that you could go so far. Discharge totally opened my eyes. And to me, they were unlike other punk bands—they sounded more like metal. But I'm a music lover, and at that time, punk was extremely raw as far as songwriting was concerned, and I always missed the music component in punk. Metal at least had a melody and a song structure—a lot of the punk at that time didn't have any melody. Although early Celtic Frost has been compared to punk many times, I personally was not into punk at all.

How did you choose your stage name?

Ain: Yes, my real name is not Martin Eric Ain; it's Martin Eric Stricker. In Hellhammer, I wasn't only Martin Eric Ain; I was also "Slayed Necros." Tom was not only "Tom G. Warrior"; he was "Satanic Slaughter." We dropped those names because we started to think of them as ludicrous, but to pick up such a name in the first place was of course trying to become a different personality than we were in daily life. The name Martin Eric Stricker was defined and chosen by my parents, my family, and this was exactly what I was trying to get away from. At the time, I was starting to read about occultism, religion, philosophy and systems of practical magic, like the Golden Dawn as taught by Aleister Crowley. I also came across Kabbalah, a form of Jewish mysticism that deals with how to decipher the Bible through numerology. And of course, the Hebrew alphabet is different than the Western alphabet; every letter can be a word in itself, or can change its meaning, but every letter has a number to it. So the way the letters are used, they have different numbers and different meanings. This was used to make sense out of the word of God, the Torah, and the Pentateuch, the word of God given to Moses. I realized that the numerological meaning to "Ain" was zero—it didn't have a clearly defined meaning, and zero could mean everything as a whole, as a circle, or as something that has been accomplished, but at the same time it could also mean that something has been nullified—and I really liked that, because you couldn't put a proper meaning to it. It was exactly what I was looking for—something that I could put myself into and make into my own, rather than a name predefined by somebody else.

Warrior: The night Steve Warrior and I formed Hellhammer, we were on one of our typical nightly hikes through the forest in the farmlands surrounding the city of Zurich. We used to spend all night hiking the forest together hatching out plans. We already knew we were going to call the band Hellhammer, and we wanted to have radical names. We were basically kids, so we didn't have much self-confidence because we hadn't achieved anything yet in our lives. We felt embarrassed about our last names; we thought we couldn't possibly play radical music with household Swiss names. Bands like Venom had adopted radical stage names, so we thought we had to do that to in order to be fully radical. Steve Warrior's English teacher's name was actually Warrior, and we thought it was such a great last name that we both adopted it.

What do you remember most about the recording sessions for Morbid Tales?

Priestly: We had no money at all. We were driving from Switzerland to Berlin in a green, loaned VW bus with all our stuff in it—the drum kit, the Marshall stacks, the whole thing. I guess it was Martin, Tom, me and Rick "Lights," the driver. Back then, East Germany was still the DDR [Deutsche Demokratische Republik], and you had to drive through the Wall to get to Berlin, which was a strange feeling. When we got there, we recorded and mixed the whole album within a week. I remember that the studio was very small, with very cheap equipment and the record company was a pain in the ass. They would come down, like, "What sound is that? You can't do that like that." As you know, we had this horror song on the album called "Danse Macabre," and they said, "No way—you can't do that! It's not a song!" But that was actually the most fun song to do on the whole record. [*Laughs*] That's about all I remember. As you know, it was a long time ago. The whole thing happened so fast. They made the Hellhammer record with Bruce Day on drums and within half a year, we recorded the first Celtic Frost record.

Warrior: It was a very difficult and liberating time all at once. It was difficult because the only proper record we had, not counting demos, was of course the Hellhammer EP, which had been ripped apart in the media at the time. Hellhammer was nowhere near the myth it is now—the band was loathed by the media and the record company as well. They told us that we could not ever record anything like that again. So we knew we had to prove ourselves once and for all with Celtic Frost, or that would be it. Nobody would give us a third chance. It was already a miracle that they gave us a chance with Celtic Frost after the Hellhammer EP. At the same time, we were aware that we had made a huge jump forward as far as songwriting. We knew this was a completely new project, which filled us with optimism and tons of energy. Above everything was the lack of funding—we had only six days to record and mix the whole album.

Ain: I remember we had about four days to record *Apocalyptic Raids*, but for *Morbid Tales* we had an entire week, so we were like, "Wow!" We went to the same studio in Berlin that we had recorded *Apocalyptic Raids* in, with the same engineer who knew our basic approach to music at that point, which made it easier. We were well prepared, because we had really analyzed the recording process and the mistakes we had made with *Apocalyptic Raids*. We already had the first three Celtic albums worked out by that point—what they would be called, what they would be about, even a couple of the songs. We even already knew that we would have the rights to the Giger painting for the cover of *To Mega Therion*.

What was it like being in Berlin while half the city—and half of Germany—was under Communist rule?

Warrior: We were in West Berlin; there was of course the wall dividing Berlin at the time. In order to get there from Switzerland, you had to drive through what was Communist East Germany, the DDR. It was just like you've seen in the Cold War movies—there were guards with machine guns, Russian tanks, barbed wire—and they would take your passport for like 20 minutes and scrutinize them. We had already done that trip by train when we did the Hellhammer EP, but we drove in a van for *Morbid Tales*. It was a fitting background for what we were doing, I think, because it was very unreal and very serious. In the early '80s, everybody talked about the possibility of nuclear war between East and West, and we were in that scenario. If war broke out, the part of the earth we were in would be obliterated. We could actually see the Wall from the studio, and if you turned on the radio, you could hear Russian broadcasts. It's a scenario that's hard to imagine nowadays, but it was very real and very intimidating at the time. West Berlin was an island in the middle of East Germany, and in that little island is where we recorded this album.

Ain: It was a completely different place than it is right now. At that time, Berlin was a one-of-a-kind place. You couldn't compare it to anywhere else in the world. We already knew the experience of traveling through Eastern Germany—which was basically a military dictatorship—when we recorded *Apocalyptic Raids*. Every time I went to Berlin in those days was a unique experience. Everything was open 24 hours, there was a big underground and alternative art and music scene—Einstürzende Neubauten was basically starting their career at that time. And I think some of that stuff sort of inspired us later on for *Into the Pandemonium*. But of course, the most intense experience we had in Berlin was during the recording of *Vanity/Nemesis*, because we were actually there when the Wall came down and the Iron Curtain fell in 1989. History was literally happening—you could grasp the feeling in the air. It was an entire nation in euphoria, and the whole world realizing that the Cold War was basically over.

Was it understood from the beginning that Stephen would be a session drummer on the album?

Priestly: Not really. They wanted me to play on the record, and then after the record was finished they wanted to do some touring and stuff like that. Back then, I was more into Boston and Journey, like I said, I didn't really want to play music like the *Morbid Tales* stuff. That's why I quit and then Reed

[St. Mark] came. I didn't tour with them until later on, during the horrible *Cold Lake* times. [*Laughs*]

Warrior: We hoped he would join us on a permanent basis, but he didn't want to. His dream was to do something really commercial, like House of Lords—keyboard-oriented heavy metal. But he was the only option we had at the time, and he was a friend, so he agreed to do the album as a session drummer. We of course hoped that the music and the album, and the possibility to actually record in an international studio and have an international record deal with us, would convince him to join. When we went back to Switzerland after recording, to our astonishment, he said that he wasn't going to join. So we were left standing there without a drummer after finally having made a mark with something that was at the time better than Hellhammer. It totally ruined everything. We had a huge tour offer for Europe and we had to turn it down because we had no drummer. It took us maybe six or seven months to find a drummer because Switzerland had no heavy metal scene to begin with, and especially no extreme metal scene.

What was it like working with Horst Müller?

Warrior: At that time, it was sensational. He had worked with funk bands and all kind of things. His father was a conductor in an orchestra, so he had grown up with serious music. There was at the time a dance/disco band called Supermax that combined disco music with reggae, and they eventually got more serious and became one of the early world music bands. They were quite big at the time—they did platinum albums in Europe—and Horst had worked with them. He had also already engineered the Hellhammer EP. We came in there as little kids, totally radical, and told Horst, "You have no idea what Hellhammer is supposed to sound like; we're producing this ourselves." Of course, we had never been in a professional recording studio, and we had never produced anything. And the results went accordingly; even we realized that the production of Hellhammer's EP was awful. But we realized that Horst had a lot of capability, so when it came time to record Celtic Frost, we called him up and said, "We've learned our lesson. We're not stupid—we want to give you a chance and we want to actually listen to what you proposed during Hellhammer. We want to let you produce the album." Horst was great—he was at that time very easy to get along with, very professional, very experienced. He had built the studio, so he knew it inside out. It was just a perfect situation.

Priestly: Horst did some backup vocals, too [on "Dethroned Emperor" and "Procreation (of the Wicked)"]. The funniest thing about him was that he was famous in the '60s and '70s for working with bands like Can. I didn't know that back then—I didn't even know those bands back then—but I found out later on.

I guess he was on drugs the whole time, but back then we were so naïve and enthusiastic that we didn't see that.

Was the intro, "Human," something you had conceived of before you went into the studio?

Ain: Yes, we had the idea before we went into the studio—we wanted to loop a scream and make it perpetual. We also wanted to use it as an intro for the live shows. A regular human scream would never last that long, so we wanted to loop it and make it sound like a scream from hell, like how you would scream if the pain was everlasting.

Warrior: We had talked about it, but we were basically still laymen, so we had no idea how we could put it together. So we told Horst what we wanted to do, and he proposed how to do it. But as I said, we only had six days to do everything. If one thing had failed, we would've gone over budget or had to go home. So, in hindsight, it's a miracle that tracks like "Human" or "Danse Macabre" came out the way we wanted them to. We couldn't rehearse some of those parts, you know? I have no idea how we did that in just a few days, especially given our lack of experience. But therein lies one of the strengths of Celtic Frost to this day: Martin and I usually visualize certain pieces of music down to the last detail without even touching an instrument.

Priestly: It's basically just Martin and Tom yelling and we put on a whole bunch of reverb and distortion. I remember them both in the vocal booth together, and it was fun to watch, because Tom had to sing later on and his voice was already gone.

You had two guest musicians on **Morbid Tales**—*vocalist Hertha Ohling and violinist Oswald Spengler. Did you know them beforehand?*

Warrior: We had absolutely no connection at the time. I mean, you have to realize we were absolute nobodies, and we weren't familiar with Germany, either. We told Horst on the first day that we wanted to record with a female singer and a violinist, and of course he had a lot of connections, so it proved relatively easy for him to get these musicians. But nobody knew what we were gonna do, because it wasn't really known in metal to use musicians like that—especially not in extreme metal, a fledgling area of metal that hadn't even been defined yet. So Horst hired these people and we tried to explain to them what we wanted. None of us could write scores, so we just had to describe it. We weren't even good enough on our instruments to be able to play, in detail, what we wanted them to do. And everything had to happen rather quickly, because we didn't have a lot of time.

Ain: I think the violinist was related to Horst Müller, and I think we got the female singer through [executive producer] Karl Walterbach; she was either the sister of a girlfriend he once had, or even maybe the girlfriend he had at the time.

Priestly: I guess Hertha was a singer from the Deutsch Opera Choir. The funny thing was that we couldn't write [musical] notes or anything, so we had to hum the melodies for her. She was a professional musician, and we were standing there like idiots, humming the notes for her. We had to do the same thing for the violin player [Oswald Springer] on "Danse Macabre" and "Nocturnal Fear." As you probably know, Tom and Martin did that later on almost every record, with a female singer who spoke on the Frost vocals. I guess we were the first band to do that in that genre. And now you see Lacuna Coil and bands like that, with female vocals.

Warrior: On all Celtic Frost albums, except for the brand-new one, it was extremely difficult to work with classical musicians. At that time, extreme metal was something totally fresh. Heavy metal in general was totally disrespected in classical circles, and all these musicians came into the studio with huge prejudice, looking down their noses at us. And of course [the fact that we were not] experienced musicians at the time made it even more pronounced. Most classical musicians would say, "You cannot do that," or "I cannot play that" or "You cannot overdub that"—just every possible denial. It was always a huge struggle to get them to do what we wanted to do, but at the end of the day, everybody was always fascinated that it actually worked. And as I said, we were totally untrained. There was even a moment when Horst, who was very open-minded, said, "You cannot do this overdub," but I was very stubborn about it, so we did it and it came out fantastic.

Who had the idea to do a song about Gilles de Rais ["Into the Crypts of Rays"]?

Ain: I had read this book about the relationship between Gilles de Rais and Joan d'Arc. As you might know, Gilles de Rais was the Marshal of France, basically the military leader of France when they were at war with England during the Hundred Years' War. I had read stories about Gilles de Rais—I knew he was burned at the stake and that he had raped and killed children—but I didn't know how much of a mass murderer he was, or that he was basically the role model for the Big Bad Wolf or for Bluebeard. It was really interesting, so I gave that book to Tom, and I think that was his inspiration for "Into the Crypts of Rays."

Warrior: Even though I wrote the lyrics for that song, we discussed the content in detail, and Martin was actually the one who pointed out the story to me,

---

which totally fascinated me. Researching things like that back then was a huge undertaking, because it was pre-Internet. You really had to be a fanatic to get into all that stuff; you had to raid libraries and go to secondhand bookstores to find it. You couldn't go to Wikipedia or something like that. And we both loved the irony and the sarcasm in the story of Gilles de Rais, which is why we put it into a song.

What was the lyrical inspiration for the song "Morbid Tales"?

Ain: That song was inspired by one of those pulp-fiction short stories— I can't recall the name or the author—but it was about Nitocrys, an Egyptian empress who was dabbling in the black arts and witchery. It might've been in *Weird Tales*, which was one of the first publications to release the writings of H.P. Lovecraft and Robert E. Howard, who both were really, really inspirational to the lyrics we did at the time of *Morbid Tales* and *To Mega Therion*. Tom and I were both very big Robert E. Howard fans—*Kull the [Fabulous] Warrior [King], Conan the Barbarian*. And I was a huge H.P. Lovecraft fan— he was my favorite fictional author at that time. I liked the supernatural horror, and I liked the philosophical and religious concepts he made up— this entire universe of gods and demons, the writings of *The Necronomicon*, and that kind of thing. I really loved his approach and his style. "Nocturnal Fear," for example, was very much inspired by H.P. Lovecraft and *The Necronomicon*.

In "Nocturnal Fear," there's a reference to the Babylonian goddess Tiamat and Lovecraft's demon, Azag-thoth, which were later adopted by the Swedish band Tiamat and Morbid Angel guitarist George Emmanuel III (a.k.a. Trey Azag-thoth), respectively.

Ain: I know . . . you have the album *Morbid Tales*, and the band Morbid Angel. Septultura's first album was called *Morbid Visions*; our first album was *Morbid Tales*, with the song "Visions of Mortality" on it. This album of course became quite influential to a lot of musicians that came after us. Of course, we didn't know that at the time. We did what we did because we believed in it.

Warrior: "Nocturnal Fear," to me, is the ultimate expression of the Martin I met two years earlier—the Martin I met at a heavy metal party in a farm village. I sat down to talk to him, and he had all this occult knowledge, and I had all the historical knowledge, and we just bonded and spent nights talking about these topics. I would tell him what I had read, and he would tell me what he had read, and we just had endless material. This song is exactly like Martin at the time— it's exactly half of Celtic Frost.

What was the lyrical inspiration for "Return to the Eve"?

Warrior: "Return to the Eve" was very much about some of the teenage angst I had due to a very difficult youth, due to a feeling of entrapment, and my only escape being desperate daydreams. I know that sounds pathetically cliché, but that's what it was. My youth was hell. As a kid, I was totally dependent on a mother who basically drifted into insanity and had me live in circumstances that you would not even believe if I would tell you. My only means of escape was to shape my own world in daydreams and dreams, and a very tiny expression of that is the song "Return to the Eve."

What about "Visions of Mortality"?

Warrior: "Visions of Mortality" expressed our view of all the people hiding behind magic or religion or sermons or church brunches on Sunday and claiming they had the better answer for the world when the reality was that they were failing just like everybody else. And yet they all think they have the formula, while abusing certain aspects of religion that they arbitrarily pick out of a larger picture. It's no different if you go into Satanism or a church mass—it's always the same. "Visions of Mortality" is a very sarcastic expression of that, and incidentally, it was the last song ever written in Hellhammer; in fact, Martin had written a completely different set of lyrics. That was when we realized we were reaching a musical standard that did not fit into Hellhammer anymore. That song was the catalyst that made us dissolve Hellhammer and form Celtic Frost. We played it for Stephen Priestly, and that's the song that convinced him to actually give it a shot.

How important was the corpsepaint to the overall concept of Celtic Frost?

Ain: The imagery was just as important as the music. Of course, we weren't the only band that had makeup at the time—early Slayer had makeup, King Diamond had makeup. The corpsepaint, the black clothes, the leather, the gun belts, using occult imagery—it was all trying to get away from where I came from, which was a stern Catholic family. My mother was a religious teacher—she taught the catechism to kids in school, including me; I was an altar boy as well. I had to go to the Boy Scouts when I was young, too, and I have fond memories it, but one of the things I really disliked was the fact that it was kind of like a paramilitary organization, but with the same organizational structure. You have officers giving orders that you have to fulfill; everybody's dressed in uniform with symbols of rank, and this is something I really disliked. I realized pretty early on that this is how society structures itself in extreme. So we were trying to structure ourselves in a different way, but also using uniform and imagery. It was really important to have that, to give ourselves a sense of belonging, of being a group or a unit—and of course separating ourselves from the rest at the same time.

Warrior: The corpsepaint was an overblown expression of where we were at a certain point in our career. It's very much an expression of our rebellion and our then-current state of mind. As you know, our image on each Celtic Frost album is radically different. That's because we were aging and progressing and changing as people, and were weren't one of those bands that wanted to hide that. We actually wanted to show we were changing. The corpsepaint was very honest—it was exactly where we were at that time. And we didn't use it to hide our identity; it was done to underline the kind of people we were. We wanted to enhance the feelings we carried inside. But it was like theater makeup, which is usually very over-the-top, so that even the people in the last row can recognize what's going on.

Priestly: We had it on *Cold Lake*, too, but in a different way. [*Laughs*] For *Morbid Tales*, we were just trying to look evil. The corpsepaint that we had back then, I guess only Mercyful Fate had it at that time, so we were one of the first. I guess it was Martin's idea—he thought it was so aggressive. I didn't really like it, but I went along with it because I thought it belonged with the music. You can't really see my face on the album sleeve, though. When I see the Norwegian or Swedish bands that do that now, I understand that it has to be like that.

Where did the cover art come from?

Ain: I designed the heptagram. If you look at the back of *Apocalyptic Raids*, the heptagram is already in place; that's the original drawing. We wanted to a full-cover-size version for *Morbid Tales*, so we went to a graphic artist, a person we knew back in Switzerland, to make it bigger and cleaner. It was of course inspired by the Crowley heptagram, and also by the Crowley tarot. You have the symbol of the swords in tarot, and there was this artist, this lover and friend of Crowley's who painted this amazing tarot following the way that Crowley taught the tarot. And so the daggers make a pentagram, each one meaning like anger, failure, triumph, success—all things that were shown with daggers. So I combined the heptagram, Crowley's seal for the whore of Babylon, with the pentagram made by the daggers. And of course in the center is the skull, as a symbol of *Memento mori*. In the realization of death, we are not eternal. We are destined to fail as beings no matter what we do.

The swords make a pentagram in the upright version, but on the skull you have the pentagram in the inverted version, sort of like yin and yang. In the writing [on the original cover, not the reissue] where Crowley would have put, "Babylon," I put "Pazuzu," who is like an ancient Assyrian demon who also surfaces in the *Necronomicon*, who also comes up in the film *The Exorcist*. When Father Karras is doing the archaeological dig in Mesopotamia, in modern-day Iraq, he finds this devil head, and there's a silhouette of the demon Pazuzu, who was actually a demon that was used to ward off even more evil spirits. The way that I experienced Satanism was a liberating experience, so I realized quite early on that the devil is kind of like a scapegoat for Christians in the New Testament. Their god is supposed to be all about good, but how can you explain everything that is evil? You need some other figure. Hence, you get this Prince of Darkness, this counter-figure.

Did you consider yourself a Satanist at the time?

Ain: When I was reading the writings of Anton LaVey, we were approached by a branch—or a grotto, as they call themselves—of the First Church of Satan. I think it was the Dutch grotto. But I had just escaped the clutches of one form of organized religion, so I didn't want to run right into the clutches of the next one, which seemed to be even more sectarian. And not all of the writings of Anton LaVey seemed to be proper to me. Some of the stuff I wasn't really certain about. I wasn't agreeing with everything he had written, and some of the stuff even seemed ludicrous to me at the time. Like for example, in *Satanic Rituals*, he was using German, and of course German being my first language I realized that a lot of things were misspelled. So here were these supposedly powerful rituals, and he's using words that have a clearly defined meaning in a completely different way. And with English, he wasn't doing it like that, so to me, that seemed ludicrous. He was making mistakes. Also, the main theme of Satanism was being an individual—trying to differentiate yourself from the rules or the pressures of a group—so for us, Satan was about rebellion, but we didn't consider ourselves Satanists.

What were the reviews like when the album came out?

Priestly: Very shitty. I think *Kerrang!* magazine gave us just one "K" out of five. Some German magazine wrote something about us like we were the shittiest band and we could hardly play our instruments—which was true. [*Laughs*] Almost all the reviews were really shitty. But Xavier Russell, who later did the *Cold Lake* videos, was very into the band and he wrote for *Sounds*, the English magazine, and also *Kerrang!* and he said he made a mistake on the first record because it was really cult and influenced a lot of bands—but he didn't realize that until later on.

Ain: I would say they were mixed. We had absolute fantastic, enthusiastic reviews, and at the same time people who were like really putting it down and bashing. Some of that still had to do with our Hellhammer legacy; I remember

Kerrang! gave it one "K," which stood for "compost," utter dirt, utter shite, and they said, "These are the guys who did Hellhammer, but it's the same shit." They couldn't believe we had the nerve to record another record. Of course, when *Into the Pandemonium* came out, they reviewed all our old records again and they gave *Morbid Tales* five "K's," officially excusing themselves for not realizing the genius. [*Laughs*] But generally speaking, it was well received, and it did sell enough for a record company to release another record for us.

At what point did you start to realize the influence that Morbid Tales had on other bands?

Warrior: A few years ago. When Celtic Frost dissolved at the beginning of '93, I really wanted a break because the band had been such a rollercoaster ride in every way—musically, personality-wise and industry-wise especially. So I left the music industry entirely and dealt with my Celtic Frost demons by writing the book [*Are You Morbid?*], and to me, that was the closing of a chapter. I did not think about Celtic Frost anymore. Later on, I came back and formed the electronic-industrial project, Apollyon Sun, and once again, that was a completely different approach on every level. It was only when I began promoting the second Apollyon Sun album in 2000—along with the Celtic Frost book that also came out that year—was it first brought to my attention by so many writers and bands that I met at that time that Celtic Frost had been an influence. At first, I was extremely reluctant to hear that because it simply seemed impossible to me. We started in such a humble manner and on such a shoestring budget—we couldn't even afford to buy guitar strings or guitar [picks] when we did *Morbid Tales*—we had nothing. It was simply what was inside of us, and it was on such a small scale that I never expected anybody to ever pick up on that, never mind claim it as an influence. It seemed ludicrous to me. There were bands I looked up to—bands that technically blew us away—who said, "Yeah, we stole your riffs." I thought this was impossible, and I had this attitude until a short time ago. We played at Wacken this summer, and Mikael [Åkerfeldt] from Opeth said something like this, and I said, "This cannot possibly be," and I explained to him why I thought that way. So to this day, it's extremely difficult for me to take that seriously. I'm very close to my roots—I have revisited the Hellhammer rehearsal room frequently over the years—which is why it seems so incredible to me that anybody on this planet, much less bands like Nirvana or Opeth, would claim us as an influence. It just seems implausible.

Priestly: For me, it was quite cool because I could see it from the outside. At the time, I was playing my own stuff with [guitarist] Curt Victor Bryant, who later played on *Cold Lake* and *Vanity/Nemesis*, and you could see all those bands like Sepultura, who were into Frost. At first, I didn't realize they were so heavily into Frost, but then they would talk about us in interviews, so later on, when I was back in the band and [touring] for *Cold Lake* and *Vanity/Nemesis*, I'd meet people from the supporting bands who would say that the first record changed their lives. I thought, "Are you nuts? We could hardly play the instruments." But yeah, it seemed like a really big influence, especially on the Nordic scene. And I have to say that Sepultura did a really good job covering "Procreation (of the Wicked)." I also really appreciate those bands who did that tribute record [1995's *In Memory of Celtic Frost*].

Ain: I didn't realize until maybe the mid '90s how influential Hellhammer and Celtic Frost were, or how important *Morbid Tales* had become. At the beginning of the '90s, I tried to get away from the Celtic Frost thing and find out who I was as a person. While other people my age went to school or lived with their parents and tried to figure out what they wanted to do with their lives, I was working hard on a career in one of the most difficult businesses in the world. Around the time of *Vanity/Nemesis*, I realized that that career, for me, was over. I literally spent myself on the music, on everything, and business-wise, it hadn't come back to me. I wasn't able to make my living off of it, because we were ripped off just as many other bands were ripped off and still are ripped off nowadays. That's just the way this business works. Certain businessmen know that music is a young person's dream, and they take absolute advantage of it. To this day, the rights to *Morbid Tales* and the songs on there are fully owned by people who will own them until 75 years after we will have died. Noise Records was sold to the Sanctuary Group, and the Sanctuary Group has gone public on the stock market, so there are people owning our creation who don't even know that they own it. They just look at it as another number on the stock market. This is the way the music business works, which is why I didn't do anything musically for the last 15 years and why we did it differently this time around.

Are there any cover versions of songs from **Morbid Tales** *that you particularly enjoy?*

Warrior: I've heard a million—from Anthrax to the two tribute albums that were released—and I hate them all, except for when Sepultura did "Procreation (of the Wicked)." They play it note-by-note, which I generally don't like, but they made it theirs by putting in an aggression that we didn't possess at the time. When I heard it, I called Martin and said, "Look, they're playing it better than we did. They're blowing our version to bits." And now, I think that's the way that song must sound. When we reformed Celtic Frost, that was the benchmark. We thought if we could not play "Procreation (of the Wicked)" that way, we have no business coming back as Celtic Frost.

What's your favorite track on the album?

Warrior: Probably "Dethroned Emperor"—I like the tempo changes, and I like the slow groove of it. I like slow, heavy music, probably because I grew up with things like Black Sabbath. My favorite is when the riffs are huge and crunchy and they have time to unfold. I don't subscribe to hectic music, where everything has to be hurried. I like music to be able to breathe. A lot of bands mistake speed for heaviness, and they're definitely not the same thing. The faster band is less heavy, because you can not possibly play heavy as a drummer when you have to have so many beats per minute. You have no time to actually beat the drums. Slower songs are much more majestic and powerful. My second favorite track is probably "Danse Macabre" because it was very daring for the time, and I totally enjoy the way it came out. I like to compare it to a theater play done just with sounds.

Priestly: Definitely "Into the Crypts of Rays." First, I like the lyrics a lot—they're really good. And I always loved to play that song live, because the crowd goes mad. "Return to the Eve" was always a good one, too, because on the *Cold Lake* tour, Tom would say "Return to the Steve" because I was back in the band. [*Laughs*]

Ain: I think "Procreation (of the Wicked)" and "Dethroned Emperor" are my two favorites. "Procreation" has such an organic feel to it; it's genuinely heavy and primitive. It was sort of like if Robert Johnson lived in our time and played heavy metal, this is what he would've come up with. It just seems really timeless, and I also like the lyrics. I think they're some of the best lyrics we've written. "Dethroned Emperor" is one of Tom's genius strokes, with these kind of fantasy lyrics. You can obviously interpret it as us trying to reclaim our throne, like we're trying to do right now—maybe that's why it's one of my favorites right now. It's a metaphor I can relate to especially nowadays.

In retrospect, is there anything you'd change about **Morbid Tales?**

Priestly: No, not at all—because we were exactly like that at that time. That's what I really like about it. I was 17 or 18 when we did that, and it's still a part of my life. The only thing I would change would maybe be not quitting the band. [*Laughs*]

Ain: It was only released as mini-album in Europe first—I wish it would have been released as a full album. That's maybe the only thing I'd do different. And I'd make certain that the lyric sheet was included in every album—that was really important to us, and it was only included in the first edition. It wasn't even included in the first CD version. But as far as the music and the recording, I wouldn't change anything.

Warrior: No. *Morbid Tales* is a milestone for us personally—even without all the people who claim it as an influence. For example, the guitar sound on that album is something we tried to reach again, and we never were able to until the new album, 20 years later. In many other ways, it became an icon for us in our career. The spontaneity, energy, authenticity and desperation of the album—we knew if we failed, we would be out of the music industry for good—all these things are captured, which makes it a once-in-a-lifetime thing.

CHAPTER 4

WHO'LL STOP THE REIGN?

THE MAKING OF SLAYER'S *REIGN IN BLOOD*

by J. Bennett

Release Date: 1986
Label: Def American
Summary: Rick Rubin finally does something good
Induction Date: November 2004/Issue #2

I
n the early '80s, four L.A. boys in huge spiked wristbands and football grease-
paint terrorized the rouged-up glam queens trolling the Sunset Strip for fake
tits and lucrative recording contracts. Having already unleashed two merciless lo-fi shredding clinics via *Show No Mercy* and *Hell Awaits*, Slayer's urban-
satanist lyrics and ultra-violent guitar acrobatics were far too inaccessible for West
Hollywood's coke-metal scene and way too sketchy for the Bay Area's newly
viable thrash contingency. But by 1985, the makeup was long gone, and Slayer
entered the studio with Def Jam Svengali Rick Rubin (at the time best known for
producing the Beastie Boys and LL Cool J) to record their third album, *Reign in
Blood*. Now widely regarded as thrash metal's definitive 28 minutes, it is as relent-

less today as when it scared the shit out of everybody back in '86. Nearly two decades later, hesher classics like "Angel of Death" and "Raining Blood" *still* make other metal bands sound like frail pussies. With original drummer Dave Lombardo back at the pulpit and a 2004 DVD (*Reign in Blood Live: Still Reigning*) documenting the band's inclusion of the entire album in their live set, *Decibel* hunted down all four members of Slayer for a romantic stroll down memory lane.

What was the general feeling just before you went into the studio to record Reign in Blood?

Tom Araya: I remember coming back from the tour we had done in Europe and really working on the new material. Jeff and Kerry had written a lot of it on their own. They rehearsed it and taught it to Dave—they did it pretty quickly, if I remember correctly. We recorded the songs ourselves, which we always did, and took the tape to Brian [Slagel, Metal Blade Records CEO and early Slayer producer/manager]. He got all excited when he heard the demos—and at that point, there weren't even any vocals on it. And then he didn't hear it again until Rubin put it out. [*Laughs*] That's my fondest memory about that.

Jeff Hanneman: Basically, we were all pretty pumped because it was right after we had met Rick Rubin, who wanted to sign us to his label. The overall feeling was just that we were excited because we spent all those years on a shitty label . . . what was it, Metal Blade? [*Laughs*] We didn't have a bus or a tour manager. It was fun, but after we hooked up with Rubin we had a manager and a real record label, so we were just excited as hell.

Kerry King: To us, it was just the best 10 songs we had at that point. It wasn't like we sat there going, "We're gonna change shit with this record." We had a new producer; we were excited about being on a new label, but other than that, it was business as usual.

What was your first meeting with Rubin like?

Araya: The first time we met him, we were out touring on *Hell Awaits*. We were playing at L'Amour in New York City, and Rubin came out to see the show. He was a fan of the band, and he said he wanted to sign us. We told him to call Brian, because Brian was our manager at the time. [Rubin] seemed like an interesting person; a genuinely nice person. He had a big old grin on his face—he usually does—but the only thing I knew about him was that he was with Def Jam, you know? In the process of working with him on that record, and then *South of Heaven* and *Seasons in the Abyss*, we heard some of the other things he was working on, which was very impressive stuff.

Dave Lombardo: Then [Rubin] came over to my parents' house. It was good to have somebody interested who knew what they were doing. I remember Glen

E. Friedman—the photographer for *Thrasher*—came over, too. He was the local punk scene photographer at the time.

Were you aware of Rubin before he came knocking?

King: Not at all. I think Hanneman might've been into some of the rap stuff, but I wasn't.

It must've been a big difference, production-wise, going from Slagel to Rubin.

Hanneman: Oh, yeah. Rubin is a *real* producer. [*Laughs*] He knows how to get the sound he wants. Slagel was a kid like us—he was going through the motions, trying to figure out how to do it.

Lombardo: Absolutely. It sounded really good. Plus, we had Andy Wallace engineering the sessions, and he captured the best of us at that point.

King: It was a different mentality. Right away, the first thing you notice is that there's no reverb on it. That allows it to be way more threatening—it hits you in the forehead. Rubin really cleaned up our sound on that record, which drastically changed what we sounded like and how people perceived us. It was like, "Wow—you can hear everything, and those guys aren't just playing fast; those notes are on time." It was what we needed to be. Before that, we were happy to sound like Venom or Mercyful Fate. We played in Reverb Land, for lack of a better term. And the reverb was the first thing Rubin took out. When we heard the mix we were like, "Why didn't we think of that before?"

Was the idea just to be the fastest, most evil band in the world?

Araya: That was about it. [*Laughs*] That's what we planned to do. I remember when Brian first heard us and asked us to put a song together for one of those *Metal Massacre* compilations. So we went and bought the *Metal Massacre* he had out at the time. We listened to it and were like, "We can write something heavier and faster than this." So we wrote "Aggressive Perfector," and just continued from there.

King: In the beginning, it was definitely about being the heaviest and the fastest because, well, you gotta be something. But by [*Reign in Blood*], I think we were just honing what we do, just looking through that window of what Slayer's gonna be forever.

Did you think of yourselves as being in competition with Metallica?

Lombardo: In my eyes, there was no competition—Slayer was an entity unto itself, a band with its own style and its own name. Whatever anybody else did was their business, and whatever success they had was strictly up to them. I just minded my own business and played the best I could possibly play.

King: Well, that was around [*Master of*] *Puppets*, and we always knew they'd be more popular than us because they sang about accessible stuff and we sang about stuff that nobody wanted to talk about. We knew that from day one, and I'm still happy with that today.

Master of Puppets *is almost twice as long as* **Reign in Blood.**

Hanneman: At that time, we always listened to Metallica and Megadeth to see what they were doing, but one thing about me and Kerry is we get bored of riffs really quick. We can't drag the same thing over and over or do the same verses six times in a song. If we do a verse two or three times, we're already bored with it. So we weren't trying to make the songs shorter—that's just what we were into. When we finished *Reign in Blood*, we had this meeting with Rubin, and he was like, "Do you realize how short this is?" And we're going, "Oh, fuck . . ." And then we all collectively looked at each other and said, "So what?"

King: I thought it was kinda neat that you had the whole record on one side of a cassette. [*Laughs*] You could listen to it, flip it over, and play it again. We'd never been about putting songs and music on our records that doesn't need to be there. Hour-long records seem to be the trend these days, but you know, you listen and it's like, "You could lose this part; you could cut this song completely—and make a much more intense record," which is what we're all about.

The first time you heard the album played back, were you like, "Holy shit, we're the best!"?

Lombardo: [*Laughs*] No way. We put it out, and eventually it got the recognition that it did, but we were in no way acting like that. That might sound like other bands I probably know—when they put out a record, they think they're the greatest. Little do they know, they gotta live up to the expectation.

King: Yeah, we're full of ourselves to an extent, but not *blindly* full of ourselves.

At the time the album was recorded, there weren't many bands doing what you were doing. The first records from the original death metal and grindcore bands had yet to be released.

King: Oh, yeah. I think we went fast to be intense. It's been misconstrued along the way, and bands are fast just to be fast. A lot of the blast beat bands—you know, three straight minutes of blast beats in a song? It takes the intensity out of it. I know a lot of people are into it, but it doesn't work for me.

How soon after **Reign in Blood** *came out did you realize the impact it had?*

King: Probably not for a long time. I mean, we just kept on going—we put out *South of Heaven*, we put out *Seasons*. So maybe around *Divine Intervention* is when we'd get the interviewers asking us, "How does it feel to keep trying to outdo *Reign in Blood*? How does it feel to have made the best thrash metal album of all time?" But you know, we didn't really think about it. And we certainly don't try to outdo it.

Some say you'll never top Reign in Blood. *Does that bother you?*

King: Not really—because in a lot of people's minds, we won't. I think [2001's] *God Hates Us All* is a better record than *Reign in Blood*—not because it's the last one, but because it's more mature. Not to take anything away from *Reign in Blood*—it's a great record.

Hanneman: No matter what we do in the future, it's gonna be *the* album. That's why we did *South of Heaven* right after that. We knew we couldn't top that record, so we slowed down and changed our style just a tad.

Lombardo: That's the nature of the business. One record is declared the ultimate record. But then again, I hear people say that *Reign in Blood*, *South of Heaven* and *Seasons in the Abyss* are the classics. It's just that one had an impact because it was the *first* one—the masterpiece. Nobody had done anything like it at the time.

When it came out, Reign in Blood *was largely ignored by the mainstream media.*

Lombardo: Yeah, we were ignored by everybody except the underground magazines, but that was normal. Look at the music that was on MTV at the time—Flock of Seagulls, Duran Duran—and here come these punks from L.A. with long hair and kind of a demonic outlook. They didn't want to acknowledge our presence—they'd never heard music being played that way. I think what really opened their eyes was that a well-known producer like Rick Rubin gave it the time. So the recognition we got was, in part, because of Rubin's interest in us. By taking on the project, he was showing that there was something there.

The first word uttered on the album is "Auschwitz." Did you think that you would attract controversy because of that at the time?

Hanneman: Oh, yeah—but I didn't give a shit. We had just gotten off tour for the last record, and since we didn't have a tour bus, there was no music to listen to, no TV to watch—we were just sitting in Tom's Camaro driving all over the place. So I was buying books to read, and I remember stopping some place where I bought two books on [Nazi "surgeon" Josef] Mengele. I thought, "This has gotta be some sick shit." So when it came time to do the record, that stuff was still in my head—that's where those lyrics came from.

Lombardo: We got dropped by Columbia because of that. I mean, "Auschwitz—the meaning of pain!" Any sympathizers with the Holocaust aren't gonna have any part of it. But they didn't see the deep meaning of it—it's just documented musical awareness. It's not necessarily *for* it—it's just something that Jeff discovered and wrote a song about.

So that must've been how all the "Jeff Hanneman is a Nazi" rumors started.

Hanneman: Yeah, probably that, and I collect medals and other Nazi stuff that my dad got me started on because he gave me all this shit he got off of dead Nazis. Next thing I know, we're neo-Nazis. It was like, "Oh yeah—we're racists. We've got a Cuban and a Chilean in the band. Get real."

King: Slayer are "Nazis," "fascists," "communists"—all that fun shit. And of course we got the most flack for it in Germany. I was always like, "Read the lyrics and tell me what's offensive about it. Can you see it as a documentary, or do you think Slayer's preaching fucking World War II?" People get this thought in their heads—especially in Europe—and you'll never talk them out of it. They try to talk *you* into what they're thinking. When they ask you a question and you give them an answer they don't want, they'll be like, "Well, don't you mean . . ." And I'm like, "No, dude, I *don't* mean that." It's just like, wake up.

Lombardo: Jeff's best friend is black, so I don't think that was a good way to portray him—although it was kinda funny. It's fine, though—it gives people something to talk about. It's better that they talk about something than not talk about it at all.

Almost 20 years later, which song holds up best for you?

Hanneman: Probably "Raining Blood." I still love playing that song live. You'd think we'd be tired of it—I mean, I'd love to know how many times we've played it live. That would be really interesting.

King: Yeah. The intro is big with the two-guitar harmony part, and then that first beat that Dave does, that double-kick thing, and it's like this backwards gallop that gets the crowd going regardless of where you are. I mean, we could be playing in front of Alanis Morissette, and the crowd loves that part.

Tom, how many takes did you need to nail the scream at the beginning of "Angel of Death"?

Araya: [*Laughs*] It took two takes. On the first one, they were telling me what they wanted to hear, and I just let it rip. After I did the initial scream, I told them to rewind the tape. They looked at me, and I just said, "I've got a better one."

The most widely available version of **Reign in Blood** *has "Aggressive Perfector" and the remix of "Criminally Insane" tacked on the end—which I always thought was weird, because the original album closes perfectly, with the rain sound effects at the end of "Raining Blood."*

Araya: Yeah, it is weird, but that's the record company's way of sweetening the deal—because it's got two tracks you really can't get anywhere unless you've got that rare single that was released in Europe. It's like them saying, "Here's two cookies. You're gonna have to buy the milk with the money you're saving."

King: Our history of changing distributors—which certainly isn't our fault—means whoever gets the catalogue puts out a new one. Although, I know people who've bought *Reign in Blood* twice because they wore out their first CD. [*Laughs*] That's the way it should be.

Hanneman: I think it was Rubin's idea [to do the "Criminally Insane" remix]. We were getting ready to leave for a European tour, and Rubin wanted to fuck with it. It was just me and Dave hanging around, and Rubin wanted to slow it down just to fuck with people, I guess. I'm pretty sure Dave did the slow parts on a drum machine. I think I did a new solo at the beginning, too. We took out some of the lyrics and put a solo over the first verse.

Whose idea was it to use that Larry Carroll illustration on the cover?

King: That's the artist, right? [*Laughs*] I'm guessing Rick Rubin, because we certainly wouldn't have known about him. We've actually been kicking around the idea of having that guy do the next album, since the original lineup is back together.

Larry Carroll: I met Rick Rubin in a coffee shop in New York—it must've been 1986. He looked pretty much the same as he does now, with the big beard and everything. I had heard Slayer, because I'm from California, but I'd never seen them. At that time, I was doing a lot of political illustrations for *The Progressive*, the *Village Voice*, the *New York Times* op-ed page, stuff like that. If I remember correctly, the band didn't like the cover I did for *Reign in Blood* at first. Someone didn't, anyway—I don't remember if it was actually someone in the band or their management. But then someone in the band showed it to their mother, and their mother thought it was disgusting, so they knew they were onto something.

Hanneman: Rubin knew the guy and was like, "This is sick. This should work for us." We ended up using him for three albums.

Araya: I thought it was amazing. I liked it immediately. I liked them all, actually—there were three variations, and they incorporated all three into the cover. They did the same thing with *South of Heaven* and *Seasons*.

In hindsight, is there anything you'd change about **Reign in Blood?**

Lombardo: Absolutely not. What it was is what made it a classic, so you'd never change it.

Araya: Someone asked me that same question the other day, but just in terms of Slayer in general—what I'd do differently—and I just told him I'd bring a video camera. [*Laughs*] People would not believe the shit we've gone through.

CHAPTER 5

SLAVES TO THE GRIND

THE MAKING OF NAPALM DEATH'S *SCUM*

by Kory Grow

Release Date: 1987
Label: Earache
Summary: The dawn of grindcore
Induction Date: May 2008/Issue #43

Without Napalm Death's *Scum*, you probably wouldn't be holding this magazine. This album—essentially a split LP between two almost completely different lineups—defined grindcore with its growled vocals, whirring, hardcore-influenced riffs and faster-than-a-locomotive blast beats. Its fusion of anarcho-punk and death metal would inspire countless bands, and every musician who played on it would go on to do something extraordinary, musically.

Co-founded in Birmingham, England, in 1981 by vocalist/bassist Nic Bullen, who would later play in Scorn and others, and drummer Miles "Rat" Ratledge, Napalm Death began modestly as a Discharge-inspired, politically charged punk band. The group would land a track on the Crass Records comp *Bullshit Detector #3*. After that, guitarist Justin Broadrick joined, and this lineup formed the nucleus for grindcore. Broadrick came from an industrial-music background; he would later form Godflesh and, more recently, Jesu. Finding a faster drummer in Mick Harris, the group kicked Rat out, and with this lineup recorded the A side of *Scum*. Harris would be the band's linchpin, later playing in Painkiller, Lull and also Scorn. Side B's lineup would feature bassist Jim Whiteley (currently in Warprayer), vocalist Lee Dorrian, later of Cathedral fame, and guitarist Bill Steer, who also played in Carcass concurrent with Napalm Death. (Steer's Carcass bandmate Jeff Walker would design the album art for *Scum*.) To this day, Steer says people in the U.K. know him better for his work in Napalm Death than anything he would do with the far-more-successful-outside-of-England Carcass.

Fame came quickly to the group, thanks to repeated airplay on BBC DJ John Peel's popular Radio 1 program. With constant spins of "You Suffer," which found a place in the *Guinness Book of World Records* as the world's shortest song, Peel's more eclectic audience started showing up to Napalm Death gigs, attracted by Harris' whirlwind drumming. Often located at dingy clubs, like Birmingham's the Mermaid, the group scrambled to keep up with themselves, both in terms of fame and musically. Shortly after the first tour for *Scum*, the lineup would change again, as Whiteley left the group and new bassist Shane Embury would join, performing on the follow-up to *Scum*, *From Enslavement to Obliteration*. To this day, Embury remains the only consistent member of Napalm from their breakthrough days. Through him, *Scum*'s legacy lives on.

PREAMBLE

When did Napalm Death form?

Nic Bullen: When we started Napalm Death, I was 12. Miles and I had been playing and writing songs together for sort of a couple of years prior to that. Because we'd been doing a fanzine together since I was 10 and Miles was 11.

How did you come up with the name Napalm Death?

Bullen: We were both interested in films like *Apocalypse Now!* and *The Ninth Configuration* and films about the horrors of war. So that fell into it a little bit as well. It was just a natural kind of movement.

What did your parents think of the band?

Bullen: They weren't very impressed . . . I suppose they'd rather I was doing that than going out smashing windows and hanging around doing nothing.

How did Justin Broadrick come to join Napalm Death?

Bullen: In the center of Birmingham, where we lived, there was a big, old market. It's called the Rag Market. And it had clothing stores and general stores, a typical big market. And it had a stall that sold cassette tapes, mainly bootlegs.

Justin Broadrick: Obviously, being at such a tender age, anyone who was of a similar age and who was interested in similar music, you would converse with. It was just obvious. Nic Bullen happened to be one of those people. One of the first things that he mentioned was that this band he was in had recorded a song released on one of the Crass Records compilations, *Bullshit Detector Vol. 3*. As soon as he told me that, I was really excited about it.

Bullen: We both just started talking about how we liked similar music, because we would see each other there every week.

Broadrick: He came over to where I lived with my mom and stepfather at the time in a really shitty part of Birmingham. We did a session of just jamming complete noise and stuff—one of those tracks is an edit on the *Final 1* CD.

Bullen: Justin played the last-ever concert with his group Final, and we played at that. He asked us to play. It was a free concert at the Mermaid in Birmingham in 1985.

Broadrick: I made some demo of Final that was a bit more structured, with drum machine and quite abstract guitar. It was really remedial, really naïve-sounding and fairly shit. [Nic and Miles Ratledge] heard this demo I did with the guitar outside of the noise stuff as Final, and they were really excited somehow by my guitar playing.

Bullen: We had reached the point where it was just Miles and myself, so we asked Justin if he wanted to play with us, and he said yeah.

What were your musical influences around this time?

Bullen: Mainly Discharge. And groups that were inspired by Discharge, so that would have been Chaos U.K. in Britain and Disorder, and then also European groups from Finland and Sweden like Anti Cimex, Chaos, Recession—those kinds of groups. And we also combined them with slower songs, which were probably more resembling of the post-punk influence we had—all of us, Miles, Justin and myself.

Broadrick: When we first heard Siege, it was exciting to hear a version of hardcore that wasn't just based around melodicism. We were enamored with the speed thing. The speed sounded extreme. It sounded like a machine.

How did the songs that would eventually become **Scum** *on your* **Hatred Surge** *demo develop?*

Bullen: The songs are strange because a lot of them date from 1985, from the lineup with Justin and Miles. And of those songs, a couple were updated versions of songs that Justin had done in Final back in 1983.

Broadrick: I think at the time there was something in [the Final demo] that Nic and Rat found refreshing, something weird. It was actually inspired by the bands in the anarcho-punk scene like Amebix and Killing Joke. But it had this bleak feeling, [a] very naïve but quite nihilistic sound.

When did you begin playing fast?

Broadrick: Every song we had at the time we sped up. We wanted to make them more brutal. Unfortunately, Rat—Miles—he couldn't drum so fast. He couldn't drum at the speed that Nic and I wanted to get up to.

How did Mick Harris come into the picture?

Broadrick: Mick came up to me at one of these Napalm Death shows and when he first [came] up, I'm like, "*Who is this guy?*" This little tattooed guy. Nobody had tattoos at the time. The tattoos, a psychobilly haircut—which is like an old rockabilly haircut—and he looked pretty aggressive. He's like, "I'm a drummer and I play in this psychobilly band that's really fast."

Bullen: [I remember] hearing the band he was in called Anorexia—they weren't a very great group, but they did play very, very fast.

Broadrick: Like an opportunistic little kid, I remember saying to Nic, "I met this guy over there. I'm gonna go down to his rehearsal and check his drumming out." Obviously, without Miles I had this conversation . . . They started playing, and immediately I couldn't believe the speed of the stuff. Musically it was shit, straight up. But the drummer, Mickey, straight away I was thinking, "*Fucking hell, this guy's fucking great.*"

Bullen: A hell of a lot of people, even in the underground music scene, did not like thrash. They hated it. Even within a minority subculture, you were a minority. So it was really good to meet other people who did like the same kind of music.

Mick Harris: When I joined Napalm Death, the whole idea of me getting in and being asked was they wanted to go a bit more thrash, and it was Justin who turned me on to metal basically. I'd never ever listened to metal. I believe the first record [I heard] was *Seven Churches* by Possessed, and I quite liked it. They wanted to bring those elements into Napalm, and the drummer that was playing with them didn't want to, and they knew that I wanted to play fast.

Mick, how did you develop such a fast drumming style?

Harris: I've always listened for the extreme end of music, whatever it be. And for me, I was always looking for the faster band. And Siege and Deep Wound from Boston were always someone that I looked up to. It was fast and, yes, Heresy took that even further. I guess I just wanted to play even faster. It just comes from what I call the hardcore beat—the Chaos U.K./Disorder beat. I just wanted to take it as far as you could go, and that was it. There's nothing technical about that beat. There's only one way to play the blast beat. As much as a crap drummer I am, I'm sorry, I played it the right way, and the only way there is to play it.

How did the changeover between Miles and Mick happen?

Broadrick: I went down to Mickey Harris' mom and dad's house and he had his drum kit set up in his bedroom; I plugged the guitar into some fucking stereo or something and we rehearsed all the existing Napalm Death songs at hyperspeed. Basically we went into his bedroom, and I said, "So, how fast can you play these songs?" We were listening to Siege, and he said, "I can play faster than that, I think." And he would do the blast beat, which was still not that fast. And I would just say to him, "Faster!" And he would just keep speeding up. And then we would get together with me and Nic and Mick and rehearse. We were doing this quite nastily behind Miles' back . . . [Miles] didn't want to go in the direction that Mick and I were going anyway. He wanted to do what the Final demo was doing.

Bullen: I think, at the time, instead of being sensible and saying, "Oh look, we really want to play some fast music, and you don't; why don't we have two groups and carry Napalm Death like this and start a new group?," we decided we wouldn't do that, and that we would basically kind of throw him out, which is really bad.

Broadrick: Nic and Miles were next-door neighbors, so it was a bigger personal thing for Nic, really. And Miles obviously is a fantastic person as well, so it was quite sad.

Bullen: It's one thing I would regret, really. I mean, it hasn't come between us. But it could have been a lot better.

Harris: At the time, I was playing in a local punk/hardcore band. And all I wanted to do was play fast, and they just wanted to play slow songs. So I was sort of getting a bit bored of that. I got the opportunity to join Napalm, so it all came together.

What were you listening to at the time?

Harris: Japanese hardcore. Stuff like Gay Akura, SOB, Gold, Geza, Systematic Death, then the American side of hardcore: Septic Death, Siege was huge, [they] obviously were and still are fast and brutal and pushing the boundaries. Deep Wound. Negative Effects. All the stuff. Washington, DC, hardcore. Minor Threat. Obviously, still British stuff like early Discharge, and Disorder, Chaos U.K., and then a hell of a lot of indie stuff, alternative. Killing Joke, Birthday Party, Test Dept., Neubauten, Throbbing Gristle—there's a whole mix of things. Dub reggae. Really all sorts. Membrane. And then, obviously, Justin turned me onto thrash, death metal, which I gave you a list of earlier—the more underground [stuff] started when I remember meeting Shane Embury. I have to say thanks to Shane because [of] the tape-trading scene, which Shane was one of the first persons [involved]; because of meeting him up at the Mermaid in mid '86, I started to discover things like Genocide, which is pre-Repulsion. And that was it. It was like, "Whoa, listen to this band." Super-fast, super-heavy riffs. They were doing the blast beat with two kick drums, but whatever. Super-heavy riffs like a super-fast Slayer. And that just went on. Master, Death Strike and all these others. From the tape-trading days, we were all just trading certain rehearsals—live, demos, Massacre, Death and Obituary when they were called Executioner—and all these classics, basically. Early Morbid Angel and Incubus. Loads and loads of things. The underground death metal scene was basically heavy and brutal; it's what I wanted. It sort of had the punk ethic. And the DIY and the raw sound, this metal sound—this underground metal thing, which I can totally relate to.

SIDE A

After Mick joined, you recorded the **From Enslavement to Obliteration** *demo.*

Bullen: With the *From Enslavement to Obliteration* demo, there were a few songs that were written in the studio on the spot: "You Suffer," "The Kill" and "Death by Manipulation." "Death by Manipulation" was only ever played at that recording. [It] was essentially modeled on early Swans, predominantly the *Cop* album. That's where the origins of "grindcore," the word, comes from. Because Mick Harris would use the term "grind." And we'd say things like "do a Swans grind" on the bass.

What about "You Suffer"?

Broadrick: "You Suffer" was largely a comedy thing, one-second song. Utterly retarded. It's ridiculous, but it was hilarious. We played that song in front of 30 local kids, like, every weekend. We played that song 30 times. It was a laugh.

Harris: There is a bit of novelty. Let's do the shortest, fastest thing you can do. And yeah, there are notes there. People think we just go, "Blllp" and that's it. And I believe there's, like, four notes or something. There's a lyric, "You suffer, but why?" And it's played quick, fast and sharp and as tight as we could. We had a bit of reverb on there. It probably makes it even longer.

Bullen: Wehrmacht, on their "Night of Pain" demo, '85, did a song called "E!" which was just the phrase "E!" So, there were already precedents, and we just did our own take on that.

The **Scum** *recording of "You Suffer" is in the* **Guinness World Records** *book as the world's shortest song at 1.316 seconds.*

Bullen: Yeah, I've been told that. It's quite amusing. [*Laughs*] I wish it had been for the first human to be able to breathe underwater, but that's quite good.

Harris: We didn't ask for it. It just got put in there. We were told, "You've made the *Guinness Book of World Records*." And we were like, "Nah, get out of here," and yes, there it is. It's sort of funny, isn't it? A bit of an achievement, I guess.

Were audiences receptive to Napalm Death?

Bullen: I think at first people were either very dismissive or felt we were a laughingstock. And that all changed from my memory when we played a thrash festival at the Mermaid in Birmingham on, I believe, March 15, 1986. And I remember pretty much the whole of a capacity crowd went really crazy for what we were doing while we were playing, and I really remember at the time thinking, "Gosh, this is unusual." It was interesting what we did in Newcastle with the group Anti Cimex. There's a recording of it. And if you listen to it, it starts off with complete silence after every song, then laughter, then at the end people screaming for more. Really strange. In the space of 20 minutes, it's like you're totally winning over a whole audience.

How did you come to record the A side of Scum?

Harris: The A side of *Scum* was gonna be a 12-inch for the promoter of the Mermaid Pub in Birmingham, which was the promoter for all the hardcore and punk events.

Bullen: When it was recorded, there wasn't any specific intent for its recording. There was talk floating around of, "Oh, we could do a record and this could happen and that could happen," but it was more of a case of just recording again.

Broadrick: I remember how silly it was, how childish it was. By then, everybody had their own pockets of friends. It had already become quite clique-y within the whole circle. There was about 20 dudes in the studio when we did it. We had Head of David in there.

Harris: Justin was very much into Sacrilege—we all were, really—and Damian [Thompson] from Sacrilege was really good to us. He let Justin borrow his guitar pedal. Justin at the time didn't have very good distortion. He was aware that this MXR Distortion would give him a real warm sound and more of the tone he was looking for. We went to Rich Bitch because you got a good discount doing the overnight sessions. I believe it was from midnight to eight in the morning. You got a good discount to use the eight-track there.

Broadrick: I remember lying under the mixing desk. Stuff like that. We put all the money for the session together from dole money, which was like social security money. It probably cost us 60 pounds to record it, like 120 bucks to record the whole of the A side.

Harris: I think it was 80 pounds. Ten pounds an hour, I believe. And then you paid for your master tape. Which, then, it was Betamax, believe it or not. That was sort of the first digital-style recording. I remember asking the engineer, "What the hell is that?" And he explained, "Well, it's binary code, 0's and 1's, and it's a better quality than analog."

Bullen: I remember it being quite brief. We were very tight then. We played a lot of concerts locally, sometimes three times a week. I remember thinking as it was being mixed that it sounded really good. And I still do like its production because the use of reverb, it bleeds at the edges. It doesn't have defined, sharp, crisp edges. And that bleeding gives it a certain element of kinetic energy, and of danger, which I really like in recordings in general, so I still like it in that recording.

What were your intentions with the recording?

Harris: Something happened, communications with Daz Russell from the Mermaid. We were like, we're not gonna give him the master because we feel we're getting a bit ripped off here . . . The reason why we kept hold of the master was [we've] never ever been paid by Daz Russell for all the shows. We never ever got paid. So we felt no guilt.

Bullen: The initial talk was with a group called Atavistic from the south of Britain who were playing in fast thrash style, perhaps to do a split record with them on a label from another part of the south of England, a label called Manic Ears. But as far as I know, they passed on that.

Harris: We sent it to [punk underground artist/legend] Pushead, who showed interest. He'd been writing scene reports in *Maximumrocknroll*, and he heard about Napalm, this super-fast band. So we thought we'd send Pushead a copy, and never heard back from Pushead.

Broadrick: We took that demo to Earache Records, who had only released a Heresy record at the time, who were nothing. They were just run out of Dig [Pearson]'s bedroom. They were sort of interested, but didn't really go through it straightaway. I think Nic had lost interest and even Mickey, I think to some extent, for a little while. Mick had gone down a different avenue socially, and to some extent musically as well, and Mickey had become more involved in the culture that Napalm Death had become not only a part of, but had also started, I guess, too. Had also become a big part of the thrash metal tape-trading scene as well, so Mickey got involved with a whole other group of people. I promptly left the scene.

Jim Whiteley joined on bass around this time, right?

Broadrick: I did a couple of rehearsals without Nic Bullen there, actually, because Nic had become not even interested in rehearsing at the time. At Nic's request, he didn't play bass again. And that was basically how we drafted in Jimmy Whiteley, who was the bass player on the B side of *Scum*.

Jim Whiteley: Mick and Justin visited me telling me that Nic had quit the band; they needed a bassist. I was into what they were doing, even though I couldn't play for shit. I'd only acquired a bass two months prior. I was more nervous than excited.

Broadrick: Jimmy couldn't even play bass. I would go to Jimmy's flat and I taught him both to play bass and play the Napalm Death songs simultaneously. Which is ridiculous. We obviously were also a punk band, so we could do anything rather badly with passion.

Why did Justin leave Napalm Death?

Whiteley: Justin was a long-standing friend of the Head of David chaps, hence them also being crammed into the studio the night the first side of *Scum* was laid down. He was already drumming in Fall of Because. It was no surprise when he left Napalm Death to concentrate his other efforts; after all, [Head of David] were already recording sessions for John Peel and playing gigs where they'd [come] away with more than the price of a pint as remuneration for their efforts. I don't remember there being any resultant hostility towards his leaving the band.

Broadrick: I was playing with Fall of Because and Napalm Death on the same nights at the Mermaid Pub. I started to feel again that I didn't want to just be making this music that was this hyper-speed thing we'd come across. I think me, Nic and Mick were all quite extreme personalities and kids; I think that makes it even worse. We were kids, really. Just mad kids. Everyone was quite an extreme personality. I knew I didn't want to be in an environment that was based on confrontation on a weekly basis in rehearsals.

Harris: October '86, Justin had totally lost interest in Napalm. And he got the offer to play drums with Head of David, a local Birmingham band. So Head of David was gonna be touring, they were going abroad. And that's what Justin wanted to do.

Broadrick: They said, "You pretty much have to leave Napalm Death, because you won't be able to put the time into it because we've got a couple tours with Head of David and we want to record a new album." And I was totally excited by that. I wanted to record a record. As I said before, when we recorded *Scum*, we weren't recording an album; we were recording a demo to try and get an album.

Bullen: We played a concert with Justin just before he left in Leeds with Sacrilege, and after every song, all the people did was shout, "Play faster! Play faster!" And I felt we were like performing bears in a zoo. And that nobody was listening to the content of the songs in terms of the politics. Nobody was listening to the conceptual reasons for creating the songs. All they wanted was a rollercoaster ride, a fairground ride. And then I was thinking, "Why do I want to be doing this, be somebody's performing seal?" And so, when Justin left, it was getting to a crisis point for me.

Broadrick: The last thing I did for Napalm Death, literally, was give that demo to Earache Records. Because they were the only people that would take it. I just gave it to Dig. He said [he] might be able to do something with it, and I just said, "Have it." I think I just sent him the master cassette and left it there. When I joined Napalm Death, I didn't think anything would come of it. I didn't think they were gonna continue on, to be honest. Because when I left, Nic wasn't interested in doing it either, and Mick didn't want Nic in the group anymore either because they'd have such conflicts already. I don't think any of us expected Mick Harris to continue on with it.

After Justin left, who was in the band?

Bullen: It was really just me and Mick Harris and Jimmy Whiteley, who later went on to be in Ripchord and various other groups. And we tried a couple of guitarists.

Harris: We went through a few different guitarists that didn't really work; Frank [Healy], who plays bass in Benediction, tried out. He just didn't click.

Bullen: So we asked Shane Embury if he would like to play the guitar, but I think he was just a bit too nervous to do it, so he said no. It was still with Frank Healy when I left. And it was only afterwards that Bill Steer joined. But again, as far as I was concerned, they really weren't my kind of people.

Nic, why did you leave?

Bullen: Because I didn't get on with any of them. And I didn't really want to be in a heavy metal band or just a rock 'n' roll band making a career. I'd been getting pretty dissatisfied through the later months of 1986. I really didn't get on with Mick Harris at all. And at the time he had a group of cronies who hung around him, who whatever he'd do they'd just kind of applaud and laugh and think he was brilliant. And I didn't really get on with any of them. So I tended to talk more to Justin. When Justin left, I really felt isolated in my own group. I was weak. I should have said to them, "It's really not for me. I'm gonna leave." But I find that hard to do because I actually don't really like conflict. And so I stayed on, hoping it would get better. And it wouldn't. And then I started not turning up to the practices, because I'd travel to go to the practice and I'd nearly get there and I just couldn't face it. I couldn't face going in and spending time with those people. I remember getting into the city center and going and buying a bottle of drink and sitting on a park bench and drinking the drink and thinking, "*I'm not going back.*" And so I didn't contact them, and then I sort of found out at some point they were doing concerts with a new singer and a new guitarist. So that was it, really. There wasn't really any big argument or bust-up or anything like that; it just sort of disappeared, really.

Harris: I just remember one day, it was like March '87, I said to Nic, "Look, you're turning up drunk. You're not into this new material, and you're not really into it no more; what do you want to do?" And that was it. Nic took off. That was the last I ever saw of Nic. OK, Nic's gone.

SIDE B

How did Lee [Dorrian] come to join as the vocalist?

Whiteley: Lee was a good friend of mine. He arranged gigs for underground punk/hardcore bands in his home city of Coventry, mostly at a pub called the Hand & Heart. In fact, it was whilst passing a secondhand goods shop on the way to the Hand & Heart that I spied the bass guitar that I ended up buying and subsequently using on *Scum*. I frequently traveled over there to gigs that he'd arranged, as there wasn't much activity in Birmingham at the time. Again, we had a similar musical interest; we were both from poor sub–working class neighborhoods and had a fair bit in common.

Harris: I was friends with Lee. Jimmy was friends with Lee. We knew him coming to the Mermaid, and also he was a local promoter in Coventry. He put Napalm Death on in Coventry.

Lee Dorrian: We were all in the scene, which was a very small scene. We used to converge at the Mermaid on Friday and Saturday nights in Birmingham.

Harris: I asked Lee, "Do you want to do vocals?" He sort of didn't really feel he could do it. I said, "Look, it's quite easy. Give it a go."

Dorrian: I had no preparation whatsoever to go into the studio. All I'd done before that is I had a bedroom band with a friend. We didn't even have any equipment. He had a small amp. I used to scream into a screwdriver, never mind a mic. The first-ever gig [I did with Napalm Death], I actually promoted the show myself. Antisect were headlining and Heresy, and then Napalm Death opened. So I was on the door one minute and on the stage for the first time the next. I was quite nervous that night.

Did it seem weird that you were in a band with no original members?

Dorrian: It felt weird, but on reflection it didn't, really. It seemed the other guys moved on and did something else that they wanted to do. Napalm had already established itself in the underground. In many ways, you could say it should have changed its name, because it was Napalm Death Mark II, really, but in hindsight it just seemed natural the way it happened. Look at the band now. Even since then, there's not one original member off that album that's in the band now. The only surviving member from that period is Shane, who is on the second album.

At what point did the idea to record a second side come up?

Harris: Dig had shown some interest towards the end of '86. He'd been coming to some of the Mermaid hardcore matinees, which were all-day punk/hardcore affairs, and just about everyone was playing them. He'd started to take an interest. I remember him phoning me up one day and saying, "You recorded this A side; how about coming to Nottingham? I'll buy the master tape off you, and I'll get you into the studio again, and you'll record a B side." So I went along to Nottingham, took the master tape. He was adamant that I took this master, and there was no contract or anything. It was just a gentleman's handshake. He said, "Do you want to go back to Rich Bitch?" I said, "Yeah!" He said, "Do you want to do one of those evening sessions?" I said, "Yeah, it's not a problem."

How did the songs on Side B come together?

Harris: I'd written what became the B side of *Scum*. I'd had this two-string guitar—I couldn't play a guitar. I couldn't hold a chord. I have little fingers, little monkey hands. I just couldn't hold a chord. I'd get that chord, but as soon as my fingers moved, the chord was gone. I just discovered this way of taking all the strings off and leaving the E and the A and sort of messing with this tuning, like, "*Well, hang on, that sounds like a bar chord.*" I just thought, "Well, someone's got to do some writing here."

How did Bill [Steer] come to join?

Bill Steer: I'd been playing with this punk/metal band or something—it was like a really weak version of Discharge. One day [a friend] showed up and said,

"You're not playing that tour; some band called Napalm Death's got it." And I [was] thinking, "I wonder who they are?" A bit later, a friend of mine who lived somewhere in the midlands got to know them and then he sent me what turned out to be Side A of *Scum*. And that point, I just thought it was fantastic. And it was really good when I saw it. To me, it was really obviously something that stood out in that scene. Mostly because there was nobody like Mick in that world.

Harris: Come February of '87, I ended up asking Bill Steer [to join], who at that time had just started university and had got Carcass together. I went down to Liverpool twice to rehearse at his house. The Carcass drum kit was there. He was only 16 and his parents didn't want him coming up to Birmingham. So I went down and he picked the songs up in no time. I said, "I'm gonna have to get you to Birmingham, Bill, because obviously we're gonna have to record this B side."

Bill, you had Carcass at the same time as this, right?

Steer: Yeah, I think so in some form. But I think it was the early form before we had Ken, actually. That's just a feeling, but I could be wrong. I think things fell apart fairly shortly after that, because that side of *Scum*, at the time, no one knew what it was gonna be—a split album or what.

What were the Side B sessions like?

Whiteley: The original Rich Bitch was a damp basement in an abandoned building right next to Selly Oak railway station. Rob Bruce, the owner—he played in a band called Rich Bitch—had a good ear for the sounds that punk bands were trying to achieve; most local punk bands recorded there at some point in their existence.

Harris: Bill came up. We rehearsed the evening before and just went over it. Lyrics were still being written as we were recording overnight.

Whiteley: Bill, Mick and I had only had a minimal amount of time trying to thrash out ideas in Bill's parents' house some weeks prior to that. It was pretty desperate . . .

Harris: It was just a matter of [turning] up at the studio. Shane [Embury] and Mitch [Dickinson] came along from Unseen Terror. At that time Shane was a *huge* fan of Napalm.

Whiteley: I remember primarily being nervous of the fact that we had only rehearsed once as a unit merely hours the previous night before we were committing all of the B side to tape.

Harris: I had to cue Lee for the lyrics every time—where it should drop in, where it should drop out.

Dorrian: That was the first time I'd been in a studio. I'd done one gig previous to that, and that was kind of a guessing game. There was like no rehearsals whatsoever. And a lot of it was just instinct, really.

Harris: The vocals were a lot more extreme with, obviously, Lee doing more growling and me doing the screaming, "influenced from Japanese hardcore" stuff.

Mick, other than the lineups, how would you say the sides are different?

Harris: I'd say it's a lot dirtier, the B side to the A side, as much as it's the same studio and same engineer. I think that's just down to the tuning. It's a lot more down-tuned. It's concert pitch for the A side. I think Bill tuned down to, I believe, C-sharp or B.

Was that it for recording?

Harris: We did have to go back to do another mixdown. We knocked it out, but there was something that was still not quite right. So Dig was sort of, "Oh, I don't want to spend any more money." I said, "I'm not happy, Dig; the drums just aren't fitting." He said, "OK, let me call them up." We managed to get a four-hour session.

Why did Jim eventually leave?

Whiteley: That old chestnut, "differences of personality."

Harris: Several months later, it was released and we went on tour, with record; we shared a van, shared all the costs and we went through Europe. Come back and Jimmy decided he wanted to quit over really nothing, as far as I'm concerned. A little argument over next to nothing. And that was it. I called up Shane.

Much of Scum's *success is owed to BBC Radio 1 DJ John Peel. What does that mean to you?*

Harris: I'd grown up with John Peel. He educated me musically, because he was the only one that was playing music that pushed boundaries and let us all discover new music, which would go onto other things . . . I think on a Wednesday night, Peel had said, "And tomorrow night I'm going to be playing some records by so and so," and I thought, "Oh yes!" Just to hear Napalm Death mentioned. And I went down to Jim's and I said, "He's gonna play it tonight." And he did. He played "You Suffer" three times.

Broadrick: Head of David did a Peel session with me on drums. The night it was broadcast, John Peel followed the first Head of David song with Napalm Death, one of the songs I was on on *Scum*. And my jaw just hit the fucking floor. I couldn't believe it. In one night, my hero that I'd been listening to as a little kid—I was played twice in two different groups in one night on John Peel. Napalm Death blew up then in the U.K.

Dorrian: From my personal point of view, he didn't play a track from side two until a week after he'd been playing side one to death. So I'd listen to it every single day, taping it and stuff, and then I think it might have been "Parasites" or "C.S." And then we got asked to do a session, and it just got better from there. Just to get asked to do a John Peel session was a dream come true.

Harris: Basically, he played "You Suffer" and there was a bit of silence, I remember, and he was like, "Wow. Oh, hang on, I'm just gonna have to put that on again." And he did! He did it three times. And he just said, "Wow. We'll, we're gonna hear some more from them in the show."

Steer: A lot of the attention we were receiving was just down to John Peel—because he brought us in really quickly and we did a session—and then, obviously, at that point, I was listening to John Peel because either a band I was in was on his show, or a friend's band was on there, and it was very exciting.

Dorrian: To this day, Napalm Death is a name that probably one out of five of the average people in the street would have heard. Back in those days and after I left the group, there was Radio 1 in the afternoons and there was this asshole DJ named Steve Wright. And it got so notorious that he used to have this competition like "open the box," or something like that, and if you got the question wrong, you were submitted to a two-second dose of punishment, which was, I think he played "Dead" or "You Suffer" by Napalm Death as your punishment. It was a really hot summer and that thing on Radio 1 was on all the time. And I was delivering furniture around really pissed off.

Harris: What was I—19, 20—and there you are, your idol and your record music teacher [Peel] plays a record that you played on, and not playing it [not] once but four times, and saying those words that you would never expect to hear: "I'm gonna have to get these guys in for a session." And he did.

Whiteley: He left a void larger than the imagination and will never be forgotten by those whom had the good fortune to be touched by his wisdom and humility. R.I.P.

Justin and Nic, since you weren't in the band when the album came out, what did you think of it?

Broadrick: I remember thinking, "*Wow, my first record.*" What was the weirdest shit for me was when John Peel had caught onto it. John Peel was a fucking hero to me. It was like going to a council-estate school where very few people could connect with what I was into; for me, my solace was listening to John Peel every night.

Bullen: What I resented was the way the group tried to paint Justin and myself out of the history of the group by a kind of brief mention of us, as if we had merely been session musicians who happened to play instruments on the first side, whereas we were the writers of the songs. Mick Harris and no one else but Justin and myself wrote all of the songs on Side A.

Do you like any of the Napalm Death recordings after you left?

Bullen: Um, no. I find it very staid, very conservative. I like danger and experimentation and mystery and excitement and the unknown, and they don't give me any of that. Putting it in context, I didn't buy records by any of their peers, either. I didn't buy albums by Heresy or Hellbastard or the Electro Hippies or any of those groups.

Broadrick: The first John Peel session with that lineup that replaced Nic and I is, for me, the best stuff Napalm Death ever did, in my own personal taste. It was way beyond what Napalm Death began as on *Scum*, and I think it was fucking incredible, and I think Napalm Death were incredible after I'd left the group as well.

Harris: The raw element's gone. I've always said it. And I'm not slagging them. I would love to produce Napalm Death. I'd do it for free. I'd love to give them that rawness back.

BLEEDING WORKS OF ART

How Jeff Walker came to do the cover art for Napalm Death's Scum

Having met Napalm Death while playing in his own group, thrash-influenced crust-punks Electro Hippies, Jeff Walker formed a friendship with the band. In addition to playing music, he designed several album covers around that time, including Carcass' LPs and Axegrinder's *Rise of the Serpent Men*, and he recently designed Liverpudlian death metallers Diamanthian's logo. Shortly after Nic Bullen quit Napalm Death, Mick Harris asked Walker to design the cover of what would become *Scum*, and subsequently the logo the band would use on future releases. Walker used cheap, fine felt-tip pens, suitable for a draftsman, to create the black-and-white image. Walker would later join Napalm Death guitarist Bill Steer's band Carcass as vocalist/bassist.

— Kory Grow

How did you come to do the Scum *album sleeve?*

Jeff Walker: Mick gave me a general idea of what the record sleeve should be. It was pretty brief, but it was pretty punk rock. I just tried to put my spin on what their influences were, which was Siege and Celtic Frost. It's got the skull from Siege flyers at the bottom . . . and then it's got the wings off a Celtic Frost flyer. In a way, I was kind of taking a piss, because they wanted it to be really punk rock, anarcho-punk the way it was described. It was kind of difficult. They were like, "Yeah, we want skulls at the bottom and all these corporate logos and businessmen." I tried to bring something a bit more interesting to it.

Sounds like you're not entirely happy with it.

Walker: Like I said, the brief they gave me was kind of lame. The whole sleeve is peppered with clichés. The skulls are from Siege flyers or Dead Kennedys records or Reagan Youth. It's typical punk rock.

What do you remember about designing the logo?

Walker: It's a take on the logo that they had anyway. It's kind of inspired by the old t-shirt. It's out of proportion. If you look at the "N" and the "M" on the end, they're not the same size.

Was this an easy cover to create for you?

Walker: Back then I was very lazy. Mick kept hassling me to do the sleeve and I started it. For a long time, it didn't get beyond two inches on bottom of the big paper I was doing it on. All I can say is I'm really happy I finished it. I'm actually surprised I still got it. I don't have the Carcass artwork. If anyone wants to buy it, just get in touch with Albert and make an offer.

CHAPTER 6

SCARED TO DEATH

THE MAKING OF REPULSION'S *HORRIFIED*

by Matthew Widener

Release Date: 1989
Label: Necrosis
Summary: Unkind grind pioneers
Induction Date: August 2008/Issue #46

Horrified. It's both Repulsion's genre-sparking album and the way enlightened metal fans will look at you should you admit ignorance of the fact—which is very well possible, seeing as how Repulsion have always been a band that your favorite bands worshipped, but were somehow otherwise criminally unheard of. But make no mistake, evangelizers like Napalm Death, Carcass, Entombed, Terrorizer, At the Gates and others will tell you—one listen to *Horrified*—to the thrashing riffs and buzz-saw bass, the desperately screamed vocals and the incessant pounding (that legitimized a new drumbeat)— and you'll see how it all started. You'll visit the haunted cobwebbed attic of the genre we call grindcore.

Recorded in '86, tape-traded for three years—beyond Repulsion's demise—and released posthumously on Earache sub-label Necrosis in '89, *Horrified* infected the burgeoning underground with an unheralded blend of hardcore and death metal, appealing to disparate scenes and transcending genre boundaries, effectively blurring them into a frenetic mess. It was a singularity, a leap in the evolution. Unpolished and unapologetic, its legacy of primitivism is just as relevant now in this digital age of perfection as it was back in the '80s, when it was shocking enough to make tape decks tremble and listeners utter, "What the fuck is that?"

Decibel interrogated Scott Carlson, Matt Olivo, Aaron Freeman and Dave "Grave" Hollingshead for the story of *Horrified*: how it came to be and what it infamously went on to do.

PART I: BIRTH OF THE BLAST

Genocide—later to become Repulsion—changed my life. No other band mattered to me after that. They destroyed every other band around at that period and were everything I was looking for at that point. I was 18 at the time; this may sound a little cliché, but I don't give a shit—to me they were and still are gods!
— SHANE EMBURY, NAPALM DEATH

I just remember hearing that first record in demo form way back in the mid '80s and going, "Holy shit, that's fast! What the fuck are those guys snorting?"
— DANNY LILKER, BRUTAL TRUTH

Horrified *was originally recorded as the* **Slaughter** *of the Innocent demo three years before its release. What was the songwriting process like?*

Aaron Freeman: At that time, most of the songs on the album were already written. Scott and I collaborated on "Acid Bath" and "Crematorium"—we were tossing a few things back and forth.

Matt Olivo: Scott and I had maybe 75–80 percent of the songs written already in the band Genocide. Essentially, Repulsion was just a—not even an evolution of Genocide—it was Genocide, but noticeably faster. We dropped a few Genocide songs, we changed the name and then we added a few more Repulsion songs. It was a seamless transition, let's put it that way. As far as the songwriting goes, there were a couple of different modes that we were in back in those days—sometimes Scott would come over with pretty much a whole song, which I would contribute a riff to. And then sometimes I would come to Scott with a couple ideas, and then he would add a couple ideas to it. I think our best songs were written that way: "Black Breath" and "Radiation Sickness" come to mind as two songs that we both had an equal amount of musical ideas, and it literally came together almost instantly—like coca powder and milk. [*Laughs*] And then there were times where I would seriously spend a weekend to myself and come to him with two whole songs.

Scott Carlson: For the most part, I think it was a dictatorship on the part of Matt and I, as far as how we rehearsed and put songs together. I'm not sure exactly how much Dave enjoyed the way we did things—probably not very much. At that point, Matt and I were extremely driven to get our stuff out of the garage or the basement. Everything was written between January of '86 and June when we recorded. We had already established the blast beat, so those songs were written with that style in mind, so they're a little less manic, I'd say, than the ones that were written to sound like Slayer and then just got sped up by the "accidental" discovery of the blast beat. "Maggots in Your Coffin," for instance, and "Crematorium"—those riffs were written around the blast beat. So we had that in mind. We were just basically trying to flesh out the album. We needed 30 minutes, we figured—we were really into punk bands—and Discharge albums were 30 minutes long, so we figured "18 songs" and that's what we were shooting for. And I think "Maggots in Your Coffin," "Crematorium" and "Black Breath" were the last three songs we wrote. And "Crematorium" was probably finished, like, a couple days before we recorded it.

Olivo: Now Scott was the lyricist. There were a few open forums where he would say [the lyrics] out loud and we would all laugh and throw in a word or two to add a little spice to it. The lyrics are pretty much Scott Carlson, and they're still amazing to me—some of them are just so good.

At that point, what were your major influences? What was **Horrified** *hatched from?*

Carlson: We grew up in the '70s and we listened to rock music, you know; there was no death metal, and there wasn't even that much heavy metal aside from heavy metal/rock bands, like UFO and the Scorpions and Judas Priest, bands that all had block structure. Most of them were four-on-the-floor, pretty straightforward, meaty riffs and catchy choruses, and we loved all that stuff. I'm sure that had an influence on us. We were big Aerosmith fans, KISS and all that stuff.

Dave "Grave" Hollingshead: My influences come from funk back in the '70s—shit my sister used to listen to. My mother listened to the Rolling Stones and Queen, Olivia Newton John and shit like that. And then I got into new wave. At that time [of the recording] I was all into death metal, anything fast—Slayer, Metallica, Sodom, COC, D.R.I., GBH, Black Flag.

Had you rehearsed much going into the studio? Did you know what sound you were after?

Carlson: If you listen to the rehearsal we did the night before we went into the studio, we were probably 10 times tighter than we are on the album. Back then, our live shows were always a mess, but when we rehearsed we were incredibly tight. We had that material nailed. But you know, recording—that was the first time any of us had been in a studio where we were isolated from one another, and that threw everybody off.

Olivo: We pretty much knew what it was going to sound like. I mean, the drumbeats in Repulsion—there are only, like, maybe three or four drumbeats that we use over and over and over again. We kind of ended up using Dave as a drum machine, practically. Of course, he put his own things in there, but we would come to him with well-fleshed-out ideas of what we wanted out of the drums.

And the drums at that point had been pushed faster than any other band had previously seen. That was probably the first album comprised mostly of blast beats. What made you go that fast?

Hollingshead: Well, Scott kept pushing me. [*Laughs*] Every practice: "Could you, uh, play a little faster?" And as far as doing a one-two beat, like the classic Slayer thing, I hated going any faster because I couldn't double time with my right hand, my hand on the ride, and it was like . . . cheating, until we got so fast it was just, you know, ridiculous. I didn't like it at first because of the cheating factor. But I can still do it. Not very long, but I can still do it.

Freeman: Scott was always pushing Dave. And sometimes it was hard for Dave to keep up. [*Laughs*] I mean, I don't know how it evolved—it just did. The songs just progressed—it wasn't something conscious, I think, and as far as the blasting stuff, I just don't think Dave could play a straight beat, so somehow it evolved into the blast. And the swing beat—like on "Bodily Dismemberment" or "Slaughter of the Innocent"—that was just something that Dave pulled from playing in the hardcore bands or the funk bands he was in.

Olivo: Dave was kind of pushed to do what Scott and I really wanted him to do. I mean, he did end up putting a few of his own trademark things on it that Scott and I didn't anticipate, like that one thing in particular—when Dave plays a blast beat, we didn't anticipate that leaning on the downbeat, that accent where it's like DUH duh DUH duh DUH duh. People just don't do that. People just go DUH DUH DUH DUH. As he got faster, I think he sort of needed his own technique to keep the time and to get a groove going so that he could physically pull it off. I mean, if you've seen him after we finish a song, the blood would drain from his face and he looked like he would pass out. Because nobody played like that in those days, you know? I guess it pushed him to do some remarkable things, and it pushed him to do something that people regard as pioneering or original.

PART II: FROM THE GARAGE TO THE STUDIO (AND BACK)

When I finally met those guys in 1990, I was pissing my pants with excitement. It was weird, because they were all absolute sweethearts and it truly didn't register to them what a beast of a demo/album they'd originally made. Dave Grave found a dead duck on a stick, though, insisted on waving it around, and he turned out to be a bit mad in the end.
— MARK "BARNEY" GREENWAY, NAPALM DEATH

I find it amazing when something as simple as a beat or tone defines a genre. With punk, the Ramones riffing, thrash metal had Lombardo's *Reign in Blood* beat, and grind had the Scott Carlson bass tone.
— KEVIN SHARP, BRUTAL TRUTH

What role did Doug Earp play in the album?

Carlson: Basically he gave us the money to record it. He gave me a couple hundred dollars to put on a hall show. I rented a hall, booked a bunch of punk bands, including Repulsion, and put on a show. I paid the bands each a hundred bucks, and I took what was left and gave it to the studio, which was, like, $300 or something like that. Doug never got paid back his money until Earache put the record out.

Freeman: He was a local guy with a record store. Anything obscure, just anything—he had. So Scott ended up hanging out there, working there, too. Doug was always the guy who would front the money for the hall shows.

Olivo: Doug was in his late 20s at that time. I think his mom passed away and left him some money, so he very smartly purchased a home and purchased a small storefront and started Wyatt Earp Records. It was a very small room, and he didn't keep lots of inventory. What he would do, though, is special order things for you. Scott was already a complete vinyl junkie, and when he found out about Wyatt Earp Records, that's pretty much where we spent all our time, because we could read about something in a magazine or fanzine and go, "Doug, can you get it?" and he would get on the phone to his distributors, and we would have it within a week. That was amazing. It was like that for years. And Doug naturally became involved in the underground music scene in Flint, and everyone went to Doug to get their punk, their metal and their underground this and that. So when we went to do our album, he'd always liked us as, you know, people, and liked Repulsion because of its uniqueness and bizarreness, and so when we asked him . . . uh, I'm not sure if we asked him or if he offered it up. But he readily offered up money.

What are your most vivid memories of the studio?

Hollingshead: I was stuck in this little room, and trying to watch Matt play through this little window so I could try to keep time with what was going on.

Freeman: When we initially went over to [engineer] Larry Hennessey's house, and we were sitting in his living room and he was really pushing a drum machine. I don't know if he thought he could program these drums or something—he was basically the only engineer with a studio within our budget. I remember Scott doing his vocals screaming into a PCM mic stuck to a piece of glass, making all these retarded faces, and Dave sitting in this other room blasting his heart out. We were all pretty excited.

Carlson: When I started to cut the vocals, the engineer fell out of his chair laughing. I think the first song that I did was "Black Breath," and he was sitting in there with Olivo and he literally fell off his chair and was rolling around laughing when I started singing. So that didn't really make me feel all that comfortable, but luckily Matt and Aaron were there, so I just looked at them and went for it.

Olivo: When Scott did his vocals for *Horrified*, he really pulled out all the stops and came to do something special, because I'd never heard him scream like that. I mean, he just went off. If you were in the studio, you would've seen someone singing the lyrics to their songs as if their life depended on it. It was very remarkable to me, and I'd been his friend for years. It was amazing.

Carlson: Leading up to the recording of the record, I had been sort of working on my vocal style. I was always really self-conscious of how deep my voice is when I was younger, so I was always trying to raise it up. My favorite singer back then was Jeff Becerra from Possessed—that was the guy that I was really into, him and Cronos. But not long before we went into the studio, I got strep throat. And I kept practicing. As soon as I got well enough to sing again, we just kept practicing, and I didn't really let my voice heal properly. And it just kind of changed after that, and I was able to get into a higher register. I definitely pushed it further in the studio, but my voice sounded different—forever—after that.

Who recorded the album?

Freeman: His name was Larry Hennessey and he was a friend of a friend who had a home studio, working in radio, doing commercials—and I think he was a DJ or something, too.

Olivo: We went into this guy's basement studio, Larry Hennessey, which nowadays would probably be perceived as a really great rapper name. He was this stoned-out dude with long hair. You think we'd all get along, but he was kind of a snob for some reason. He was a total burnout, but he was snobbish the whole time and laughed at Scott's vocals, and was made ill by his bass sound, and didn't understand the drums. He just threw up the mics on everything and we got in and got out. Three to four days, total. I seem to remember one to two days tracking drums, one to two days on guitars and vocals. It was very, very quick.

Carlson: The drums were in the utility room, and I think Matt was standing in the control room, and I was in the little room in between where Dave was and Matt was. And we tracked everything—bass, drums and guitar—like that. And then we went back and I know we re-recorded all the guitars from the scratch tracks. And the bass was re-recorded, but lost.

Olivo: Scott made a scratch bass track by plugging his bass into a Boss distortion pedal directly into the recording console, and then we went right to tape with it, and it was supposed to be scratch—why we bothered to do that, I don't know. Maybe Larry read in *Mix* Magazine that it was a good idea or something. Anyway, the sound that came out was this . . . insane fuzz; we ended up keeping it on some of the songs and I can't remember why. So the bass that you hear before "Festering Boils" is a direct-to-console recording. That's why it sounds so fuzzy and gnarly—because it was a direct signal.

Carlson: I don't want to incriminate [Larry], but he was doing a little smoking when we were recording the album, and I'm not exactly sure how experienced he was, but he blew over some of the bass tracks when we were overdubbing guitar solos, so the rough mix that got circulated back in '86 has a different bass track on it than the one that's on the finished product. The bass that's on the album is the scratch track, which is basically just a distortion pedal plugged directly into a DI [direct in] box that went straight into the board. Luckily, I recorded it with distortion or else we'd have no bass on the album.

What gear did you play?

Hollingshead: Tama Rockstar, from the early '80s, brandy wine color, beat to hell.

Olivo: Vantage Flying V guitar with DiMarzio Power Plus pickup; Marshall Mark II 100-watt head; a total no-name 4x12 cabinet; an Ibanez Tube Screamer, one of the original ones.

Freeman: Sunn Beta Lead 100-watt head; a homemade 4x12 cabinet; Gibson Flying V; Boss Super OverDrive.

Carlson: I never owned a bass cabinet in Repulsion—borrowed from a friend; Acoustic bass head; Squier P Bass.

PART III: INFECTING THE SCENE

Me and the guitarist of Dishonorable Discharge/ex–After the Bombs decided to get our *Horrified* tattoos. I took the logo and he took the face. So when we meet, we can actually be the *Horrified* album cover! When we met Dave Grave at the Skitsystem gig at Garage Oslo last year, we could actually show him this "circus trick." What a fuckin' freak I am.
— FENRIZ, DARKTHRONE

My fondest memory about *Horrified* is blasting the album in my walkman on the way to school. It efficiently blocked out the noise of other kids on the bus and eventually blew my ears to hell! Alongside early Napalm Death and Carcass, *Horrified* remains a grindcore milestone and, to me, a true classic I'll forever enjoy.
— DIRK VERBEUREN, SOILWORK

You circulated the recording, but labels were unresponsive. In that frustrating three-year interim, how did you not give up?

Olivo: We did give up! We recorded it and said, "OK, this is our demo, this is the *Slaughter of the Innocent* demo." We made a cassette demo and we traded it and sold it, and our friends, Shane [Embury of Napalm Death] and people like that, eventually got it. We had critical acclaim from people we respected, and we were really happy with that. But back then, labels were way more interested in bands that sounded like Exodus and Death and stuff like that. So, yeah, we weren't going to get a record deal. [*Laughs*] I think we probably hung around for another year or so after it was recorded, and then we started going our separate ways. Scott became more interested in playing a different kind of music, I started thinking about joining the service, Dave actually joined the Army, Aaron had a kid, so it fell apart pretty quickly. Repulsion was only together for like a year, you know. And then it was done.

Freeman: At that point, Matt had already joined the Army, Dave was in the Army, Scott and I were working together at some factory; so at the time the band was pretty much done. We sent it out and didn't really get a response— got a few rejection letters—and we were just getting burned out on it. It wasn't going anywhere, no one was picking it up and we couldn't figure out why. I don't know if we were just too far out there or what—there weren't too many bands doing that back then.

Then the album was finally picked up after Repulsion had disbanded. How did that happen?

Carlson: Around the time we recorded it, I had done so much groundwork, like sending out demos and making contacts—I was obsessed with that whole scene, that's all I did. I used to run my parents' phone bill up calling people in California to talk about music.

Freeman: We'd be hanging out at a friend's house and Scott would have to run home to flip the tape over of a demo he was duping, start a new tape. [*Laughs*]

Carlson: At one point the mail that was coming back to us just got to be so overwhelming that I couldn't deal with it anymore. And one day I took a garbage bag full of unanswered letters over to Aaron's house and said, "Here, you can do the mail now." And at the time he was enthusiastic about doing it, so I was really happy to put it off on somebody else. Because back then it wasn't about shooting an email off to somebody; it was opening letters and handwriting a reply and stamping them and taking them to the post office. So I think all that mail sort of snowballed into those guys in England getting their hands on the demo. I remember Shane [Embury] writing me a letter when he was a kid, and it was very naïve where he just kind of honestly said, "Hey, we just heard you guys and we're totally changing the sound of the band." I completely forgot about it until the day when I was working at a record store and this kid I was working with slapped on the first Napalm Death record and I heard that intro—what's that song?—and my first thought was that it was just a bizarre coincidence that somebody came up with the same riff, and then I heard the duh-duh-duh-duh-duh-duh-duh-duh, and I ran over and grabbed the sleeve and started examining it, and I was calling all the guys in the band and saying, "You're not going to believe this!"

Freeman: Initially, Digby [Pearson] from Earache called me, and Shane and I were corresponding a lot back then. I got a letter from Shane and he said he was pushing Dig to put out *Horrified*; I really didn't think anything of it. So, sometime in early '89, I got a call from Dig and he wanted to put it out. I didn't know what to think, so I passed it by Scott and Scott said, "Yeah, let's do it."

Carlson: At the same time, Bill [Steer] and Jeff [Walker of Carcass] were starting a label and they wanted to put it out. Jeff was trying to get this label off the ground, and he went to Dig and they both agreed to put it out on Necrosis.

Freeman: I got back with Dig and he was willing to send over some cash to remix it. So initially we had a guy, the engineer who did the *Slaughter of the Innocent* demo, we were going to have him do it, and he agreed to do it, and then once we got the cash from Dig, the original engineer was nowhere to be found. So Scott hooked up with a guy named Jonas—how he got hooked up with him, I don't know. Scott and I went down there and did the best we could on it.

Olivo: I went to Germany in the Army. I was just hanging out one day and I got a package that looked like a record from Aaron, and I opened it up and I could not believe my eyes. It was on Earache Records, too—a label I thought would be perfect for us. And I was, like, "Wow, this is amazing."

And they changed the name of the album from **Slaughter of the Innocent** *to* **Horrified***?*

Carlson: Oh, that was my idea. The concept I had for the cover, initially, was different. It was supposed to be a kind of comic book, and I just thought that the *Horrified* title fit it better. The lettering on the cover I did myself, and it's supposed to look like an old E.C. comic.

Olivo: As far as I know, the original *Horrified* cover art, the head, was an homage drawing that Scott had done to an old, I think, E.C. comic book—there was a panel in a comic book of a kid that was all burned up or something like that.

Freeman: Initially the cover art wasn't that head. We let another guy do the cover for us—his name was Mike Grossklaus; he also did some of the layout stuff on the album, too—and I don't know if Necrosis didn't think it was good enough or if the head was a better choice, which looking back I think it was.

Carlson: I drew the original illustration. I believe Jeff Walker is the artist who did the cover, even though he didn't take credit for it. It looks like he just took a Xerox of the sticker and blew it up and painted over it. I don't think he realized my idea was for it to be a burned-up kid, and he made it look like a rotten, green zombie. [*Laughs*] I took it mostly from a comic book called *Twisted Tales*, you know, I just redid it and changed a few things. There was a story in a *Twisted Tales* comic book about a burned-up kid who comes back from the dead on Halloween and goes trick-or-treating.

Freeman: That's our Eddie, I guess.

PART IV: THE AFTERMATH

Taking Slayer and Death to the next level was what Genocide [later to become Repulsion] did. Two thumbs-up for what was a big influence for me and early Napalm Death — *Horrified*!
—MICK HARRIS, NAPALM DEATH

My first experience with Repulsion's *Horrified* was at Tomas [Lindberg]'s house almost 20 years ago. That was also my first contact with grindcore/death metal in general. I instantly liked the rawness it offered — almost like punk, but way more brutal. A classic band that will always be safe in my future record collection.
—ANDERS BJÖRLER, THE HAUNTED/AT THE GATES

What was the response to the album after its release?

Freeman: I really didn't hear too much about it. I'm sure in Europe it might have done better than here in the U.S. We really didn't get any reports on how good or bad it was doing. Always seemed to get a good review, though. At that time I think I was drifting away from that style of music, too.

Olivo: It was pretty positive. We had friends like Chuck Schuldiner, and our friends in Slaughter up in Toronto—I'm not quite sure if those guys got it. [*Laughs*] The sound that people were so into in that day was Death and Possessed—very metallic and theatrical and thrashy—but what we were doing sounded like a chainsaw and an anvil. And it wasn't really musical—it wasn't apparent that it was musical to some people. But the people who got it, loved it; they just loved the shit out of it. It just wasn't very wide.

But it was only a matter of time—at what point did you realize the influence it would have on extreme metal?

Hollingshead: That would've been the '90s when Relapse picked it up.

Olivo: That came after we would read in interviews with Napalm and Carcass and Entombed. It was a delayed reaction—it wasn't immediate. I think one of the reasons was that it influenced people who were influential—and because we weren't around anymore. It was like a secret people could have, like, "Man, these guys were around for one fucking album."

Freeman: I think when we initially got back together, which was 1990, we started getting a little mail, and the show that we did in Buffalo—that was our first really big show outside of Flint. The place was just packed and, of course, everybody was going apeshit, wanting to meet us, wanting to talk to us. It was really strange. [*Laughs*] From playing little hall shows in Flint where you know everybody to somewhere where you don't know everybody and they're coming up to you.

Carlson: As much as Napalm Death walk around professing Repulsion—if it wasn't for Repulsion—we could say the same thing about them. You know, if it wasn't for Napalm Death and Entombed, nobody would know about Repulsion; it would've been completely obscure. They definitely put us on the map. Only musicians and a few tape-traders knew about us. Whatever Napalm Death and Carcass and Entombed and all these bands took from us, they gave back to us in spades.

In retrospect, how do you think Horrified *holds up? Would you change anything?*

Freeman: No, I don't think I would change anything. It's good the way it is. It shows the raw intensity of the band as a whole. And looking back, I think we maybe should have left the feedback in on the vinyl mix, I don't know.

Carlson: I think the fact that it's such a basic recording, and the songs are so simple, it gives it a sort of timeless quality that triggered drums and seven-string guitars can't really—not to knock that stuff, it's just very of the moment. I don't think you listen to *Horrified* and go, "Oh, it's an '80s record!" The idea was to make the ultimate death metal album of the time. And that has something to do with it—at the time it was the ultimate death metal album. It was recorded around the time of *Reign in Blood* and some other amazing records, but it's far more extreme. Obviously, the recording isn't as good. If Rick Rubin had recorded *Horrified*, I dare say it would be a lot more influential than it is now.

Hollingshead: I don't know—I mean there are some mess-ups on there that Scott had to cover with a scream or something like that. If I could do it over— like, the whole album, with what I can do now on a drum set—I'd probably be more pleased with it. For what it is, it's—well, it is what it is. [*Laughs*]

Olivo: I don't think any of [the songs] hold up in terms of sounding modern then or sounding modern now. It all sounds pretty dated. We were really influenced by punk music, like the chorus would just be a repetition of the name of the song over and over. We love that. That was our punk influence and our rock 'n' roll influence. So I think when you listen to Repulsion songs, some of them are really, really catchy. When you hear "You are rotting, maggots in your coffin," it has a certain rhythmic punchiness to it—it still feels like a song as opposed to some of the bands of those times, and it's such a general thing to say. There's just a lot of bands when you listen to them many years later, if they're not Slayer or the others—real leaders—that sound really derivative.

Carlson: Most of the recordings I've done over the years, I don't go back and listen to. But every once in a while, I can listen to *Horrified*.

Olivo: It's still amazing to me. You only spend a year of your life on something, and it's still hanging around.

CHAPTER 7

IMMORTAL RIGHTS

THE MAKING OF MORBID ANGEL'S *ALTARS OF MADNESS*

by J. Bennett

Release Date: 1989
Label: Earache
Summary: Death metal game-changer
Induction Date: April 2006/Issue #18

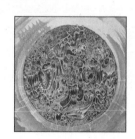

The sweltering heat and merciless humidity of mid-to-late '80s Florida proved a fertile breeding ground for a burgeoning genre that would announce itself to the world as death metal. Led by Chuck Schuldiner and Death, the DM Army proliferated quickly, as bands like Obituary, Deicide and Morbid Angel emerged full-grown from the Floridian swamplands to compete for the title of Fastest, Heaviest or Most Technical Band on Earth. Morbid Angel guitarist and mastermind Trey Azagthoth would settle for no less than all three on his band's 1989 debut, *Altars of Madness*. After recording—and shelving—the *Abominations of Desolation* LP in 1986 with *Altars* guitarist Richard

Brunelle and an assortment of other musicians who were summarily fired, Azagthoth and Brunelle hooked up with bassist/vocalist David Vincent and Terrorizer drummer Pete Sandoval, and prepared to tear death metal a steaming new asshole with unorthodox time signatures, dizzying arrangements and hallucinogenic shredding. Forgoing the gore-bore lyrical style favored by many of their peers, Vincent and Azagthoth pored over the *Necronomicon* ("The Book of Dead Names")—an allegedly ancient occult text that H.P. Lovecraft (who probably authored the book himself in the late 1920s) claimed was written in 730 AD by "the Mad Arab" Abdul Alhazred—while Sandoval honed his double-bass chops. In early 1989, Morbid Angel entered Morrisound Studios in Tampa to record *Altars of Madness*, an album that would turn death metal both upside down and inside out.

***What's the first thing that comes to mind when you think of the recording sessions for* Altars?**

Richard Brunelle: The first thing that pops into my mind is probably that it was one of the most awesome times of my life. I was living the life of a blessed musician, and I was making my dreams come true. I loved being around the guys—they were probably the sickest bunch of guys around, especially in Tampa. We were playing music that, at that time, there were a few bands around doing it, but it hadn't reached the whole world yet.

Pete Sandoval: It was my first experience in a professional studio, and I didn't know what to expect. But we had a plan, you know? We practiced, and we were ready, but I was still very young—like my early 20s, I would say—and I didn't know the other guys too well. I was new in the band, so I was still pretty shy. I would do just about anything they would tell me to do in order to make the music better. But the studio is a challenge, physically and mentally, because recording is a lot different than live performances. There was a lot of pressure because I knew I had to deliver.

David Vincent: I don't wanna say it was a trial run, but it kinda was. It wasn't a super-high budget, and as prepared as you think you might be, you never are. But I feel really good about that album. We worked real, real hard to get to that point, and we were definitely ready to do a record. I'm really pleased that everything came together when it finally did. I mean, we got rejected by so many labels. It was always, "Slow it down—it's too fast," or "You should have more melodic leads, more melodic vocals," or it was a problem with the subject matter—it was just one excuse after the other. In fact, one label sent us a rejection letter—and I still have it—that said, "After listening to your tape, all we can say is that you do for music what King Herod did for babysitting."

With so many bands emerging at the same time—Morbid Angel, Obituary, Death, Deicide, Cannibal Corpse—the Floridian death metal scene seemed like a competitive atmosphere. Were you concerned about being the fastest, the heaviest?

Trey Azagthoth: Back then, I really wanted to destroy everybody. I wanted people to have to work a lot harder after the fans witnessed what we had going on. I wanted to smoke people. I really believed that bands were challenging each other, trying to outdo each other and make each other quit—almost like the rivalries with East Coast and West Coast rappers. I really kind of thought people wanted to write parts that would engulf the whole world. I wanted to get onstage and have people go, "Holy shit—what the fuck is going on?" I wanted to write stuff that would make other bands run and hide. It's not really very nice, but that's what drove me. [*Laughs*] I never wanted to shoot anybody, though.

Brunelle: It was frustrating in a way, because we were playing stuff that was so fast and intricate, yet the tempo patterns made it sound slower than it actually was. We were really doing stuff that nobody else was doing at that time, but some songs didn't sound as fast as they really were because they were in 3/4 timing instead of 4/4 timing. When you start getting into double time as opposed to 1-2-3, 1-2-3-time, it has a whole different feel. A lot of the grindcore bands were doing real fast 4/4, and it was frustrating because we really wanted to be the fastest.

Vincent: You have to remember that this was back before death metal was even something that would be dreamed of having any validity whatsoever. It was really a groundbreaking thing. In all fairness, we were very confident that we would do well with it, just because we had the strength and the focus within the band to marshal this thing through. You get told "No" so many times, and some people take rejection as, you know, maybe that makes people start questioning themselves—but we were empowered by that. It strengthened our resolve to push things further. And there were a lot of people who said no, who, once they saw what *Altars* and the subsequent recordings did, probably wish they would've said yes.

Trey and Richard recorded the **Abominations of Desolation** *album with different band members prior to* **Altars,** *but they weren't very happy with it, so it didn't come out until years later. When you went in to do* **Altars,** *was there anything specific you were trying to avoid, based on your* **Abominations** *experience?*

Brunelle: Well, with that kind of music, it's really difficult to hear everybody while you're playing. Trey envisioned the music a certain way, and when we got in there for *Abominations*, it wasn't quite coming out like he had envisioned it—including my parts. I had to go back after that and relearn all my picking; I had to basically go relearn guitar. It was like that way for everyone after *Abominations*, actually—except Trey. He had his parts down. He knew exactly what he wanted.

Azagthoth: Most of the songs [on *Altars*] were recorded on *Abominations of Desolation*—I think we did that in like '86 or something, so certainly some riffs changed and stuff, but mostly it was just timings and drumbeats. We were able to get more out of Pete than we had on the earlier thing, but everybody grew and expanded, too.

Brunelle: We recorded *Abominations* with another drummer, Mike Browning, and we went through a couple other bass players. Then we met David Vincent, and he invited Trey up to North Carolina to continue Morbid Angel with him. I got invited, too, so Trey and I went up there, and that's where our musical foundation really took place. When we were in Tampa, it wasn't really possible for Trey's vision to come true. By moving to Charlotte, it was able to take shape, because that's when David and eventually Pete came into our lives.

*You recorded **Altars** at Morrisound, which would eventually become a legendary studio for death metal.*

Vincent: We went to Morrisound because we lived in Tampa, you know? It was the preeminent studio at the time, and it still is. The staff there was very helpful, too, but you know, people latch onto things—whether it's producers, or labels or studios. Yeah, Obituary recorded there, but they also live in Florida. Deicide recorded there, but they also live in Florida. But then next thing you know, there were a lot of bands coming because Morrisound had the reputation as the place you wanted to go to record this type of music. I've always believed that any competent engineer with good equipment could do it, but, you know, reputation goes a long way. And good for them—they made a lot of money off of it over the years.

Brunelle: It was really professional, you know, but time is money in that place. You're paying a lot of money to go in there, so you had to just go in and bust out your stuff. There wasn't really any partying or visiting or anything like that going on. Occasionally, we'd have a magazine come down for a photo session or something, but it was pretty much right down to business. The people there were very helpful and easy to work with, and they were good at hearing stuff and knowing what was right and what was wrong, even though they didn't have a great understanding of death metal at that time.

Were you well rehearsed before you went into the studio?

Sandoval: Yeah, but it was hard for me, because I had to learn to play like a death metal drummer. Before that, it was all grind—with one foot. I was in L.A., jamming with Jesse Pintado and Oscar Garcia in Terrorizer, but not doing much because grindcore didn't really exist and death metal was just being born. I'd never played double-bass before I joined Morbid Angel in 1988, so that was a learning experience before we went into the studio. I only had like two and a half months to learn double-bass and how to play all the songs—like "Blasphemy," "Maze of Torment" . . . so to learn double-bass like that, in that amount of time, was a big challenge. In the first month and a half, I think I quit like three times, because I thought I couldn't do it. But those guys pushed me, like, "C'mon—we know you can do it." And one day, after like a month and a half, the magic happened. I guess practice makes perfect.

Brunelle: I was pretty much along for the ride. I was just in awe of Trey. He was a god, and I was doing everything I could to keep up with him at that time. I could have [kept up] if I had lived my life differently, but it was almost like being a running back for an NFL team, you know? You gotta totally work out every day. Trey has muscles in his arms that I couldn't even begin to describe. In the time it'd take me to learn one song that he wrote, he'd write three more songs.

Azagthoth: That record has so many riffs, and the way they're played today has a little more fullness. Back then, everything was kinda rushed and fast, so it didn't really come together as well, I guess, as far as the atmosphere and trippiness. I really wanted a feeling of like going backward or playing sideways and dragging—just all these weird feelings that I wanted to put in the music that I think later albums have. But I think that record had more cool riffs than any other record anyone's ever done, if you count 'em. There's probably, I don't know, 50 or 100 riffs on that record, it seems like to me. I didn't want just a couple of cool riffs and a bunch of filler in each song—I wanted parts where there's actually singing over complicated riffs rather than an easy riff for the vocals.

The credits say "Produced by Dig and Morbid Angel." What did [Earache Records founder] Digby Pearson do to earn a production credit?
Azagthoth: As far as I remember, he gave input about different things, but I think he just wanted to be there because we were one of his earlier bands, and I guess he was just excited to come to America and hang out.

Vincent: I'd say Digby executive-produced it. He paid for it. He fronted the money.

Sandoval: Digby was there, and I think he had something to do with the production, but I'm not sure. Back then, he had bands like Napalm Death, Carcass and Bolt Thrower, you know . . . but a lot of those bands didn't go too far. I mean, what can I say?

Brunelle: He was in the studio the whole time, and he'd give advice or something on stuff that he thought sounded good. If I had a lick or something that

I was unsure of, he'd give it the thumbs-up—stuff like that. If we were spending too much time on something because it wasn't coming out the way we wanted it to, he would sorta say, "That's good enough for me," you know? We would sometimes get carried away with wanting things to be too perfect, so he helped out a lot. We respected the fact that he was the record company helping us out, so we respected his opinion.

Where did the lyrical ideas come from?

Vincent: Mostly [H.P.] Lovecraft-type stuff—*Necronomicon*, definitely—and in some ways adding a little bit of real-world things just to tie it in for reference. "Lord of All Fevers & Plague," for example, is straight *Necronomicon* incantations. I was really super into Lovecraft at the time, and a lot of people attribute the *Necronomicon* to him, but his whole doctrine of the Cthulhu mythos is, you know, some of the names are spelled or pronounced a little differently, but it's the same "Unspeakable Ones, the Ancient Ones, the Old Ones"—there's a lot of parallelism there. I read a lot, and I'd always been into the occult, even from an early age. Everybody in the band was. The type of inter-band humor that we'd have was often like, we'd get a rejection letter and go, "Oh, the Ancient Ones are just challenging us." We'd find a way to bring it back to something that we could rally around.

Azagthoth: The *Necronomicon* was really interesting—I got a lot of inspiration from it at the time. I wanted the songs to be like incantations, like a ceremony with the music setting the mood and the lyrics invoking the energy of a spirit or something. Rather than narrating the situation, I wanted it to actually *be* the situation in real time. I thought that would be the most dramatic, powerful approach. "Bleed for the Devil," for example, was mostly invoking as opposed to narrating. But some songs tell stories, and others are actual real-time rituals. I was into real-time rituals, rather than just talking about people having rituals.

Sandoval: I've never been a lyric type of guy—I've always just been concerned with the drums and the melody. But when I heard songs like "Maze of Torment," "Immortal Rites," "Suffocation," "Damnation"—all those fucking classic songs, who gives a damn what the lyrics are about? The lyrics were powerful no matter what, but I didn't pay too much attention, to be honest with you. I know the first couple of albums were very, very satanic, though.

Brunelle: I loved the lyrics—I thought they were great. They gave me power; they gave me energy. And I loved that there were foreign words in there—words that only we understood unless somebody happened to look into the *Necronomicon*. That book was really twisted and sick, and it really appealed to me and Trey. It was so foul and anti-life. It was against everything that had to do with this world. To us, it seemed like the ultimate in rebellion, because the *Satanic*

Bible and stuff like that still kinda cherished life somewhat, but the *Necronomicon* just wanted death to everything.

Did you have all the guitar solos worked out beforehand, or did you improvise certain parts?

Brunelle: Everything was pretty much worked out. I'd write a basic lead, but I wouldn't write an exact lead as much as Trey would. I'd always kinda just play until I found something that I liked and that everybody agreed on.

Azagthoth: I had a few patterns worked out, but you know, back then I didn't really have a lot of time to spend on my soloing. I'd actually like to go back and have more time to do better solos, because they're a little too painful for what I would've liked them to be. But that's just the way it goes. Some people like them the way they are—all atonal and painful-sounding and all that—but I'm more into flowing solos, like on our last record, *Heretic*. There're some painful elements to those solos, but then there's still a lot of nice flowing going on. It's just a different approach to the guitar, I guess—different scales, matching certain types of riffs to rhythms and stuff. I've got much better solos for all those songs now, anyway—at least for the ones we play live. Like for instance, the solo on "Chapel of Ghouls"; on the record it's one way, but live it's completely different. It has a lot more cool parts. Nowadays, "Lord of All Fevers & Plague" has one solo with all this really cool tapping across a big three-octave scale. Back then, Richard actually played that solo spot on the record.

How did you end up choosing Dan Seagrave's art for the album cover?

Vincent: When I flew over to England to deliver the masters, Dan had submitted that piece. I can't remember if it was completely finished, but it was already in his portfolio. I saw it and I was like, "That's it. That's what we need." I can't remember if we just ran with it, or if we discussed it afterwards, but it really seemed like a no-brainer. It's this heaving earth with a billion different personalities.

Azagthoth: I don't know—I guess it looked cool. I thought some of the faces looked stupid, but overall I thought it was pretty cool for the time.

Sandoval: I think it was perfect—it's the earth, but it's full of faces. It made an impact, and I think most people liked it. A lot of people have even got tattoos on their body of those faces on the cover.

What's your favorite song on the album?

Sandoval: That's hard, but I would say "Maze of Torment," back then, had a very nice feeling to me. I like "Visions From the Dark Side," too—that song had some pretty cool riffs. Favorite song, though? I can't tell you. The thing is, that album is full of hits.

Brunelle: I'd say "Immortal Rites," because it has a classical feel to it, a bigger-than-life feeling. It makes me feel like there's more than just music, like it's an expression of the heavens.

Azagthoth: I like all those songs, but I think they're all done so much better now when we play them live. As far as songs and riffing and the ideas, I thought they were all good songs. When I wrote them, I wanted stuff that was really aggressive and extreme, but I wanted to have really trippy timings—stuff that was swinging and offbeat. But on that record, everything pretty much had a straight-line aggression, because that was the type of drummer Pete was. Later on, we got a lot more grooving, so later albums were more balanced. *Altars* had those parts, but they just weren't played like that. Now those songs have more contrast. But we did the best we could. It was some pretty rough stuff, and it was pretty unique for that time. I think it's still unique, actually—I think the riffing and the arrangements are still unique to the genre.

Vincent: I like all the songs. There're some we haven't played for a long, long time—you can't play every song from every album when you do a live set. People would be bleeding after four or five hours of music. I like "Visions From the Dark Side" and "Immortal Rites" a lot, though. Actually, "Immortal Rites" may be one of my favorite tracks on the record. There was tons of pot smoking during the writing of that song. I can't say that I really smoke that much anymore, but when we were doing these records, we were all constantly smoking pot.

It seems like there's always been a psychedelic element to Morbid Angel—was that something you were thinking about when you were writing the **Altars** *songs?*

Azagthoth: Oh yeah, I think about psychedelic stuff all the time when I'm writing. I was really into Pink Floyd, but what I enjoyed about it was probably different than what most people liked about it. I was drawn to the feeling of things—like a guitar player using some effect and not even playing some proper scale. That would make me see things in a different way—it was something that transcended a bunch of notes on a piece of paper. When I write riffs and rhythms, it just turns out differently, you know? In a lot of ways, it goes to back to why I even wanted to play guitar. When I was a fan, I had an idea that certain guitar players were the best, and the riffs on their records were ones that no one could play but them. I know it's not really like that— the reality is that when someone can't tour, there's 20 people waiting to fill their shoes. I don't think anyone can play my stuff right, but maybe they can. I'll put it this way, though: When Randy Rhoads died, I thought there was no way they'd get anyone as cool as that to replace him, and then they got that Bernie Tormé guy, and he supposedly played all the solos fine. I thought that was weird—I thought Randy was the only guy who could play those solos. I know that's not right, but I was a kid then, and I'm still kind of a kid at heart, so that's how I look at stuff. Back in the day, I'd listen to music and think the guitar player was doing way more than he really was. What I thought was the guitar was really the guitar, bass and drums all together. That sounds silly, but it was actually very useful, because it made me become a very percussive guitar player. I guess I just think about things differently than most people, but I'm just being me.

In the liner notes on the **Altars** *reissue, you mention that you had already abandoned traditional musical scales by the time you wrote those songs.*

Azagthoth: Oh, totally—there's hardly any kind of scales going on in that record. I just didn't have enough time to get the best out of me for the solos. I like to have an environment where I'm just there by myself, and it doesn't happen when people are bothering me or looking at me or whatever. I could've done a lot better, even with what I knew on guitar back then. A lot of people take a scale, put some theory behind it and that's their lead, whereas I would just pick an area on the guitar and play it without really looking at it. I'd connect it in a different way. I think a lot of the solos on that record were pretty jagged-sounding—they weren't as flowing as I would have liked them to be, but I think that's because I just wasn't able to get in the right state of mind.

Why did you decide to do remixes of "Blasphemy," "Maze of Torment" and "Chapel of Ghouls"?

Vincent: They're not really remixes—they're more like alternate mixes. It's not the easiest music in the world to mix, you know? Everything is on 10, and it's all at once. To try and pull out articulation in and amongst the different instruments is a challenge, so when it came to the mixdown, we tried a few different things. Dig felt like maybe he wanted to have some extra stuff for the CD version, because this was right when CDs were coming out on the market, and they were more expensive than cassettes. "Lord of All Fevers & Plague" is not on the vinyl or the cassette, either.

Brunelle: I think we had the opportunity to see if we could make it better, so we tried it, and decided to leave it to the listeners to decide. It was also an opportunity for me to improve some of my leads, and I think a couple of them came out a little bit better on the remixes.

Sandoval: I think the drums were a little bit louder on the remixes. That was the only difference, I think. It doesn't really do anything for me, though, because I play those songs differently now, and they're much faster live.

When did you start to notice the influence or impact **Altars** *had on other bands?*

Vincent: I don't know that I was tuned into it. We kinda did our own thing—we were off in left field. Prior to the record coming out, we were kinda into the whole underground scene, the tape-trading and stuff, but once things started rolling for us, we just didn't have the time to do that anymore. So I don't know that we spent a lot of time thinking about what other people were doing. But taking all of our stuff as a package—not just this record—and thinking about what kind of impact Morbid Angel had, I probably didn't even really consider or realize it until I rejoined the band [in 2004]. We just did what felt good to us, so we didn't consider a lot of things. If somebody ever said, "Well, I wonder what somebody's gonna think about this," one of us would always go, "I don't give a shit." We just wanted to play music. It's not like we could say we were part of such-and-such a club. There wasn't one. That came later. But if I listen to different bands, I can hear Morbid Angel, and it's kind of a compliment.

Sandoval: Well, not just *Altars of Madness*, but the whole Morbid Angel thing, you know? And a lot of people will tell me that if it wasn't for me, they would not be playing drums. I don't know why they say that, but the only thing I saw is that death metal became popular in 1990, and that's when it started to get ruined. A lot of the bands just sounded the same. That's why I don't even listen to death metal.

Azagthoth: I don't know—I think by the time that *Blessed [Are the Sick]* came out, there were some bands that expressed that they were motivated by some of the things on *Altars*, or even the *Thy Kingdom Come* demo that came out in '87 or '88. Some people think *Altars of Madness* is our best record, and they love everything the way it is, and probably wish that we'd play it exactly the way it is on the record—which we don't.

Brunelle: There was a lot of competition back then, and everything was happening pretty fast. We were struggling to make a name for ourselves and find our niche. I personally didn't realize at the time what was happening. It was fun; we were doing what I wanted to do, there were a lot of people praising us for it and I was really enjoying it.

In retrospect, is there anything you'd change about the album?

Sandoval: If we recorded the album over again, the songs would be tighter. Back then, I wasn't very experienced, but now I know what it takes to get a good sound. I don't think I'd change anything, though. Back then, you know, there were none of these computers that could fix drums. On *Altars* and the first Terrorizer album, everything you hear is what I hit. There wasn't any cheating going on. Nowadays, you can take a part of a song, and use the same drums on another part. Back then, it wasn't just about playing fast; it was about having the stamina to last.

Brunelle: Well, one thing that I'd definitely change is that I would've worked a lot harder to stay with those guys. Those were some of the best times of my life, and sometimes people don't realize what they've got until it's too late. I am so honored to have been in that situation. I was given an opportunity to be a part of history, and I am so thankful to Morbid Angel for giving me that opportunity.

Azagthoth: I'm always so critical of stuff—I always want it to be better. And that goes for every album, including *Altars*. It's hard to find a comfort zone, but I think that's part of my nature. It's tougher as it goes on, too. On the first record, the sky was the limit, because we hadn't done anything. At this point, I've written 80 or 100 songs, and every time I do something, I want it to be unique, so I've had to dig really deep. It gets tougher and tougher to come up with something that's gonna outdo it. I want everything in my life to be over-the-top, or I can't bother with it. But once you've already done stuff over-the-top, it's hard to be over-the-top yet again.

Vincent: I don't even wanna answer that question, because it would be rewriting history. Yeah, if we re-recorded the album, it would come out better sonically, but everything's an experiment, you know? That's the beauty of art. We did it, we made it happen and it opened up a lot of doors and opportunities for us, as well as a lot of other bands. I think it was the kindling that started the forest fire. It's an important record. When we saw the finished package, we were elated. We knew chumps would be silenced.

CHAPTER 8

MEMORIES REMAIN

THE MAKING OF OBITUARY'S *CAUSE OF DEATH*

by Kory Grow

Release Date: 1990
Label: Roadrunner
Summary: Guttural incoherence + wild solos = DM classic
Induction Date: May 2007/Issue #31

When Obituary's 1989 debut, *Slowly We Rot*, infected record stores, death metal had never sounded so guttural and primal. Having only previously released a few songs on demos and comps under the names Executioner and Xecutioner, the group fulfilled the potential Roadrunner A&R Monte Conner had seen in them with their debut. John Tardy's bass-heavy, nonsensical lyrics—kind of a collage of grunts and occasionally coherent horrific-sounding words—combined with the rest of the Tampa-area band's relentless, pounding riffs had taken what fellow Floridians Death had released two years earlier on their debut and mixed it with a near-European Hellhammer-like delivery. Without even touring, the band—then comprising singer John, drummer Donald Tardy, lead guitarist Allen West, rhythm guitarist Trevor Peres and bassist Daniel Tucker—inspired reverent chatter among death metal's burgeoning literati. All this, and they'd only just graduated high school.

After Roadrunner asked them to record a follow-up, 1990's unfuckwithable *Cause of Death*, everything changed. Bassist Tucker disappeared, found months later as a victim of partial amnesia from a car crash. In the meantime, Obituary drafted new bassist Frank Watkins, who quickly learned the group's repertoire, and would play on every album since. Soon after, guitarist Allen West left the band to pursue family life, prompting the group to enlist ex-Death member James Murphy, who'd later become recognized as the closest thing death metal had to a guitar hero. When Obituary finally entered Tampa's Morrisound Recording to work with producer Scott Burns, they had no idea they'd leave with a death metal masterpiece.

TURNED INSIDE OUT

What stands out to you about the time between* Slowly We Rot *and* Cause of Death*?
Donald Tardy: That's all when it started moving quickly. We were 20 years old, and I was allowed to go write more music and write another album. *Slowly* was where we just basically learned what we were doing and kind of became the band that we were, but *Cause of Death* was a true focus on writing an album. It was an exciting time.

What do you remember about Daniel Tucker disappearing?
Donald Tardy: I don't know. I honestly don't know. It was probably more confusing for band members than most people around Brandon, or around Tampa, FL, because we never really looked for him.

John Tardy: [*Laughs*] He wasn't in the band for very long. He really was just with us long enough. I don't think we even got the copies of [*Slowly We Rot*] before he just disappeared.

Trevor Peres: Daniel was a friend of mine. At a party or two I'd jammed with him just for fun or whatever. So I called him up and he came in, learned the songs, played on the album and he played a couple shows with us locally and he just kind of vanished.

Frank Watkins: I actually met Daniel like in 1997 or 1996 at a show in Tampa, and he just walked up to me like, "Hey, what's happening? I'm Daniel Tucker." And when he said that, the name was familiar, but it didn't click. That sounds so familiar, Daniel Tucker? I go, "And you are?" And he goes, "Oh, I'm the guy who played bass on *Slowly We Rot*."

How did you meet Frank?

J. Tardy: Frank found us.

Watkins: I went on a road trip with a bunch of my friends to see Morbid Angel play in Tampa, and Obituary was opening. And I was watching them play and I was like, "Wow this band is like the heaviest thing I've seen in my life." My jaw hit the floor. While I'm standing there watching them, the guy that was playing in Cynic back then, Tony Choy, just out of nowhere he comes up to me and says, "Bro, you need to be playing bass for this band." And I was like, "No way." And 10 minutes later when Obituary was done, I walked to the front of the stage. John Tardy was standing there handing out autographs to people and, I'm like, "Yo, I heard you need a bass player."

D. Tardy: We met him and just instantly got along with him real well and just kind of set up some jam time after that.

Peres: Actually the first day I met Frank, we bonded pretty good. Me and him hung out and partied and I think we tripped on acid together. [*Laughs*]

Did you do a lot of drugs back then?

Peres: Pretty much just drinking beer and smoking pot. Every once in a while, we used to trip a little bit here and there. But like I said, that was when we were young. We were 19, 20 years old, experimenting with whatever the hell. Did mushrooms a little back then. Hell, in Florida you could pick 'em yourself.

Did you guys play often while stoned?

Peres: Yeah. Even today, still. It's almost like a ritual. [*Laughs*] We always get one rolled before the show and burn one and go onstage and after, during, before. Writing music. Recording. [*Laughs*] You'll see me and Frank with a bottle of Jack half the time onstage. [*Laughs*] As long as we got one on the rider that night, we'll have one.

What do you remember about your first rehearsal?

Watkins: We were gonna meet them in their garage and jam and kind of teach me songs. One of the songs we did, 'cause they were like, "All right. This is a new one that we're just working on," it was the song "Cause of Death." So they start playing it and I learned it right off the bat and they were like, "Damn, you know that even better than we have it down."

D. Tardy: Allen wrote the song "Cause of Death." He didn't end up recording the album with us. But yeah, he wrote half of those songs.

Watkins: When I drove back to Fort Lauderdale, I mulled it over for a few days and I called up Trevor to see when they were jamming again. I went up there and we jammed again. And I said, "You know what? You guys never said to me yes or no if I'm in the band." And they're like, "Well, you're here. You're in." And shortly after that, Allen was gone.

Why did Allen leave the band?
D. Tardy: His wife at the time was having a baby and he was young and he was afraid of money and paying for a child, so he kind of freaked out for a little bit.

J. Tardy: We were together, wrote all the songs and stuff like that, but he just had some issues he had to work out and stuff like that, so he was really just unavailable for us to get in the studio with him.

Peres: And he had to work and stuff. We were all kind of working, but he wasn't prepared to be able to tour or do all kinds of stuff that we needed to.

Watkins: I just remember [Allen] and Donald arguing about something and Al just stormed off. And I remember it was a couple more weeks before we had to go to Mexico. And I remember Donald looks at me and goes, "Well, it looks like we're going to Mexico as a four-piece."

Peres: I pretty much finished up the writing of the music. And we went in and recorded it. I guess we didn't really think about another guitarist until we were in the middle of the studio.

CIRCLE OF THE TYRANTS

What was the songwriting for this album like?
Peres: We don't really think about it. It just kind of comes out of you. You just sit around and sometimes I'll have an idea and I'll bring it to Donald and we'll start jamming . . . It's really an unconscious decision to write, really.

How did you come up with the lyrics that you have?
Peres: To be honest, still to this day, I have not seen a lyric sheet of a whole entire song. No one ever has. Not even his brother. So we never will know. Maybe the day he dies we'll find a folder with a bunch of notes in it.

J. Tardy: [*Laughs*] No, he probably hasn't. They're few and far between . . . I don't know if I just get to the points in songs where instead of trying to make up some words or write down something that means something, I'm more concerned with the way it just sounds. So I have to just put something together that I have to make up as I go along.

D. Tardy: And when a signer says that, he's actually progressing.

J. Tardy: Yeah. I'm working on it. [*Laughs*] Get off our backs!

Peres: You'll hear in "Cause of Death," he says "cause of death" in there. But lyrically, we never did have a concept like, "Let's sing about world peace."

Watkins: I never really cared what he was saying. I loved the concept that it was just so guttural and you couldn't even understand it, and I remember talking to Donald way back then. And Donald was like, "Yeah, we came up with that. One day our dad came down to the garage yellin' and screamin' at us saying, 'God, I can't even understand what the hell you're saying,' to John. 'What kind of stuff you singing? I can't even understand a goddamn word you're saying.'" So they were like, "You know what? Maybe I should sing where you can't even understand what I'm saying." So that developed him into singing even more brutal. If you know their dad, Jim Tardy, he's a crazy old redneck guy and I can totally see him yellin' and screamin'.

When did James Murphy enter the picture?

J. Tardy: Scott Burns was like, "You know James Murphy? He might play some solos."

Watkins: I wanted to call up Trey from Morbid Angel, because he was a good friend of mine, and I was like, "Man, he would be perfect. He would just really shred on this album." But the rest of the guys were like, "Yeah, but Morbid Angel's a big band. We want somebody that's not in a band."

James Murphy: I was on the road supporting [*Spiritual Healing*] with Death, when I came to realize near the end of the tour that I wasn't gonna be sticking around in the band. So I left with my money and my amp head and my clothes, and as I was waiting for the bus, I happened to call Scott Burns, 'cause he was a buddy of mine at the time. He was like, "Wow, man. That's crazy. Well, I happen to be in the studio with Obituary right now and they need a lead guitarist." And I was like, "Wow, really? They're pretty cool. What's their new stuff like?" And he said, "It's really great stuff. We started recording. Let me talk to the guys and call me back."

Peres: I guess we were pretty much halfway done with the recording of the album and James Murphy called me one day. We knew he was a good guitarist and we knew whatever he did would be good, so we just let him go for it. John already had his vocals finished, and he was like, "Here's spots here and there."

Murphy: I came off the road with Death. Got home. Unpacked my stuff, and next day I was in the studio meeting those guys and that night I was recording—that night or the next day. It was bang, bang, bang—right off the road with Death into the studio with Obituary. No time to hear the material prior, other than [a] quick cursory listen, and then I was in.

Watkins: When I first was listening to his style and the way he plays, it just seemed to me, I hope this doesn't turn into like a guitar masturbation kind of album, like a Marty Friedman record or something crazy with death metal behind it.

Peres: As far as James goes, we kind of threw him to the wolves. He came in, did the album. I went to the beach with him a couple of times, and we drank some beers before we all really knew him.

Murphy: One of the first things they ever said to me when we sat down in the lounge at Morrisound to get to know each other, I don't remember if it was Trevor or Donald, but one of them said to me, "You know, Allen is our bro. And you've got to understand if he decides to come back, we'd like to take him back." I was like, "OK, fair enough."

Peres: It was kind of a weird situation, because we just kind of threw him in and recorded him. And shit, I think we recorded that album in March or April, and in June we were on tour doing the *Slowly We Rot* tour.

Did you write any songs with them, James?

Murphy: What happened was, at some rehearsals I tried to introduce my riffs. They were so not Obituary-like. Pretty much all the riffs that I ever showed to Obituary that they were kind of like "eh" about ended up on my Disincarnate album.

What was Morrisound like at the time?

Watkins: When we were at Morrisound, it was like a bunch of our buddies got together and snuck in there and recorded a record; meanwhile Jim Morris, the bosses and the guys that were there, were kind of like our parents that would show up every once in a while, like at five o'clock or something. "Hey, what's going on guys?" "Oh, hey. How ya doin'?" We'd have to hide the bong and everything. And then they'd check it out and then they'd leave. And it's like, "OK, mom and dad's gone."

CHOPPED IN HALF

What do you remember about recording the album?

Watkins: Back then we were real into cassettes. When I bought *Reign in Blood*, you'd put your cassette in your car or your truck and *Reign in Blood* would play the whole album through and when the cassette would flip, it would play the whole album again. And we wanted Roadrunner to do that for *Cause of*

Death, and they were like, it's too long to keep it on one side, and we thought, maybe we'll shorten it.

Peres: When I was getting ready to do my final takes of the guitar parts, Scott was like, "You ever thought about tuning down to D? I think you should. You'd sound sick." It didn't make a damn difference to me. So we did. We tuned down and I got some fatter strings and recorded it that way. And it sounded cool.

D. Tardy: It was also the album that started a lot of what is going on now, which is sound replacement and triggered bass drums and snare drums and stuff. I don't think that was ever even heard of for bands to do that at any time earlier than that. That was the one thing about that album that still bothers me.

Watkins: I used to always mess with the dudes. We're real physical guys. And I think me and Trevor were wrestlin' or something and he kind of threw me back and I tripped over myself. And they always call me Goofy because I'm kind of a big dude, but I'm always, like, always fallin' over everything. And boom, I fell right on the tape machine.

Murphy: You hit a tape reel when it's spinning on that flange, those things are balanced really well. It made the machine just lock up, totally stretched a piece of tape like it was Stretch Armstrong. It took that tape and warped it to hell.

Watkins: And the whole place was like, "Whoa! What the fuck?" They thought I ruined the whole freakin' thing.

Murphy: Scott, with a razor blade and some creative editing, was able to save it. It was certainly a frightening moment for all of us. We were all trippin'.

D. Tardy: One time with Scott, John did the craziest, heaviest built-up scream thing, and when he was done with it, John's look was so proud. He knew it sounded so good, and Scott was like, "So, did you want me to record that?" And John said, "You're gonna die."

Monte Connor: Something very curious about the sound of the album, the actual mix of the record and the sonics—I believe the rhythm guitar tracks on that record are recorded out of phase. A way that you can tell something's out of phase usually is that something sounds very, very stereo, like more stereo than it should. It wasn't until we were remastering the record in 1997 with George Marino, the mastering engineer, and he's the one that pointed it out. Scott Burns, to this day, will deny it, because it's the type of thing a producer's not gonna want to admit, because it's basically a glitch in the recording.

Watkins: They had this guy at Morrisound [Kent Smith], he would make commercial jingles and stuff. And we needed some ambient music or ambient shit behind our stuff. We wanted our record to go from the beginning of an intro into the second and first song, and all the songs kind of mesh, so it plays one continuous way. This guy is like a 40-, 50-year-old guy and he had no clue what death metal was. And I just told him, "Just think evil. Just think horror and scary movies and that kind of stuff." And the whole time he's doing these keyboard parts, he's giving us these crazy, evil looks and he's going, "Yeah, I feel it. I feel it, I feel it." And we were like, yeah, this is perfect.

How did your cover of Celtic Frost's "Circle of the Tyrants" come about?

Peres: Donald and I were still in the studio room and I started playing the first riff off "Circle of the Tyrants," and Donald kicked in. He knew what it was because we used to play it live, as well as other Celtic Frost songs we used to play. We didn't know it and Scotty hit record, just playing around, and we came in the console room after we were done just playing around and Scotty said, "Check this out," and he hit play and we said, "Oh shit, that sounds sick." Everybody was like, "Damn dude, we should do that on the album."

Did you ever hear from Tom G. Warrior about your cover?

J. Tardy: I talked to him. We were in a hotel, down at the bar and, for some reason, he and one of the other guys in the band, they walked in and we started talking to him. He had heard the cover and did say he liked the cover. I bet he got some four or five dollars in royalties from us playing his song.

D. Tardy: He got to buy a six-pack of beer, probably, at least.

INFECTED

Did you notice a big difference between Slowly We Rot *and* Cause of Death?

Murphy: Oh yeah. It was very evident. And I was very happy that I had been able to add something. And all the guys commented on it at the time. Later on, they made public comments that Allen's [style] was theirs. And I can't really disagree. I think I added something unique and special to *Cause of Death* that made that a very special record.

Connor: I think *Cause of Death* is by far the band's best record. It's definitely the most creative thing that the band has ever done. Even though *Slowly We Rot* has an amazing brutality and raw edge to it, I really think *Cause of Death* is the best of both worlds.

How did you get the artwork for Cause of Death?

Peres: It's something we didn't really know about, really. I personally had found some artwork we wanted to buy from Time-Life. I was in the library looking at books and stuff, and I found this piece of artwork. It was an old Civil War scene in the woods and all these ghosts of dead Civil War veterans were walking around. It was kind of creepy. We tried hard to get that piece, but Time-Life would not release it without selling it. So I basically told Monte, on a whim, I said, "Hey, do you have any artwork laying around that no one's using yet?" He said, "Yeah, we got this piece by Michael Whelan, it's pretty sick. Let me send it to you."

Connor: When Sepultura was first signed and when we were recording the *Beneath the Remains* album, Max sent me a copy of the artwork that eventually got used on *Cause of Death* as the cover that Sepultura wanted for *Beneath the Remains*. Michael wound up sending us a book of other artwork in it besides this Obituary painting. We wound up seeing the [*Beneath the Remains* cover] and we wound up thinking that "Wow, this would be a better-looking cover for *Beneath the Remains*." So we wound up pretty much just convincing Sepultura that the skull would be a better painting for them. We ended up using the other cover as the cover for *Cause of Death*.

Peres: I opened up the FedEx envelope and pulled it out and it was the *Cause of Death* cover, and I looked at it and I was like, "Holy crap, this is our cover. I don't care what anybody thinks . . ."

Watkins: As soon as I saw that eyeball, I was like, "Man, that's different. That's really fuckin' different." And it was a big discussion between us because some of us liked it and some of us were like, "You know what? I could live with it, but . . ." There was a big cockroach on it. We were like, maybe if you took that off, moved this here . . . Finally, we decided that's the one we wanted to use.

Connor: That's not the full painting. The other section of that cover was sold to another band, that band Demolition Hammer [for *Epidemic of Violence*].

Peres: Later we found out Sepultura was planning on using that artwork and none of us had a clue. I kind of felt bad in a way. It had nothing to do with us. It was Monte. Monte did it. It was really his mistake in a way by giving it to us.

Connor: It was definitely me that sent the artwork to Obituary. At the time, they didn't know that Sepultura wanted it for *Beneath the Remains*. Neither band knew what was going on until the albums came out.

D. Tardy: [Sepultura] knew it had nothing to do with us. There's never been any bad words, and I don't think there's really any bad feelings 'cause it was our record label's mistake, not necessarily band members fighting over something. I wish I would have talked to 'em about it, but obviously it was much more fun moving on and touring with each other like we did.

Connor: For years later, Igor [Cavalera] from Sepultura was upset with me, really pissed off about that whole incident because he wanted the cover of *Cause of Death* to be the cover of *Beneath the Remains*.

Peres: Later on we found out Igor had part of the thing tattooed on his arm.

As you were finishing recording the album, you took your promo photos. What do you remember about the coffin pic?

J. Tardy: Not wanting to do it.

D. Tardy: Not wanting to do it and that Scott Burns built those coffins.

J. Tardy: [Scott and photographer Tim Hubbard] concocted this whole idea and we all looked at it like, "That's the stupidest thing I ever heard in my life." And they all worked so hard and they were so proud of it. "Just try it. Please!" And we try it and of course it was just dumb, and of course Roadrunner will use anything you give 'em.

Murphy: They looked pretty cheesy in the picture, but they looked *really* cheesy in person. They were like the thinnest plywood you could get, spray-painted black and tacked together. I was like, "Wow, are these things going to break if I lay in it?" We were very, very skinny kids at that time.

D. Tardy: We were so young that we a) got talked into it, b) realized how stupid it looked and c) actually gave it to a record label thinking they might not use it. That's what you call 18 years old.

J. Tardy: Don't fart onstage and give it to a record company, because it will be used.

Peres: I think those photos are kind of silly of us laying in 'em. Even today when I look at it, 'cause we're all just wearing jeans and freakin' t-shirts and freakin' Vans tennis shoes, lying in this frickin' coffin. It looked silly as hell. A lot of people think it's cool. But, you know . . .

Watkins: I think Trevor and I took one of them home and we used it as a coffee table in our apartment.

GATES TO HELL

Almost immediately after you finished recording **Cause of Death,** *you went on the first* **Slowly We Rot** *tour with Sacred Reich and Forced Entry. What do you recall about your first national tour?*

Peres: I remember even Sacred Reich, they were like "Oh, what's this shit? A death metal band touring with us?" They were like old thrash metal guys, thinking we were gonna suck. By the middle of the tour, we had their respect. They were like hanging out with us, partying with us and loved us to death. The crowd loved us. Everywhere we played, we crushed and sold tons of merchandise.

Murphy: One day, it was at the Eagles Hall at [Milwaukee Metalfest]. I think we had been told not to do pyro, and so [Big Daddy, our roadie] was just like, "The hell with that," gonna do it anyway. This was a place that had huge ceilings.

We had 30 feet to the ceiling. And we were 20 feet to any wall. This stage was huge.

Watkins: What we didn't really calculate on was that some of the people that we brought to put it all together, some of Big Daddy's buddies, were drunks and idiots, and they left some of the gaffer tape on top of the pipes that shot the flames up. So when Big Daddy ignited everything, everything instead of shooting up imploded down, and the stage completely blew up and stuff went flying.

Murphy: I think it knocked Donald off his drum stool. It threw wood out into the crowd, like jagged, sharp pieces of wood everywhere. I saw a piece fly over the crowd's head and land behind the soundboard. I got shoved forward, and I thought it was just a concussion at first, but it hurt really bad. And I turned around and there was a piece of wood laying right behind me. And it was completely sharp and pointed on one end. And someone said, "That piece of wood hit you flat across your back, dude. I thought you were going down." It hurt really bad and I was deafened, but we actually continued playing and finished the set. If that piece of wood had spun around, that sharp point certainly could have killed me.

How was your first European tour—the first official **Cause of Death** *tour—with* **Morgoth** *and* **Demolition Hammer?**

D. Tardy: That was our first time in Europe. We flew the day Stevie Ray [Vaughan] died.

Murphy: I remember we had to stay an extra day, and the airline put us up in hotel rooms and gave us meal tickets at this cafeteria. And we were in line getting our food at this cafeteria, and the radio playing over the PA announced that Stevie Ray Vaughan had died in a crash after this concert in a big mountain somewhere. His helicopter had crashed. I don't think any of us finished our food.

D. Tardy: I thought, "Damn, I just got out of the air and Stevie just died trying to fly, and he's been doing it for a decade and this is my first tour." I was like, "I hope I get to live for at least as long as he did."

Murphy: I think we just picked at [our food] and were just blown away, and our hearts were sunk to our feet and it was one of the most tasteless, bland meals that we've ever had.

D. Tardy: It affected John and I, because we were some of the biggest Stevie Ray fans ever. We saw him that year, live, with Steve Vai or someone opened for him.

How did everyone get along on the tour?

Murphy: I was a little set apart from the other guys in that I didn't partake in all the "party utensils." That wasn't my thing, and still isn't to this day. They did enjoy quite a bit. So that put a bit of a distance between us a bit. I certainly never complained openly. At the same time I realized, hey, I'm in a metal band. And this is par for the course.

Watkins: That tour kind of showed us the demise of James. Because when we first met James, he was a really cool guy. He was outgoing. He was talking with us. We just really got along. We got on tour and we finished the record and we started doing shows, and he started coming out to us. And he would always complain about everything. I was like, "It's gotta stop, man. We can't handle it." It got to the point where it embarrassed us a few times with other guys in some of the other bands, he embarrassed us. And it got to the point where we were like, "I don't think we'll be able to hang with this guy anymore." He [had] turned into a separate person in the band.

What do you remember about returning home from Europe?

Watkins: When I got home from that tour, I had a military duffel bag that I kept all my clothes in and all my stuff. I get to the front door of my mom's house and she wouldn't let me in the door. She made me put my bag in the yard. [*Laughs*] And she hosed me off because I stunk so bad. Because we wouldn't shower; we were just going crazy, man.

What lead to Murphy's departure?

Watkins: We did a U.S. tour with him, with Sepultura and Sadus; it was like immediately after that European tour with Morgoth. Right when we got home, I drove up with the guy from Roadrunner, this guy "Psycho" came to visit me. I pull into the Tardys' parking lot and I see Allen West's truck sitting there. I walk in and Al's playing guitar. And I'm like, "What are you doing, Al?" And he's like, "What do you mean, what am I doing? I'm playing my fucking guitar." And I was like, "Killer!" And I turn around and here comes James pullin' up in the driveway. And I was like, "Oh shit. I wonder what's gonna happen here." And me and the guy from Roadrunner kind of walked outside and walked around and waiting and James went in there.

J. Tardy: James went and did the European shows with us and then we came home and Al just kind of hung out. It wasn't like we never talked to Allen or he quit kind of thing; he just had what he had to do at the time.

Peres: We had never wanted Allen to leave the band, obviously. After we got back from those tours, it was ironic. Allen called us and was like, "Hey." His baby was born and he was mentally stable and ready to jam again. Right after that, we wanted him back in the band, because he was a big part of the band at that point.

D. Tardy: It probably sucked for James. It probably hurt him a little bit, but he had to have seen it coming, only because it was obvious to us that Allen was Obituary. He was the beginning of it and he's been on every album with us.

Murphy: I was agitated, obviously, to show up at what I thought was going to be a rehearsal and Allen was there. I was like, "Oh, what's going on?" And then that's when I think it was Donald came out and told me, "We're getting Allen back." At that time, I think I was like, "Whatever. Let me get my stuff."

Watkins: James walked out and said, "I'll see you later, Frankie. I'm out." And that was the last time I saw him.

Murphy: Definitely moving on from that band was the right thing for me and it was the right thing for them.

Watkins: It's unfortunate because I really did think of him as the guitar player in the band. Musically, he was amazing. It fit like a glove. And we could have done some really crazy shit in the future as far as the leads, but it kind of brings us back to what Obituary was and still is, which is we're just in-your-face death metal. And that definitely prolonged us to make *The End Complete* and the rest of the records we did.

Looking back at Cause of Death, *what are you proudest of?*

D. Tardy: It was the album that really started kids to realize what the two words mean when they say "death metal." With Venom and Hellhammer and Slayer back in the day, to us that was death metal. That was metal. We didn't know what it was. So as a band we just started writing music that our heroes would probably want to write. *Cause of Death* was the album that really made the idea that, "You want to see a death metal record? You want to hear it? Go get *Cause of Death*!"

CHAPTER 9

LEFT HAND LEGACY

THE MAKING OF ENTOMBED'S *LEFT HAND PATH*

by J. Bennett

Release Date: 1990
Label: Earache
Summary: Swedish death metal starts here
Induction Date: August 2005/Issue #10

Death metal was still in its infancy when *Left Hand Path* came roaring out of Stockholm like Satan's official theme music—a deafening cavalcade of impossibly thick guitars, guttural vocal incantations and gore-drenched lyrics that struck a considerable contrast—well, the guitars anyway—to the burgeoning Floridian death-swarm (Obituary, Death, Morbid Angel) of the day. Entombed began as Nihilist, which was in itself the product of two other Swedish bands: Singer L.G. Petrov and guitarist Ulf "Uffe" Cederlund were refugees from Morbid (Petrov played drums), a group that also sacrificed its infamous vocalist Per Ohlin, a.k.a. Dead, to Norway's burgeoning black metal insurgency, while future Entombed members Nicke Andersson (drums), Alex Hellid (guitar) and Leif "Leffe" Cuzner (guitar/bass) played in hardcore outfit Brainwarp. (Before Cederlund's official involvement, Nihilist enlisted bassist Johnny Hedlund, who would go on to form Unleashed.) Nihilist recorded three demos—recently released on CD via Entombed's Threeman Recordings—before Cuzner moved to Canada (and was replaced by Cederlund). Shortly thereafter, the group kicked Hedlund to the curb and changed their name to Entombed. By the time the new band's demo appeared in late 1989, the teenaged Swedes already had an offer on the table from Earache Records. Upon its release in early 1990, *Left Hand Path* became Sweden's first "proper" death metal album, the primary influence for countless death rock commandos, and the world's official introduction to the savage guitar tone that would become the legendary "Entombed sound."

PART I: SUNLIGHT SYMPHONY

What's the first thing that comes to mind when you think about the making of Left Hand Path?

Nicke Andersson: We did it really fast—it couldn't have been more than a week. I think we actually recorded it in late '89, maybe December or something like that. I know we did the first Entombed demo in September. I must've been 18.

Uffe Cederlund: I think I was 18 or 19, and I remember we were really happy that we got a record deal. Earache wanted to sign Nihilist, but we told them we had a new band called Entombed, and sent them the *But Life Goes On* demo.

Alex Hellid: We had a budget of a thousand British pounds, which was about 10,000 Swedish crowns or something. It was a cheap album—and now it's extremely cheap—but at the time it was more money than we had spent on anything. I think the *But Life Goes On* demo cost the equivalent of a hundred bucks or something. The album was more time, too—with the demos, you recorded and mixed everything in the same day and you were outta there. I think I was 15 at the time. That whole period—'89–'90—felt like 10 years, but it was actually quite a short time.

L.G. Petrov: We were very young—I was 17, I think. The songs went with us from the Nihilist days, so we had most of the songs. We didn't think about it too much—you just went in and recorded the stuff. [*Laughs*] I didn't think about it, anyway. When we were recording, if it sounded good, we just went on to the next song.

How was working with Tomas Skogsberg at Sunlight Studio?

Andersson: The first time we went there was for the second Nihilist demo. We went because Morbid—well, the mark II lineup of Morbid, when Dead wasn't in the band anymore and they were more like a Testament thrash band—had recorded there. The singer lived in the same apartment building; Sunlight was in the basement. But we weren't satisfied at all, so for the third Nihilist demo, we went somewhere else. Then we heard the Treblinka demo [the band that would become Tiamat]—they had just been in Sunlight, and we thought their demo sounded awesome. So we went back to do the *But Life Goes On* demo. We got along with Tomas really well, even though he didn't really seem to know what the hell we were doing. If you think back, though, it makes sense. Everyone was like, "What are these guys doing?" But people probably thought that about Metallica at some point. Still, he made us feel really good about everything. And by the time we did *Left Hand Path*, he seemed to know how to make our guitar sound even better.

Petrov: It was great. Good old Tomas was sitting there with a cigarette in his mouth all the time—and I mean *all the time*. We were one of the first bands to do an album there—Tomas was still a little bit new to that kind of music. I guess we were a bit lucky, because the sound turned out to be so in-your-face. We were very excited—and nervous, of course. But as time went on in the studio, it got more comfortable.

Hellid: I remember it being very, very small. People would be surprised that he made it sound like it sounds coming from that studio. The first Sunlight Studio was a really small demo studio—he didn't even have real drums because the room was so small you couldn't fit a drum kit, a drummer and another person. It was the '80s, too, so he had digital drums, and we actually used them for like half the kit on the first two albums. It wasn't until the third album that we used all real drums. On *Left Hand Path*, I think the snare is real and the toms are real, but the kick drums are d-drums. And it's hard to play on those things—there's no skin, you know? It's like hitting a wall.

Cederlund: I think the entire kit except the snare and the cymbals were d-drums. Tomas didn't want to use real drums because he thought it took too much time. I remember Nicke had a hard time playing on them. It took a while to get used to them, because the drum sticks bounce differently. We never really questioned Tomas, because we thought he knew better—we figured he was the studio guy. But you know, when I listen to the album, I don't think about it. If I listen to the *But Life Goes On* demo, I can hear [the difference], because on that, we used the d-drum for the snare also, which sounds really bizarre. Bands these days do the same thing, pretty much, but with triggers. It's the same thing, only with real drums.

Hellid: It was a very primitive studio, but we hadn't been to a lot of studios, so we didn't know. The mixing board didn't even have VU meters. I don't know how Tomas decided when the levels were right. Mixing *Left Hand Path*, *Clandestine* and even *Wolverine Blues* was a three-man job, because you needed more than two hands to mix. There were no computers or anything, and there were only so many effects you could put on things. If you wanted, say, *two* reverbs, you'd have to unplug cables, put them into other inputs, and raise faders during the mixdown. So we'd have it split up three ways, and if somebody fucked up, we'd have to do it over again.

In **Choosing Death**, *the Entombed guitar sound is attributed to Nihilist bassist/guitarist Leif "Leffe" Cuzner's Boss Heavy Metal pedal.*

Andersson: Yeah, there're four knobs on it. One of them is all mids, and if you put that on 10, that's how you get the sound. If you just have the regular Boss distortion [pedal]—the orange one—there's only high and low. But this one had the "mid" setting. First we thought the sound was his guitar or his speaker, but it was the pedal. When we found that out, Uffe started using one, too. Then Dismember bought the same pedals. [*Laughs*]

Cederlund: Everybody had that pedal, but Leffe was the guy who cranked everything to 10 first. That pedal is a really bad distortion pedal, but everybody had it because it was the cheap pedal to buy back then. Leffe was playing through a Swedish amplifier on the *Only Shreds Remain* demo [1988]. Nicke had a Peavey combo, and I also had a Peavey combo. Then Leffe moved to Canada.

Hellid: Uffe inherited that sound; I go with the Boss DS-1 distortion pedal. His whole sound is very overdriven—I've always had a little less distortion to try to balance it out a bit. On the early albums, we'd always have four guitars. I remember Tomas would put down two or three really distorted guitars—like a wall of guitars—and then we'd put one down so you could actually hear what the guitar was playing.

Andersson: Alex had the more—well, traditional is not the word—but a sound that we'd blend with Uffe's sound. Alex is great, but Uffe is probably the best guitar player I've ever played with. We'd double-track his guitars—always—so you'd have him on the left and the right, with Alex in the middle. [*Laughs*] I don't think Dismember did that.

You didn't have much time in the studio, so you must've been pretty well rehearsed.

Anderssson: We must've rehearsed at least two times a week at that point. How these rehearsal places in Sweden work is that they get funds from the government—like a cultural fund, you know? And you enlist, I guess you would say—it's almost like being in a club. We hadn't played a lot of shows, because this music was not considered acceptable. If you wanted to play shows, you had to promote them yourself. So it was just shows here and there that we put together, or friends put together. We didn't play outside of Sweden at all until the album came out.

Petrov: I remember some lyrics were changed in the studio. Nicke was standing beside me with the lyric sheet, and he would point at what I was supposed to sing.

Cederlund: We didn't have [all the songs] ready when Dig [Pearson, Earache founder] said, "Let's make an album." So I think there are three songs we wrote a couple of days before we went into the studio—"Left Hand Path," "Drowned" and "Bitter Loss." When I listen to the album, I think those are the three that don't sound finished. We knew what we were gonna do with the others, because we had recorded them before—it was just about trying to make them better than the demos. I think those three are really sloppy, though.

You didn't have a bass player at the time, so Nicke and Uffe played bass. Do you remember who played on which songs? The liner notes don't say.

Andersson: I don't remember who did which songs, but I think we were pretty good. I have to pat ourselves on the back, because we'd never played bass before. But we knew the riffs. I mean, I wrote a lot of them.

Cederlund: I think we played every second song. He's playing on "Left Hand Path"; I play on "Drowned" and "Revel in Flesh" . . . fuck, I can't remember. When we did the bass in the studio, it took an hour, tops. It was more like, "Do you wanna do this, or shall I do it?" We worked pretty fast back then.

PART II: KNIGHTS IN SATAN'S SERVICE

Whose idea was the album title?

Cederlund: Alex came up with it, I think, but it was Nicke who decided it would be the title—he was the big boss. Before *Left Hand Path* came out, we wanted to call the second album *Left for Dead*, but we skipped that.

Andersson: I think it was an Anton LaVey thing. It could've been Alex—he actually read that book [*The Satanic Bible*]—I just looked at the pictures. Although, maybe there were no pictures. [*Laughs*] I just thought the idea of it was cool. I guess I was never a real Satanist—it was just a pose. It's like the Norwegians told us: We were "life metal"—and I guess they were right.

Hellid: I think it was from *The Satanic Bible*, because I was reading that a lot at the time—but you know, I've gone back over the years, and I can never find the part where I took the actual line from. I wanted to call the song "Left Hand Path" first, but when Nicke saw the title, he said we should call the album that, too.

Did you specifically request Dan Seagrave to do the cover art, or did Earache suggest him because he had already done Morbid Angel's Altars of Madness?

Hellid: I guess when Digby or someone at Earache suggested Dan, we thought, well, of course. We loved the Morbid Angel artwork, so we thought if we could get this guy to do it, then great. I remember Nicke doing a sketch and sending it over—when it came back, we were so happy with it.

Andersson: I really wish I still had the sketch—his artwork is almost exactly like my sketch. The grave is exactly where it was in my sketch, and I drew some trees and a path or whatever. It's really close—and I specifically told him what kind of colors we wanted. Looking back, I like the Morbid Angel art he did, but it was kind of comic-like. It was kinda funny—and we didn't want *that*.

Petrov: It's really great artwork. If you look closely on the left of the path, there's a little happy frog there. There are a lot of faces there, but I like the frog.

What about the inscription on the tombstone: "Rest in Festering Slime: Here Burns the Souls of a Thousand Generations"?

Andersson: Dan did that. It had nothing to do with us, but it was great. [*Laughs*] I like the "Rest in festering slime" part.

Hellid: We still don't know what it means—it was just something he put on there. But I remember we were pissed about the back sleeve—we had nothing to do with that. I don't know if Dig had some friend in art school or something. We had a back [cover] that we thought was perfect—just the photo [from the inside], it looked like the back cover of Slayer or Autopsy or something. But when it was done, it came back with that weird photo. It's kinda funny now, though. I still have no idea what it is. It feels like the old days when bands didn't even get to choose their own covers. I'm not comparing us to Black Sabbath, but it's the same thing they had with the inverted cross. [Unbeknownst to the band—until its release—the gatefold of Black Sabbath's first LP contained an inverted cross.] Nowadays you have more control.

Andersson: Yeah, it's got some teeth and some plants going on. [*Laughs*] We didn't like that, because it interfered with the colors on the front. I looked at it the other week, actually, and I kinda like it now—'cause it's weird—but it still doesn't fit. I think it was the same guy who did the first Hellbastard cover. [*Laughs*] We didn't get anything to approve, you know—and nobody liked it. We were probably a bit pissed off.

Petrov: We were like, "What the hell is this?" But you didn't complain much back then—first record and all. To get a record deal was the greatest thing that ever happened to us. Nowadays, people just spit out records, but back then you'd show it to your mom, like, "Oh, is that you?"

Cederlund: The back of the album is really ugly. We hated it—I still hate it. We told them what we wanted, but they just didn't respect us. That band Hellbastard got the guy who did our back cover to do their front cover—so at least we got Dan Seagrave on the front. Another thing that's weird is that the album was supposed to be called *The Left Hand Path*, but we didn't seen anything of it until it came out, and when we did, the "The" was gone.

What's the story behind the band photo inside, with the giant cross?

Andersson: Oh, that's a really nice cemetery in the suburbs of Stockholm [Enskede]—it's called Skogskyrkogården. It means "the forest cemetery." The whole place is really beautiful. Obviously, it was the perfect place. There's no graves in that area—just a big cross. It's kind of majestic.

Hellid: We met the photographer [Micke Lundstrom] in the studio. The local newspaper had just sent a guy down to take pictures while we were recording. We liked him—and the way his pictures came out—so when it came time to do a photo for the album, we asked him. He suggested the graveyard—we had no idea where he was taking us. None of us had even seen the place before. It turned out to be kind of a classic. It's kind of hard to find those places nowadays, where nobody's been before. The place is huge, and in the middle is this big cross.

Cederlund: We were really lucky, because it had just started snowing—that's why the shot is a bit blurry. Young kids trying to look tough, you know?

In the liner notes, you thank Fred Estby of Carnage/Dismember for a riff, and you refer to him as "Milli-Vanilli Fred."

Andersson: Yeah, he did something with his hair at one point—like a braid, or cornrows, you know? It was some kind of fake dreadlock, which is why we called him that. He didn't have that for a long while, though. [*Laughs*] Now it's been so long that he's not gonna get offended—he doesn't even have hair anymore. We were probably trading riffs back then. He's still one of my best friends, you know, and we were really close at that time.

Cederlund: I got pissed off at Nicke because he gave away lots of riffs to Dismember, and I was like, "Why are you giving these riffs away? They're great riffs." So when Nicke and I wrote "But Life Goes On," we stole a Dismember riff for the slow part. It was on one of their rehearsal tapes, I think.

How did Uffe get stuck putting his home address on the album?

Petrov: We did a lot of tape-trading back then, so that was just a thing among friends. I don't think we would do that nowadays. I don't think he got millions of letters or anything, but it was cool, you know? It was underground—you'd give your address and exchange letters with people. I don't have a problem giving my address out to people, you know. Some people who play music are scared, but I don't care.

Hellid: I think we had put mine and Nicke's on the demos, so it was Uffe's turn. [*Laughs*] He lived there for a few years afterwards, and people would come and knock on his door—people from Germany and places like that would want to see if he was home.

Cederlund: I liked to write letters back then and stay involved in the scene. Nobody else wanted to put their address on the album, I think, so I agreed to put mine. All the bands we liked—Napalm Death, Carcass—had their addresses on their albums, so we thought we should have one of our addresses, too. That was my mom and dad's place, that address, and during the summer, people from Spain would come knocking on the door. It was pretty weird—they expect you to be their pal. There were a lot of bands sleeping at my house back then, like Disharmonic Orchestra and stuff. Whoever we played with ended up staying on the floor. My parents must've wondered what was going on, because I'd get 20 or 30 letters a day. The mailman must've wondered also. But I was only able to keep up [with the correspondence] for maybe six months after the album was released. It got to be too much, so I just stopped.

PART III: GUIDED BY GORE

Alex and Nicke are credited with the lyrics—who wrote for which songs?

Hellid: I wrote "Left Hand Path" and "The Truth Beyond"—they're both about being your own master, which I guess is what we still write about. *The Satanic Bible* is about thinking for yourself, so a few of the lyrics are from that. A lot of Nicke's lyrics had more of a gore/horror movie thing.

Andersson: I know I did "Revel in Flesh." I think I did "Abnormally Deceased." I did "Supposed to Rot," too—that's from *Evil Dead 2*. It's about somebody burying someone in a fruit cellar or something [*laughs*]—I guess that was a big influence on the lyrics. I mean, I laugh a little bit about it now, but at the time it seemed like the right thing to write about. I can still watch *Evil Dead 2*, you know? It's when the listener starts taking things too seriously—that's when you're in trouble. Part of me was very serious when I wrote that stuff, but it was kind of ironic, too. I mean, when you're 18 years old, what the hell do you know about the world? You're thinking about a hundred things at once, and your music taste changed every week. Such and such a band was too wimpy, but at the same time, you'd listen to the Ramones. It was a weird time. Within this genre, we had very strict rules—even down to which chord progressions were cool. It was like a scale that we thought we made up. If there was a band that was fast and had the energy, but had lousy chord progressions, they were out the window. The blueprints were Autopsy and Repulsion. Like, you couldn't play A, D and E next to each other—that'd be a pop song. Almost all our riffs were in E—but it's not really E, because we tuned down to C or B. So you'd consider your B to be an E. So E to F to G-sharp—that's great. And you can also have a G in there—with those four chords you can make killer riffs. But if you had E, F-sharp, G and A, that was totally fucking gay. It would never happen. But by the third album, we'd loosened those rules up a bit.

What other things were influences?

Andersson: *Hellraiser*. The first two, actually. The third one hadn't come out yet, I don't think. It was definitely my favorite, because it had the Cenobites and the other realms. H.P. Lovecraft was a great influence, too—although I probably didn't read that much. I'd read maybe three novels or short stories, even. They were a drag reading, because they weren't translated into Swedish. But the biggest influence was the dictionary, obviously. If you look at the lyrics, there's no way that a Swedish-speaking person would know what any word means.

Did you ever consider writing a song in Swedish, or was that against the rules, too?

Andersson: Never. That wasn't even talked about. It's like if *Hellraiser* had been a Swedish movie—with Pinhead speaking Swedish. It's hard to explain, but Swedes would know what I'm talking about. Then again, some of the black metal bands sing in Norwegian, and that totally cracks me up. To a Swede, a Norwegian accent sounds really happy—and I think they think the same thing about Swedes. Then again, accents don't come across very often in these growls, except in the mispronunciations. But some English-speaking people I know love the mispronunciations in the lyrics. Then again, you're not really listening to the words. But it's great when you hear someone yell, "Die!"

Half the songs on **Left Hand Path** are from Nihilist demos; Leffe has writing credits, but not Johnny Hedlund.

Andersson: He never wrote a single riff—not one. [*Laughs*] Well, he wrote a few, but he never had that chord-progression rule down. Eventually he got it, though, with Unleashed—there's stuff on there that could've been Entombed stuff. He wrote some really good stuff with Unleashed, but with us he never did.

PART IV: LEFT HANDED LEGACY

Do you remember when you first received a copy of the finished album?

Andersson: I remember when Uffe and I went to the post office to pick up the test pressing—that was the first time we were on actual plastic, you know? I remember it was a sunny day and it was kinda magical. I mean, there was no plan to make an album. If you made a demo, and people in fanzines mentioned it, that was success. None of the bands we liked made albums. There was [Death's] *Scream Bloody Gore* and [Slayer's] *Reign in Blood*, and that's it. Even Repulsion didn't have an album until later.

Petrov: I have my test press right here. It's black and "Entombed" is written on it with just a regular pen. It's the kind of thing you want to keep for the rest of your life. Just holding it and seeing yourself on a record was like, "Yes! We did it!" Every time you put out a record, you have a little bit of that feeling, that you accomplished something new again.

How soon after it came out did you realize the influence it had?

Hellid: I think it took a long time. We didn't really feel like we were doing something so different from what other people were doing. We felt more like we were ripping off all these other bands—which we were. Repulsion was out there, Autopsy, Morbid Angel, Obituary—or Xecutioner, as they were called at the time. I mean, we just took the *Phantasm* theme and used it for the end of "Left Hand Path" without even asking anybody for permission. It was total ignorance. But I think we took the pieces and made it into something of our own. Still, it was a little bit of a surprise when people said it was so influential.

Andersson: Well, *we* thought it kicked ass, obviously, because there was nothing else around that sounded like that. So *we* were all content with it, but I don't know . . . it was so strictly underground at the time. I grew up on punk rock before I started listening to metal—and I think Uffe did the same—so there was no aim to be a star. We wanted to play the music that we liked—if nobody else does, we didn't care. The goal was to be mentioned in the same sentence as Repulsion and Autopsy. If somebody was asked in an interview what they were listening to, and they mentioned us together with other great bands, that was cool. But if they liked us and bad bands, that was terrible.

Petrov: People would be like, "Oh—how did you get that sound?" That happened straight after the album came out. *Still* people ask what we used to get that sound. It was just a little Peavey amplifier and a Heavy Metal pedal—all at maximum. The guitar sound—that's the main thing. Everyone says it rules. We're just grateful that Tomas was there and we had an opportunity to do it with him.

You can hear some other records that are pretty similar—I don't know if it's the studio, or if they used the same amplifiers, but it was great for Tomas, too.

Hellid: It was one of those things where you're so into what you're doing that you don't even realize what it is you're doing. In a lot of ways, the album was no different for us than doing the demos. When the reviews came out, I was surprised they were so good. I don't think we realized how well it would be received.

In retrospect, is there anything you'd change about it?

Petrov: No, I'm happy with it. It's so in-your-face, that thick guitar sound. If there was anything negative I could come up with, I would tell you right away. But I can't.

Andersson: No. I'm proud of it. We were really young, and without knowing it, we did something that nobody had really done. I mean, we thought people had done it before, but no one had heard of Autopsy or Repulsion—it was weird. It never became that fun again, you know? Those goals were reached on a really low level. We never even thought about making an album. Of all the Entombed albums, *Left Hand Path* and the last one I was on [1997's *To Ride, Shoot Straight and Speak the Truth*] are my favorites.

Cederlund: Dig didn't give us too much money to record. If we had maybe one more weekend in the studio, so we didn't have to rush things so much, the album would've been a bit better. The entire thing was recorded and mixed in eight days—four weekends in a row. But I'm proud of it—it's probably the best we could've done back then.

Hellid: I don't think we could even do it nowadays. To create that thing now would be impossible for us. It was then and there.

CHAPTER 10

AN ETERNAL CLASSIC

THE MAKING OF PARADISE LOST'S *GOTHIC*

by Scott Koerber

Release Date: 1991
Label: Peaceville
Summary: Gothic metal benchmark
Induction Date: June 2005/Issue #8

orthern England, 1990. Amid the cacophony of blast beats echoing from the speed-obsessed world of U.K. death metal and grindcore, five lads from the grim North were feverishly gathering songs and ideas for the follow-up to their doom-laden debut album, *Lost Paradise*. Marrying the grittier sound of the down-tuned, death-doom heaviness of their 1989 demo *Frozen Illusion* with the icy majesty of the early '80s U.K. gothic scene, the band emerged with a monolithic slab of metal unlike anything the underground had ever heard. *Gothic*, released through Peaceville Records in 1991, stunned headbangers everywhere with a dark, innovative sound that seized listeners within seconds of dropping the needle onto the opening track. The album became an absolute cult classic, approaching religious stature by countless underground fans and bands alike. In its wake, the *Gothic* album single-handedly opened the gates for countless trends within the metal world, which sought to incorporate melancholy and—above all—melody within heavier sounds. We gathered the band's original five members—vocalist Nick Holmes, bassist Steve Edmondson, drummer Matt Archer and guitarists Greg Mackintosh and Aaron Aedy—to reflect on all things *Gothic*.

What was the general feeling within the band around the time you were writing and recording for Gothic?

Greg Mackintosh: In those days it was the grind scene, so we were playing with bands like Extreme Noise Terror and Napalm Death and Carcass, and we were the only slow band around from that scene. We'd play gigs and people would shout, "Play a fast one" and so, of course, we'd play an even slower one. Our first album, *Lost Paradise*, didn't really sound how we wanted it to sound. We thought the *Frozen Illusion* demo was better than the first album. So, with *Gothic* we wanted to make it sound more like the demo, but we'd also been listening to the *Reptile House*–era Sisters of Mercy stuff, and bands like Trouble, as well as all the tape-trading death metal stuff, and wanted to bring in some new elements.

Nick Holmes: Around the time of *Lost Paradise*, the Sisters of Mercy were pretty big in England, and I liked the sound they were doing. On the early records, they kind of captured a real sort of depressive gothic sound, and we really liked that. We thought we could try and capture that element and put it in with the kind of noise stuff that we did. Plus, at that time, Matt, our drummer couldn't play fast anyway, so we were kind of restricted even if we wanted to play fast. I think we tried playing fast and it was just a disaster and so we said, "OK, we'll just go the opposite and play as slow as we can." [*Laughs*] First and foremost, though, we were totally obsessed with death metal and doom metal. We were such big fans of it. Just like today, I see teenagers totally into it. We were no different.

Aaron Aedy: I think what we were trying to do with *Gothic* was combine the majesty of gothic music with the miserableness of doom music. We heard Celtic Frost's *Into the Pandemonium* and *Morbid Tales*, and they were using orchestrations on metal music, and we thought that was cool to take it in another direction.

Matt Archer: In those days, we listened to so much death metal and all the bands we played with were death metal bands. On tour, we'd put on our old compilation tapes and stuff just to hear something different. So, when we did *Gothic*, we wanted to do something that was heavy and somewhat in line with *Lost Paradise*, but we wanted to expand the sound into other genres of music that we were listening to: Celtic Frost, Trouble. We were young enough and naïve enough to have that sort of "let's just do it and see what happens" attitude.

All of that aside, **Gothic *was certainly something much larger than the sum of its parts. Where were your heads at back then to be able to create such intense atmospheres with your music?***

Mackintosh: Part of it comes from the area where we grew up. Not sure why, but all the other bands that also came out of the Bradford/Halifax/Leeds area also made very depressing music: the Sisters of Mercy, the Cult, New Model Army, My Dying Bride. Lots of bands from that area went for a sort of bittersweet tinge to their music. I think it's because we're all just miserable. We've all got this quite dark sense of humor where you can laugh at everything, but the area has still got this grim, miserable edge to it. There's a saying around here that goes "It's grim up north," and it was very true for us. We were always pretty miserable about stuff. We've lightened up a bit now, I think. I think it's an acceptance that life is a bit shit. [*Laughs*]

Aedy: Leeds is where gothic music came from really, so there was quite a strong following for darker music in our area, and a lot of the pubs and clubs sort of reflected that. In Bradford we used to go to a number of clubs where one minute they'd be playing serious gothic music, and the next minute they would have Kreator on or something. Between that and the Frog & Toad, which was the venue where we played our first-ever concert, they really mixed everything up, which kind of helped because you were hearing these things in the clubs as well.

Holmes: I had a friend at school who gave me the Sisters of Mercy *Reptile House* vinyl, and I remember going back and listening to tracks like "Black Planet" off the first Sisters' album *First and Last and Always*. I did like that sort of music very much, but outside of the Sisters, there really weren't too many other gothic bands that we knew of. We were also into the Melvins at the time and they played really slow. I remember an album they did called *Gluey Porch Treatments*. It was so slow. We liked the idea of combining the sort of Sabbath riffage, but making it even slower and getting the whole doom thing going. But honestly, we were so obsessed with the death metal stuff in those days that we didn't really venture that far outside our own musical field.

Who came up with the album title?

Mackintosh: The title for the album had come about because I had seen the Ken Russell film *Gothic* and I remember saying to Nick, "Hey, what about calling it that?" And he sort of went back and forth because he didn't want people thinking we were a gothic band rather than a doom whatever band, but eventually we agreed on using it.

Holmes: It was more to do with gothic literature and gothic architecture. That was more in our minds than any actual musical movement. Greg's very much into grandiose titles. He came up with [1995's] *Draconian Times* as well. For *Gothic*, it had more to do with architecture. We just like looking at gargoyles. Even now, I still like looking at gargoyles. It's kind of like the ultimate heavy metal thing, really. [*Laughs*]

How much of the record's sound did you have down prior to going into the studio?

Mackintosh: We had all the songs down beforehand. As far as sound, we knew what we wanted the record to sound like, but we didn't know how to capture sounds in those days. The only thing we had down beforehand was my guitar sound, because I had all the effects that I wanted to use ready to go before we went in to record. Aaron had a lot of trouble when we went in to record *Gothic*. He was trying out a lot of different guitars and different amps and he never really got the sound he wanted, so I ended up playing some of the rhythm stuff as well, until he sorted out his sound. I think Keith [Appleton], who owned Academy Studios where we recorded *Gothic*, was instrumental because he played the keyboards on *Gothic*. He had this Proteus rack thing that we used, and we were like, "Oh my god, that sounds amazing! Yeah, use that!"

Holmes: Songwriting in those days was just a case of gluing riffs together. A lot of the old metal stuff is like that anyway. It's like eight minutes of riffs glued together, which is cool. One after the next, after the next, and then come back to the original riff right at the end there. And then for the studio, we'd just buy a bottle of bourbon, plug in and see what happened. It was all very kind of rock 'n' roll. I mean, when you're a kid, you just think about being in a band and just getting drunk and having a good time, and that's all we really did in the first few years. Even Hammy [founder of Peaceville Records], who had done some production for us on *Lost Paradise*, all I can remember during *Gothic* is him buying a bottle of whiskey and sitting there smoking spliffs. There was no massive sort of sterile recording environment like there is now. With the song "Rapture," Matt couldn't get the timing right on a certain drum fill. We were under tight time constraints, and in those days drummers didn't have a click track. So in order to wrap up the song, I remember pushing a key on the keyboard right at the time when the drum fill was supposed to come in. It was the sound of a bomb going off, or a nuclear explosion or something, and it covered up the drum fill perfectly. If you listen back you'll hear it.

Aedy: I seem to recall back when we did *Lost Paradise*, Hammy was actually reading a book called *How to Be a Producer*, which I've never forgotten. But he did seem to know more about it than we did. Basically, he just sort of sat there with a bottle of whiskey and some marijuana and just headbanged. The great thing about Hammy was he was really into music.

Steve Edmondson: As for the time spent in the studio, it was hard work. I mean, we weren't brilliant musicians then. It was only the second time we were in the studio, and I just remember it being hard to nail the parts. Looking back, I can say it was genuinely innocent times, really. We were having a lot of fun.

In addition to the orchestrations, the presence of a female vocalist complementing the death growl was also more apparent on **Gothic** *than* **Lost Paradise.** *How did you meet vocalist Sarah Marrion and what was her reaction to the music she was asked to sing on?*

Mackintosh: We got Sarah through an advertisement we placed in *NME*. She was from Manchester. I remember seeing a surprised look on her face when we played some stuff back for her. She had never heard anything like it in her life!

Archer: I'm not sure the band sold itself extremely well in that instance. [*Laughs*] Here we were, a death metal band on a small independent label, and here was this quite prim and proper young lady. I don't think she knew what she was getting into, but she went in and when we heard her vocals with the rest of the music, we just thought it sounded absolutely fantastic.

Aedy: I think she got what we were trying to do, but it wasn't her thing. She was more into house and dance music. But I think she kind of got it because she had a bit of classical training. If you take away the guitar sound and Nick's vocals, we were just playing chords and melodies in minor keys, so she was able to catch on to the atmosphere we were going for.

Edmondson: We used her again on our next album, [1992's] *Shades of God*, so she must have liked it somewhat since she came back to the studio with us to do it again a year or so later.

The lyrics on **Gothic** *were a mature departure from those on your first album. What were you going for?*

Holmes: I always felt that psychological subject matter sort of gave you more space to work with. Back then, lots of bands were discussing evil or the devil. I've always tried to avoid the satanic stuff because once you do that it's hard to get out of that. Back then, it was just death metal growling, so I could write the lyrics at the same time or even before the music was written and just make the words fit. Basically just like writing down poetry or something, because you don't have to make it fit to a melody. It's actually easier to write lyrics like that. You can be as pretentious as you want if you're growling lyrics. If you're writing in the context of a melody, you have to think about words you're using and syllables, but in the old days you could be the Poet Laureate—you could be the death metal Poet Laureate if you wanted to. [*Laughs*]

Do you remember your reaction to the playback of the finished album while you were in the studio?

Mackintosh: Oh, we were loving it. We were all very young at the time and as soon as we played any of it back we were all going mental and headbanging along to it and saying, "Oh, this is ace. We've got another record out!" As far as the sound, there's a phrase that Nick always uses: "Weep openly at the sea of pomposity." It's the whole over-the-top thing. There's a fine line between sounding majestic and being pure cheese, and it's a line that we've always been very aware of and been very conscious of not crossing, which is unfortunate for a lot of other gothic metal acts today because they seem to err on the cheese side of the line.

Holmes: I think because it came through the huge speakers we were more impressed with the fact that we could play it so loud; plus, we had had a few drinks, so yeah, it just sounded phenomenal.

Archer: Rehearsals for the record were held in this shitty little room, which was noisy and distorted, so we really didn't know what the finished product would sound like. Listening to the playback, the album definitely had a sort of raw sound to it that added to the overall feel of what we were going for. Today most metal bands opt for a strictly regimented sound, but we loved the raw feel of what we had with *Gothic* and we felt that any overdubs or re-mastering would have killed some of the magic we had managed to create.

Edmondson: The ultimate reaction came when we actually got a tape of it and you put it in your car stereo and went somewhere quiet. We went to the rocks in Halifax, which is sort of a local beauty spot, and we sat there playing the album; that's when it hit us all.

Prior to the release of **Gothic**, *there were no death-doom or gothic metal scenes, but there were some bands [Cathedral, Winter] that picked up on what you guys had done with the* **Frozen Illusion** *demo and* **Lost Paradise**. *Were you paying much attention to any of these bands?*

Mackintosh: When we were doing *Frozen Illusion* and our first album, bands like Cathedral weren't in existence yet. Lee Dorrian was still in Napalm Death before Barney [Greenway] had joined. Back then I hadn't heard of bands like Winter or Cathedral or any others. The death metal stuff that we knew of was just the early Earache stuff and the early Peaceville stuff, and all the stuff from our tape-trading days from death metal bands. After *Gothic*, I remember we fast became a band's band. I remember Lee Dorrian and bands like Bolt Thrower were into it, and we got letters from bands like Entombed who were writing to say that they were really into it.

Holmes: In those days we didn't know of any other bands pursuing the sort of sound we were doing. Most of the bands we played with during our demo days and around the time of our first album were bands from the U.K. hard-core/grindcore scene—bands like Doom, Concrete Sox, Extreme Noise Terror and Napalm Death. Around the *Gothic*-era, the scene had sort of fractured into divisions of punk and metal. For *Gothic*, the concerts were reasonably turned out, but still very underground. It was like 50 guys from each town; death metal tape-traders who came to all the shows. We were tape-traders ourselves so we'd all just sit around and try to name bands that no one else knew and see if you were better than the next guy because you knew this really obscure band. I mean, we didn't think about girlfriends or anything back then. It was just guys and hair and tapes.

Early Peaceville bands like My Dying Bride and Anathema quickly picked up on the sound of the Gothic *album, and subgenres like death-doom/gothic metal/funeral doom largely owe their existence to the* Gothic *album. In many ways,* Gothic *single-handedly spawned an underground metal movement.*

Archer: On tour people used to hand us demos, and we started seeing bands with names taken from tracks from the *Gothic* album. While touring Europe, I remember suddenly we started hearing bands with that same sort of death metal sound, with orchestrations and female vocals. Here in the U.K., I remember Aaron [Stainthorpe] from My Dying Bride telling me that My Dying Bride was formed after seeing Paradise Lost play live at a gig in Bradford in 1990 or 1991.

Mackintosh: Over the years we had a lot of bands saying they liked *Gothic*, and it's really flattering. I remember Anathema at the time, I think they were supporting us for their first-ever gig. They were a bit younger than us, maybe 14 or 15 years old at the time. During their set they did a cover of our song "Eternal," and then we had to go on and play that song as well! We hadn't ever heard of Anathema because they weren't on record at the time, but afterwards we talked to them and we were like, "Oh yeah, really good. I think you're version was better than ours." The same thing happened with the Gathering when we played Holland. The Gathering opened for us and they also played a cover of "Eternal" before we went onstage, and it was like, "Crass, can these bands stop doing it, because their versions sound better than ours!"

Aedy: After *Lost Paradise*, we noticed some bands were picking up on the sound we were after, so what we tried to do with *Gothic* was to up the ante by putting all the orchestration and female vocals on. When we did *Gothic*, it wasn't like a massive commercial success, but there seemed to be a whole explosion of bands that were inspired by the *Gothic* album, so I think we sort of reacted to that when we went to do *Shades of God* by dropping the female vocals and having no orchestrations. In a lot of ways, *Gothic* was the answer to people copying *Lost Paradise*, really.

So was the influx of bands that were trying to capture your sound an impetus to change your style and move in a different direction on subsequent albums?

Holmes: For us, when everyone else starts to do it, we really set out to change what we're doing. It's the same now as it was then. Once everything starts to sound the same and you can't differentiate one band from the other, it's time to move on. We've always wanted to be on our own little island. The thing with growling is that it is so one-dimensional. You can only go so far with it, because you can't get any melody in there, so it's hard to get across what you want to. When we did tracks like "Shattered" on *Gothic*, I remember doing the sort of cleaner voice just to try to slightly break away from the total growl. We went on to do the *Shades of God* album, and it was kind of like "growling in key" as opposed to "just growling." And then we moved on from there. Not to say there's anything wrong with the straight-on death metal sound. I mean, even today, I like good death metal bands, and I can still totally appreciate that sound; but for us, we wanted to sort of expand out of that, but still keep it heavy.

Mackintosh: At the time when *Gothic* came out and when we did some gigs after it and went on to write more stuff, there wasn't that big thing surrounding *Gothic* where loads of bands were copying it. That came maybe a couple of years later. So, by the time *Shades of God* came out, there were bands starting to copy *Gothic*, but at the time we weren't really aware of any of that. We get bored quickly, I think that's what it is. We do a record and then sort of say to ourselves, "OK, we've done that, so what are we going to do now?"

So what is that image on the cover anyway?

Edmondson: It's literally Matt Archer's pocket. It's a close-up picture of his chest pocket with a bit of Greg's arm. It was Nick's idea. We had taken some band photographs and we blew a few of them up to bigger sizes. The section between Greg and Matt looked really weird when we had the big photograph, so we turned it upside down and chopped it out and blew it up larger. Nice and cheap! It fit what we were going for much more than the cover on our first album did.

Aedy: We wanted to stay away from the typical "heavy metal painting." Around that time, we were seeing a number of album covers with some sort of

Viking warrior holding a Flying V in his hands or something. So, with the *Gothic* cover, it was a reaction against what other bands seemed to be doing back then. It worked; I mean, the *Gothic* cover stood out because it looked different and had a dark feel to it. I remember at the time getting letters from fans asking what the cover was. People thought it was a picture inside some cave or inside a tomb or the inside of a coffin lid that had been scratched apart.

Holmes: I did the cover. If you look on the inside sleeve of the gatefold and look at the cardigan that Matt is wearing, I saw a picture within the cardigan. I saw a stream with molten lava coming out of it. It sounds like some kind of fucking schizophrenic thing or as if I'd been smoking some weed or something, but I saw this image within the picture. I don't think anyone else can see it, but I just thought it would be great on the cover. Now when I look at it, I can still see the image, but it wasn't elaborated on. It was supposed to be more elaborated on to make it look more like what was in my mind, but that never happened. We just took the film and blew the image up larger and that was it.

Mackintosh: Yeah, it's ludicrous when you hear the story behind the cover, but it all seems to fit into place now. A lot of people think it was some big plan, but really it was just a bunch of young kids just fiddling around in the dark. Back then we didn't have any art direction or anyone saying yes or no to us. Hammy just let us do whatever we wanted. Same thing goes with the Christ image on the back of the *Gothic* album. My brother did that. He came up to me and said, "Why don't you put this on the back of the record?" And I said "Yeah, OK."

Archer: When we had the completed cover, we all thought it looked pretty cool and pretty dark. It took on a whole atmosphere of its own. I've seen the cover hung up on people's walls and we used to get comments like, "That's such an amazing piece of art," and so at the time we didn't want to advertise that it was a lock of my hair and a bit of a jacket. We didn't want to shatter the illusion or anything. Everything from the cover to the songs to the sound of the record— it all sort of fell into place for us.

DOOM OVER MY HAMMY

Q&A with the Peaceville Records founder

The singularly named enigma Hammy not only discovered Paradise Lost way back in 1988, he also produced the band's early demos and their debut album, *Lost Paradise*. But PL's *Gothic* album was the breakthrough release for his now legendary Peaceville Records.

— Scott Koerber

How much input did you give the band on Gothic?

Hammy: Paradise Lost evolved very quickly from the days of the demos to the second album, *Gothic*. With *Gothic* they felt extremely confident when they were going into the studio. The songwriting was really down. It was extremely precise. They didn't need me to produce or anything. I didn't really feel the need to help anymore. *Gothic* was the last record they were contracted to record for Peaceville, and the band knew damn well that the world was their bloody oyster afterwards. They felt the big label stardom coming. It was absolutely a concrete thing, and that was such an exciting time for those guys. They were buzzing around like mad at the time. They knew they were flying off to major label-dom!

The record was really experimental at the time of its release. What was the vibe in the studio like?

Hammy: Not all of the bands sat too well with Keith Appleton [owner of Academy Studios] because he was quite uneducated in metal and rock and punk. Keith was coming from a pop background, and sometimes the two worlds just collided. But with *Gothic*, we just hit it right that time. It was the first really well-recorded album at Academy Studios. Being a studio-based guy, Keith had the technical knowledge to be able to pull off a lot of the experimental stuff that Paradise Lost were intending to do. The marriage between Greg's songwriting and musicianship and Keith's technical ability really came to the front, and the pair of them worked together extremely well to create the whole event and atmosphere that is the *Gothic* album. I remember running into Keith and Greg while out doing some Christmas shopping on Christmas Eve during the time when they were mixing *Gothic*. They both seemed really happy. I just felt that was a brilliant sign. Peaceville didn't really have the funds to re-record albums or go for endless remixes or anything like that. It was pretty much a one-take sort of thing.

What did Gothic do for Peaceville Records?

Hammy: *Gothic* made Peaceville. It had a massive influence on the scene full stop. It made a lot of waves. Even from the white label promos going out to radio stations and the press, people were just really turning their heads because you could just feel the shockwaves. It affected tons of bands in terms of how bands were writing and how they wanted to sound. Soon you started to see a "Paradise Lost effect" on the new bands. Lots of bands started to say they wanted to sound like *Gothic*. Same sort of thing that happened after Slayer's *Reign in Blood*. After *Gothic*, there was a massive flood of bands that went to Academy Studios for the *Gothic* sound. Cradle of Filth and everybody else started turning up after that.

Do you have a favorite track from Gothic?

Hammy: Definitely "Eternal." "Eternal" was the first time Peaceville had sort of what we could class as a single. We put "Eternal" on a flexi disc on the cover of *Metal Forces* magazine in 1991. As a song, it stood out as the first really big song from *Gothic*.

CHAPTER 11

ROTTEN TO THE GORE

THE MAKING OF CARCASS' *NECROTICISM—DESCANTING THE INSALUBRIOUS*

by J. Bennett

Release Date: 1991
Label: Earache
Summary: Deathgrind comes of age
Induction Date: September 2005/Issue #11

L iverpudlian grind titans Carcass may not have invented grindcore with 1991's *Necroticism—Descanting the Insalubrious*, but they certainly opened it up to a magnitude of previously unfathomed possibilities. After releasing two well-received but sonically blurry (and visually controversial) grind shitstorms in *Reek of Putrefaction* (1988) and *Symphonies of Sickness* (1989), guitarist/vocalist Bill Steer, bassist/vocalist Jeff Walker and drummer Ken Owen began writing longer, infinitely more complex and compelling songs before recruiting future Arch Enemy guitarist Michael Amott (then of Carnage) from Sweden and entering Amazon Studios in Simonswood, England, with producer Colin Richardson. The result was an eight-song psychedelic metal colossus with song titles like "Lavaging Expectorate of Lysergide Composition" and "Corporal Jigsore Quandary," bizarre samples culled from British TV programming, and medically/disease-themed lyrics (penned by Walker) that cleft a fine line between morbid obsession and rarefied genius. But *Necroticism* isn't just the crucial transitional album between Carcass' muffled past and their highly refined death-rock future—it also happens to be the latest inductee into *Decibel*'s Hall of Fame.

⊕

PART I: NECROTIC CONCEPTION

What's the first thing that comes to mind when you think about the making of Necroticism?

Bill Steer: I guess the studio where we recorded it—in those days it was known as Amazon. We'd been there before; we did a track for a compilation there. We really liked the place and it was relatively local for us, on the outskirts of Liverpool. It was in a really weird neighborhood, though—not a particularly pleasant area. It was almost on the edge of an industrial estate. The studio itself didn't look like much from the outside, but once you went in, it was really nice. It later moved to the center of Liverpool and became Parr Street Studios, where we recorded *Heartwork*. Later it became well known for Coldplay and stuff like that.

Michael Amott: It's the first time I was in a professional studio. The first record I did, we spent five days recording and mixing it in Sweden, so that wasn't really professional. The Carcass thing was a bit more; it was spending quite a lot of money—for back then especially. I just knew that the other guys in Carcass, they definitely wanted to step it up on that record.

Jeff Walker: I remember Amott drew a swastika on a tiny Polish flag he had on his Charvel for a laugh—taking the piss out of Jeff Hanneman's guitar that had an S.S. death's head insignia on it at the time—which pissed off the engineer, 'cause his wife was black. [*Laughs*]

Steer: There was a weird sense of humor in the band—people were into saying and doing things they didn't actually believe just to get a reaction. [*Laughs*] That Amott story might have been one example—I can't say I remember it, but something about it sounds familiar. It was mostly good-natured ribbing, though—people just making fun of each other, as they do.

Walker: The first thing I thought when the album was finished was that it wasn't fully realized. At the time, a few things happened that I wasn't happy about. But then, I'm the lazy bastard who should've spent more time in the studio. A couple of things got changed, or edited, that should've remained. [*Laughs*] For me, that album was our . . . *And Justice for All*. It's the calm before the storm.

You'd worked with Colin Richardson previously on **Symphonies of Sickness.** *What was it like this time?*

Ken Owen: For me personally, it was quite a struggle because Colin was a real stickler for getting it precise. I had to do my tracks several times—like 10 or 15 times per song, probably. He certainly put me through the wringer, but if he hadn't, we wouldn't have been able to come up with the goods. It was very important to have someone there who could sit back and analyze everything. Colin's extremely patient, because listening to the same track over and over again can really wear you down and make you wanna give up. But the amount of energy he put into it was incredible. He's an amazing producer; he had a good sense of humor as well, which Carcass always had.

Steer: To me, Colin wasn't a taskmaster—he was an incredibly patient person. He had an almost autistic obsession with the details of a recording. To me, he was more obsessed with the sonic picture rather than the actual performances. I mean, he'd react if there was an obvious mistake, but—beyond that—he was usually listening for sonic quality. From what I can remember, that's the way he always operated in the studio. He had so much patience that he'd go for hours or days to achieve whatever result he was after—budget permitting, obviously. For that record, somehow or other we ended up with a little more money—not a huge amount, but we definitely had more time to nail certain sounds or whatever we wanted.

Amott: It was exciting because I obviously knew he produced some bands that I was into and stuff, and I'd heard a lot about him through the Carcass guys. I was just excited; it was kind of, I don't know . . . I was surprised how down to earth he was; he didn't have this big-shot producer-type attitude at all. He was very laid back and almost shy in a way, but he took us seriously. I was, I don't know, I guess I was 20 years old then, and to be taken seriously, that was amazing.

Walker: When we brought Colin in to produce, I think he felt being a producer meant sticking your bloody nose in and convincing people to change things. Some of the songs got cut up when I wasn't there. For example, "Carneous Cacoffiny" would've been even longer. [*Laughs*] But probably it was for the best. I was 21 when we did that album, and when you're a kid, you think you're always right. Some of the samples as well—there should've been more between the tracks, but they got cut because I wasn't there. But that's what you get for having a girlfriend and going to the pub.

Where did all the samples between the songs come from?

Walker: They're all off TV shows. One was from a pathology program. The main guy, the pathologist, still lectures at [the University of] Sheffield, and I wish I could remember his name. He's quite a humorous guy; I still see him on TV. One's from John Waters—the one about "you can hear people puking" [intro to "Pedigree Butchery"]. Another one's [Herschell] Gordon Lewis—he's the one who says "prepare to die" [intro to "Symposium of Sickness"]—he directed *Blood Feast* and *Two Thousand Maniacs!*, these gory 1960s exploitation drive-in movies. That quote is from an interview he did that I taped off the TV. He's talking about the arty, pretentious bullshit he's being asked to justify, but he's saying it's just exploitation. It was the same thing with us—compared to *Reek of Putrefaction* and *Symphonies of Sickness*, *Necroticism* is pretty mainstream. It's kind of a more accessible version of Carcass.

Necroticism is the first Carcass album that doesn't have a bizarre medical/gore collage on the cover. You used photos of the band members instead.

Walker: To be honest, we wanted something we could get into the shops. It was getting a bit boring that people couldn't buy our records in Germany. After *Symphonies*, we realized we couldn't just churn out the same shit.

Steer: By that time, Jeff had made that side of the band his own—the lyrics and the imagery. It was very much in his hands. I'm guessing what he had on his mind was a way to move forward. We couldn't just stick a collage on every cover, you know? We had those black-and-white photos taken. I'm not entirely sure of the circumstances, but I think they were taken at my parents' house. Later, Jeff had the big prints done and tore them up a bit to use as part of that picture that Ian Tilton took. That was what you see on the front of the album. It was actually shot in Ken's dad's veterinary surgery. That's Ken holding the hammer.

Walker: I feel like I'm trying to take all the glory, but I've got to be honest—it *was* me. I got a photographer, Ian Tilton, who used to work for *Sounds*. It was all sort of cobbled together. We went to Bill's house to do [the band photos], and I only had a basic idea in me head. The only thing I *knew* I wanted to do was shoot somebody in the bathtub, which Amott, the poor sod, ended up doing. But they're killer photographs. I think nowadays people would assume the [album cover] was done with Photoshop, but it was four actual photographs laid on Ken's dad's veterinary gurney, and then another photograph was taken. The hammer belonged to Griff from Cathedral—we lived together and I nicked it from under the kitchen sink. And that's my hand coming out of the bin.

PART II: TOOLS OF THE TRADE

Whose idea was the album title?

Owen: Jeff did. I thought it was a really clever play on words. Jeff's real inventive with language, though.

Walker: "Descanting the Insalubrious" was Ken. "Necroticism" was me. Bill and Ken wanted to add the "Descanting the Insalubrious" part, but I thought it was too middle-class. But mine was poor grammar—it should've been "Necrotica" or something.

On previous Carcass albums, Jeff used his sister's medical dictionary for lyrical ideas. It seems like he did the same thing here, only he took more liberties with the terminology.

Walker: Yeah, I think that book was probably my first choice for getting clever words. But that's another reason why I think the album is half-baked—there's so many typos in the liner notes. I remember being at our manager's house, and literally the artwork had to go off the next day. I was forced into a corner with a lot of the stuff, even song titles. I still can't get past the fact that that song came out as "Incarnated Solvent Abuse." It's supposed to be "Incarnate Solvent Abuse." I won't take the blame for typos—I swear it's not me. It happened all the time—I mean, even with *Heartwork*; it makes me cringe. Americans are terrible with their grammar anyway, and I hate to think I'm responsible for making your literacy even worse.

Amott: [There were songs about] making dog food out of humans . . . I just thought it was turning things upside down. A lot of the death metal that we were listening to or had been listening to was about zombies or mutilating women and stuff like that, and he kind of turned that thing around. I don't know if it was on that album or the previous album, but he had a song about a sort of male rape—just, like, horrific situations for men or young boys. I thought that was cool, just to fuck with people. I think it was deliberate in that way. I thought the words that he was using—or sometimes even making up on his own—I thought it was kind of psychedelic at times. I think [Jeff] went through a period where he was very, very creative for a few years, and he was definitely taking it to the next level all the time. I think that's probably his best record.

Steer: The lyrical direction of the band was actually kicked off by Ken in the beginning. When we were kids, he started writing all these weird lyrics, and I thought they were hysterical. Once we put a band together, those lyrics became the foundation of what we were doing. Later on, Jeff just completely took over and twisted it into all kinds of new directions. Things were kind of compartmentalized that way. Besides the lyrics and visual atmosphere, he was the driving force in a lot of the practical matters like gigs and various business-related matters. By [*Necroticism*], I was purely interested in the music. I don't have a lot of patience for the other stuff—I'm just not that kind of person.

Owen: I helped come up with the lyrics on *Reek of Putrefaction*, so I was involved with the lyrical content from day one. We didn't take ourselves too seriously, though—our tongues were firmly in our cheeks.

In the liner notes, all the guitar solos have names. One of Bill's solos on "Inpropagation" is called "Humanure," which Cattle Decapitation used for an album title.
Steer: [*Laughs*] That was Jeff's idea. He was wacky in that sense—he'd throw in any kind of spice he could think of that would make things weirder.

Walker: Obviously, I'd like to take credit for everything, but honestly, yeah—again—it was probably me. I think maybe we named the solos on *Symphonies*, too. It was sort of . . . what's the word? Pretentious.

Necroticism *was the first Carcass record with Michael in the band—how did that change the dynamics?*
Steer: Becoming a four-piece was part of our development. With two guitars in the band, we could do harmonies, solos . . . you know, widen our scope a bit. That turned out to be the case, because he came up with a lot of ideas, some great riffs . . . he helped the spirit of the band along. I just loved it in the beginning, because all of a sudden there was another guitar coming from the other side of the stage and, you know, [*laughs*] I like guitars. He played well in the band, so it just immediately made us sound better.

Amott: I contributed a little bit on one song, "Incarnated Solvent Abuse," and I think one more riff in another song. They had most of the album already written when I joined the band. I guess I've always had a . . . maybe they were still a little bit more caught up in just being more sort of, I don't know . . . you know, *sick*. Just sick-sounding riffs; we used to call it "sick" then. I don't know what it's called now, but just odd stuff, you know, like random combinations of notes that just sounded really twisted. I think I brought in more of the wimpy stuff. [*Laughs*]

Walker: It's funny, because most of the album was written before Amott joined, but the two tracks that save the album are obviously "Incarnate Solvent Abuse" and "Corporal Jigsore Quandary," which he helped write. They're mostly Bill's songs, but I played him Arch Enemy's version [of "Incarnate Solvent Abuse," on *Dead Eyes See No Future*] and Bill's only comments were, "I forgot how much input he had in those songs." But it was good, because they started to write together. And without those two songs, the album wouldn't be as popular as it was. They're quite good, catchy songs.

Did you have all the songs finished and rehearsed before you went into the studio?

Steer: Well, I could be wrong, but as far as I remember, everything was written before we went in. We got to eight songs, and we knew they were kind of lengthy, so we figured we had an album, and we just went in. I think seven of them had been demoed at home. Ken and I definitely had access to a four-track at that point. We'd play in a spare room at my parents' house and put down a really rough four-track. Then I'd maybe put down some extra guitars and Jeff would stick a vocal on there—just to get a feel for how the track was going to turn out. I guess at that stage we were getting to the point where we were a little more organized as a band.

Owen: I remember I wrote "Symposium of Sickness" at home on an acoustic guitar using only single notes. Then I'd pass it over to Bill and he'd transpose it to guitar chords. Then we'd play the original melody in chords.

Steer: I remember this was the last record where Ken contributed any riffs. He'd write very odd-sounding riffs, and I always had a lot of fun playing anything he came up with. They were just warped—I don't know anybody who could come up with stuff like that. He wasn't really playing guitar per se; he'd just pick up an acoustic, find these bizarre finger patterns and put them down on cassette. I'd take the tape home and try to transcribe it, which was really difficult because he was doing things you wouldn't naturally want to do. But that was part of the fun. Sometimes I'd alter it to make it a bit more playable for us. Ken was a funny guy in those days. Even before Carcass, he'd do these bedroom recordings—I think one of them was called "Torn Arteries" and the other was called "Despicable"—and they had those really sick note combinations that you hear in early Carcass.

Walker: Yeah, the music was done, and most of the lyrics. But we'd never rehearsed the vocals, so that was all done on the spot. When it came to the bass, I quickly realized I hadn't learned half the bass lines. The beauty of Carcass is that, with the exception of Bill, we were pretty sloppy—but we could get our shit together when we needed to.

It probably took me a day and a half to do the bass, because Colin was really putting everything under the microscope. I don't know why we bothered, 'cause you can't hear the bass, anyway—that's another reason it's our . . . *And Justice for All*. I remember Ken got flustered 'cause the money and time ran out, and we only had the basic tracks done, but what are you gonna do?

You ran out of money?

Walker: When we started doing this record, we were doing it with our own money. We had like 16 or 18,000 pounds, and after about two weeks we ran out of money and time. We'd done the drums, the rhythm guitars and about half the bass. We weren't signed to Earache at the time; our contract was up, so we were doing this off our own backs. We were negotiating with Earache and Roadrunner at the time—in fact, I've still got the offers that Roadrunner sent us. I remember Roadrunner asked us, "Do you want to make money, or sell records and be famous? You can't have both."

PART III: INEVITABLE PROGRESSION OF SONIC MALFEASANCE

It seems like there was a point in Carcass where the band was more concerned with being sick and fast, but by **Necroticism**, *it seems like that attitude had faded a bit—it was more like you wanted to shape something.*

Amott: That's definitely something I noticed when I joined the band—how progressive they were in the true sense of that word. I was trying to learn as much as I could, especially from Bill Steer, who was my mentor at the time. I mean, I guess I liked bringing in more sort of classic metal–sounding riffs and melodies for the guitar. The song that I did write, "Incarnate Solvent Abuse," was also the most straightforward song on the record.

Steer: Yeah, in the early days, we definitely wanted to push it as far as we could. But I guess we suddenly realized a couple of years down the road that it wasn't really a goal worth pursuing. Where can you go when you get to that point? When we first started doing this kind of music, there were a handful of bands doing it, and at some point you realize that there isn't any particular reason to spend your musical career chasing that one dream. It's something that can't be quantified, anyway. Who's to say which group is fastest or heaviest? You can't really measure. So, yeah, third album onwards, we were looking for new things. We were trying to get more musical, really. Half of it was listening to other music. Our days of being bigoted about the stuff we listened to, that died out with the first record. Even by the second record we were listening to Thin Lizzy and Guns N' Roses—which people might find shocking if they've heard that record, but that was the case.

It seems like **Necroticism** *was the first Carcass album that had a certain degree of clarity and focus to it.*

Owen: Certainly, yeah. I think it was because we'd been playing live quite often, and that really tightens you up and pushes you to the limit, playing-wise. If you can play it live, you can play it in the studio. You only get one chance live.

Steer: I suppose we were restless in a way, because we didn't want to make the same record twice. The first one just disappeared in a load of mud; with the second one, we had gotten a little more proficient, but it was still a noisy record, with a load of fast parts and a lot of distortion going on. By the third one, I suppose we got more into in playing riffs on strings other than the bottom one.

Amott: The first time Carcass asked me [to join the band], they only had their first album out and I didn't really rate that. I didn't think it was worth leaving whatever I was doing at the time for. When they came out with *Symphonies of Sickness*, they became my favorite band overnight. But I wasn't actually prepared . . . the music that they'd written for *Necroticism* was so far beyond that. The band was really making huge steps. It was quite exciting because, I mean, back then everybody was making such big leaps forward as musicians in between recording sessions. A year passes and you think, "Wow, this guy's become really, really good." Those things slow down after a few years, you know, actually learning to play. I guess Carcass was definitely an example of a band that grew up in public.

Is there any one song that you think holds up particularly well?

Owen: "Corporal Jigsore Quandary" is excellent. Bill came up with the riff, showed it to me, and we worked out the drumbeat. The drums fit exactly with the guitar riff, so it was quite a precise track to write. Most of the songs worked that way; we'd rehearse at Bill's parents' place until we felt we'd achieved something.

Steer: To be honest, I've hardly heard that record since we did it. Of course, you're in the studio and straight after you get home, you listen to the album a bit just to check it, but none of us tended to listen to it much after the fact—except for Ken. I lived with Ken for about half a year in Liverpool, and I actually heard him listening to [*Necroticism*] just before we were supposed to go in to do the next record. I was a bit freaked out, because I've always had a bit of a phobia about listening to our own stuff once it was done and dusted. I just doesn't seem healthy to me. But it'd be very funny to hear it, actually, after all these years.

PART IV: PROPAGATION

How soon after it came out did you realize the impact it had?

Walker: Pretty straight off—probably because people figured we'd spent a fortune on the production. Back then, a lot of the recordings were still primitive, for death metal bands or whatever. Immediately, it had quite an impact, because things started to take off for us. We were playing more, and more people would turn up at the gigs. It's weird that you're doing this piece on *Necroticism*, because a lot of people would consider the classic album to be *Heartwork*, but purists would probably say it's *Reek* or *Symphonies*. Nobody's gonna say it's the last album [*Swansong*], but that album was very misunderstood. If there's one thing you can say, it's that no two Carcass albums sound the same. Not many bands can say that.

Steer: I don't really recall meeting anyone who had much to say about that record—certainly not at the time. That's my general memory of being in the band, actually. We'd do records, and they'd sell well enough that we could tour and maybe get a tiny bit of press, but didn't really feel like we were getting anywhere with our career in that scene. There was a load of bands, and we just got carried along with the wave. It enabled us to do things and travel, but we never felt like the band was any more significant than it was. I don't know . . . occasionally, once or twice a year, I'll be somewhere on my own and I'll run into someone who mentions that stuff. It's quite a rare occasion, though. The impression I've got is that it's looked upon more fondly now. To be really honest, the two records that seem to be big now—this one and *Heartwork*—weren't rated very highly by people. A lot of people said we'd sold out. People were very conscious of anything creeping in that was too musical or too mainstream. But we'd got to the stage where we wanted to do something different—we didn't care if people thought it was wimpy. Looking back, it wasn't particularly wimpy, but those were extreme days, I guess.

Amott: We were very young at the time, so we were very big-headed and we thought a lot of ourselves, I think. We had that cockiness and we basically despised everybody that wasn't trying to push boundaries. There were a lot of real sort of bog-standard death metal bands at the time. There were a lot of people just happy to imitate Death or Obituary or Morbid Angel. I didn't really notice that we influenced anybody, really, but I knew that we had a breakthrough with the media, especially in England. We got some people behind the band, like Malcolm Dome and, you know, serious music writers, and we would actually be featured in these kinds of magazines—that was kind of a new beginning in a way. I think that was the beginning of Carcass becoming media darlings.

Do you think about the album differently now than you did back then?

Owen: Yeah, especially with what happened to me. Six years ago, I had a cerebral hemorrhage, which changed my life. It was very close to being the end of my life, to be honest. I was in a coma for a long time. There was no warning whatsoever. I bent over to stroke my cat, and I passed out. It was caused by an aneurysm. I had to go in for surgery a year after the initial hemorrhage because the aneurysm was still there, and I was told I wouldn't survive another one. Of course, that kind of surgery is like a massive head wound. I wasn't able to walk after that, so I was just struggling to get on my own feet for a while. But the doctors are really happy with my progress. I'm playing drums again live—with a blues band in Nottingham—but it's not quite as intense as Carcass.

Walker: Yeah, because at the time I was kind of, well, not *disappointed*, but I was kind of on a downer about it. I like it for what it is now, but at the time, I had more emotion wrapped up in it. For me, it was half-focused, half-envisaged. Not literally *half*, but there were things in there that were taken away, and that left a bad taste in me mouth. But I've only got meself to blame. Colin, Ken and Bill made these decisions when I wasn't around. Which isn't to say I wasn't wrong . . . if you put the stuff back in now, I don't think it'd necessarily make it a better album.

Amott: I think it sounds kind of tame now today, actually. But it surprises me now . . . I heard it a while ago, and it surprised me how long the songs are. There was a complete disregard for the listener back then. [*Laughs*] There really was. I can't even remember that ever coming up in conversation—what people would think about it. It was all about keeping ourselves happy, and also trying to impress other bands at the time. I think there was quite a competitive spirit, like, "Wait 'til Morbid Angel hear this," you know, that kind of attitude.

Steer: Well, I couldn't comment directly because it's been so long and I couldn't even count the years it's been since I've heard the thing. Like I said, every once in a while I'll run into someone who seems to rate it very highly, and for me, that makes it all worthwhile. I distinctly remember the talk in the band— even in the studio when we were recording this album—we thought, "Oh, this scene hasn't got long." We felt it was way past saturation point already and there really was no future for it. I guess we were completely wrong about that.

Is there anything you'd change about it?

Steer: [*Laughs*] No, definitely not. It was all part of our learning curve. It was definitely a transitional phase, you know, going from that really muddy-sounding three-piece grindcore act to something more musical. I think [*Necroticism*] was where we realized we had six strings on our guitars, not two. Ken got into some super-developed drum stuff, too, which is why the recording took so long. When you get into a studio, those things suddenly become a lot harder to play.

Amott: I'd like to remix the album. [*Laughs*] I can understand that people are interested in it, but I'm not really that interested in it myself because I was there and . . . [*laughs*] I don't know, I guess maybe when I retire, that's when I'll just sort of look at everything I've done. I think it's too early to look back now; I mean, you know, I can't really rate what we did with Carcass as classic or anything like that, you know what I mean?

Walker: Nothing. There's no point. It is what it is, and people enjoy it for what it is. There's nothing that offends me after all this time. I've got no beef with it. I don't have to listen to it, and I didn't pay for it, so . . . [*laughs*] It was a good time doing it, and that's the bottom line. Maybe I'd make it longer, though. [*Laughs*]

Owen: No, I personally don't think it'd be right to change anything. You can't take away any part of your history without changing who you are today, and I'm very happy with the person I am these days.

CHAPTER 12

THE CRYPTIC STENCH

THE MAKING OF CANNIBAL CORPSE'S *TOMB OF THE MUTILATED*

by Chris Dick

Release Date: 1992
Label: Metal Blade
Summary: Indecent death metal exposure
Induction Date: June 2008/Issue #44

"To crush your enemies, see them driven before you and to hear the lamentation of the women," so said a sword-wielding Arnold Schwarzenegger as Conan in 1982's *Conan the Barbarian*. The aforementioned quote could've come from Buffalo's Cannibal Corpse after they released the all-powerful, superlatively offensive *Tomb of the Mutilated* 10 years later. See, *Tomb of the Mutilated*, as lauded and reviled as it was, altered death metal. It was the future, immediate and long-term, and nobody saw it. To be fair, Cannibal Corpse weren't the first to use horror movies, serial killers, the evening news and an overactive imagination to power music and image. That honor goes, in part, to Repulsion, Autopsy, Impetigo, Macabre and pre-*Heartwork* Carcass. What Cannibal Corpse unwittingly did, specifically on *Tomb of the Mutilated*, is take disparate concepts (music, lyrics, art, touring, merchandise, distribution) and roll them into one gigantic, pus/bile-gushing machine that everyone from the record-buying public to idea-starved bands wanted a piece of.

As a record, Cannibal Corpse's third splatter-platter runs like a no-no highlight reel at PMRC and 700 Club meetings. Musically, it's jarring, alien and nearly incomprehensible. Lyrically, well, the Germans, who enjoy scat porn and strap-on sex with animatronic dinosaurs, felt it was verboten. And artistically, as in Vincent Locke's gut-wrenchingly good cover, it proved the Germans weren't the only ones getting kinky in candlelight. Basically, *Tomb of the Mutilated* was the most grotesque yet commercially viable death metal album ever. It made soccer moms run screaming—Birkenstocks smacking like machine gun fire against expensively massaged heels—back to their Volvos and kids like impressionable high schoolers, wonder if sheer possession alone could lead marathon family counseling sessions. I mean, if songs like "Entrails Ripped From a Virgin's Cunt," "I Cum Blood," "Addicted to Vaginal Skin" and "Necropedophile" don't offend, then pinch your balls really hard. If you yelp in agony, then you're not one of us. Your senses haven't been whittled down to bloody nubs. And you should just go home now.

Of course, for every mention of "Entrails Ripped From a Virgin's Cunt" what really set Cannibal Corpse apart was album-opener "Hammer Smashed Face." Heavy, heavy, heavy. And catchy, too. As in H5N1 catchy. This is one of those songs you can't forget. It's death metal equivalent of "Stayin' Alive," with less Gibb and more giblets. And then there's the movie deal. While Slayer jammed in front of Giza, the Corpse landed an appearance in *Ace Ventura: Pet Detective*— the movie with future supercalifragilistic star Jim Carrey. They only got a few frames in the theatrical release, but "Hammer Smashed Face" was given worldwide exposure. Big-time stuff for a small-time band. This alone is Hall of Fame–worthy, but we must be judicious. *Tomb of the Mutilated* is this month's inductee simply because it ruled. Cannibal fuckin' Corpse, dudes!

I remember a friend of mine slamming the audio cassette of **Tomb** *on my desk in high school saying, "Dude, this makes your Bolt Thrower sound gay." That was my first memory of the record. What are yours?*

Jack Owen: The main thing I remember was putting the album together— the final touches, seeing the song title "Entrails Ripped From a Virgin's Cunt" and saying, "Dudes, we've finally gone too far!" When we got the artwork back, which was a male zombie going down on a female zombie, it's like, "Oh, man! We've *really* gone too far!" I remember writing it in Buffalo. It went smoothly. I don't remember [Bob] Rusay contributing much. Well, not as much as he had on *Eaten Back to Life* and *Butchered at Birth*. By then we were a machine. We didn't have jobs. I think it was after the first European tour in 1991, we thought, "Why go back to work? Let's keep writing albums!" We'd practice every weekday. Me and Alex lived about 45 minutes from the practice room, so we'd carpool in every day.

Alex Webster: For *Tomb*, we wrote more on our own than on previous records. The one thing for me is that the bass is more prominent. I had started practicing a lot more after the first tour for *Butchered*. I was hanging out with a friend of mine, Greg St. John, who was friends with Cynic. He was in the band Solstice with Rob [Barrett]. Well, Greg had moved back up to Buffalo from Florida and was like, "Listen to Atheist, listen to this Cynic!" He was getting me into that stuff. I was very much into brutality, but it was around this time I started getting into the more technical side of music. Some of the stuff I ended up writing, like "Hammer Smashed Face," was the result of me practicing. That was where I was at. I wanted to improve as a bass player.

Chris Barnes: From working on the album [and] being in the rehearsal space to putting together the artwork and going back to Morrisound to record, I had a lot of good memories of that time. It was a blast. It was an important album for me at the time. The band was finding its particular style and nailing that down.

Paul Mazurkiewicz: Fond memories, really. It was a critical point in the band's career. We took it to the next level on *Tomb of the Mutilated*. It was a good time for the band. It pushed us forward. We were a young band, too. We were formed in December '88 and signed our contract with Metal Blade in July of '89. We were together seven or eight months. It was overwhelming. We were just kids playing music. We never set goals higher than playing a few shows. By the end of '89, we were down in Florida recording *Eaten Back to Life*. Those three records came together pretty quickly. Most of the touring started on *Tomb of the Mutilated*. It was our last album during what I call the "innocent times." We got more serious with everything on *Tomb of the Mutilated*.

Bob Rusay: It was the last album I appeared on. It was a pretty stressful time in the band. We were on the outs at the time. At least with me. It wasn't a happy time for me, but the scene was exploding. It was taking off. We were having a lot of fun on tours. The European tours were huge. Writing the actual album was a little different from the first two. On the first two, everything was new and fresh. By *Tomb*, for me, things were a little tense. We weren't getting along. Some of the guys wanted to get technical with it. Sadus was really popular at the time, and they were great musicians. None of us were anywhere near their level of playing. Alex wanted to write all these goofy guitar parts and Paul was coming up with some pretty simple parts. They sounded good. Alex was like, "No, you're a drummer. Stay behind the drums." There was always pressure to write music. I remember when Alex came up with the intro to "Hammer Smashed Face." It was really intricate. It was a scale broken down and mixed. The whole direction of the album went in that way. On the first two albums, I wrote a lot of music. With *Tomb*, I hit a wall. I wasn't coming up with fresh ideas. I couldn't get inspired.

Your first two albums were intense, but **Tomb of the Mutilated** *took all things Cannibal Corpse one step further. Why do you think the album was so strong in comparison to its predecessors?*

Rusay: It was a much better collaboration from the group. It's a much better album, as far as the material. Everyone had a hand in it. It was a good direction to go in. Everyone wanted to have a say. It was more stressful, but it made for a better product.

Owen: I remember making the band more refined. Finding our identity. *Eaten* and *Butchered* are so different. *Eaten* is more thrashy and *Butchered* is just riff after riff. Some of the stuff doesn't make much sense. With *Tomb* we took our time. Some of the songs took a week to write and some other songs took five. You know, to rot. *Tomb* was more song-oriented. Chris had taken over the lyrics, so we could concentrate on the music. We really wanted to write music that made sense, in the end.

Webster: It's more song-like. To me, if you have interesting and brutal riffs that were put together in a memorable way, then it's OK. During *Butchered at Birth*, we were convinced the more unorthodox the music, the less mainstream it was. It was heavier to be off-the-wall as far as arrangements go. When you look at some of the records that really inspired us, like *Reign in Blood*, they're heavy records, but they're conventionally arranged. That was how we approached *Tomb*. There's still some weird stuff, like on "Post Mortal Ejaculation." That's pretty far from being a mainstream arrangement.

Barnes: It was a natural progression. You learned more as you went. *Tomb of the Mutilated* was no different. Jack and Alex started getting more interested in the technical aspects of writing, excelling in each of their instruments. We'd always been into bands like Sadus and Possessed. Cynic was also a big-time influence. It was a natural extension from *Butchered at Birth*. For me, it's hard to lyrically or vocally decide if *Butchered* or *Tomb* is the most intense. Both are lyrically obscene. And vocally they're on the verge of alien. Either one of those records is about as heavy as we ever were going to get. Some like to say *Tomb* is the pinnacle death metal release of the time. That's an honor when people hold the album in such high regards.

Mazurkiewicz: It was the next step forward. It was more technical. A song like "Hammer Smashed Face," with the bass line, was new to us. When you look back on that song, that part was considered tech. It was a little primitive. Back in '92, it was pretty cool. The writing was still brutal, but we never wanted to write the same album over and over. That was the start of things getting more and more technical. And catchier.

One of the **Tomb***'s signature traits is its groove. It's heavy, fast, but insanely catchy. Groove wasn't even a factor on* **Eaten Back to Life,** *and* **Butchered at Birth** *had a few booty-shakin' moments. Where'd it come from?*

Rusay: Well, the first couple of albums, it was all about speed. We wanted to slow things down a little bit—get more groove parts in there and change up the tempo a little more. Speed was still a primary thing, but we wanted to see the pit explode. You want to see the pit grow. You want a couple of circles forming around the primary circle. You had that in Europe. Like three circle pits.

Owen: Not sure where it came from. I don't think more influences came into the picture. We were into Exodus and Bay Area thrash, at least on my part. Autopsy was a big influence. The low tuning and doom element. We were still playing six-string guitars, so we were limited in tuning. But we didn't know that back then. We were better musically, had better gear and better practice facilities. Everything kind of came together. You can hear we finally found our identity.

Webster: That was the goal from the beginning. We had some pretty obscure stuff early on. "Living Dissection" on *Butchered at Birth* goes all over the place. More unorthodox. On *Tomb*, things started get more song-like. For sure "Hammer Smashed Face" is a song. I wouldn't call *Tomb* catchy by mainstream standards, but it definitely was put together in a way you could remember the songs.

Barnes: It *is* very catchy and heavy. We were inspired. We were just trying to make it interesting for ourselves while making things as heavy as possible. It just worked out that way, the way those guys wrote. They're talented musicians. It's orchestrated and echoes back to bands we listened to growing up. More verse-chorus-type stuff. We put that whole idea into hyper-motion, with a thousand things going on at once. We wanted to have it rhythm-based, though—a catchy-type of groove going on, especially in the middle parts of songs. *Tomb of the Mutilated* is filled with groove tangents.

Mazurkiewicz: It took things to a whole new level. It was technical, heavy, but it had a groove. We were starting to groove out a little more. The song-writing was getting better and better. "Hammer" is a pretty catchy song. I can't say how or why it happened; it just did. I mean, why is Slayer popular? You can think of almost any reason, but the fact is they wrote amazing riffs. They're catchy. Memorable. I think things really took off on *The Bleeding* when we focused as individuals on writing actual songs. With *Tomb of the Mutilated*, it was the last album where the songs were written as a collaborative effort.

At the time, most bass players in death metal were basically underperforming guitarists with four strings. A few guys stand out, like Steve DiGiorgio, the late Roger Patterson, Scott Carino and Tony Choy. On Tomb, *Alex made the following statement: "Hey, I'm not a guitarist! I'm a bass player!"*

Webster: I definitely didn't play guitar very much before I picked up the bass. It didn't grab me. I started playing bass around 13 or 14. I thought, "Oh yeah! This is it!" It felt good. Bass was the right instrument for me. I could tell right away. By the time I was good enough to play in a band, bass was the only instrument I knew. I was completely fingers by the time Cannibal got going. I fooled around with a pick in my old band, Beyond Death, but it always seemed more natural to play with fingers. The finger bass players are always going to sound less guitar-like. The right hand approach is entirely different. A pick-playing bass player is more like a guitar player. I definitely wanted to be a bass player.

Mazurkiewicz: When you listen to it, he stands out. He was becoming a better bass player. If you look back on videos of yourself you think, "What the heck? Look how far we've come." Alex was always a good bass player, but over the last 20 years he's become a monster. A great bass player. *Tomb of the Mutilated* was his stepping-stone. He wanted to be heard.

Owen: Alex became better and more unique out of necessity. Before then, it was just guitar players who were given a bass and forced to keep up. He came from a traditional school, so he developed finger patterns in order to keep up with us. We all wanted to be heard, but the bass pokes out on that album. You can actually hear him.

Barnes: Alex has always been 100 percent tech, using his fingers trying to get all five going. He was driven as a musician. I've never met anyone as driven as Alex when it comes to trying to learn an instrument. That's for real, man. He was always trying to outdo guys he thought were amazing. He pushed himself. On *Tomb*, Alex became more vocal, as far as being a songwriter and being involved in the recording process. He really got on Scott [Burns]'s nerves. He wanted the bass turned up. Scott walked out of the room a couple of times. Alex was pushing Scott to the limit as far as how loud the bass should go. That went on into the next album, *The Bleeding*, too.

I think it's a given you were influenced by Slayer, Possessed, the Bay Area bands, Death—the usual suspects. Were there more contemporary influences coming into Cannibal *around the time you started writing* Tomb of the Mutilated? *The arrangements on* Tomb of the Mutilated *are way more advanced than on* Butchered at Birth.

Rusay: I remember Chuck [Schuldiner] did some interesting things. We did five shows with Death in Europe. It was fun hanging out with those guys. Apart from that, I don't remember anything new. Death metal is something that's still developing.

Webster: I started listening to Atheist a lot. We toured with Atheist. We also toured with Pestilence and Death. Getting to see Scott Carino and Tony [Choy] play every night was very inspiring. Those guys were fucking awesome. Then, right after that we toured with Atheist and Gorguts. Éric Giguère was a great bass player and Darren McFarland, who was with Atheist at the time, was fantastic. I listened to DiGiorgio and Roger Patterson a lot as well. Roger unfortunately, as we know, passed away by that time, so I never got to see him play. But, boy, he was a big influence. The playing on *Piece of Time* is phenomenal. This was more or less during the writing of the album.

Barnes: I was never influenced by Sadus or Cynic, but I'll say Cynic influenced a whole bunch of bands from the death metal scene. Around '93 or '94. They were the silent influence in a lot of players. Paul [Masvidal] and Sean [Reinert] were such amazing musicians. If you were a musician in death metal at that time, you were just in awe—with your jaw to the floor. I remember watching those guys and I couldn't believe what I was seeing. The guys were good friends. The scene fed off itself. For me, I was influenced by how I was feeling inside and how heavy and erratic the music was. The music was so groove-laden and technical. That's what inspired me—to push myself—to come up with the sounds I did. I liked Obituary, Death and Pestilence, but those bands didn't really inspire me vocally. I just wanted to destroy everything I thought was right. It was insanity put to music. A madman's brain on tape. I was really into true crime.

Mazurkiewicz: Not really. Nothing inspired me other than what we were doing. We were narrow-minded in those days. If it wasn't death metal, we weren't listening to it. The bands of the day that we were playing and growing with like Deicide, Malevolent Creation and Suffocation were, like the fans, inspiring. The band and scene were going great, and I couldn't wait to get back in and tour, write a new album, be with the guys.

One of the first reactions to Tomb of the Mutilated *is that it's shocking. From cover to music. Were you trying to provoke?*

Barnes: No, I don't think so. I wasn't trying to provoke. I was trying to invoke thought in some way. Hoping someone would see the twisted dichotomy. To be sickened by it and yet entertained by it. Like watching a horror film. There's an underlying theme of paraphrasing society, people's sickness, and putting it to music. I was feeding off the music. I see words in the music. If I can get through the first line, it pretty much writes itself.

Rusay: We definitely tried to push that. The name itself, Cannibal Corpse, pushed the envelope. We wanted to be on the edge. The blood, the guts and the gore—that's what it's all about. We always tried to translate a horror movie into reality. If you do read the lyrics and pay attention to what's going on, a lot of it's based on real-life events. There's some really sick people in this world. Art sometimes imitates life. It's the media that's hypocritical. I mean, it's OK for the evening news to show a kid going crazy, shooting people. Like in Virginia. But they way they report it glorifies it. We had lyrics about Jeffrey Dahmer and Ed Gein, real-life killers, and all of a sudden what we have to say is taboo. Why is it OK for you to glorify a school shooting, when it's not OK for us to tell a story based on true events? From our view, the way we see it? This stuff is out there.

Webster: I think it was more of the same. As far as provoking lyrically, that's all Chris. He gets the credit. We told him nothing was off-limits. Boy, he sure took our word. We concentrated on the music. I've always been more focused on that. For *Tomb*, I focused on writing and my instrument.

Mazurkiewicz: We were trying to be over-the-top. I don't know if we were trying to provoke. We thought we should have the same freedom to put out whatever we feel. If people can't understand it's fiction, then I don't know what to tell them. It's no different from movies out today like *Saw*, *Hostel* or some crazy Stephen King novel. All the bands we were listening to, like Kreator's *Pleasure to Kill* and Slayer's *Hell Awaits*, had similar subject matter. Well, we took that to another level. It had to be as extreme as possible. Luckily, [Metal Blade owner] Brian Slagel was cool enough to let us have that control.

Did you ever think Cannibal Corpse—or, more specifically, **Tomb**—*was controversial? This is different from provocation. Too much to take in one sitting.*

Barnes: I never did anything for controversy. That was more a nuisance. I wanted to just write something that was exciting to me. Controversy was secondary. I just thought it was cool I had fans who were into what I was writing about. They thought it was well written. It wasn't meaningless jargon written down to fast music. I've always taken pride in writing a storyline. It is brutally sickening, but there's always a story in my lyrics.

Owen: I guess mainstream-wise, yes. As far as death metal, no. I mean after people saw "Entrails," I don't even think they questioned "Post Mortal Ejaculation."

Webster: Not back then. It didn't even cross our minds. Fuck it, we went for it. We loved horror movies, heavy shit, extremities. We wanted everything as extreme as possible. That was the mission back then. I guess you can't make records like *Tomb of the Mutilated* without people noticing. As the band got more and more popular, do-gooders were bound to notice us.

Mazurkiewicz: Not then. We were doing what we wanted to do. When we released *Tomb of the Mutilated*, we had only been together for four years. It was all relatively new. We didn't have many problems releasing *Butchered at Birth*, so by the time *Tomb* came around, it's like, "Well, it's sick, but this is what we do." I don't think there were any regrets. Looking back now, it's like, "Whoa! This *is* extreme!"

Lyrically, Cannibal Corpse were intense, but Tomb *took the whole concept to extremes. I mean "Entrails Ripped From a Virgin's Cunt" or "Addicted to Vaginal Skin" aren't exactly subtle. I remember reading the lyrics in Humanities class in high school. Not only did they make me feel ill, I thought if I was caught with the sleeve I'd be expelled or placed in some type of protective custody.*

Barnes: I just felt the music was so extreme and the beats Paul was putting down represented the sickness that kept creeping out of me. I had great song titles going. I was just living my life at the time. I was influenced by friends of mine. A friend of mine had a lot of drug problems, so I'd go to unsavory neighborhoods with him just to see how those types of people lived. I put myself in weird situations just to get something out of it. I was working at a warehouse and one of the delivery guys used to work at a prison. He knew I was into horror and would start telling me stories about guys who were locked up for murder. "Entrails Ripped From a Virgin's Cunt" was based on two brothers, one of whom was semi-retarded, who were serving life. They captured some girl and the semi-retarded brother was talked into putting a coat hanger up her pussy to pull out her intestines. That story freaked me out. I started to think about fear at that point. To just shock someone doesn't really work, but trying to write something that invokes an emotion, like fear, is what interests me. I put it out there raw. I felt it complemented the music, 'cause it was so far out there on all levels. "I Cum Blood" is probably my most disturbing lyric though.

Mazurkiewicz: It was the most extreme album we had done. "Necropedophile," "Entrails," "Post Mortal" and "I Cum Blood" were pretty extreme. "Hammer Smashed Face" is pretty mild for this album in retrospect, isn't it? Lyrically, Barnes took over on *Tomb*. They were as crazy as possible. I don't think we did anything like those lyrics on albums after *Tomb*. I haven't read the lyrics in a long time, so if they still shock me then I know it's a job well done. Vocally, he was so guttural.

Rusay: Around that time, *Silence of the Lambs* was really popular. We were really trying to push the envelope. Take things one step further. You wouldn't think of combining words to get "Hammer Smashed Face." The following album had song titles that people thought were too much. Like "Fucked With a Knife." It's as blunt as you can get.

Owen: It kind of became a postcard for the band. "Entrails" isn't even that great. People were so floored by the song title. It was so over-the-top, but then again I guess this is what we're supposed to be doing. I just went with it.

Webster: Like I said, we held nothing back. Chris did the lyrics and we helped come up with song titles. He went for it. He worked hard, reading books about serial killers and doing research. He busted ass to take it to the limit. For sure, our grossest lyrics are on *Tomb*. I mean, it's pretty hard to beat "Necropedophile" and "Entrails Ripped From a Virgin's Cunt." "Post Mortal Ejaculation" isn't too friendly either. If you wanted our most offensive album, lyrically, it's *Tomb of the Mutilated*.

The song titles made me cringe. I thought, at the time, nothing could top those song titles. Did you guys just sit around and whiteboard gross shit?

Owen: Right, the titles either came from lines in the lyrics or brainstormed in a smoke-filled room with poster board. I think all Chris needed was a song title or a few words. He'd work from there.

Webster: Unless Chris had come up with something on his own, we'd sit around the practice room and come up with titles. We still do that. We put a piece of paper on the wall in the Cannibal practice room and think up titles. Stuff that's cool. It's hard to remember who came up with what. I might've come up with "Hammer Smashed Face." It's honestly hard to remember at this point.

Mazurkiewicz: We always brainstormed. There were definitely titles that belonged to Chris or Alex or me. It was mostly us three that came up with titles over the years. It was like the songwriting back then. Everything was collaborative.

Do you remember much of your time with Scott Burns recording **Tomb of the Mutilated***?*

Rusay: Scott Burns is a really great guy, but I'll tell you—the three albums I worked on with him, I couldn't find a guitar sound I liked. We got close on *Tomb*. We used two heads—a Marshall Valvestate head and ran that through a Carbon head. Everything was monotone. There was never enough crunch for me. I think

Scott did a great job on Morbid Angel and Deicide. Their guitar sound crunched. It popped. For some reason, I was never really happy with my guitar sound. When we were in our practice room, it was really crunchy. There was a lot of high end. More tones involved. I like working with Marshalls, 'cause they're really warm sounding. I put a lot of effects in front of that to get the crunch and high end. When we went into the studio, it seemed to go away. I mean, Chris' vocals are so deep—from his stomach—it drowns a lot of details, the tones, out.

Barnes: Scott was the man. From day one, I was the closest with him. I set up things for us to go down from Buffalo to Morrisound. He was the coolest guy in the world. On *Tomb*, it was really comfortable working with Scott. I think people miss the sounds he put on tape.

Owen: Once we finished drums, I remember it being smooth. On *Eaten* we didn't get to punch anything in. This was the first time we could actually over-dub and double-track the guitars. We simply had a bigger budget.

Webster: I remember it was the first album where I got to spend a lot more time recording. I was afforded more time. On *Eaten Back to Life*, I did all the bass tracks at the exactly same time as the drums. It was all one take. On the second album it was like that except for one or two punches. I went back and redid "Innards Decay." You can see the footage of that on our box set. For *Tomb*, I played with the drums and then went back to re-record. We did scratch tracks for Paul. It was the first time I got to re-record my parts on every single song. I got to go back and make sure everything was right. We were just learning how to make an album tight on *Tomb of the Mutilated*.

Mazurkiewicz: He was with the band since the beginning, watching us transform. The time at Morrisound was great, apart from some of the stuff with Bob.

Scott worked overtime to finish* Tomb. *You went over your scheduled time. He was like a sixth member of Cannibal. He looked after you guys.

Owen: He lived about maybe an hour from the studio. So, if he worked late, he'd just stay in the studio. He was definitely a sixth member of the band back then.

Webster: Scott did that with pretty much all of our records, but he spent the most time with *Tomb*. We were supposed to be done at midnight, and he'd stay until two or later. He wanted us to sound great. Everything he did and everything he recommended for us to do was only to make the record sound good. He was definitely a sixth member. It was clear he wasn't punching the clock. He wanted us to succeed.

Barnes: He an opinion about things. Scott was a very highly regarded person, as far as how we wrote things. He pushed us. Not in a bad way. Scott wasn't one of those guys who'd yell and scream. He's a really great guy. You didn't mind listening to him, 'cause you couldn't help but love the guy. That's what his personality was like.

Mazurkiewicz: He was one of the guys. [We had] a lot of fun working all those years with Scott. Looking back, yeah, he was the sixth member. He worked a lot of overtime. We went over a couple of days and he fought for extra time. He always worked for the band. I think we had three weeks on *Tomb*, but I think it ended up taking like 21 days.

"Electronic Harmonizer was not used to create any vocals on **Tomb of the Mutilated.** *"That was the statement on the inside sleeve. What was the purpose of that statement? Was it important to tell people you didn't pitch the vocals?*

Barnes: It was out of frustration, something that stems back to *Butchered at Birth*. I was coming into my own—my own sounds, my own tones and my own vocal patterns. I've always got questions from people about my vocals. Like, "What effects do you use to get the vocals to sound like that?" I'd tell them it was natural and they wouldn't believe me. Even my sound guy at the time got sick of hearing it. I put it right on the record, so people who had the record knew what the story was. My vocals were always raw. We'd do effects on accents and intros, but never a broad spectrum of effects throughout. No flange or reverb on a vocal throughout a song. I've been fighting that my whole career.

Rusay: The point was [that] he didn't add anything to spice up the vocals. When Chris went at it, he didn't put anything on his vocals. He mic'ed in and went for it. There wasn't really anything added to get him to sound like that. That's what he sounds like. The stranger story is if you listen to our demos before *Eaten*, Chris sounds like Blaine [Cook] from the Accüsed. Apparently, the singer for Morbid Angel was in the studio laying down tracks, so when he came back with our sound and the Blaine vocal style, it didn't sound right. He went back the very next day and changed it to a barking death metal style. That evolved. He was in his groove on *Tomb of the Mutilated*. So, there was a change early on. A lot of people from Buffalo knew it. The biggest question we got after we finished the first album was the change in Chris' vocals. Eventually, we wanted people to know that we don't spice things up. If there's reverb on there, it's to appease Scott Burns. Scott had to turn a knob somewhere.

Owen: It was important to him. To let people know those were his vocals. He used a little on *Tomb*. Screw it! The guitars are good. Those are legit!

Webster: There were other bands that used harmonizers at the time. Chris wanted to be clear it was just him singing. No studio trickery. If there's one thing where there was friction with Chris, [it's] that the vocals are completely dry. He never wanted any effects on the vocals. He was definitely subterranean on *Tomb of the Mutilated*.

Mazurkiewicz: I think it was important. A lot of bands were using it at the time. What you hear is natural. No question. He's making the sound naturally through a microphone. We knew Deicide used it, so we were well aware of the statement we were making.

The songwriting is credited to Cannibal Corpse on **Tomb of the Mutilated.** *Was it really a collaborative effort where everyone was involved?*

Owen: Yeah, there was a lot of camaraderie back then. If somebody was stuck on a riff, somebody else would step in. Rusay wrote a lot of "Post Mortal Ejaculation" and "Beyond the Cemetery." Alex and Paul wrote "Hammer Smashed Face," which was about the mini break-up. You can imagine whose face they wanted to smash. Barnes. I contributed a lot to "I Cum Blood," "Addicted to Vaginal Skin," "Split Wide Open" and a lot of "Necropedophile." "Necropedophile" was a total rip-off of a Danish band called Invocator.

Webster: We were a band. We'd practice all the time in a room at a place called Absolute Storage. It's what we did after work. We'd drive to the room and start working. Practice was from 6–6:30 p.m. to 10:30 p.m. five days a week. We worked 'cause we loved it. It didn't feel like work at the time. We'd come up with riffs at home and bring them to the practice space. I remember Bob came up with the intro for "Beyond the Cemetery" that way. "Hammer Smashed Face" was mainly me and Paul. Jack did one riff on that. "Entrails" is mostly me. "Cryptic Stench," I think, is the same. Bob wrote most of "Post Mortal Ejaculation." That stuff was written in 1991 and 1992. That's a long time ago. I wanted to step up and be the best band we could be.

Barnes: The songwriting kicked ass. I guess it was like it always was. I don't remember it skipping a beat. Bob came up with a lot of riffs and those guys had to take their time to figure them out.

Mazurkiewicz: The album came together naturally. We learned along the way. We were taking things in a direction of being more aggressive and technical. The way the band needed to head. We never had any major lull in our creativity. We just wrote what was in our heads at the time. We're always growing as musicians and people.

Cannibal Corpse actually broke into two separate groups for a short while before the writing of **Tomb of the Mutilated** *commenced. It was never publicized at the time, but what happened?*

Owen: There were differing opinions in the band, so me, Rusay and Barnes split for a while. Paul and Alex kept it together. They wrote "Hammer Smashed Face" during that time. I was always in the middle. Like in Deicide, Steve is always between the Hoffmans and Glen. I didn't really know what to do. I was with Rusay and Chris, but I think I was trying to keep the whole thing together. If I would've stuck with Alex and Paul, we probably would've gotten another singer and guitar player. I think it was the recording contract and our tour obligations that eventually pushed us back together. It was too good to pass up.

Webster: We never publicized it. Chris was tour managing. It was the first time he had ever managed a tour and there were questions about what was going on with the money. We argued about that. I mean, our practice space was like four rooms away from Cannibal's practice space. We just moved down the hall. There was a lot of friction. Me and Paul started writing "Hammer" during a brief exodus from Cannibal Corpse. We were like, "Fuck this! We're out." We were so pissed at each other. Who knows what it was about now? We were a bunch of young guys doing things like touring for the first time. We were stuck in a van for a month, and by the end of the month we were ready to quit. And that's what we did. It lasted less than a week.

Barnes: I have a hard time remembering that. I couldn't even tell you what it was about. There have always been speed bumps.

Mazurkiewicz: There was inner turmoil at the time. It was mainly Chris. We had just got back from the road and all the issues from the road sort of came to a head. We felt like we didn't want to deal with it anymore. So, Alex and I quit the band. We moved down the hall. Alex and I split the cost of the space. Officially, we quit the band. We moved our stuff out, we jammed, and like two or three days later we had "Hammer." It was written more out of anger. After a few practices, we reconciled and moved on. We just wanted to get another album out and move on.

The vocal cadence on **Tomb** *is unique to Cannibal Corpse. Did you write lyrics or music first?*

Barnes: 99.9 percent of the time I wouldn't have an idea of what to write until I had a tape of the music. Then I could start writing lyrics and vocal parts.

Owen: It was piece by piece, but I think the music came first most of the time. This was before the break-up.

Webster: The music came first. Almost always. When I look back on it, as a lyric writer, I realize how hard we made it for Chris. Like on "Hammer Smashed Face." At no point is there a vocal part where you're hearing the name of the song title again and again. The hook is in the music and vocal patterns, not the lyrics. He wasn't writing standard verse-chorus-verse lyrics, 'cause we weren't writing like that. Well, most of the time. He reacted to the music rather than us reacting to the lyrics.

Mazurkiewicz: A lot of songs were written with the title first. Sometimes we just had music and no title, but all the lyrical concepts came from Barnes.

How the hell did you guys get the **Ace Ventura: Pet Detective** *gig? Do you remember much about the shoot? I can't think of anything more random than Cannibal Corpse appearing in a Jim Carrey movie.*

Barnes: It was awesome. I got a call from the record company. The Vice President of Metal Blade, Mike Faley, called me and said, "Chris, we have this crazy offer from Morgan Creek for this movie with a comedian named Jim Carrey." They asked for us. Jim wanted Napalm Death to do it at first. I guess we were his second-favorite band. I think Alex didn't want to do it at first. He was concerned we'd be taken as a joke, 'cause the movie was a comedy. We talked him into it. It didn't take much coaxing. The funnier story was, after we finished *Ace Ventura*, we got another call from Mike two weeks later. He was like, "Hey, I got another offer from a film called *Airheads*." I was like, "Awesome, dude! We're there!" A few days later they had found out we did *Ace*. It worked against us, but we picked the better movie.

Owen: Jim Carrey was a big fan. We didn't believe it until we met him. I remember saying, "Who is Jim Carrey? Oh, the white guy from *In Living Color*." We had a choice between *Airheads* with Brendan Fraser and *Ace Ventura*. *Airheads* sounded too cheesy and, of course, we couldn't appear in two movies in the same year for some reason, so we picked *Ace Ventura*. We were familiar with the Cameo, the venue, in Miami. We had played there before. I remember meeting Jim at sound check. He asked us to play "Rancid Amputation." It's like, "Dude, we don't even play that song anymore. We've forgotten it." He then rambled off a bunch of song titles. It showed how much of a fan he was. We shot for two and half days, so there was a ton of footage. It was nice to see the NBC cut, with an extra five minutes of us.

Webster: That was right after the whole Bob thing. Rob Barrett had just joined. It was a great experience. I was visiting a friend in Dallas. I got a call on the answering machine, "Hey, man, we're gonna be in a movie. Give us a call." I called Chris and asked to be filled in. It was a movie called *Ace Ventura*, starring Jim Carrey from *In Living Color*. I remember when I heard the full name of the movie, *Ace Ventura: Pet Detective*, I thought, "How is our music going to fit into this movie? How in the world is this going to work?" We set some conditions for ourselves. We shouldn't be up there acting stupid. If they're using Cannibal Corpse in the movie and our music, then we should behave the way we normally do onstage. If we're representing ourselves in this movie, then it has to be as a serious death metal band that happens to have very unserious things happening nearby. Jim Carrey was so cool. He had a couple of our albums. He knew the names of our songs. We had no idea he'd be more famous after that. He was totally nice. The guys from Malevolent Creation are in the crowd. Jason Blachowicz is in the slam pit. I can always spot him. Jimmy [Ferrovecchio] from Brutal Mastication, a band from Fort Lauderdale, is also in there.

Mazurkiewicz: That was a *huge* thing. Surreal. We thought it could be really cool or really bad. I mean, it's a Jim Carrey comedy. It ended up being amazing. We were portrayed as ourselves in the movie, which was important. It was supposed to be funny seeing a band like us in the movie. The network version of *Ace Ventura* was better, though. That's when Jim gets up onstage and jumps around with us. He didn't know the lyrics, but it didn't matter. I remember thinking, "Pay attention. This has to look real." It was so hard, 'cause Jim was going insane. I couldn't take my eyes off him.

Rusay: It was a bitter pill to swallow. I had no idea the shooting of that scene was even going on. It's good for the band and good for the music. I'm sure they had fun doing it. Anything good for death metal is a good thing. I thought it was great. There was a part that wasn't in the movie, where Jim gets up onstage and jumped around with the band.

Did Ace Ventura *increase sales or profile for Cannibal?*

Barnes: People asked us that at the time. I don't know that it did. Our fans were just blown away that we were in it. Not many people wait around for the end credits to see who the bands are just to rush out and buy the albums. Until it's on, at that time, VHS, you didn't have time to research that stuff. Our record sales were going up on each release, so it's hard to say how *Ace* impacted the sales of *Tomb of the Mutilated*.

Webster: Definitely. I've met a lot of people who said it was the first time they'd ever seen us. It surprised me. I take it for granted that people are as interested in music as I am and they're gonna look for the heavy stuff. Some people need it in front of their faces to realize it's there. That kind of mass media and exposure is incredible. For a few seconds, whether they like it or not, everyone is watching a really brutal death metal band. It was a good advertisement. We weren't that big back then. We weren't Anthrax. They got on *Married With Children*.

Mazurkiewicz: It definitely had to. There were kids who came up to us saying, "I got into death metal from *Ace Ventura*!" A lot of people got into us from that movie. The movie was huge, so I guess we were burned into their memories. I think *The Bleeding* benefitted the most from *Ace*, though.

Why did you choose Possessed and Black Sabbath covers for the Hammer Smashed Face EP? Do you remember the selection process? There's a lot of potentially cool cover tunes out there.

Owen: It took forever to decide what songs to cover. The four of us decided on "The Exorcist." Chris wanted to do "Zero the Hero." All of us were total death metal heads at the time. It's like, "What? You want to do a slow song?" It worked out pretty good, 'cause people still ask for that song to this day.

Webster: It was pretty easy on the Possessed track. The Sabbath track, which is from *Born Again*, is from an album my big brother had. I wasn't totally into Sabbath like I was Maiden. Sabbath was Chris' suggestion. That song received such a strong response. People loved "Zero the Hero." Here we are busting our asses playing all this fast stuff on *Tomb*, and "Zero the Hero" maybe got the best reaction. It's like, "Damn, there's five notes in that song! And it's super-slow." It didn't surprise me that Chris eventually got into Six Feet Under.

Barnes: Me and Paul picked the Sabbath song. We liked *Born Again*. We slept out for tickets when they toured for that record. It's my favorite Black Sabbath album. It turned out awesome. The arrangement of it stood out to me. I've done a lot of cover songs over the years, and that's still my favorite. The Possessed cover was a no-brainer. It was my most comfortable vocal session.

Mazurkiewicz: At that point, the record label wanted an EP. We loved it when other bands did covers. Like Metallica. So, we did something new and something old. Possessed was easy, but Black Sabbath was a little different. "Zero the Hero" was pretty much the same, except for the vocals. Obviously, it doesn't sound like Ian Gillan on our version.

The photo on the back of **Tomb** *is nuts. It's totally typical of the time, but the statue in the background gave it an eerie vibe. What was that thing?*

Rusay: That was at the old Buffalo train station. It was a piece of art that they tried to remove with a bulldozer. They just gave up on it. Left it there. All the pictures in the album were from the Buffalo train station. It's one of the better pictures we had. It's a little bizarre.

Owen: It was originally supposed to look like an angel holding a baby. The train station had been shut down since the '60s and everything was decrepit. Once we got there, we thought, "Oh, man, we gotta get a picture of this!" It was half-uprooted. There was rebar all over the place. I liked that we looked all scummy.

Webster: Chris, Bob and Paul were from closer to that area. Me and Jack weren't from that area. They probably had gone there to party. There was graffiti everywhere. It had this statue. It was a religious statue, but the eyes were gouged out and it was tipped forward. It was an eerie thing. The suggestion was great to go down there to take those pictures.

Barnes: It looked like a medical center inside. It was all run down.

Mazurkiewicz: At the time, it wasn't being used anymore. It looked it was hit with a bomb. We probably were trespassing, but it was our best photo session ever. That statue was in the front near a roundabout. It was half tipped over. It was an alien-looking, pentagram-like thing. Killer! We took pictures near it and with the wind blowing our hair, it turned out kind of eerie. I love that photo. We thought about going back and doing another photo shoot there, but I think it's being renovated now.

The cover is legendary. The imagery is so disgusting it begs to be looked at over and over again. The detail is phenomenal. Since this was the third cover with Vincent Locke, do you remember how it came together? What were your reactions like after Vincent had finished it?

Barnes: Since day one, I've always been impressed with Vince. The way he drew corpses, zombies and stuff spoke to me—his take on it artistically. I found him like you found Bob. Just used the phone book. I remember suggesting a corpse eating out another corpse. He's like, "OK!" I think he was having problems positioning the bodies, and that the perspective of it was a challenge for him. I remember when I first opened up the artwork—to approve it before it went to the record company. The blue-ish, slate gray tones. The white tones. It affected me. It was creepy and cold. I didn't think it was as shocking as *Butchered at Birth*. It's more zombie pornography. He portrayed death really well with that cover.

Rusay: The first version we sent to the label was sent back to us because it wasn't gory enough. That's where all the slash and cut marks on the lady came from. She was originally white. The label said it wasn't bloody enough. Brian Slagel is a really good guy. He knows how to put a product out there. Chris worked with the label on the cover. We'd give Chris ideas and he'd relay those ideas to Vincent. I think we had the same vision. We wanted the zombie to be more sexually involved with the corpse. The way he pulled it off was perfect. I mean, zombies have to eat and the best place to on any female is the pink taco. It had to be more sexual. The first album, we didn't even have a song title called "Eaten Back to Life." We just wanted a zombie tearing himself apart. And he's eating himself while he's doing it. *Butchered at Birth* was totally Vincent's creation. I love that album cover. When you look at her lying on the table and her arm sliding off at the bone, it gets you.

Owen: It was so brutal it was comical. So over-the-top. I didn't think we could get away with it. It's like, "I can't show this to my mom! She'll freak!" Barnes hammered him a little more on *Tomb*, 'cause we needed two pieces of art. We wanted it to be completely sick. Like zombies having sex. The censored cover is like a beforehand shot.

Webster: We loved it. We had so much trouble with *Butchered at Birth* they wanted a second piece. The regular version shows the zombie cunnilingus, but the censored version shows the single zombie just standing there. I was never sure if the girl was alive and enjoying it or just dead and the zombie was literally eating her. Either way, it's a great piece of art. Vince was the perfect choice. I'm also 100 percent sure it was Chris who got Vince in the first place.

Mazurkiewicz: I was like, "This is crazy!" *Butchered* was the sickest thing we'd ever done. We wanted to keep it going. Barnes talked to Vince about it. He came up with the title, *Tomb of the Mutilated*. Vince comes up with crazy stuff regardless of us giving him ideas. He's always done great art. *Tomb* was utter insanity. Complete gore.

The voiceover on "Addicted to Vaginal Skin" is revolting. It's rumored that it's the voice of Arthur Shawcross. Where'd you get that from? Also, what's up with the kids screaming on "Necropedophile"?

Barnes: I snuck that on the record. We'd get sued for that in this day and age. I was reading a lot of true crime stuff. I was reading a book about Arthur Shawcross, the Genesee River Killer in Rochester. It came with a cassette tape, an audio confession of a killer. I was listening to his voice. It creeped me out. I boosted it from the tape. It was icing on the cake. For "Necropedophile," I'm a late sleeper. I was living next to a church when I was writing *Tomb of the Mutilated*. Whenever I write lyrics it's always late at night. Like at 4 a.m. Every morning around 11, the church let out the daycare for recess. I was getting woken up by screaming kids. It was every day while I was writing that record. It was pissing me off. So I put my boombox next to the window, pressed record and got those fuckin' kids on tape. I wrote a song about murdering the kids who were waking me up every morning.

Webster: I'm not sure if we're supposed to say who it was. It's Arthur Shawcross. Chris did all the research, trying to learn what was going on in these freaks' minds. I honestly don't know if we were supposed to use that. It was Chris' idea. It definitely fit the lyrics for "Addicted to Vaginal Skin."

Mazurkiewicz: All that stuff was Barnes. It's Arthur Shawcross from his confessional tapes. It was cool to do intros and snippets like that in the old days.

I gather there's a lot of bad blood with Bob.

Rusay: When we recorded *Tomb of the Mutilated*, there was a big argument about the guitars being recorded. But it started before then. I think it was mainly Paul. When we'd play live and he'd do his monitor checks, he'd always tell the guy to turn my guitar down. So, we get into the studio and they all say, "We want Jack to do both guitars on the album." I was like, "Fuck that! This is a band." When they had Jack do both guitar parts, the whole thing broke. It was the final straw. People need to know I wasn't able to record my own fuckin' music. Shit I wrote. They did the same thing on the *Hammer Smashed Face* EP. After about two weeks, I got the call that I was fired. I don't think Chris had too much to say about it. It took me by surprise. I was working a club, Chris showed up, punched me in the arm, and then the next day I get a call, "We don't wanna jam with you anymore." It's like, "What? Do I have a choice here?" The way it was handled was pretty bad. I called Paul and he was frantic. Like a little girl. That's how they got rid of me. I tell people it was a mutual break-up and we weren't getting along, but now that we're talking about it I want to set the record straight.

Owen: I think his playing wasn't tight enough to where we wanted to progress with the band. We tried to be professional. We were under the microscope. The budgets were getting bigger. He wasn't tight. It's not where we were at. It goes back to *Butchered*. I played more than half of the rhythms on that album, and on *Tomb* I did 95 percent of the rhythms. I don't think he was regressing. He just came from a punk background and wasn't concerned with tightness. It was all aggression. We wanted to be more focused. I think it was in the middle of tracking the album, Alex told him I was going to do the rhythm guitars. Next thing you know, Bob was back at the hotel, drinking beers and getting sunburned. I remember Alex called Bob right after the Bills won the AFC Championship game. They were going to the Super Bowl. Alex isn't a sports fan, so he didn't know what was going on. So he called Bob. There's a big party going on in the background and Bob said, "We're going to the Super Bowl!" Alex responded, "Bob, you're out of the band." The Bills ended up losing the Super Bowl, so it was a bad couple of weeks for Bob. I was in the middle. I wasn't going to break the news to him. I really thought he'd kill me. Bob was a badass.

Webster: He was a good friend of ours. And the fact that he hasn't wanted to communicate with us since that happened isn't something we feel good about. To this day, we feel it had to be done. Nobody wants to part ways with a friend in that way. It's not fun. He's the guy I called up to start the band. Bob, me and Jack were friends when we were in Beyond Death. We went out and partied and shit. He was in Tirant Sin with Paul and Chris. Paul and Chris had steady girlfriends, so Bob went out and partied with us. He was our buddy. So when things didn't go well, it wasn't fun to deal with. Nobody else wanted to call Bob, but all four of us agreed on the decision for him to go. So I called him and said, "Dude, we don't know what to say. You're out. Sorry." He hung up on me and that was the end of it. I haven't talked to him since then. It's not a good memory for us, but I'm sure it's a really bad memory for Bob. He wasn't asked to leave the band until after we recorded the *Hammer Smashed Face* EP. The deal with that is we went up to Niagara Falls—we lived in Buffalo until 1994—in January '93. We recorded the cover songs. Again, we were having problems with Bob. Shortly after that is when we fired Bob. Bob was the tough guy in the band, for sure. He was in great physical condition and was really into martial arts. When you're young, you tend to solve your problems that way instead of talking it out. That was something to think about. He could've found us if he wanted.

Mazurkiewicz: It was really unfortunate. He was an original member. It's hard to kick a guy out of the band you grew up with. There was no easy way to do it. We had a lot of problems on *Tomb of the Mutilated*. When it came down to it, on the EP specifically, we needed a very melodic, Iommi-esque solo for "Zero the Hero." Bob came in and slopped through it. He left this bad solo for "Zero the Hero." We were distraught by it. Jack had to fix it and do it properly. What you hear is all Jack. That was the last straw with Bob. Alex wasn't watching football at that point. Alex is still the least interested in that. Myself and Rusay were football and hockey guys. It didn't make it any easier for Bob to accept. From elation—"Yeah! We're going to the Super Bowl!"—to, "Aw, man!"

Barnes: Things just started to decline. Alex had a specific vision for the band progressing. He took it seriously. He put a lot into learning his instrument and being a better songwriter. I think he felt Bob wasn't working hard. I didn't really agree with the decision, but I was out-voted. I didn't have much say in it. I was just the lyric writer and vocalist. It wasn't my favorite decision. We were such good friends. It helped the band progress, but in a way something was lost when Bob was let go. Bob was an awesome songwriter. He was unconventional in the way he laid things out. A lot of the songs on *Tomb of the Mutilated* wouldn't have been written if it wasn't for him. You can see a change in the band after *Tomb of the Mutilated*. I guess it worked out on a different level, in the end.

Did you think Tomb of the Mutilated *would go on to influence so many bands? At the time, the media used a specific term, "Cannibal Clones," for the glut of bands aping your sound. It was insane. I used to get a lot of demos back then and nine out of 10 bands clearly had listened to* Tomb of the Mutilated.

Owen: I guess there was a confluence: the extremity of the band and how much touring we were doing. We were the next new thing. I remember being the same way. I was listening to Metallica, Venom and Motörhead, thinking how sick they were. I can relate to where the kids were coming from. They were just looking for the next extreme thing. We happened to be it. Scott Burns called us Elvis.

Webster: I think Suffocation had a big influence on the death metal scene as well. Give credit where it's due. I think you can still hear it in American death metal. You can hear Deicide, Suffocation and us. If anything pushed this album

---

over the top, it's "Hammer Smashed Face." I'm not saying the song is better than any of the other songs on the album, but it became our most popular song. Whenever I go to YouTube, I search for Cannibal Corpse. Half of it is people covering "Hammer Smashed Face." It's only that song.

Rusay: We had no idea. We were playing what we wanted to play. We were doing the things we felt would get the music recognized. One of the main reasons death metal appealed to us is because not very many people were doing it. We didn't want a label that would say, "Hey, we need a couple of longer songs and we need more solos." We had no idea *Tomb of the Mutilated* would impact the way it did. We didn't go into it thinking the record would turn the industry around. Our primary goal was: How can we better *Butchered at Birth*?

Mazurkiewicz: It's a great feeling to know we've left a mark. *Tomb* took things to the next level. When you talk to people in the scene they will tell you *Tomb* is a pivotal album. To a lot of people, *Tomb* is their favorite album. It's awesome for us. We can be proud of knowing we inspired a bunch of people. It's flattering for people to follow the template we laid down. One day Cannibal isn't going to be here. We need young bands to keep it going. That way the future of death metal is secure.

Barnes: Imitation is the highest form of flattery. *Butchered at Birth* and *Tomb of the Mutilated* were the heaviest death metal records at the time. People started using us as a template. I do think a lot of bands just liked the novelty of Cannibal Corpse and never did anything with it. As long as bands make it work and grow from it, then that's cool. A band like Chimaira was influenced by us, but you can't hear that influence now. I like that.

ZOMBIEGEDDON

Q&A with Tomb of the Mutilated *artist Vincent Locke*

Discourse on Cannibal Corpse wouldn't be complete without descanting the group's predilection for zombies and their unfortunate victims in various states of duress. In fact, we'd be remiss not going to the source. So, we did. *Decibel* talks to artist and *Deadworld* illustrator Vincent Locke. — Chris Dick

How did the idea of the zombie performing cunnilingus come about?

Vincent Locke: It was a long time ago, but I believe it was the band's idea.

You worked closely with Chris Barnes. Was there anything that was considered no-go territory as far as explicit material goes?

Locke: This cover was a little hard for me. Not because of the subject matter, but because it was another victimized woman. We had gone pretty far with *Butchered at Birth*. I liked that cover a lot, but I wanted to do something different. I didn't want there to be a pattern of covers depicting violence against women. Around that time, some female friends were beat up by a group of frat boys. [I was] sickened by their cowardly hatefulness. I enjoyed painting horrific images, but it made me think that maybe not everyone was going to view these pictures in the spirit intended. They are just little horror stories meant to shock. I was afraid that if the covers became one-sided, some kids would get the wrong message. I tried to put the woman on the cover in some position of power, with her sitting up, and the male zombie groveling on the floor. In the end, I was able to come up with a cover that we all liked. The cover to *Vile* was meant to "round out" the subject matter. We had showed self-mutilation, and the torture of women and children. With *Vile*, we attacked the men as well.

Did you use a model or photograph for the pose?

Locke: No. I rarely use a model. I do use a few good anatomy books and skeleton models.

What medium did you use for the artwork?

Locke: Watercolor, acrylic and colored pencil.

What was the most challenging aspect of Tomb of the Mutilated?

Locke: Trying to come up with two covers that worked together, and were both interesting.

What were some of Chris' ideas you keyed off to get the scene, setting, blood, candles and staring head?

Locke: The oral sex was Chris' idea; beyond that I don't remember. Chris would call me up with his idea and a title for the album. Then I would do a few sketches. I would send them the sketches to get more input from the band before I started the painting.

Brian Slagel originally rejected the cover. He wanted more blood. Do you recall that? What did you change?

Locke: If the band wanted anything changed, it had usually been a call for more blood.

What kind of impact do you think the cover had?

Locke: I don't have any idea. When I'm working on a cover, I'm just trying to please the band and myself. Trying to come up with something that will grab your attention and maybe shake you up a little bit. Hopefully, the artwork is as memorable as the music.

CHAPTER 13

HAZARDOUS PRESCRIPTION

THE MAKING OF EYEHATEGOD'S *TAKE AS NEEDED FOR PAIN*

by J. Bennett

Release Date: 1993
Label: Century Media
Summary: Southern-fried sludge classic
Induction Date: June 2006/Issue #20

Drugs, disease, crime, abuse, poverty, paranoia, drugs, alcohol, alcohol, alcohol: Such are the cornerstones of Eyehategod's time-honored New Orleans aesthetic. The band's first album, *In the Name of Suffering*—a lo-fi, doom-ridden disturbance bashed out on a broken drum kit and cheap guitars with missing strings—was originally released on the French label Intellectual Convulsion in 1990. When Century Media re-released it two years later, they also commissioned Eyehategod to make what would arguably become the band's defining album. A series of buzzing, lurching dirges steeped in feedback and contempt, *Take as Needed for Pain* was released in 1993, spawning countless imitators as vocalist Mike Williams, drummer Joey LaCaze, guitarist Jimmy

Bower (also of Down and Superjoint Ritual), guitarist Brian Patton (also of Soilent Green) and then-bassist Marc Schultz lashed a Sabbathian groove to the muck-ridden undertow of the Melvins' *Gluey Porch Treatments*, drowned the whole vicious slab in disorienting noise, and proceeded to give everybody the finger. Song titles like "Sister Fucker" (parts one and two), "White Nigger" and "Kill Your Boss" may have launched the band headlong into a shitstorm of cultural controversy and confusion that follows them to this day, but then again, that was always kind of the idea.

It seems like Eyehategod didn't really become what it is today until Take as Needed for Pain. What happened in the five years between the original release of In the Name of Suffering and Take as Needed for Pain?

Marc Schultz: I played guitar on *In the Name of Suffering* and then we got into some shit on tour with the bass player at that time, Steve Dale, and when we got home we couldn't really find another bass player who could hang with us, so I switched and for a while we were a four-piece band. We played a couple of shows like that, but we didn't really have a one-guitar sound. So we hooked up with Brian from Soilent Green and I stayed on the bass. Back then, we were all about no outsiders. We were very into preserving the unit. If you weren't part of our little gang, it was like, "Fuck you." We all knew each other since we were little kids.

Brian Patton: I didn't play on *In the Name of Suffering*, but me, Jimmy and Mike had played together in a band called Drip for a year or two. Eyehategod was started as a way to piss people off. All the heavy music around here was fast, thrashy stuff, so Eyehategod slowed it down as much as possible and made a bunch of noise, basically. It was a way to say fuck you and make everyone hate them. And it worked, man. People fuckin' hated 'em. For the longest time, I was one of the few guys who actually enjoyed the hell out of it. So they were still in that frame of mind on the first record. It was just a thing to do. That's why the band's relationship with Century Media turned into such an unfortunate thing. They were young and naïve and didn't really give a fuck. It was like, "Fuck yeah, send us to Europe." They took the music seriously, though. Obviously, the influences were there—they were ahead of their time. People just couldn't grasp it.

Jimmy Bower: We were known to be like, "Fuck speed metal." We'd open up for like some big speed metal band like Exhorder or New Religion in front of like a thousand people and Mike would make his own flyers that said, "Eyehategod with special guest A Very Nice, Talented Metal Band." We were making fun of these bands, but we were friends with them, too. We were kinda like the class clowns of the whole scene. In New Orleans at that time, people still thought of us as a joke band—even though we had an album out, people wouldn't give us a shot. I remember giving Phil [Anselmo] and Pepper [Keenan] a tape, and they were like, "What the fuck, dude? We thought y'all were a joke band." They loved it, though.

Mike Williams: We had gotten into the Melvins, too. *Gluey Porch Treatments* is still my favorite album by them. I mean, there're a few fast parts on *In the Name of Suffering*, but with *Take as Needed*, we started writing more structured, mid-paced stuff. It wasn't necessarily all slow. But our first live shows were like that. That was the concept of Eyehategod in the beginning: To play as slow and aggravating as possible and just destroy people.

You were into bumming people out.
Williams: Oh, fuck yeah. I mean, the people that got it liked it, but for us, that was great. We were ecstatic that people hated us. We just wanted to hurt people's feelings—and it worked. I mean, I'd be lying if I said we wanted everyone to hate it—that's not true—but it got weird when people started liking it. When we started getting recognition, we'd go up to Boston and play with Grief and Anal Cunt—the two most extreme forms of that type of music—and fights would always break out. Always. It was great.

Bower: Totally. You hit the nail on the head. Bumming 'em out, still to this day. Sometimes we get onstage and feel miserable, and we wanna make everyone else feel miserable. It'll be real silent and Mike will be like, "I love this! Uncomfortable silence is fuckin' awesome!" He'd just verbally abuse people, and it ruled. When we played Baltimore on the *Take as Needed* tour with Buzzov*en, some dude in a Vitus t-shirt with, like, goggles on was spitting on us. I went up to him after the show like, "What the fuck's up, dude? You got a Vitus shirt on and you're spitting on us?" He was like, "That means I like you guys." But where we come from, you don't spit on *nobody*. So I got in this big argument with him, turned it around, and he ended up buying like two shirts and a CD.

Patton: We had toured with White Zombie before we did *Take as Needed for Pain*—right before they got really big. That was pretty much one of our first tours, along with another one we did with Buzzov*en, after it came out. Those were some wild fucking tours, man. Jesus Christ. *Take as Needed* was kind of the calm before the storm. Everyone was still rooted here at home, but then things started getting out of control. No need to go into too many specifics, but we made good and bad impressions on many people. [*Laughs*]

What's the first thing that comes to mind when you think about the time period around **Take as Needed for Pain?**
Patton: That was the first real album I had done. Soilent Green was around then, but we hadn't recorded anything yet. Eyehategod and Soilent played their

first shows together, actually. We opened up for Exhorder. After a while, Soilent was the only band that would play with Eyehategod.

Schultz: When we first started the band, I was living at Jimmy's house with him and his mom, 'cause my parents were gone since I was a little kid. From the time I was like 16 or 17, I stayed with Jimmy and his mother. Miss Linda—Jimmy's mom—I love this woman, man. She's the most beautiful woman in the world. She totally took me in and took care of me like I was her own son. Then Joey's mother let me live with him and his family, too.

Joey LaCaze: I remember it was the first record we kinda wanted to take serious. When we did the first record, we didn't really know what the future of the band was gonna be—we were just doing it for fun. But for *Take as Needed*, we were like "OK, we've got a real fuckin' record here."

Bower: We had just gotten back from touring Europe with Crowbar, and then we did four shows with White Zombie, which was a big deal for us. That was right when Brian got into the band, so we showed him everything we already had written, and then we started writing with him as well. We were practicing out at the Soilent Green practice room in St. Bernard Parish, which doesn't exist anymore. It was just cool times, man—a lotta acid, any opiates we could find. [*Laughs*] We were all like 23, 24 years old and out of our fuckin' minds. We were burning a ton of grass, too—obviously—and that really hooked it up for the record.

Williams: At that point, I had been kicked out my house by an ex-girlfriend, and I was living in the French Quarter on the street. I was totally homeless while we recorded that entire record. I would stay at people's houses every now and again, and sometimes I'd stay above this strip club on Bourbon Street called Big Daddy's. There were these horrible, horrible little apartments up there—me and my friend, this girl Jessie, had like half of a room that was infested with fleas. The cool thing was that the studio was like a block or two away, on Canal Street.

What was Studio 13 like?

Williams: It was on the 13th floor of the Maison Blanche building on Canal Street, which used to be a department store, but it was totally closed down and abandoned, so the only thing that was going on down there was this studio on the bad-luck 13th floor. I'm sure the dude rented it really cheap 'cause no one else wanted it, you know? It was a nice place, though.

LaCaze: I remember when we first went up there, you could see right over the city.

During the '20s and '30s, Maison Blanche was the real popular department store to go buy all your shit, you know? Most buildings don't even have a 13th floor, but it figures, in New Orleans, you know? It had a cool atmosphere, though: It was all real lush and cozy and stuff, with all these old rugs, and when I first saw it, I just knew we were gonna do something cool.

Bower: It was weird, because the dude who ran the studio, Robinson Mills, was our age, and I guess his family had money because it was beautiful, man—all old wood, like Victorian-looking. I think we gave him like three grand and he let us have the studio for an entire month. So we had plenty of time to track everything. I remember Brian and I did two guitar tracks apiece. I mean, it was a magical period, man. I know that sounds stupid, but we were all so into it.

LaCaze: Robinson was used to recording all the jazz and blues bands that are popular down here, and then we'd go in there and it was all feedback. He was just blown away, but I think he was interested because it was something totally different, though. But we kinda had to, like, teach him what we were going for. I remember we brought in some Saint Vitus records and *Gluey Porch Treatments* to kinda give him an idea of the heaviness. I don't think he really understood it, but he did a good job. He really captured the rawness of it. It was cool to do it on two-inch tape, too, because that helped capture the full sound.

Williams: Robinson wasn't familiar with our type of music at all. In fact, nobody was at that time. People assumed we were death metal or like a punk rock band—they couldn't figure out that it was something totally different than either of those. When we did the first album, it was impossible to explain to these guys that we *wanted* the feedback, that it was part of the song. But Robinson was open-minded. He didn't know what was going on, but he tried to learn about it. There were a few things he did that were strange—like sometimes he would just let us have the mixing board and he would go take a nap or something. And the very last song on the album, it says "Laugh It Off"—that's not one of my titles. He put that on there. It's a sample of some crazy guy laughing, and he took it upon himself to call the outro "Laugh It Off." So after all these titles like "Sister Fucker," "White Nigger," "Crimes Against Skin," it's like, oh, but "Laugh It Off." That's fuckin' stupid. I was pissed, but it doesn't matter, you know?

So the drug situation hadn't gotten out of control yet.

LaCaze: At the time, everybody was young and, you know, life hadn't progressed too much then. We were in our early 20s, and everyone was in their prime at that stuff. We were drinking and smoking, maybe doing a little acid, and that's about it. It was before various things got in the way of people's vision of it.

Williams: At that point, we were just smoking pot and drinking, pretty much—and maybe a couple lines here and there or a couple pills or something. It wasn't a big problem. I actually remember a big argument I got into with Jimmy, because we totally scraped money off the advance to buy whatever we needed. So they were getting all this band money together to go buy a bunch of weed, but I wasn't even really smoking then, so I was like, "Look, man—I need some alcohol money." But nobody else was really drinking, so Jimmy got pissed and threw some money at me and goes, "Here—go buy your fuckin' alcohol!" But as far as the drugs go, that's all that was going on.

Bower: We didn't drop acid in the studio, but we smoked a lot of weed. We'd go out at night and do acid, though. We jammed a couple times on acid, but not in the studio, because we were trying to make a real good record. But we ate Rohypnol and Xanax like candy back then. I'm off all of that shit now—all the opiates. I was on methadone for like five years. We all quit—Brian even jogs now. It makes me feel like a loser.

Patton: We dosed up on much coffee, smoked tons of dope in there, and Robinson didn't really give a fuck. We were in there having a good time. I think when Mike did his vocals, some glass ended up getting smashed around up in there, so [Robinson] had to do a little cleaning up. [*Laughs*] But beyond that, it was all good. Back then, Mike was big on alcohol. He would get in that mode when he was doing his vocals—he would need to get obliterated. Whenever we played, he wanted to get obliterated, too. Obviously, we've all grown up now and it's not quite the same. It's good to have fun now and again, but at the time, we'd just get pissed and loaded.

Schultz: That was before any of the tragic shit started happening. That was when we still used to have fun.

A few of the Cash Money rappers were recording at the same time, right?

Schultz: Those guys would be in another room down the hall, hanging out and talking shit. I worked in production for a while, so I worked with the Cash Money dudes on some of their videos. They're all totally cool, but they were fuckin' scared of Eyehategod, dude. They didn't know what to make of it. These big ol' tough, gold-teeth, tattooed rapper dudes thought we were going to hell.

LaCaze: Those dudes were funny, man. You know, they're like totally ghettoed-out motherfuckers. If they weren't getting enough bass in the mix, they'd pull a gun on the dude, you know? [*Laughs*] It's funny, years later I read [infamous New Orleans musician] Dr. John's autobiography, *Under a Hoodoo Moon*, and he'd explain how, back in the '60s, they'd have to rob somebody at gunpoint to get their money from some session, and then two weeks later, the same dude would rob them at gunpoint because they owed him some master tapes. In a way, that still goes on. It's a New Orleans tradition, you know? We've always been the murder capital. But now those New Orleans dudes are huge—Juvenile and Lil Wayne have sold millions of records. They got the money for their records from slingin', you know? But they've totally got themselves out of that rut, and they still come down here on the holidays and provide all the projects with turkeys on Thanksgiving.

Bower: They were total project dudes—I'm talking drug-slum, 75-bucks-a-month-rent. They took all their coke money and look what they did. It rules. I love it, man—it's a New Orleans success story. Juvenile bought this house in a rich white neighborhood and had all these strippers over. Some chick left the sink on, and the water ran down onto his new carpet, so he beat her up in his front yard. When we heard about it, we were like, "Dude—that rules!" I mean, we didn't want the girl to be hurt or nothing—we just thought it was a good story. They had all kinds of problems with him in that neighborhood—he'd park his tour bus out front, and you know he did it on purpose. Those dudes were super-cool, though, man. They used to live in this place called the Magnolia Housing Project, and they wanted to buy it from the city of New Orleans and let everybody live there rent-free for the rest of their lives. It was kinda like their payback. But it's all state-run housing, so they wouldn't sell it to a bunch of rappers. Now they probably would, though, because it's fuckin' empty since the storm hit. Weird, dude, weird.

Were all the songs written beforehand?

Patton: Me and Jimmy and Marc wrote most wrote of the songs. We had played a bunch of them live, like the "Sister Fucker" songs, "Kill Your Boss" and "White Nigger." Those songs were written for months and months before we went in. When it became crunch time, it turned into me and Jimmy sitting in his room, because we had to put together like three songs, I think it was, right before we went in. "Crimes Against Skin" was one, "Blank" was one and I think "Take as Needed" was the third one. We wrote those in Jimmy's apartment, ran 'em through like two or three times and then brought 'em into the studio. They were thrown together, but it all worked out great. Sometimes when you're rushed, you come up with the best shit.

Bower: Me and Marc wrote "White Nigger" and "Sister Fucker" in like 10 minutes. I mean, those songs aren't brain surgery, but for Eyehategod, they were good songs compared to the first record, which was a lot more doomy. Joey writes, too, so when Brian got in the band, we had four people in the band actively writing riffs.

Patton: We were determined to use every bit of tape that we possibly [could] so we kept going 'til the tape ran out. That's why "Who Gave Her the Roses" gets cut off at the end—it was just a riff we had left over that we just ended up jamming out.

Bower: When Mike came in and did vocals over that song, I thought it was fucking genius. All I had heard him do before that was scream, but then he comes out with, "I love her heart as well as her warm piss and the cuts and bruises on her body . . ."

What's the story behind "White Nigger"?

Bower: "White Nigger" is about Marc. On tour, we'd get so baked and I'd have to do all these like eight-hour drives because Mike and Marc didn't have licenses. And Marc would put N.W.A on like, 10, and just sit there like, "This is the shit, bruh." So that song's about him. [*Laughs*] He's a white nigger. When we went to Europe, we actually caught a little flak for that. Even Century Media was like, "Y'all sure you wanna put this on there?" But at the time, there was this black dude down here—he actually came up with the name Crowbar—and he called himself Adolf Nigger. He was this pissed-off black dude who grew up in New Orleans—people like that were our friends. I mean, the high schools here are like 75 percent black. When you see your black friends, it's like, "Damn, nigga, what's up?" But it's kinda hard to explain that to someone in Germany who comes up to you at a show and goes, "Vat is the meaning of 'White Nigger'? Not gud, Not gud." I'd be like, "Fuck you. Y'all killed six million Jews. We ain't killed nobody. All we did was say 'nigger.'"

Williams: Honestly, the title was just meant to be offensive. It'd be bullshit to say there was a deep meaning behind it. There's this '70s punk rock band called the Avengers—I think they're from San Francisco—and they had a song called "White Nigger." I totally took the title from them. We just liked the reaction it got—of course you can see how people will take it wrong. I mean, Patti Smith had a song called "Rock N' Roll Nigger." And Lester Bangs, the writer, had a t-shirt that said "100% White Nigger." Plus, the lyrics to the song don't have anything to do with the title of the song. You know, we *are* from the South—and we're proud to be from the South—so people just assume we're racists. But it's not like we didn't expect that to happen when we called the song "White Nigger." We enjoyed the negative publicity, of course, but honestly, I have regretted that title. I stick by it, and I'm not gonna take stuff back, but there's times when I think it's not worth all the bullshit. And I definitely don't want people to think I'm a racist—that's horrible.

What about "Sister Fucker"?

Williams: Honestly, "Sister Fucker" has no meaning, either. I don't even have a sister. But then again, that's in the third person, too. And it is offensive, but that stuff does go on. But people think, "Oh, you're from the South; you're all in-bred." So we were like, "Let's play that up. Who cares?" I know it's terrible humor, but at the same time people think that just because you give a song a certain title, that must be what you're thinking about—like you can't write something that's outside your point of view. But people wanna attack you, and we thrive on that. We still do.

LaCaze: The second part was so slow, you know, that we kinda figured that if anyone was gonna play it on college radio or whatever, they wouldn't go all the way through. That was kinda Phil and Pepper's deal, because they came up and they were trying to put their two cents in—even though we ended up scratching most of what they did, anyway. [*Laughs*] But yeah, it was Phil's idea to cut it in half. I don't think that really mattered, though, because I don't think anyone was gonna play our song, even on college radio, with a name like "Sister Fucker."

Who came up with the samples and the noise track, "Disturbance"?

Williams: The "Disturbance" thing is totally Joey. He'd go to thrift stores and buy these crazy records, and he had one called *Care of a Patient With a Catheter*, and that's where "Disturbance" came from. I don't know where he got all the rest of that stuff, though. Jimmy would do that stuff, too, though—he'd tape these crazy radio talk shows and just edit them together all crazy. I think some of the seven-inches have that stuff on there.

Bower: We had done samples on the first record—the [Charles] Manson thing. We used to take practice tapes and put cut-ups in 'em. Marc and Joey made the one with that sample that just goes, "alcohol, alcohol, alcohol," over and over again. We put it over "Blank," and it just worked out perfect.

LaCaze: At the time of that record, I was living at my mom's place, and across the canal are some really fucked-up areas, and every night we'd hear gunshots. I mean, like, automatic weapons and shit. You could literally hear people shooting each other, and it was weird, because it'd be totally quiet and in the silence of the nighttime, you'd just hear gunshots and you'd think, "Someone probably just got fucking killed." So "Disturbance" was inspired by that. I had these police scanners set up, so I'd hear the gunshots, and then I'd hear the cops on the scanner responding to the call. At the time, I was into doing a lot of experimental recording—like short-wave radios and shit like that, no instruments, really. I even had a piece from this Volkswagen hood miked up in my room. [*Laughs*] People would think I'm insane if they saw the shit I had in there. I'd be sitting up at three in the morning, sitting in a box with all this shit miked up. I was never a big person to go out or nothing, so I'd be up there recording every night.

Where did the cover art come from?

Williams: The photo of the girl is by this guy Jan Saudek—he's this really great photographer/painter. I know Rorschach and Soul Asylum used some of his stuff, too. But we didn't get permission or anything, so I hope he doesn't come after us. I guess we kinda figured he'd never see it. When we submitted it, Century Media freaked out because they thought it was Jodie Foster. The funny thing is that, once they figured out that it wasn't her, nobody worried about getting the rights for it.

Bower: Mike and Joey basically did all the artwork, and they blew my mind. I think it's totally demented and totally original, but our label freaked on us. We went out to California, and Oliver, the owner of Century Media, brought us into his office and goes, "You trying to get me fucking sued?" We were like, "What the fuck are you talking about, dude?" He goes, "How dare you put Jodie Foster on the cover of your record?" [*Laughs*] You gotta be fucking kidding me. That ain't Jodie Foster. That picture is from the '50s, and he fucking yelled at us, dude. I remember he had, like, an air hockey machine, too, and he kicked it over. [*Laughs*] I swear to god, man. We would fight with Century Media so much back then, and I know we've given like 80,000 interviews where we say "Century Media sucks," but we were like a fucking degenerate kid giving their parents problems. We probably started half that shit, but not that one.

Williams: The other pictures on the cover are from this insane medical manual. I love old, black-and-white medical books. I got the idea from Discharge—their stuff was all old war photos, but I wanted to do medical stuff. The old SPK stuff, like *Leichenschrei* and *Auto Da Fe*—they had all that stark, black-and-white stuff. I think it just hits you harder than color. I collected old photos like that for years, and I did that type of art before I even had a band that I thought would put out a record. I'd just go to the library for hours at a time and dig it all up. The girl on the back cover, I don't know where I got that photo, but she just looks so sad, you know? And what I love about it is that it's not even black and white; it's that sepia tone. She looks like she's either at a horrible wedding or an even worse funeral.

I like that the fan club is called Negative Action Group/Foundation for the Retarded.

Bower: Joey and Mike used to drop acid and ride around in Joey's car with ski masks on just screaming at people—that was the Negative Action Group, NAG. Fuckin' weirdos, man—they were lucky they didn't go to jail. Not even jail—a fuckin' mental institution.

Williams: We had these police scanner radios that we'd turn all the way up, and we'd put ski masks on and drive around, pulling up next to people walking on the street. They'd hear the static on the police scanner, and when they'd look over and see us, they'd start running and shit. We called it the Negative Action Group, so we thought NAG was a good name for the fan club. The Foundation for the Retarded thing, though—we only used that once because I think there actually *is* a Foundation for the Retarded. The funny thing is that Joey put his mom's phone number on the record, so he'd get all these calls from local pastors asking us to accept God.

Bower: Joey's mom's phone number is on the fucking record. Dude put his fucking home number on the album. I know his mom got fed up at one point—it became one of those 867-5309 things.

Schultz: Joey's mom used to get calls and threatening letters because people thought we were making fun of retarded people—which we were. [*Laughs*] After a while, I think she learned to go with the flow. She knew we weren't bad kids—we were just into some crazy shit.

LaCaze: Originally, you know, we were on such a small level that we would put the phone number on there so people could call us to book shows. There wasn't no Internet back then—for years, I was writing people back by hand and doing shit over the phone. This one woman called from Puerto Rico, and she was fucking crazy, dude. I think she saw the pictures in the record of the people with the skin diseases. At the time, my mom was working for a dermatologist, so we had all these weird books at my house—that's how we got into the medical shit. So I think this woman must've been suffering from one of these skin situations, and I mean . . . I could tell she had nothing to do with this kind of music. I think she thought it was some kind of place to get treatment, and I'm on the phone with this woman thinking how insane this is, like, "What the fuck are we creating?" People were taking all of our sick sense of humor for real. She's asking me about how to get flown over here for treatment, and I'm like, "No! Don't call back—I'll relay the message." I was trying to explain that it was a band, but she didn't understand.

Williams: After that, Joey was like, "We cannot put this number on here anymore." I mean, what band does that nowadays—puts their home phone number on their record? We actually did make a lot of friends by doing that, though. Kids would call from the U.K. or Germany, and we'd end up going over there, meeting them and staying at their houses. So it was good and bad, I guess.

What's with all the text that's mixed in with the lyrics in the CD booklet?
Williams: That's just more confusion. People couldn't figure out which song each set of lyrics was to, and it drove them insane. Nobody could go away from the form of, you know, "Here's the title and here's exactly what the guy's gonna sing." I just like the idea of throwing something different into the mix. I like making people think, though. It confuses them and probably frightens them a little bit, but I think it opens people's minds to different things, and I'm just glad that I could do that. Plus, Joey put that thing in

there about how "all followers of the path should make one hallucinogenic trip per week and every day with marijuana." People would come up to us at shows and go, "We're doing like you guys said—taking LSD once a week and smoking pot every day." [*Laughs*] We were totally corrupting everyone. Which is great, though.

Do you have a favorite song on the record?

Patton: I've got a couple of favorites. "Blank" is a really good song, just because it's really dense and I love playing it live. "Kill Your Boss" is a really good one, too—I just love the riff at the end. That's why we usually do medleys live. We'll break the songs into pieces, take our favorite parts and make our own new song out of them. Sometimes we even add new riffs just for the fuck of it. We don't wanna bore the fuck out of everybody.

Williams: "Shoplift." I just like what I came up with, I guess, and how it starts off. It's actually got a slight melody to it, too. I like "Sister Fucker Part 1" and "30$ Bag," too—that's one of my favorites to play live. People love it. We actually still do a lot of stuff from this album live.

Schultz: I love 'em all, man, but "Who Gave Her the Roses" is cool. It's not even really a song—it's just a piece of music, a jam, you know? I'm into shit like that. It doesn't necessarily have to be a fully constructed song with verses and choruses and shit.

Bower: I like "Kill Your Boss" and "30$ Bag" the best, I think, but I really like 'em all. Those two songs had what we called "the drops"—you know, we're playing one tempo, and then we slow it down and it makes your knees buckle.

LaCaze: I always liked "Take as Needed for Pain," but I don't know—every Eyehategod song has a different meaning for me. Some we don't even play live, and others, like "Blank," we play every show. Now that I think about it, that record has a lot of songs that people wanna hear. I mean, I wouldn't feel complete doing an Eyehategod show without playing "Blank."

When do you think you first started to notice the influence the record had on other bands?

Williams: When the record came out, I think people were still confused about what was going on, and we weren't helping the situation, either. I think the first time we went to Europe was after *Take as Needed* came out—we went with Crowbar—and there were fans already. But we didn't see all the bands that were starting to sound like us yet. I think it was still very underground. But I guess I didn't really realize what was going on—and maybe that's because of my alcohol and drug abuse at the time—until Iron Monkey came out. And [Iron Monkey guitarist] Dean [Berry, currently of Capricorns] is a great friend of mine, but their artwork was similar, and their music is totally similar, but I never had anything against it. It was flattery, to me. But people we know will get mad about it. Like Seth from Anal Cunt used to call up Iron Monkey and threaten them. [*Laughs*] I'd be like, "Dude, don't do that." I mean, I admit my influences—that's how things evolve.

Bower: The first American tour we ever did was with Buzzov*en, and I remember talking to Kirk [Fisher] and he'd be like, "Dude, we listen to your record all the time." I thought he was just being nice, but when we went up to Richmond to meet them for the tour, we met all their friends and it seemed like every dude had our album in his car. They were like, "Man, this is our Bible up here." It was cool because there were little pockets of people who were into that style—you know, Witchfinder General and [Saint] Vitus, but to meet a whole other group of people who were into it was killer.

Schultz: The people who said, "Eyehategod sucks," are the same people who are ripping our shit off today. It cracks me up. I laugh about it whenever I see someone who used to talk shit and now they play in a band that sounds like a terrible Eyehategod rip-off. I don't wanna sit here and name bands—I mean, I'm friends with some of these people—but almost every single fucking band in New Orleans went through that whole deal back then. And they know who they are and how I feel about them.

Williams: I'll say it: There are a lot of bands that try to do what we do. There's a band called Sofa King Killer that even has samples about heroin in the middle of their songs, and there's another band called Lickgoldensky—they don't sound anything like us, but the name of the band is taken from my lyrics. That's actually from *Take as Needed for Pain*, which brings me back to the point. I hate to even say stuff like this, but it was obviously influenced by me. Shit, there's another band called 99 Miles of Bad Road. Another band wrote me a letter and asked if they could call their band Ruptured Heart Theory. Even Grief and Cavity, who came out around the same time as us, started having more groove parts on their second records. We'll play with one of these bands and somebody will come up to me and go, "Listen to these motherfuckers," but, you know, I can't be a dick about it because I support these kids, man. If they're playing something that we started, that's just incredible.

In retrospect, is there anything you'd change about it?

Patton: Fuck no. I'm completely happy with it. I'm real critical about things, you know—there might be a few transitions I would've done differently—but I wouldn't change a fuckin' thing. The way you gotta look at it is that's where you were at the time. You grow as a person and as a musician, but why change the feel, or a riff, or anything? To be honest, it's my favorite record we did.

LaCaze: No. We never really gave any of our records much thought at the time—I mean, we'd do 'em in a couple weeks, tops. Some songs we did in one take. It ain't nothing like these six-month, one-year recording situations where it takes two months to get a guitar sound or something. And that's what works for us, because usually your first instincts are the best.

Williams: I don't think I'd change anything about it. Maybe I'd make the noise song a little shorter, but then again, we did that to irritate people. When anybody asks what I think is the best Eyehategod record, I say this one.

Schultz: No, man. Nothing. It's not perfect, but I wouldn't change it. I'm totally happy with it. I always have been and I always will be. I don't care if I go on to make 50 more records before I die. If *Take as Needed* remains the best one, I am so totally cool with that because I love that record.

Bower: I'd leave that bitch the exact same way it is. It's a trip, man—we wrote that record so fast. And looking back on it now, it's vocal-oriented, it's verse-chorus, and we weren't even trying to do that. It's ironic how it came out. I look back at it now, and it's funny—the lengths we would go to just to escalate our ignorance.

CHAPTER 14

HUNGER STRIKES

THE MAKING OF DARKTHRONE'S *TRANSILVANIAN HUNGER*

by Albert Mudrian

Transilvanian Hunger

Release Date: 1994
Label: Peaceville
Summary: Isolationist black metal starts here
Induction Date: Previously Unreleased Bonus HOF

I t was the fall of 1993 and the Norwegian black metal scene had formally ratified the mystique that would forever surround it. But, musically, it was now pretty much fucked. Burzum mastermind Varg "Count Grishnackh" Vikernes had just been hauled off to the pokey for the fatal stabbing of Mayhem guitarist and scene Svengali Øystein "Euronymous" Aarseth. Within weeks, Emperor's Tomas "Samoth" Haugen and Bård "Faust" Eithun would each be arrested for arson and murder, respectively. And although they weren't involved in any of the aforementioned criminal activities, Darkthrone were on the verge of falling apart, too. Guitarist Ivar "Zephyrous" Enger had already begun drifting away from the band following the 1992 recording of their *Under a Funeral Moon* album. Vocalist/guitarist Ted "Nocturno Culto" Skjellum was still residing in a remote area of the country—several hours from the band's home base of Oslo—and growing more emotionally distant from Darkthrone drummer/founder Gylve "Fenriz" Nagell by the day. With free time on his hands and rehearsal space in his living room, Fenriz rejoined his old doom metal band Valhall and appeared—for all intents and purposes—dethroned.

Then it happened—a postal prophecy and a two-week whirlwind of inspiration that saw Fenriz conceive and record the entire framework of what would become ground zero for isolationist black metal. When it was finally released in 1994, however, *Transilvanian Hunger* was anything but an instant classic. Instead, it was derided for its raw, lo-fi, almost nonexistent production values, and further disparaged for the inclusion of the phrase "Norsk Arisk Black Metal," which loosely translated to "Norwegian Aryan Black Metal" on its original back cover. (Darkthrone maintain that they profess no white power ideologies, and in response to the controversy, the band's next album, 1995's *Panzerfaust*, bore the legend, "Darkthrone is certainly not a Nazi band, nor a political band. Those of you who still might think so, you can lick Mother Mary's asshole in eternity.")

Fifteen years and nine more studio albums since its release, *Transilvanian Hunger* is now the most emulated of Darkthrone's seemingly endless canon. For this Hall of Fame "bonus track," *Decibel* corralled its architects to find out why a new wave of black metal bellies will never be full.

What was the state of Darkthrone after you recorded Under a Funeral Moon in 1992?

Fenriz: We weren't huge on communication then. We didn't really start rehearsing another album after we went to the studio to record *Under a Funeral Moon*, which was in the summer of '92. When we recorded *Soulside Journey* in the summer of '90, we started to make another album pretty soon. And in the summer of '91, when we recorded *A Blaze in the Northern Sky*, we quickly went on to make a new album, but we didn't in '92. We'd been in the zone for two years, partying hard and being, you know, maniacs like you wouldn't believe. There wasn't really an established black metal scene until the mid '90s, so I guess we were all strange and freakish. We were having day jobs and living ghoulish lives on the side, and I guess it took its toll. After *Under a Funeral Moon* was recorded, everyone went on to do what they wanted.

So, you didn't immediately start working on new material as a band for a while?

Nocturno Culto: I moved from Oslo in late '91, and I never looked back, actually. What I did was, every week I was driving three hours to get to Oslo and rehearse, and that was during the rehearsals for *Under a Funeral Moon*. And Zephyrous still [lived] just outside Oslo, so he was like a natural in the band. I was the one that was weird, moving away and everything.

Fenriz: Yeah, we didn't start making new material. It was also the fact that Ted moved, so it would become impossible, and it was all a blur, really. As far as I remember, in summer '92 we recorded *Under a Funeral Moon*, and then I guess I was hanging a lot at the Helvete store that Euronymous had. 'Cause that had opened a year before in August '91 with help from the few left in the scene. My help would just be giving 60 records, so he had something to have on the shelf. This was really low . . .

Low-budget, barebones?

Fenriz: Yeah, yeah. It wasn't a fancy store—it was a freakish hangout. I was thinking about it, and I just sat in the store and had a beer after work always. But then, after *Under a Funeral Moon*, that store, it was open some months after, and then Christmas '92 it just shut down; that had sort of been a little center-point for all of us, like, in this freakish time from August '91 'til Christmas '92. And then when that sort of fell apart, the store closed and you had sort of all the problems that I didn't know about that just perfectly led up to a lot of, well, you know, the whole murder incident in '93. I guess '93 was *extremely* confusing for everyone involved here, because we weren't really that many people, but everyone was really strange and weird, and then when '93 came, then we just lost the store and it was every man for himself. It was crazy. It was almost, you know, different unions for different bands, going and trying to keep contact and stuff like that. But I guess in '96, three years after, everyone was going their own direction more or less. So, that was sort of the start of the total anarchy after the '93 thing—when we didn't have the record store of Euronymous anymore. Then it was like back to normalcy, but everyone was like, "We were all crazy, so we just fend for ourselves." And then after the murder, then everyone suddenly knew that, yeah, we're really on our own now, and we did get more popular from that in this neat little country.

Did you consider replacing Zephyrous before **Transilvanian Hunger?**

Fenriz: I guess I wasn't used to Zephyrous because we were like different guys. I'm this really gesticulating, typical Italian, hyper dude, while he's really calm and easy. I guess it was hard to handle my escapades. And I never really— it's not something I want to sit down and talk to any of them [about]. As far as I remember, I was not hanging out with those others a lot, like Zephyrous— we got a bit too close maybe. Just answering this is forcing me to try to remember something I haven't remembered before. And, of course, at work today I was like, "What the hell happened in '93?" I know what happened on a personal level. I know that I had quit Valhall—we started Valhall in '87. And after I got the record deal with Peaceville in '89/'90, I said, "Valhall, I don't have time to do both bands now; I have to really concentrate on Darkthrone." And Valhall said, "OK, that's a shame." And then in '93, I realized that Darkthrone was not active, and I probably didn't want to make songs, and Zephyrous didn't want to, and Ted—I don't know if Ted really wanted to make songs after *Under a Funeral Moon* either. It felt like we made something really total, and that's really our most total black metal album, *Under a Funeral Moon*.

So, in '93, I just joined Valhall again, and we had been rehearsing with Darkthrone in my living room ever since we got the record deal—it was like '90 to '92 we were there—and then when *Under a Funeral Moon* was recorded, then there was no music being made there anymore in the room, so now that I think about it, it's not strange that I was twiddling my thumbs there and thinking, "Hmmm . . . maybe I should ask if Valhall needs a drummer again," 'cause they've always had problems with drummers. So, I was back, and that meant also that they had their portable studio with them, so the portable studio now was a part of my living room. And whenever we were not rehearsing, then I could make everything I wanted with that studio, so it became that I continued the Isengard project—that's how I got started on that very same studio in the summer of '89. But . . . at that point Ted was living far away—we're talking '93 now—and I had gotten married, too, and he . . . I don't know what Zephyrous . . . I think he was still sort of, maybe he moved. I don't remember when Zephyrous moved away, but it's clear that at one point he really did move away. They both moved far away. They both just thought that the Helvete scene that I was sort of in sucked because they were really into just being on their own, and I am also a loner, but even the thing with me being there, it was just pissing them off, I guess. So it was [that] they're *really* die-hard loners.

Nocturno Culto: Zephyrous actually came to the same small village I was living [in], and we would just basically have a good time, you know, usually just partying. Also, when I moved, I was experiencing things that were kind of larger than life, especially after the *Under a Funeral Moon* album. I was this dude drifting around in mountains and woods and fishing, and there was the wilderness—I kind of forgot everything else. I had this amazing time. Zephyrous did come up, and we just continued partying and things like that. And you what? I don't think I even thought about Darkthrone that much, except for that Zephyrous and I probably did have some slight plans for new material.

You mentioned in an earlier email correspondence that the music for **Transilvanian Hunger** *came to you in a vision while you were at your day job at the post office.*

Fenriz: Yeah, that's how I remember it, and that's how I remember it the year after and the year after that, and every time I talked about the album, it's the same vision that came up at work. I had this really intense feeling, and with that came the lyrics to the "Transilvanian Hunger" song. And as I told you . . . I'm just going to put in some mouth tobacco here, one moment . . . oh yeah. I stopped smoking. The first thing I did was mouth tobacco, then I started smoking, then this. I have this stupid, incredibly rare lung disease, too, so I can't smoke. Not to worry, though—I can ski well, and hike.

So, how fully formed was the vision for the record at work?

Fenriz: So, I [should] mention now that we had lots of instruments in my living room; it's a rehearsal space, and it has been for years. And then, suddenly, [the] Valhall guys took with them the whole studio that I knew how to work from before, because I did the first Isengard demo on it in summer '89, and then I also did a Valhall demo on that studio, so I sort of knew the ropes for that little piece of shit studio called Necrohell studio. So I was ready to go. I was coming home after work and I started making the music, and the vision I had for the music was to . . . I can only know this by thinking about the album now, so that's what I'm talking from, that sort of memory, because I haven't listened to the entire album in years, and I didn't do that now before the interview. If I had the album at work today, I would have listened to it, but I didn't have it; I really should have, I'm sorry about that. I sort of remember four or five of the songs and the main things to talk about it.

OK, then what do you remember?

Fenriz: Drums . . . let's see, first I had to make song number one on the guitar. And then I would know it in my head, and then I would sit down at the drum kit and go "chick-chick-chick-chick" while usually humming the riffs in my head, and that's what a one-man band is. It always starts with the drums, but you have to have made the song in advance so you can hum it in your head while you play the drums. So, that's how it works, OK? I figured out different ways to record the drums, because when I had recorded the demos before in another place, here I had, this is a portable studio—only four channels—so I can only use one mic for the drums, and I had to put it high up, behind my back, in front of the kit, and then do checks afterwards to see that it sounded good. And I ended up having the mic—I was sitting next to the wall, you know, like usually drummers do with their back to the wall—and I had the microphone lowered, sort of like behind my head, and that would work best for the drums.

Then I had to find a guitar sound for the riffs, but I sort of found that when I was making the first song. Let's say that, in all probability, "Transilvanian

Hunger" was the song that I made first for [the] *Transilvanian Hunger* album, with the finger-moving technique that had been started by Bathory on the *Under the Sign of the Black Mark* album, and been used on the *Blood Fire Death* album. This sort of technique was one of the styles that became known as Norwegian black metal, but that particular style that I'm using is not a typical Norwegian [style]; it is more that Quorthon started that style, and what I quickly found out was that guitar sound that I had was working very good with those sorts of riffs. And in retrospect, you can see that it was right; it sort of works because it gives that exact sort of attack on the strings, and it totally worked. Also, it was a strange kind of effect that I used, so when I turned off the effects pedal, the amp would still be going "kkkkkssshhhhh" on a level of five out of 10 decibels. So, it was sort of crazy. It was a special thing.

And then for the bass, I had to create a bass sound that would fit with the other two guitars, so now we have established that Necro studio has four channels— so number one on the drums, number two on the guitar, number three on the second guitar, and then I had to find a bass sound that would match, to bring out the magic in those finger movements that I use. Because I don't really use chords like Euronymous and Snorre [Ruch]. Euronymous from Mayhem and Snorre from Thorns were the ones that made the typical Norwegian thing, you see—they made chords, and they would play all the strings, like more than one string in the chord, but would they be clean together? No, they would resound together. That was their style, and that you can hear on Mayhem's *Live in Leipzig*, and Mayhem *Deathcrush*, and on the Thorns demo—and the Thorns demo was really, really important. And I guess also Count Grishnackh or Varg, we all [listened] to the early and new style of Mayhem and Thorns stuff. But I am not a good guitarist, so instead I use the technique that Quorthon already did in '87 and '88. OK?

The vision that I had was that this is winterish—this will be the "longing" that I already knew from Burzum, and I will have that sort of trance, and [an] entrancing tempo that was monotone. A band that was important for both me and Varg was called Von from the United States. Von was extremely important for Burzum, but not for Darkthrone—only on the *Transilvanian Hunger* album was Von important. Yeah, because we have to see the '80s as a whole now. Would you say the '80s was a decade when metal was really monotone, or was it really hectic? I mean, everyone knows it was damn hectic. You'd have like, riffs and riff changes and tempo changes from the NWOBHM, until death metal and even grindcore. What was the world ready for? More hectic stuff? I don't think so! So, when Von started doing their thing, we're all clicking like, "Holy shit! They're doing the monotone thing!" That was the freshest thing [we'd] heard since we were born. Suddenly the monotone thing was allowed, and we would be like, "Yep, we will open up to that." And with all due respect, it was Count Grishnackh who understood this monotone thing first, and he understood it from Von. And I thought, "This lyric I got in my head at work, and what I'm starting to work at now will be this tempo, [these] sort of riffs, and it will be monotone." And it turns out I completely entered the sound, and that's why I made all the songs and made all the takes and laid everything down on tape in two weeks—[it] must have been maximum two weeks. And you can also hear that it's a very monotone, very concept album, and usually that sort of music is made by one person. Whether it's electronic or not, when it's really sounding a bit totalitarian, then you know it's the work of one guy, one dictator.

Did Fenriz tell you about the vision he had at work, or did **Transilvanian Hunger** *just show up in the mail one day?*

Nocturno Culto: The latter. Fenriz just sent a tape in the mail, and said this could be our new Darkthrone album. To me, it was really strange, because I hadn't really thought about it, but when I heard the album, it was like an echo of the things I was doing in the middle of nowhere. It was a weird sensation of, "Well, this is exactly the sound—if I could create an atmosphere on tape of what I've been doing for the last two years now, this is it." Even though it sounds strange that he did the album himself . . . who can blame him, you know? Everybody was moving away, and he was just sitting there with all the equipment saying, "What am I supposed to do now? Well, I have to play it." It's probably only natural. And especially after the fact that this was in the day and age where there were no cell phones. There was no email. I didn't have a phone. I had to travel for half an hour to get a phone box, so it was not easy. It was also difficult when I'd go to the phone; it was not necessarily very easy to get a hold of Fenriz anyways, so the communication wasn't really top-notch back then. But if all these things that happened today, all the communication and stuff, it would probably have been a different situation. Also, I think Zephyrous felt kind of very left out. But he couldn't do anything about it, because he was the guitarist really, you know? Since I do the vocals anyway, I could do the vocals. I remember he was not very pleased about it, but I don't think this is the entire reason for him leaving the band, actually. He was actually getting sick, and probably, I don't know why, but suddenly, I mean, he was driving a car one day, and everything went black and then he woke up in the hospital with a lot of things attached. It was kind of dramatic stuff going on. He recovered kind of slowly and moved to another place where his relatives were living. But, yeah, he tried to cope with it— I definitely understood then that he's not going to play anymore.

I've heard the drums were done in one take?

Fenriz: Well, I couldn't go in and stop myself or anything like that since this was a very primitive studio. Of course, I made the next song; I don't know what song I made after that—it's one of the seven others, I'm sure—but I learned that song. I'd sit down and play it on guitar, and I'd decide for myself, *this would go eight times, this will go 12 times*, because in the '80s you would never play a riff more than four, six or eight times. Burzum and Von were also experimenting with playing stuff 12, 16, even 32 times before changing, and that would mean the change would be of the essence, the change would be really noticeable. And as I said, this was very fresh in the early '90s. We'd had a decade where this was not done. There was not a single album except the Bathory stuff that was doing this sort of thing in the '80s. So yeah, those who hadn't heard Bathory were really thrilled by the new stuff we were doing. So, of course, I had to do the drums in one take. If I was doing a mistake, I would just go back and start again, and that's how we always work. I don't stop in the middle of a song saying, "OK, I finished part one now; I can do part two tomorrow." That's not how we roll. That's how the big guys roll, I imagine.

So, that's not really impressive either. Because, as you know, the really special thing with *Transilvanian Hunger* is that it's the first metal album that has the same pace on Side A, except for Von, of course, again—but that was not an album, it was only demos. So, the first four songs, as far as I know, have the same tempo. And that's really extreme. That's really, really extreme. But I have always decided that the riffs I was doing were fitting these kind of riffs, and that's where I was going. And then the fifth song, finally [makes drumming noises with tempo change], and of course when you listen to four and a half songs with one tempo, then the tempo change is gonna make an impact—it's the monotone over the monotone. But it was only me, so there was no one there to argue or anything.

When we interviewed Grutle Kjellson from Enslaved for **Decibel's** *Darkthrone cover story, he mentioned the idea of making "pure Norwegian music"—not in the Aryan sense, but in the sense that all the lyrics [except the title track] are in your native tongue. Was that something you were trying to accomplish with* **Transilvanian Hunger?**

Nocturno Culto: No, definitely not. But it's cold, and for us, we have to admit that our country, and the feeling, and the cold weather—the autumn, the bleak and gray light—sometimes, it all inspired us to do a lot of things. I think especially I was inspired by desolate places. Because it's such [a] more powerful experience than being around where so-called things are happening. But today it's, of course, different.

Fenriz: Yeah, it was the coldness and the nature and the winter forest walk that we did a little of. Both me and Varg were into that—walking into the forest—but now I just laugh at it, because we didn't really walk long distances or anything like that, like I do now. But sadly, everyone thinks that. All the rich white kids of the world think this is really exotic, and want to do it, too, and put on a bit of corpsepaint and go back into the yard when it's winter, but this is not really wildlife. And then you've sort of had a distance to it and a little taste for it, and that was enough to spawn that incredible sense for both Varg and me to sort of play an ode to that, I guess. Yeah. Simply enough, it was candles in the snow, man.

Now that you're an experienced hiker, it's kind of funny that you guys used to go on some of those forest walks.

Fenriz: Not together, though! That would be really lame.

This was the first Darkthrone record to feature a guest lyricist. Why did you share lyric responsibilities with Varg Virkernes on four of the tracks? Moreover, what did Varg contribute, at the time, that you didn't or couldn't?

Fenriz: We should go into the whole ordeal about the murder [of Euronymous]. We'd been getting threats from the Scandinavian North, though I assume it was some Swedish person that went totally crazy, because just two weeks, or three weeks, or a month before Euronymous' murder, I got a letter from Sweden anonymously, like a tombstone that said "Euronymous" across it. So it was logical that I would think that. You know, Varg wasn't arrested for the murder until weeks after, as far as I remember, and those weeks, man, I was nervous as hell. I would arm myself with the *Bonded by Blood* album by Exodus playing on my walkman, which got me through the battle it was to go to work and to go to my house—even around in the city, you want to watch your back and have your knife at hand and stuff like that. The situation for me, it was nerve-wracking; and then, you know, Varg was even visiting me and we were trading. I got some shirts and CDs, and he would get some Darkthrone merch for free from me, even after the murder, and I would say, "Man, I got this letter from Sweden," and he would just say, "No, don't show the cops that." And he'd go off driving back to Bergen, and a couple [of] weeks later he was arrested for the murder, and I was like, "What?!" thinking I don't know if it's true or not, I don't know any of the circumstances. I did the album, or had the album done. I don't really remember when in '93 I did this album—maybe it says on the album.

It says it was recorded in November and December of '93.

Fenriz: OK. I had sent the album to Ted, also along with the lyrics. The thing [was] when Varg was in prison, I was thinking more and more how he now could not speak to the outside world. I thought, this is a very extreme situation—we've never had anything like this in Norway before, or the metal world at all. So I was writing [Varg] a letter, and I said, "Do you want to communicate via Darkthrone in any way?" I offered him to write it in the lyrics, and then he sent the lyrics, and then that was the lyrics. I don't even know what the lyrics mean. I'm never a curious person that asks why. I've had some people around me always asking why, and it always bothers me. I don't want to bother anyone. And I never wanted [to] in my entire life. I don't want to be a bother, so I don't ask.

Ted got the lyrics and spent a long time to listening to the album, and I was also sort of explaining to him to what this album was, and I was sure he would find some great way of singing the stuff. Later, we would take the tape—because now it was full, the four tracks were full—we had to take the tape to the studio, get Ted down from where ever he lived at the time. I think he was definitely in the North somewhere, or in Trysil; he hadn't moved maybe at that time, which is an important place for us, Trysil. Up northeast. We record there and [we've] rehearse[d] there since '98. He's been living there, his wife's from there; we have a lot of history with that place.

Did Peaceville have any objections having Varg contribute to the record?

Fenriz: I don't remember that at all. I guess [Hammy, Peaceville founder] is a people person—he has to do that, he has to be like that, and being from England it's more like, you don't have those hermits like we seem to be. They have a lot of interaction and stuff like that. He probably knew we were going through an extremely insane period in our lives, and he saw the shit hit the fan, I guess. In retrospect, I see that happened as well. He didn't want to tamper with that at all. The album was under contract—see, we had signed a four-record deal. So the album had to be done; it's in the contract. *Transilvanian Hunger* was probably a little bit doomed from the get-go. It was an extreme outing from extreme times.

Why is only the title track written in English?

Fenriz: Oh, it was? Oh shit . . . I guess I didn't know what language Varg would use, so that was of course out of my hands. I didn't know, so that's a co-incidence. When it came to my stuff, we have to go back to a gig we did in '89, with Darkthrone. It was in the movie theater where we grew up, Kolbotn—a good place for metalheads. I'm kidding, but there has been a whole lot of bands from there, throughout, and it's a really small place; it's strange. But you know, this area is where Mayhem is from, too, just a couple of miles down the road, and we had another cool band in the '80s that was really, really great called Vomit. I remember the first Mayhem rehearsal I attended was in October '87, 'cause I'd been in touch with Necrobutcher in '87. So that was my first contact with any other Norwegian band. So I went to see them, and at that time it was only Necrobutcher and Euronymous, and there were two guys from Vomit that were helping Mayhem out. That was before Ted joined [Darkthrone]. It was before Jan [Axel Blomberg]—Hellhammer—joined [Mayhem]. And Mayhem's old drummer, Torben [Grue] went on to become an opera singer, a real character at that, too—we were all weird. You had to be to make it though the '80s metal scene in Norway because there [were] none. We were the ones taking care of any global activity.

So, at a gig in '89 that we played, Torben—he was laughing, because he's always been like that—would come up to us and say, "Hey, why don't you extreme metal acts start singing in Norwegian? Now *that* would be extreme." And I was mulling this over in my head for the rest of the '80s then, and then in '90 and in '91. And then in '91, when we'd finished *A Blaze*, I was writing the first lyric for the next album, which was "Inn I De Dype Skogers Favn"—a song from *Under a Funeral Moon*, obviously. And I felt it was really hard to crack that sort of code, 'cause even growing up with the rock 'n' roll and the heavy blues-based stuff from the '70s, it was always "yeah, yeah, yeah" and "baby, baby." Everything was . . . let's say that the international language for the postal system is French, but the international language [for] rock 'n' roll is English. So maybe that's why I went two years after receiving that idea from Torben. I finally thought, "Now is the time, now I will do it, now I got the courage. I've been writing lyrics for five years—I'll do it now." And I was very pleased with the result. It worked perfectly well with Ted's vocals, and so I guess that's why I did three more on the *Transilvanian Hunger* album.

Where did the title come from? Is it a reference to former Mayhem vocalist Dead and the "I ♥ Transylvania" shirt he was wearing when he committed suicide?

Fenriz: That would be very logical. You'd think that would be a really sound way to try to figure out a reason for the title. However, I'm not sure that it was, because I think it would come sooner after Dead's suicide, like if that would be a song on *A Blaze in the Northern Sky* or *Under a Funeral Moon*. I thought of it with the whole concept of the icy and the cold landscape. Probably it must have crossed my mind, obviously, about Dead, too, and his whole take on Transylvania, and the real hunger he had for it. I don't remember now, but I would actually prefer [if] it was like a tribute to Dead, but I'm not sure that's all of it. When I make a title—or an album title, at least—there's never just one meaning behind it. There are several, because I mull it over in my head, and, what I'm good at here in life is quick associations, so when I get a title, I quickly come up with a lot of different ways out of the little box that the title is in. And then I stuff that box full of different meanings—so it's very potent for me. I never talk about lyrics much, or not when I have the artistic side to myself anyway. Then it's better not to explain too much. Lately, I've been explaining a little bit about the lyrics 'cause it's no problem. I'll just write about my feelings containing some fucking topic or scene politics, but at that time it was all dark and serious, really. You know, the simplest thing in the world is for white kids that are a little bit troubled to go really pompous on it all—like you get a splinter in your finger and suddenly you have a whole grindcore album. That's how it is—adolescence and early 20s. I guess people feel really strongly in their lives at the time. Most artists, they make their most vital music early and spend the next 20 years sucking.

***How did the cover art come together? The illustration is a bit different from* A Blaze in the Northern Sky *and* Under a Funeral Moon.**

Fenriz: It was a continuation of it, though, and it was supposed to be a continuation. I was thinking, "Yeah, of course, what photo would be *Blaze*?"—just having a photo as a cover at that time was also preposterous. No one did that. It had to be some sort of Ed Repka painting or what have you. So I wanted to take it really back to the '80s when we did *A Blaze* and all the influences on the album are of the '80s, and so are the others really, except that when it comes to *Transilvanian Hunger*, it was more of the same mood that Burzum had, and then a mix of that, and then Von, and both those bands were like '91, so that's how far we went into having inspirations; all of the rest of the way we play our instruments, and I play drums, is '70s.

OK, the cover. We chose the photo of Zephyrous for *Blaze*—immediate shock value, I guess it had, or reminiscent for people going though vinyls in the store, going like, "What the hell is this in the new section? That's like from . . . that's from the '80s." And we continued with that with *Under*, and we didn't Photoshop away that little bush in front of Nocturno Culto there. And then finally it was time for one of the shots of me. And this was a photo session that was done, I guess, in '92, so now it was time to find a photo from that photo session; but I had lost the original photo, like from when you deliver the film, and then you get back the print and the negative, and I couldn't find this either. But what I had done in '92, I had photocopied a lot of the photos, so I could send [them] around to magazines and stuff, because we didn't work on that, this was beyond DIY. So there were photocopies, and that is all that was left. So I said, "I got to search longer, I can't just send a photocopy to England and imagine that they'll go with that for the cover." So I searched and searched—nothing. Well, then I just sent the photocopy, like have the logo up in the corner please, and put *Transilvanian Hunger* on there—boom, it's your cover. I don't remember if they thought it was strange or if they tried to protest or anything. I think, again, they sort of knew that everything was blown to hell over there in Norway. They just said, "Yeah, whatever."

So, no, that was it, and it wasn't a normal thing to do, I know. It was just a photocopy. No one would think that it would work or anything. Today, when I send photos to magazines and stuff, they're all like, "Oh, we need it better, we can't use this seriously, it's too bad," but they don't know the whole icon, which is from a photocopy of a paper copy. So that always freaks me out a little bit.

People often describe **A Blaze in the Northern Sky, Under a Funeral Moon** *and* **Transilvanian Hunger** *as the "black metal trilogy." Do you view those albums as linked in any way beyond the fact that they were all released one after another?*

Fenriz: No, it's just because human beings as a species are really visually led. Like, you could put Anthrax and Celine Dion in a box with the same type of album cover, and they'd go, "Yeah, this is a natural progression, sure; I can see how these are linked," 'cause the cover is clearly almost identical. No, the thing is the three album covers are black-and-white photos, and that's why it's viewed as a trilogy. If the *Panzerfaust* album also had that kind of cover—like the black and white instead of black and gray—then they would have to say it's a "four-ology"! It's so easy to think of it as a trilogy instead of this four thing, so everyone's going, "Oh yeah, that's a trilogy." But the thing is, those albums are really far between, the productions are very different, the music is very, very different on these albums. Ted's vocals are [mostly] the same, but that's always, that's the only thing that ties them together. Also that they were number two and three and four in our chain of albums, but there's nothing else combining these albums. Different lineups, different studios—not the first two—but different engineers and sound. And the thing with the first one, *A Blaze in the Northern Sky*, in this so-called trilogy, is a mixture of death metal and black metal; and number two of the so-called trilogy, *Under a Funeral Moon*, is basically pure black metal of the '80s style; and then I did the *Transilvanian Hunger*—part three—which was just me, so there again, it has really nothing to do with the vibe of the two other albums. I see it as a very, very different album. Actually, there are so few things that combine them and so many things that divide them.

Nocturno Culto: Yes, I do, actually. When it comes to being a musician and being in a band, I don't think those three albums connected to each other in any way, really, but they're connected in the sense of that time period. I would say there was definitely a new era after *Transilvanian Hunger*, and we never looked back. To me, [there were] very, very fruitful years between *A Blaze in the Northern Sky* and *Transilvanian Hunger*, because lots of things did happen, lots of things in my life changed. Also, it was totally Darkthrone on the darkest day, but that was a really important time also, because I think since Fenriz and me obviously are the only two left in the band since '93, I think those years are without the rehearsals, especially *A Blaze in the Northern Sky* and *Under a Funeral Moon*; of course, [that] did get a solid platform for us to stand on in the future as well. Musically, everything worked perfectly. We never really after that encountered any problems playing together, because when you're the only two left, you have to rely on probably experiences from the past, and there's less argument when you're the only two in the band, and you don't have to stand in line to record.

Do you view it as a special time period for the entire Norwegian scene as well?

Nocturno Culto: Yeah, I would say so, because you have to remember that people also like to call it the second wave of black metal, which pretty much started off—and we were kind of early on in there—with *A Blaze in the Northern Sky*. It really did cause a stir. All kinds of reactions came. It was a time where things were actually misanthropic and dark. The bands that did do stuff then had a lot of attitude, and even though we never did see any of them as competitors, it was cool. It was a great time, actually, because metal bands did have a lot of attitude back then. There were, of course, a lot less bands back then as well, but it was a great time. It's a different time today. I don't know. People are just literally killing everything they have just to have some news headlines. There's a lot of things going on today that are not misanthropic, to say the least. I mean, I'm kind of living a misanthropic life, even though we realize that everything today is more difficult—especially when it comes to spreading your music around in a sea of bands. So we have to do more stuff—do interviews maybe, do some fielding and do exclusive stuff and everything.

In the **Decibel** *cover story, you state that 1994 was "a horrible year for black metal." To your credit, nothing else in the black metal scene that year sounded anything like the* **Transilvanian Hunger** *record.*

Fenriz: Well, there were other bands on the brink of doing this, probably. I can see that if I didn't make an album that was so hypnotic, other people would, but then again the other bands were more like bands, and I was alone at that time with that album. But I've always said that everyone in the Norwegian scene of '90, '91, '92, '93, '94—everyone was doing those kinds of riffs. Gorgoroth was also doing them, Enslaved was doing them. Emperor was doing them. Immortal was doing them. And I was making some sort of riffs like Mayhem and Burzum and those guys. All of us were listening to the same bands of the '80s. Of course, this was the early '90s—there were no other bands to listen to. There was Master's Hammer. Master's Hammer was the first Norwegian black metal album, but they were from Czechoslovakia, and we all listened to

Master's Hammer a lot, the *Ritual* album. So I don't think there is much originality about the riffs on *Transilvanian Hunger* at all. The whole originality of it is the production, the die-hard monotony of it, the whole execution, the thing that it was an icon was that it was structured that way; it's the structure and the sound, and, I mean, I'm the executive chief on the album, so I had to make all those choices, but to me they weren't like choices at all. It was made, it had to be that way—there was no other choice. I realized I had made an album that was entirely in one tempo.

But I didn't know, I thought maybe more of it like, "OK, I got the inspiration, so I did the album. I am proud of it, but I am keeping Darkthrone afloat with this album." I was even considering, when I had done the first Neptune Towers album, to release that as a Darkthrone album, just to keep Darkthrone afloat as well, or just to confuse people, because I had started to detect in '94 that it was turning into a trend, and that was the thing that was [most] horrible about '94—it was the trend. You'd see people from other countries really tuning into what we were doing and trying to do it, but misunderstanding it. And making it with better sound, more synthesizers. Where before, the riff—and you would sort of hear the riff so many times that you would sort of make the synthesizer sound in your head, but then the other people from other places would take that tone that you would get in your head while listening to a riff long enough—they would put a synthesizer on top, and I was sort of like, "That wasn't really the intention." And then the whole sad thing about it became inflated, too. There's a sadness in it; I don't think *Transilvanian Hunger* is very extreme, but there's a lot of emotion there, and there's also a sadness, and that's why the whole thing started to go a little bit haywire, because there was suddenly an emphasis on the sadness; and that's why Gezol [of Sabbat/Metalucifer fame] from Japan started saying [in faux Japanese accent], "What is happening to black metal? It's too much black and not enough metal!" and this is what I am currently . . . I'm paying my debts. Every time I make a new song, I'm paying the debts, man. Because I had to do *Transilvanian Hunger*, but realized I was veering into the "too much black and not enough metal." Although, on the third song—I think it's called "Skald Av Satans Sol"—that was a song with a very metal riff, which is what Merciless would play. Merciless from Sweden had an album called *The Awakening*, and this was the first album that Euronymous released. And the first album that we released on the label Tyrant Syndicate was also a black-thrash album, but when we released a black-thrash album, we [got] a whole lot of people going, "Why aren't you releasing standard '90s black metal?" But do you think Euronymous got the same reaction when he released Merciless? Of course not. This again proves that the scene now is completely horrible compared to when we grew up, because we didn't have this attitude from people that were locked in a trend. The last time I visited Euronymous, what were the bands he was about to release? No, it wasn't Gorgoroth; it was Sigh, and it was Mysticum, which are both really not trendy bands. We were never locked in a trend, and that's why it was so horrible for us to see it all become a trend, and that really kicked in in '94 and '95, and the last part of the '90s were horrible for absolutely every metal style on the planet. We'd been through seeing thrash metal die, and then we saw death metal, which was once a part of thrash metal but branched out. Death metal would be [at] first really great, and then would start to become [a] trend, too. And then death metal just crumbled before our eyes; I think I maybe had five death metal albums from 1990. It was just not something we listened to in 1990. We had been stuffing our heads with death metal in '88 and '89, so it was time to take the old Sodom and Destruction albums again in 1990, and then we started to listen to more *Motörhead* and Venom, too, of course—also *always* Bathory and Celtic Frost, and Hellhammer as well. But those two were always the most important bands for us: Bathory and Celtic Frost. Nowadays, there's not a lot of Bathory left in us; it's a lot of Celtic Frost and Hellhammer, though. We sort of changed Bathory with *Motörhead*—the spirit of Quorthon lives on through us as we continuously refuse to play live.

How do you think Transilvanian Hunger *holds up today?*

Nocturno Culto: Well, it's for those who are really fucked up, 'cause there's not really any entertainment there. And if you are going to like that album today, you either would have heard it many years ago, or you are a complete misanthrope for liking this stuff. Because it does not have anything to do with "modern sound." It's monotone. It's very misanthropic. It's dark, and it's an album that's not easy to get into, especially for kids today that are used to *that* sound and a lot of things just going on, and "Oh, did you hear that? That was really cool." It's not like that, so it's for people that are especially interested in that kind of far-out, distant kind of riffing. And even though I know a lot of people have a hang-on to the *Transilvanian Hunger* stuff, I like to think that it's—well, not to be harsh, but nowadays I think it's like . . . I think it's a good album, by all means, but you know, it's more like emo-goth kid stuff. So, that album is actually the reason there's emo kids. Just kidding!

Fenriz: Now something finally popped into my mind, like, why so many bands copy that exact album. I'm thinking maybe because it's damn easy. My mother could play that. She couldn't create it, but she could sure play it. I've been a fan of many hundreds of thousands of acts throughout the years, and I never really felt like I would copy one of them and send them a tape and say, "What do you think?" That's not me. I said earlier that I don't wanna bother people, but it seems like other people are not like me; they are perfectly willing to make me listen to themselves copying me! They sort of think that that's the thing I need to hear most in the entire world. It's like, no, I made that, I don't sit around and listen to that all the time. I prefer to listen to Burzum. I don't know, that just makes me sort of lose the faith in humanity—not that I had much from the get-go! But it's really horrible, man.

To make something that sticks out like that—well, I'm sure not everyone can do that. Usually it's a coincidence that leads to someone making a punk album that stands out or something like that, because it's really difficult, right? But there's a time and place for everything. And suddenly I was thinking I was doing what everyone else was doing when I made *Transilvanian Hunger*, but it turns out now it's really distinct; but as I told you, that really hurts when people copy it, because then I find it truly loathsome. I'm really much more comfortable with playing a varied style like we did on *Blaze* or *Funeral Moon* or later albums, 'cause then [if] you'd have people copy those albums, at least they will be playing three, four or five metal styles instead of just that one type of album! It's so limited, what can I say? It hurts. It hurts my ears. I mean, it doesn't hurt. It's cool that someone's listening to what I was making—it was two weeks of my life, man.

I couldn't have made that two weeks without having gone through my musical life up to that point, or the life in the scene and the creation of—or the continuation of—the '80s black metal, but it's still just two weeks of my life . . . that is haunting me on a daily basis, mind you. I discovered MySpace through a coincidence two years and three months ago, so I quickly started surfing around, and discovered how easy it was to find new crust bands I never heard about. I'd find one crust band and then, suddenly, on their "top friends," there were 12 others, and I'd heard about six of them, and then: "Yes, this is great!" But earlier this year I was thinking, I was asking my girlfriend, maybe I should check into our MySpace page, maybe see what people left—messages and stuff. And then I sort of figured that it was really easy to answer a lot of people on a daily [basis], but [the] result is that I got more and more bands that had played for a couple of months and they choose *Transilvanian Hunger* style. It's just more of what I was bored of already in '95 and '96. I was bored then and now. Twelve years after that, I still get it on a daily basis.

CHAPTER 15

1993: A DESERT ODYSSEY

THE MAKING OF KYUSS' *WELCOME TO SKY VALLEY*

by J. Bennett

Release Date: 1994
Label: Elektra
Summary: Sorta s/t stoner smash
Induction Date: November 2008/Issue #49

olling from Los Angeles into the parched sandbox of the Mojave, anyone familiar with *Welcome to Sky Valley* will see almost all the relevant
landmarks along the 10 East freeway. The rows of windmills with 20-
foot blades, the same ones that dominate the inside and back cover of the album;
the sign that lets you know you're about to hit White Water, the unincorporated
territory with which *Sky Valley*'s final (listed) track shares its name. For Kyuss
die-hards, it's like entering hallowed ground. For guitarist Josh Homme, vocalist John Garcia, drummer Brant Bjork and bassist Scott Reeder, it's the physical and psychological precipice of the proverbial High White Note, the

humming lifeforce of a hundred ultimate riffs and mountainous power grooves. For still others—legions of weedians, longhairs and music critics, it's the birthplace of "stoner rock." And *Sky Valley* is the album that perfected the then-nonexistent form. (Full disclosure: It's possibly my favorite album of all time.) Recorded in early 1993 at Sound City Studios in Van Nuys—after Elektra Records swept in and bought the band's original label, Dali/Chameleon—it wouldn't be released until over a year later. Foreshadowing what would happen in Queens of the Stone Age over a decade later, Homme and the band had recently kicked perpetually wrecked bassist Nick Oliveri to the curb and poached Reeder from the Obsessed. (Homme and Bjork had grown up watching the insanely talented southpaw play in desert rock progenitors Across the River.) *Sky Valley* also marked the departure of Bjork, who split the band immediately after recording his drum tracks. What he left behind is one of the most deserving Hall of Fame legacies in the history of forever.

How did Scott Reeder end up joining Kyuss?

John Garcia: When we were touring the West Coast with the Obsessed, Nick wound up riding in the Obsessed's van and Scott rode with us. I remember one day Josh was driving, I was sitting in the middle and Scott was sitting in the passenger seat. We had had it up to here with Nick at that point already—he was just getting wasted all the time and being Nick. We had already decided, you know? So Josh, without even consulting anyone, pretty much asked Scott right then if he wanted to join. He dropped a huge hint, anyway. And I didn't care, because I knew that Scott was badass. He's just as sick as Nick, but in a different style. As soon as Josh said it, I was thinking, "All right, I'm in." Brant and Scott were already friends because Brant was a big fan of Across the River. When we were growing up, Across the River was the only band around that was badass.

Brant Bjork: For me, it was kind of a no-brainer that the only person who could fill Nick's shoes would be another desert legend, so to speak. We all grew up knowing Scott Reeder as the bare-footed beast. Had Scott not been there, who knows what would have happened?

Scott Reeder: With the Obsessed, things were great in one sense—Columbia was getting ready to sign us. But Wino was on his way down. When Kyuss asked me to join the first time, it was about five or six months before they kicked Nick out. I politely declined and stayed with the Obsessed. But when they fired Nick, Josh asked me to fill in for a couple of shows. I dug Kyuss—we'd toured together, and I liked those guys, so I was like, "Sure, I'll do it." The first show I did was the record release party for *Blues for the Red Sun*. After that we did a thing with Body Count. [*Laughs*] That was weird. Kyuss hadn't really done much at that point, so I felt like it was taking a step backwards because the Obsessed had been to Europe a couple of times and things were going really good. But musically, it seemed like life was gonna be better for me back home in the desert. So I left the Obsessed. It just felt right.

What's the first thing that comes to mind when you think of **Sky Valley** *and the period leading up to it?*

Josh Homme: I think of two worlds happening, and that somehow symbolized the end of the three musketeers attitude I had when I was a kid, because music was always like a religion for Kyuss. We rehearsed every day, but it wasn't so much a rehearsal as a chant or a mantra. By the end of the band, we were rehearsing for six hours, six days a week and it got to the point where we had all these possibilities of where we could go. We could play each of the songs about four or five different ways. And it was unspoken, all based on cues, like a pitcher and a catcher. So when I think of *Sky Valley*, on one side it's our moment of triumph. The way we sounded live was exactly how we sounded on that record. But I also think of feeling, like, how could it be so misunderstood within our own band? Because Brant left.

Bjork: Probably conflict. I was already aware of the fact that the band was devolving in a way that I couldn't do anything about—on all levels. I used to be bitter about it, like anyone would be in that situation, but as I get older I start to understand that it was a natural de-evolution, a natural situation, when you've got different personal and artistic backgrounds, different experiences or lack of experience, different agendas or hang-ups. Kyuss was kind of a miracle to begin with. It was a miracle that we even left the desert, so suddenly being involved in big rock business was a lot to digest.

Garcia: We had a pretty tight rehearsal schedule. That was all we did. We practiced four or five times a week leading up to that album. We generally rehearsed in someone's garage—Josh's parents' garage, my parents' garage. So I remember constantly rehearsing—especially "Demon Cleaner." That song was really hard to get together for some reason. Even in the studio, at Sound City, I spent 14 hours in the booth singing that song because it was so hard to sing. Josh was so meticulous. He's very intelligent—one of the most intelligent guys I've met in my entire life. And he's a great songwriter. I loved all of his ideas, vocal-wise, lyric-wise—but leading up to that, there was a lot of rehearsal, because he was a perfectionist. I was, too, you know, because when you play in a band you don't wanna suck.

Reeder: After I officially joined, the first thing we did was a crappy tour through sports bars and pizza parlors all over America. When we got home, we got a call asking if we wanted to tour with Glenn Danzig and White Zombie. Once that tour happened and we had an agency and things started rolling, we got a Faith No More tour right after that. When that ended, we got a call asking if we wanted to go to Australia with Metallica in a week. Nobody had passports, but we somehow got them in time, got our laundry done and caught a plane to Australia. That was when we stopped using set lists onstage, too. Not to talk badly about anyone on that tour, but when you have explosions and stuff going on during your show, it's pretty important that you have the same set list every night. So I think not having a set list was a rebellion against that. We wouldn't discuss it beforehand, either. We'd be in the middle of the stage, huddling in front of 16,000 people going, "What do you want to play?" When we got home from Australia, we pretty much went right into the studio to record *Sky Valley*.

How did Scott's presence affect the band?

Homme: We were getting so much better just from playing with Scott. I remember thinking, "Holy shit—this guy shreds me. I better play more." He was doing things that I didn't yet understand were available. Scott is one of the best bass players in the world, hands down. And he's also extremely musical—we never really reached the ceiling of his ability. He was older and had more experience, but he's not the type of guy who would ever shove that up your ass. There's always been a real mutual respect there. In all honesty, I've never been a huge fan of what he wrote, of the marble he would bring in to carve, but for someone carving marble that someone else brought in, there's almost no one better.

Why did Brant eventually decide to leave?

Bjork: Josh and I were the creative force of Kyuss. We had a very deep understanding of the need for each other in getting the band to exist musically. At the time of *Sky Valley*, I was smoking a lot of pot. I was young, probably about 18 or 19, and I certainly had a lot of artistic vision for Kyuss. I exercised that with *Blues for the Red Sun*, but when it came time for *Sky Valley*, there was a conflict in direction between Josh and I. That had never really happened before, and I didn't know how to handle it. And I was too exhausted to put up a fight. But musically, *Sky Valley* was more focused, and with the exception of the opening track and the closing track and maybe a couple pieces within, it's primarily Josh writing and arranging and really starting to exercise his power within the band at the time. He made great music—he's talented and he writes great songs—but it wasn't exactly where I was looking to go.

Homme: It was a complex situation, because it had always been Brant and I writing everything, but I wanted to allow Scott and John to write with us. And now Brant was saying that he was thinking about doing something else. I was saying to him, "Well, what do you want to do? We can go in that direction." Because from age eight until then, Brant and I were like that [*crosses fingers*]. So it was the first time that I sorta felt shut out by someone close to me, where I was like, "Explain it to me. We can sit down and figure it out." It wasn't that we weren't getting along—it was that he had this thing that was his that he wasn't sharing or explaining. But to me, being the masters of our own musical destiny, we could go in whatever direction we wanted, and I was open to whatever. And to be honest, one of the reasons Brant told me he wanted to leave was that he didn't like Scott as a person. He said, "I can't stand Scott and his wife." And I didn't know what to do about that. But it was true—when Brant and I were around each other and Scott would come in, Brant would bail. And I knew there were other things going on inside him that he wasn't sharing. But he wasn't willing to. Making money didn't matter, so it never came up, really. But not talking about it also became a problem—I mean, that's how secrets get their power. And I think that's where secrets were starting to take over. We'd always been a unit, like us against the world, and now one of our people was against the world alone and we were on the outside all of a sudden. So when Brant confided in me that he didn't know where we were headed, but didn't know where he wanted to go either, I didn't know what to say.

Bjork: Josh and I had been jamming together since we were 12, so it was known, even when Nick was in the band, that it was the Josh and Brant show. Musically speaking, it never broke down. Josh and I have a very interesting relationship to this day because he and I hold the keys to each other's musical hearts, which is an interesting position to be in. So the music always prevailed. The hang-ups were always more political, more personality shit. And that had been going on for a while—that wasn't something new when *Sky Valley* came along. But by then it got to the point that I was exhausted with it. I was bummed for a long time that I probably wasn't going to be involved making music at that level—certainly not behind the drums—ever again. All due respect to Fu Manchu—I just don't want to play drums.

Garcia: Nobody really knows what it was like to have Josh and Brant in the same room together. When they were together and their relationship was tits, holy shit—talk about magic. It was like, "How the fuck do you guys do this shit?" I remember thinking about how lucky I was to be in a band with those two guys. I was completely blown away by them. Even when we were really young, back in the Katzenjammer days, when it was me, Chris Cockrell, Josh and Brant—they were fuckin' animals, man. It was badass. They were each other's conduits. Looking back, I think nobody really knows what those two guys were capable of together. They were un-fucking-believable.

Bjork: Josh and I just had that thing, man. I knew it the first day we jammed, and I'll never forget it. Two guys growing up, same small town, opposite sides of the tracks, he had a guitar and I had drums. It was the process of elimination, you know? There wasn't any other dude. [*Laughs*] It's fairy tale shit, man. But we just couldn't get it together on a personal level. We came from such different backgrounds that it was hard. When you get older, you can create art with people and put things into perspective, and you have more room for other people's personalities. But when you're at the age we were at, I didn't understand that. When you've got a dude you can rock with, but you can't understand him on a personal level, that's a trippy thing.

Homme: During *Sky Valley*, I wasn't living in the desert full-time. I moved to Orange County for about half a year. I was living there with some friends—they were going to school and I was playing guitar. I was experiencing all sorts of things there, too. I was setting up lights and sound systems for raves—back when raves were just ecstasy, loud music, girls and water. So I was experiencing all this other stuff I'd never seen. In a way, I think I was looking for punk rock without all the political screaming or guilt. The punk rock guilt thing of "Do well, but don't do *too* well" was so permeated through Kyuss. We had made a commitment to originality and being different, and in my opinion, we almost took it too far. Instead of a mantra and something to pay attention to, it became something that was almost enforced. If we had a song that was kinda catchy, we had to make sure to pervert it. By *Sky Valley*, there were certain rules. And I didn't think we should have rules.

What were the sessions themselves like?

Garcia: We went back to Sound City in Van Nuys to record with Chris Goss and Joe Barresi. Fleetwood Mac did *Rumors* there; Nirvana did *Nevermind* there—everybody and their mother recorded there. The Neve boards they have in those rooms are unbelievable. No Pro Tools back then, just splicing two-inch tape. When I saw fuckin' Joe Barresi pull out a razor blade and make some of those edits, I swear to god I had no more nails left on my fingers. It was like, "How the fuck did you make that cut?" It was awesome.

Reeder: I remember I always had my jug of this really cheap burgundy wine and a little can of EZ-Cheez sitting near my amp. We were like kids in a candy shop—it was so fun. I'd been in a studio before, but the vibe for *Sky Valley* was just so awesome. We had oil wheels on the wall, incense, candles all over the place, just getting baked and going for it. We were giddy as fuck. It felt so good, and it all went pretty fast. I've worked on records that take months and months, and it's like beating your head against a wall. But we blew *Sky Valley* out so fast—recorded and mixed in under three weeks. That sounds like a long time to me now, but for a major label record, that's pretty incredible.

Homme: The sessions were amazing. I think it took something like 23 days to do the record. The rehearsals we'd done beforehand at my parents' house were great because I was bringing in stuff like "Odyssey" and Scott was bringing in the most monumental bass lines ever. Brant had changed the tempo to a faster tempo, so it really felt like—to use that song as an example—yeah, I brought in "Odyssey," but they also changed the face of what it was. So we were writing and working together in a way that was better than it had ever been prior.

Bjork: We were in the same room we had done *Blues* in, but there was frustration because things weren't moving like they did with *Blues*. *Blues* was very natural. With *Sky Valley*, I remember thinking, "It ain't moving because you're choking it." The only songs we had done when we went into the studio for *Sky Valley* were "Gardenia," "Whitewater," "100°" and "Odyssey." So there were two of mine and two of Josh's, so there was a good balance of creative input. But the rest was written on the spot, pretty much, and Josh was just like, "All right, this is gonna be the rest of the record. Let's go." And I was like, "Whoa, man—I've got stuff, too. Let's work this out. Let's make the best record *we* can make." But it was clear—I'd already seen the disintegration out on the road with other members. It was turning into a power struggle and I just didn't wanna be involved. I'd rather go home and rock out in the garage.

Reeder: Things were pretty loose going into the studio. It was actually kinda scary. We got to the jam part on "Whitewater" and we really didn't know what was gonna happen. "Odyssey" was the same way—the studio version was actually a total accident. We'd been rehearsing it a different way, but someone spaced out for a second, Brant kept going and that was that. Sometimes the best things are accidents, though. One thing about Brant that was awesome was that he made it so obvious when it was time to go to the next thing. He'd throw in some fill that was really easy for dumb, drunk, stoned guys to pick up on, like, "Oh, OK." He was an awesome fucking drummer.

Homme: Kyuss always recorded everything live. Vocals were overdubbed only if John didn't get it in the take, but the rest of us did. Goss and Joe Barresi had to talk us into punching in for little corrections, because we were against that. That was one of the rules. It's like, "No way—that's fucking cheating." Even though no one would know, it didn't matter, because *we* would know.

Bjork: When I did my drum tracks, there was so much anger. I was pissed, because I knew it was the last thing I'd do with the band. I dropped my tracks, shaved my head and we went out and played our last show with me in the band out in the middle of the desert. I moved up to Humboldt for a year, and Josh sent me a copy when it came out. I couldn't even listen to the record for a while because it was so painful. It was probably a year before I heard it.

Homme: The show where he shaved his head was before we recorded *Sky Valley*. In a lot of ways, I only made one more Kyuss record because of how Brant left. He did his tracks and said, "I gotta go to the desert and see the dentist." That was the last time I saw him [for] two years.

Reeder: I didn't realize there was any intent for Brant to leave, but as soon as his tracks were done, he was gone. He was the main reason I joined the band. I loved his drumming, and I think the other guys felt bad because I had burned my bridges with something that was pretty cool. So I think everybody kinda kept it hidden from me, because I was blindsided. That was a huge blow. We got Pete Moffett from Government Issue to play drums on "Asteroid." That one hadn't been recorded yet.

The lyrics aren't printed anywhere in the booklet. What were they about?

Bjork: There were a lot of inside jokes. Josh is a funny dude, man. That's what a lot of people don't realize about him. He's fuckin' hilarious. I always thought he'd be a comedian, like Will Ferrell or something. But I always wrote the lyrics for the songs I wrote musically, which on *Sky Valley* were "Gardenia" and "Whitewater." Josh wrote the rest. "Gardenia" is just named after my favorite flower. A lot of times I'd give songs titles that had nothing to do with the lyrics. We were driving home from the studio with Chris Goss one night and we had just gotten the basic track and I needed to write lyrics for a scratch vocal. I saw some old bikers at a stoplight next to our car. Like *real* bikers, one-percenter dudes. I don't know what club they were, but this was before the helmet law. Seeing them inspired me to write a "forever stoned on the road" kind of thing, a total Motörhead vibe: Live for nothing, but "riding fast away from it all" kind of vibe. "Whitewater" came from missing the desert whenever we toured, so that's just a song about home.

Homme: I like the lyrics for "Space Cadet" because they were kind of listless, but at the same time the most confessional on the whole record. They were written by all of us, with the understanding of what we were headed towards. Overall, I felt like there was starting to be good lyrics on *Sky Valley*. Not all of 'em, though. I don't want to harp on Brant, but the lyrics to "Gardenia" weren't my favorite because singing about cars and shit never really made sense to me. "Cro mags / a million drags / it never lags" . . . I don't know, I wanted to do things that were more inward turning. Because, really, to have a great lyric, you have be vulnerable. You have to say it and let it fall wherever it's supposed to fall. That's why I like the "Demon Cleaner" lyrics—the song is cryptic, but at the same time, it's admitting everything.

Garcia: Nobody knows that "Demon Cleaner" is about brushing your teeth. I didn't write that song; Josh wrote it, and it meant something totally different to me. But when it goes, "You get the back ones . . ." he's talking about brushing your teeth.

Homme: I have a tooth obsession. I've had everything done to my teeth that you could have done. I used to dream about teeth all the time—I've had nightmares about them since I was a kid, like horrible night-terrors. I even went to the doctor about it, and that's why I hate going to sleep even to this day. I still always have nightmares. So I'd have this recurring dream where I'm getting my teeth pulled out and then I'd flash forward and I'd be in a giant mouth with these teeth bleeding everywhere. And I'd be cleaning these giant teeth while the blood was coming down and I'd be drowning in a sea of toothbrush foam and blood. So "Demon Cleaner" was this metaphor for, you know, you gotta keep yourself clean, you gotta keep yourself tight.

What about "Conan Troutman"?

Homme: Movies and books have always been as much if not more of an influence for me than music, because the idea of Kyuss was to not let yourself be influenced by any music. That's why I never listened to Black Sabbath. People said we sounded like Black Sabbath and I was like, "Fuck you—I never heard 'em." And it seemed important to not listen to them in order to maintain that wall, so movies and books ended up being more influential. I watched *Conan the Barbarian* and also the first *Rambo* movie, you know, *First Blood*? There was that character Colonel Troutman, played by Richard Crenna—he overacted more than William Shatner. But both of those movies were badass in a weird way and the song needed a title. It has nothing to do with the lyrics—the lyrics were about taking things to get somewhere else, which is the subject of many, many songs by many, many bands. It's like trying to find the perfect potion to get lost. I've always had what may be a bizarre fascination with the retarded in that they're always happy. I used to sometimes eat lunch with them at school, and it was awesome because they could get away with things that if I did, I would get in big trouble. But the worst they got was a slap on the wrist. So I started thinking that maybe that was why people drink or get high—to be retarded. In the hopes that they won't get called out on it, either—that they'll just get a slap on the wrist. So there are a lot of songs about the attempt to get retarded, to find the right elixir that takes you to the right retarded place. [*Laughs*] That's gonna read really interesting.

"Supa Scoopa and Mighty Scoop"?

Homme: That song was actually about Brant. But moreover, it was about anyone who thinks someone else can't live without them. It's also one of my favorite riffs on the record. It felt so good to play live—it felt like you were killing somebody. And the bass line was so fucking sick. Watching Scott play it, I'd wanna high-five him if I had a free hand. We've played that song with Queens before. The way the song ends, you know, that's actually the kind of thing I'd do in Queens now.

"Odyssey"?

Homme: I wrote that on my first ecstasy trip. I was walking through the back alleys of Irvine—really glamorous—for hours, not knowing where I was, but being totally stoked, and then ending up being chased by the police. There were three of us, and we tried to walk into a garage party, but it was a bunch of people who all knew each other, and they were like, "Who the fuck are you?" And we were so fucked up, we were throwing stuff around in an alley, and I guess someone called the cops. So it was about that journey, that odyssey, and finally making it after walking about 10 miles to my place. But then Brant and Scott altered it forever by making it better. And when that happens, you don't get in the way.

I'm guessing "100°" was literal.

Homme: Yeah, "100°" was very literal, like, it's so fucked up to be out here in the desert. I'll do anything to get out of here. But how do you escape the inescapable? You can't go anywhere.

"N.O." was an Across the River song. You even brought Mario Lalli [from Across the River and Fatso Jetson] in to play the solo. Whose idea was that?

Reeder: I think that was Brant's idea. I guess Brant and Josh were into Across the River back in the day, but they would've been pretty young. I think they were at the gig that was on my 21st birthday in the Palm Desert with Saint Vitus and D.R.I.—May 16, 1986. They had to be around 12 or 13 at the time, because they're about eight years younger than I am. Actually, come to think of it, Josh turned 13 the very next day. We always had our birthdays back-to-back. When I joined Kyuss, we'd pop into Denny's just before midnight and get the free birthday meal. You gotta do what you gotta do on the road.

Bjork: Because Kyuss got signed and left the desert, people think they're the premier desert rock band, but in actuality, the band that probably deserves that title was Across the River. They influenced me a lot, and I definitely brought that to Kyuss. They were insane, but they never recorded anything, you know? That was another thing about the desert—no one recorded, there was no real focus or ambition. Across the River got close—they were talking to SST for a while. When punk and metal crossed over, you got bands like Slayer and COC and DRI and Metallica, but Across the River went straight to Sabbath and Mountain and Blue

Cheer. Saint Vitus was the only other band even doing anything close, and they played a lot of shows with Across the River. In fact, Wino's first show with Vitus was in Palm Desert with Across the River. And Kyuss was on the next level of the path that Across the River had already burned.

Homme: Every musician from the desert reveres Mario. He's one of the few guys I've ever ripped. I've taken one Hendrix thing that no one ever seems to notice, a Billy Gibbons thing and a couple things from Mario. He was always so original. Every single band Mario has ever been in is about two and half years ahead of its time. Across the River is a great example—they broke up, and two and half years later? Grunge. I got the whole idea of "Be original or be gone" from Mario. And it's not that he was so militant about that attitude—he just *was*, and that was it. To him it was like there was no question that he would be original. So it was total dumb luck that Brant and I—speaking for him—got the start that we got. We both kind of got into the same thing separately and came together over that common interest. Because we were standing next to each other, we witnessed a lot of the same things together, and we both had the same direction at the exact same age.

Reeder: At one point, I think Brant actually wanted to call the record *Across the River*, but I would've been kind of uncomfortable with that. I wanted to call it *Pools of Mercury*, and that was the working title for a while. We actually had a couple of mock-ups done of artwork with pits of mercury shining. Years later, a live bootleg [from a 1995 show in Texas] turned up called *Mercurious Pools*. But *Sky Valley* is officially self-titled. That's what it says on the spine. The words "Welcome to Sky Valley" just appear on the sign on the cover.

What's the story behind "Lick Doo," the hidden song at the end of the album?

Homme: That little thing is a perfect example of what we learned in between *Blues* and *Sky Valley*. We used to have some songs that were almost like jokes. We played that way because when words failed to express something, music always worked—especially when we started playing in L.A. in the early days. We had stuff like "Thong Song" or "Writhe," where we were singing about something that was almost ridiculous. And in truth, songs like that were a total joke. But then you realize that it wasn't working—the joke is on you, actually, because people are taking it seriously and you're actually attracting the kind of person that you're trying to repel. Kyuss was trying to hand-pick its audience and going, like, "It's OK that there's 10 people here. We'll take our time." And if there were 10 people there, it really didn't matter. It was full-on the same thing no matter how many people showed up. So, *Sky Valley* was learning not to pay for "Thong Song" by putting "Lick Doo" at the end. It was an important lesson, too.

Bjork: I thought that was gay. I would've never put up with that shit, but I had already left at that point. That's all Josh and Chris Goss, man. They have their little trippy sense of humor thing going on that I never really got into. You know, Josh and I did a little acoustic thing that they omitted from the record that I was really bummed about. For me, it was kinda like my goodbye to the band. It was this rad acoustic thing that had kind of an Allman Brothers vibe. It probably had no business being in the batch of the songs, but we did it anyways. I played the guitar and Josh played a lead over it. We called it "Juan's Day Off" and it was just kind of an ode to John, because he liked to fish and stuff. But they didn't use it, and instead they put that goofball fuckin' song at the tail end of the record. I thought that was just kinda weak and lame.

How did suddenly being on Elektra affect the band?

Homme: We were 19 years old and none of us were happy about being on a major label. The only thing we knew for sure was that there was no way off. We signed a contract with Chameleon for six records when I was like a week out of high school. All I knew is we got money to make six records from this label that had John Lee Hooker, Ethyl Meatplow and Dramarama. I mean, we walked into the President's office the day we signed and he had all these squirt guns around, so we picked 'em up and started shooting them. We were kids. And the President of the label was like this billionaire's son who was a kid, too. We'd go into the office, they'd buy us booze and we'd hang out all day. So we signed to that idea. But then Chameleon got crushed by Elektra and Elektra just took us, basically. All of a sudden we're on Elektra and it's like, "How do we get out of this?" We were told we couldn't, unless they dropped us.

Bjork: We didn't know what it meant to be employed by a record label, like, "OK, guys—go write some songs." That's not how we worked. Kyuss was an extremely organic band, and not to toot my fuckin' French horn—I'm not saying I was more important to the band than anyone else—but I just felt that I had become consciously aware of us being an organic band. That's what made us special. The more we tampered with the way things naturally evolved, the more we would be at risk for ruining what was special about it. That's just the pressures of working for the man, and everyone reacts differently to that. I wasn't even gonna do the record at first; I was over it. I told Josh I wasn't down with the scene. I was brokenhearted, but I didn't wanna go down with the ship. I felt the spirit was gone. I was upset because I knew we were just inexperienced enough not to know how to protect what we had. It's tough when you're a kid and you're touring with Metallica and you've got bigwigs telling you you're gonna be the next big thing. But those weren't goals of mine, man. I was interested in being what we were, which was a good band.

Reeder: Those guys were so young—they were probably 18 or 19 when I joined the band. I'd been around the block a couple of times and realized that they had it together pretty fucking good. But it was kinda confusing, because they were doing this thing as a hobby—they had no intentions of becoming rock stars—and all of a sudden they've got a record label telling them where they're gonna be, how long they're gonna be there and sucking them into this life that I don't think anyone was asking for.

Who came up with the idea to arrange the album into three movements?

Garcia: Josh had that all planned beforehand. I remember him talking to me about it before we went into the studio. I thought it was a little weird at the time, but Kyuss wasn't about rules, you know?

Reeder: I think it was right after *Nevermind* came out, and there was that hidden bonus track. We thought, "What could we do to fuck things up?" At first, we thought of having no track indexes at all, but that was a little too severe. We actually spent more time sequencing than we did recording or mixing. We put together these mix tapes and tried so many different combinations. It ended up that three movements seemed like the right thing to do. It really flows the way it was put together. I had a copy that the European branch of Elektra made for radio, I guess, with each track indexed. I let some film director borrow it, and he lost it. To him it was no big deal: "Oh, you've got another one, right?" And I'm like, "Uh, no—not exactly." Fucker.

Homme: When Elektra took over our contract, they asked for three singles. [*Laughs*] I remember seeing their faces when we handed those three parts in. It stemmed around fucking with them initially, but there's also an instruction on the record that says, "Listen without distraction." I mean, there was radio and all this stuff going on, but we're not that, so it was like, "Since you're already over here, here's our recommendation." So the three movements ended up having nothing to do with them. That was just a collateral benefit. Initially, the label sent a whole movement—I think it was part three—to radio. But really, as far as taking care of business, Kyuss' theory was, "Ignorance is bliss." And it truly was. We did not give a fuck.

Did you ever play the entire record live, front-to-back?

Reeder: No. Not yet, anyway. [*Laughs*] Yeah, right. I think we only played "Demon Cleaner" like twice. I think Tool has played it as much as Kyuss did. So I've actually played it live four times. I remember I had a really shitty day at work and I got home and there was a message on my machine from Adam Jones. He was like, "We wanna do a Kyuss song live—you should come out and play it with us. Just pick a song." That was in like '98, I think. So we did it twice—

in L.A. and San Diego. When I came out onstage, I think people were like, "Who is this fuckin' guy? Cousin It?" But you know, there are so many Tool nuts out there who want to know every little bit of trivia, so I think those shows actually turned a lot of people onto Kyuss. It's funny, though, because "Demon Cleaner" never really had an ending—it just faded out—so Danny [Carey] from Tool pretty much organized the end. He's such an amazing drummer. It was awesome being in the mix with those guys.

Were you consciously trying to conjure the feeling of the desert with Sky Valley? Because that's what it sounds like.

Reeder: No thought went into that—it just happened automatically. The stereo in my car didn't work at the time, so when I'd be driving around the desert, I'd just have stuff going around in my head. We were products of our environment. We loved stuff like Helmet—it was so tense and wound up—they were obviously a product of their environment as well.

Homme: The funny thing is, I've met a lot of people that have said, "I took a pilgrimage to the desert and listened to the record there." But I gotta say, I didn't listen to any of those records for years and years, actually. But some of the only cassettes I have are Kyuss, and I was driving home from somewhere after Kyuss had broken up and put in [*And the*] *Circus* [*Leaves Town*] and *Sky Valley* and *Blues* and as I started to get into the desert, it totally made sense. Everything worked right—it was the phase opposite of its environment—it filled in all the gaps. It made sense to me there. Before that, I'd just assumed it worked. But I got to step back and say, "Yeah, it works. It sounds like that place looks."

Do you have a favorite song on the album?

Garcia: Probably "Supa Scoopa and the Mighty Scoop." When you start singing those lyrics, like, "By the lately / try to someone / we've been laughing / since you've been gone / and I wanna know / did you all enjoy the show?" It's like, what the fuck are you talking about? The way Josh wrote that song lyrically, it was really fun to sing. But it was so high-pitched that I had to go down to a lower register during the live shows because it was just killing my voice.

Reeder: Oooh, that's tough . . . I'd say "Whitewater" was the most exciting to play live. When we'd get to the jam section, it was anything goes. Sometimes it would blow up in our faces, and sometimes it was the raddest thing. But you never knew if it was gonna suck or if it was gonna be great. The jam sections were always evolving.

Homme: "Asteroid" was my favorite because it reminded me of Wagner. I started listening to classical music around this time and rediscovered marching bands. I had marching band vinyl since I was a kid—and Celtic drum-and-fief stuff, too. I loved that stuff, because the idea behind it was, "How do you inspire an army to overcome their fear, jell as one and kill everybody?" They always use music. No war has been fought without it, because it draws images in your head, but doesn't finish them. It demands that you paint the picture, but the picture is getting fucking painted, and that's all there is to it. Also, asteroids are what I'd want to roll into battle with.

Bjork: I've got two favorites—"Gardenia" and "Whitewater"—because they're the ones I wrote.

In retrospect, is there anything you'd change about Sky Valley?

Homme: No. I haven't made a record yet that I'd change anything about, and I hope I never do. I put everything I have into every record I've ever made. I think *Blues* was a classic record for Kyuss, too, but I think *Sky Valley* was a little more understood in a way. To me, it stands the test of time a little bit better. But when you're done with a record and you agree to give it to the rest of the world, no matter what happens—I don't care if it's downloading or critical failure or acclaim or sales or no sales—it's not up to you and it's not your fault. You don't have to feel anything about it. A good review or a bad review, I don't feel anything about. It's nice to get one or the other, but it's not *that* nice.

Garcia: I don't think I'm happy with my vocals on a single song. I haven't heard that record in years, but anytime I hear Kyuss, I cringe, man, because I can sing so much better now. It bugs the fuck out of me. My voice right now would smoke all over that John. I hear it now and I wanna be like, "Step aside, kid. Let me show you how it's done." But that's where I was, you know? I was still learning how to sing.

Bjork: I'd get rid of "Lick Doo," obviously. That was cheesy. But other than that, I think it's a good record. I wrote a lot more on *Blues*, but the irony is that I don't necessarily prefer *Blues* to *Sky Valley*. I just prefer to rock. I prefer to let things naturally take their course. *Blues* was a very natural record, and I feel like *Sky Valley* was a very calculated, fabricated record. And when I hear *Circus*, I hear how it became even more calculated. Don't get me wrong—still great songs, great sounds—I love all the Kyuss records. But sometimes you have to sacrifice a certain feeling when you're being more calculated. Less feeling, more thinking.

Reeder: I wouldn't change a thing. Somebody emailed me just a few weeks ago, asking, "On the second chorus of 'Gardenia,' did you play a wrong note?" Man, I don't know! There are probably wrong notes all over the place on that record. But I enjoyed that things weren't taken too seriously. It wasn't like a band trying to make it big, careerists or whatever. We were just having a good time, getting free beer and wondering who fucked up and let us through the door. It seemed like a joke, like, "Uh, I think somebody made a mistake. We're not supposed to be here." It always felt like that to me. Good times, though.

It seems like **Sky Valley**—*and Kyuss in general—wasn't widely appreciated until a couple of years after the band broke up. Do you ever wish you'd gotten your due while Kyuss was still around?*

Homme: No way. I feel so lucky that no one gave a fuck, because until you've learned to play for yourself, you haven't learned to play at all. In my way of thinking, you don't play for girls, money, fame or attention. You play for respect. It's the only gift you give yourself, and it can't be taken away. If you pay respect to yourself and those close to you, you're untouchable, un-heckle-able. And that's all I've ever wanted to be—to have someone look and go, "I don't like it, but I know it's real, so I'm just gonna shut up." Nothing else really seems worth it. And if people were into us, I might not feel that way. So, who cares? It's also why I'm not trying to milk the fuck out of it. I've never tried to dry-hump Kyuss' good name. I've been the source of stopping it for years.

Reeder: I don't know. I didn't seem like a big deal or anything back then. We were just shitting out the next batch of stuff. To have it still being talked about 14 or 15 years later just blows my mind. You know, I went to this thing a couple of weeks ago—it was Mike Watt improvising on bass and Raymond Pettibon improvising on canvas. Afterwards, there were these two 20-year-old kids there who saw me and were like, "Scott Reeder!" They wanted to take their pictures with me and stuff like that. I was like, "What the hell?" I haven't exactly been out there in the limelight, you know? It's weird.

Bjork: I think everything happened in its appropriate way. Kyuss was what it was because of where we came from and where rock music was at that time. We weren't from Seattle; we were too lowbrow for that. We were dope-smokers—I was listening to Cypress Hill back then. Other than Monster Magnet, rock bands weren't talking about weed when we were around. A lot of that just had to do with the time. Black Flag was what it was *because* punk rock wasn't totally into their trip. That's what made them do the things that they did. I mean, if the whole country is partying and smoking dope and you're Led Zeppelin, you're playing sold-out arenas. Black Sabbath probably played to 10,000 people a night after *Master of Reality* came out. Why isn't High on Fire doing that shit now? It's just the way it is—it was a different time then. But we didn't need it. That was kind of my whole trip when I was in Kyuss.

Garcia: It's weird, man. These days, people are like, "Kyuss this and Kyuss that," and it makes me wanna go, "Where the fuck were you when we were together?" Now that Kyuss is disbanded, it's this legendary fucking band, but back then, we just did what we did. I'll tell you, though, when I hang out at the merch table after Hermano gigs, some of the younger kids will have all this Kyuss stuff, and it makes me feel pretty good about being 37. They'll ask me to sign *Sky Valley* and I'll see Josh's signature already on there—at the bottom, he'll write something like "Kyuss lives." So I started writing the same thing on the Kyuss records that *didn't* have his autograph on them, because I know that some of those kids will bring those records to a Queens show for him to sign. [*Laughs*] So that's kind of my way of sending him a letter, like, "Hey, dude—it *does* live, just to let you know."

CHAPTER 16

ALTERING THE FUTURE

THE MAKING OF MESHUGGAH'S *DESTROY ERASE IMPROVE*

by Kevin Stewart-Panko

Release Date: 1995
Label: Nuclear Blast
Summary: Modern metallic trailblazer
Induction Date: November 2006/Issue #25

E veryone remembers that one episode of *The Osbournes* some years ago where Ozzy's ungrateful male sprog took it upon himself to use Meshuggah's *Destroy Erase Improve* as a thrust and parry in the suburban war against his Beverly Hills neighbors. Considering how the Swedish (not Norwegian, Jack!) quintet was suddenly on everyone's lips following that one particular act of revenge, it's hard to believe that upon the release of said album in 1995—an album that has come to be widely considered as one of the '90s' definitive metallic works—Meshuggah were pretty much still an unknown quintet hailing from Umeå, a small town in northern Sweden. However, once Fredrik

Thordendal and Mårten Hagström's dissonant shots of staccato guitar detonated album opener "Future Breed Machine" before locking in with Tomas Haake's polyrhythmic kick drum patterns, the silence was soon shattered, as was the scope of metal's boundaries. It also didn't hurt that the band finally got their mitts on a North American release and some decent label backing overseas. Falling somewhere between incendiary tech-thrash, angular math rock and brutal death metal—and accented by the slick fluidity of Thordendal's fusion-influenced leads—*Destroy Erase Improve* set a new metal watermark, and continues to immeasurably influence to this very day. *Decibel* tracked down Haake, Thordendal, Hagström, vocalist Jens Kidman and former bassist Peter Nordin to reminisce about our latest Hall of Fame induction.

What are your most vivid recollections from the time leading up to **Destroy Erase Improve?**

Tomas Haake: Well, first of all, it's really hard now, more than 10 years later, to remember any specifics. I do, however, remember feeling we had something cool going on, with somewhat of a shift in style, or maybe more of a shift in approach to our own music. Even though the style was still kind of similar to that of the *None* EP, we still felt that we were treading on new ground with some of the songs on *Destroy Erase Improve*. I remember feeling that we were creating something—a style and a way of thinking—that was genuinely our own.

Peter Nordin: I agree with Tomas. We had struggled for many years and things were finally beginning to go our way. I guess we all felt that something was about to happen.

Mårten Hagström: Honestly, I really don't remember all that much. I remember us being very excited about the songs and about going into the studio with [engineer] Danne Bergstrand. As always [in the time] before an album, most of one's life revolves around the songwriting.

Was there anything you were deliberately striving for or attempting to accomplish with the writing, recording and presentation of **Destroy Erase Improve?**

Haake: As far as the writing went, we always wanted to stand out from the rest of the scene. We wanted to accomplish something people had not heard before. With the songs on *Destroy Erase Improve*, in combination with a pretty tight and crisp production, we felt—and still feel—we managed to do so.

Hagström: Of course, we wanted to make the best album we could and make it sound great. That's always the ambition, but we tried not to have that ambition harness the writing process in any deliberate way. I know we wanted it to be energetic and aggressive.

*Do you feel that being able to maintain a steady lineup in the couple of years after your debut album [*Contradictions Collapse*] helped with focus and cohesion going into* Destroy Erase Improve?

Hagström: I don't know. I joined after *Contradictions Collapse*, so it's hard for me to say. But no one left the band during that time, so maybe.

Haake: Absolutely! I don't think this band would have existed for long if we weren't such a tightly knit bunch. You need to be true friends to have a good and healthy working environment in a band, and such friendship and understanding of each other is not usually something you can accomplish overnight.

Nordin: Yes, and this also explains our musical development. We were able to focus on the music instead of members. Plus, at this time, we were doing everything together.

Contradictions Collapse, *while unique in its own right, was still comparatively thrash-based as opposed to the more jagged, polyrhythmic approach of* **Destroy Erase Improve**, *where the guitars were locking in with the bass drums and Jens Kidman was able to focus more on his vocals because he wasn't playing guitar any longer. When did you stumble upon this style? What was influencing you at the time and at what point did you realize you were onto something fairly unique?*

Haake: We didn't really stumble upon this certain style, but it was more like we "oozed" on over to it over a period of many years. We're still on that "slippery surface," going sideways in a lot of ways, and we all hope we never hit something to stop that lateral motion. Around the time of *Destroy Erase Improve*, I was listening to a lot of different music, from things like jazz/rock fusion to industrial and metal to softer things like Björk and Pink Floyd, as well as a lot of movie scores. Whether this was actually influencing me or us much as far as our own music went, I don't know. There was probably no specific point in time where we started feeling like a unique band. I think we always felt unique in the sense that we were doing something we had never heard anyone else do before us. Even as far back as *Contradictions*.

Fredrik Thordendal: I think it's always been in the making. Even if you listen to the *None* mini-LP, you'll hear us searching for the same things we're still searching for today.

Nordin: We always wanted to do something different. It takes a couple of years to get it right and to go on from there.

Jens Kidman: The polyrhythmics already started to show on *Contradictions* and *None*, but on a smaller scale. From there, they just developed and still are developing. I don't know what made us go for this style more than the thrash, but we like it like that. We've always tried to renew ourselves a bit on each album but still keep the essence of Meshuggah visible. *Destroy Erase Improve* was the next step, but it still had a pretty wide mix of song styles since it has songs on it that were written all the way back in 1991. I don't think we reflected that we were onto something unique, 'cause that's what we try to do on every album. It's normal for us to explore.

Hagström: To me, the first step toward that style was made between *Contradictions Collapse* and *None*, although it was present on *Contradictions* as well. So, *Destroy Erase Improve* was just moving even more in that direction. As far as what influenced us, it's hard to say. I can't pinpoint any one or two things that influenced us at the time; everything around us back then, I guess. Our style has always felt like our own to us. Not that it's music from Sirius or anything.

Did the on-the-job injuries that Fredrik and Tomas suffered after the recording of **None** *play any role in your veering towards a more rhythmic playing approach? [In 1994, while working as a carpenter, Thordendal cut the tip of his left middle finger off and had it sewn back on, enabling him to continue playing. Soon after, Haake had one of his hands mangled in a grinding machine.]*

Haake: Absolutely none whatsoever! You play music, you hurt your hand, you bleed, you stitch up, you heal up, you start playing music again!

Nordin: I agree 100 percent. Accidents happen and then you go on.

Thordendal: No, I think we already had that rhythmic playing approach even before we suffered those accidents.

Was the band looking to explore any particular lyrical themes on **Destroy Erase Improve?** *What was going on in the world or in your lives at the time that may have been impacting the lyrics you wrote?*

Hagström: That's a question for Tomas, really, but they were less metaphorical and philosophical in nature. Even though they still were in a way [metaphorical and philosophical], they were still dealing with more practical issues than some of our later lyrics have.

Haake: There was no particular theme to the lyrics of *Destroy Erase Improve*. In a way, I guess the lyrics were reflecting less of a personal view or standpoint on things and leaning more towards the fictive and imaginary. And as such, they were more open to interpretation.

Fredrik, how much of an influence did jazz and fusion musicians—in particular, Allan Holdsworth—have on your lead work at the time, and what sort of effects/toys do you remember experimenting with?

Thordendal: Well, let's just say it like this: Even if I took all the money I could get my hands on while alive, took all the insurance money I got from cutting off my finger and bought as much "Holdsworth tone equipment" I could, I'd still be a complete moron [compared to him]! The only effects I was experimenting with that are worth mentioning was my first breath controller prototype that I ended up using on "Future Breed Machine," the outro to "Beneath"/intro to "Soul Burn" and "Sublevels."

Haake: I remember those "trippy" effects on the guitar and that part was done almost like a conversation of sorts on Fredrik's guitars.

What's the significance of the album's title? How does the artwork tie into this idea?

Haake: The significance of the title is only loosely tied in with the lyrics of the album. The phrase "destroy erase improve" is a line from the lyrics to "Future Breed Machine" and as that one became somewhat of the main track of the album, and was the leadoff song, we just went with some artwork that somewhat reflected the theme of that song.

Kidman: It's a strong title, and it fit the pictures we cut out and stole from reference books at the library.

Did the recording process go smoothly, or was it a nightmare? Were there any parts that were improvised in the studio or was everything completely written beforehand? What are some of the more memorable moments about your time in the studio recording **Destroy Erase Improve?**

Haake: As I remember it, it went pretty smoothly. We didn't have all the songs/parts completely done, but we had most of it down. The song "Sublevels" was something we kind of jammed up while in the studio. That whole session was kind of retarded; we rented a tiny cabin just outside of the city Uppsala on camping grounds. We could barely fit inside the cabin! I also remember that we were out on the town one night and this guy comes running up to me—for no apparent reason—and puts a running speed, full-on, hard-hitting fist to the side of my face! KNOCKOUT!!! The incident later turned into this court thing and blah, blah, blah . . . The other guys kept laughing at me over the next few days because my lips looked like two loafs of polished, red bread and I couldn't eat solid food for a week! Fun, fun, fun!

Nordin: Yes, the cabin was kind of weird. I worked at the time and missed a lot of the guitar and drum sound-checking in the studio. I can tell you that Tomas' lips really looked bad and we surely had a laugh at his expense!

Kidman: I remember I got a really bad flu in the middle of recording the vocals and had to get treatment for it. My tonsils were swollen like a horse's testicles.

I think we did the song "Sublevels" during our eight-hour trip from home to the studio. Our old blue Volvo from 1971 took us safely to the studio and to where we slept every day. It was a real piece of shit car.

Thordendal: Apart from "Sublevels," which we actually wrote in the car driving to Uppsala the evening before the first day of recording, we actually had time to rehearse all the songs before we recorded them.

Hagström: *Destroy Erase Improve* was special in the way that the oldest songs for that album were written back in '91 and '92, but some of the material was also written in the studio. So, yes, on some level there was improvising, but there always is to some extent. I most clearly remember recording "Sublevels" and "Acrid Placidity" because they were basically written in the studio and they went from nothing to something really special in front of our eyes/ears just like that.

Speaking of the mellow, interlude track, "Acrid Placidity," the original promo copies of [follow-up album] **Chaosphere** *has a similar interlude track entitled "Unanything" that was reportedly taken off the final release in order to maintain a full-on relentless and brutal assault. Was taking "Acrid Placidity" off* **Destroy Erase Improve** *for similar reasons ever considered?*

Thordendal: No, never.

Haake: No, not that I can recall. For *Destroy Erase Improve*, we definitely went for a more diverse output with a lot more dynamics to the album. You're right about "Unanything," though. As the rest of *Chaosphere* was really relentless and intense, we felt that a soft track would kind of rid the album of that intent.

Kidman: No, it's too groovy.

Hagström: Not that I remember. We thought "Acrid" was a real good way of breaking the pace of the album.

In the few years after **Destroy Erase Improve**, *you guys took to writing songs at home via your computers and trading MP3s over the Internet. Was* **Destroy Erase Improve** *created in the old-fashioned way of jamming in the rehearsal room? Was there something about the* **Destroy Erase Improve** *writing sessions that made Internet writing more attractive for future albums?*

Haake: At that time we were still writing and recording on small four-track porta-studios, as well as jamming and writing together in the rehearsal space. We did not start using computers until '96, so it was still "old-school" with us sharing tapes, etc. The only thing special in the air would have been the sweat and fart smells in the rehearsal space.

Kidman: I think we more or less sat at home separately with porta-studios and drum machines most of the time. We'd then meet up every now and then and show each other what we had done, whether it was good or bad. Then, when the Internet came, we didn't have to meet.

Thordendal: We wrote in the same style back then as we did those few years after *Destroy Erase Improve*; the only difference was, instead of using a computer, we used a porta-studio, and instead of sending the demo via Internet, we played it for each other in the rehearsal room. I think what also made *Destroy Erase Improve* kind of special from the later albums was that we wrote the songs over a longer period of time, and that made them sound a bit different from each other. For instance, "Soul Burn" was already written when we recorded *None*.

Hagström: No, not for *Destroy Erase Improve* in particular. I mean, we were writing stuff on four-track portas at home as well as jamming on the first couple of albums, including *Destroy Erase Improve*. So I'd say the computer just replaced the four-track. Of course, the technical aspect made the computer superior to the four-track, so I guess that steered us towards working in a little bit of a different way. It's a misconception that we switched from jamming songs out 100 percent of the time to computer writing 100 percent. *Destroy Erase Improve* was written, to a large extent, on four-track. We just changed gear after *Destroy Erase Improve*, but it's true that the jamming part decreased a lot when we started working with the PCs.

In '95 Peter developed an inner-ear nerve problem that had him feeling constantly nauseous and off-balance, forcing him out of the band mid-tour later that year. Were there any signs of his illness previous to this, and was it ever an issue during the creation of Destroy Erase Improve*?*

Kidman: No, those problems came up on the European tour we did with Machine Head after we had recorded the album.

Nordin: It was on the tour that I became ill. It had nothing to do with the album.

What's being said in the double-tracked spoken-word part on "Inside What's Within Behind"?

Haake: Oh, I can't really remember the exact words, but I remember we used leftover lyrics for that song and just read the sentences in opposite order than how they were written; i.e. the last word of a sentence first, and so on . . .

Kidman: The same lyrics I'm singing, but backwards. Neat.

What were the initial reactions to Destroy Erase Improve *upon its release? Were you surprised by any of the attention the album received?*

Haake: The way I remember it, the reactions were all really positive. We got a ton of really good press and reviews for that album. Even though we knew we had done something cool with that album, we were still surprised with the reactions.

Nordin: We sort of knew the album was good, but the reactions overwhelmed us.

Kidman: I don't think it got a super-amount of attention. But at that time we didn't really have anything to compare to except for *Contradictions*, and it definitely got a better response than that album.

Hagström: I remember reviews being really good. It's funny; *Destroy Erase Improve* didn't really do that much to begin with. Today, a lot of people speak to us about *Destroy Erase Improve* and how influential it was when it came out and so on, but in reality, it was a much slower process than that. We were glad it got a good response, but it actually took some time for the album to creep into people's heads. It's interesting, because the same thing has happened with *Chaosphere* and the rest of our albums as well, even though I personally think that *Destroy Erase Improve* is by far the most accessible album we've made so far.

The North American release of **Destroy Erase Improve** *has both logos from Nuclear Blast and Relapse on it. Having those two labels co-release something these days would be pretty . . . well, let's just say it'd be unlikely. Can you offer any insight into that association or what was going on at the time?*

Kidman: I don't remember. Mårten?

Hagström: I have no clue. We were never aware of what was happening with us in the States at that time. We were going to tour Europe and hope for the best. I was over in the States at the Relapse office in '95 doing some press, but I never got anything but good vibes from [owner] Matt [Jacobson] and the guys there. If anything, I think the split between Nuclear Blast and Relapse was more of a turf thing than anything related to the band.

Haake: I believe that, because Nuclear Blast didn't have an office in the States at the time, they cooperated with Relapse for distro, etc. I could be wrong, though.

Destroy Erase Improve *is continually referred to as your best album by many fans and critics. Do you agree and what are your thoughts on it being as praised as such, especially since it's been 11 years and six releases since?*

Kidman: I definitely do not agree with that. Wake up.

Haake: Well, it's cool if people think so and I think that it has a lot to do with the fact that it was released at the right time, when there was nothing like it on the market. Over the last decade and more, the whole metal genre as such has diversified and become so immensely huge that, for every year that goes by, it's getting harder and harder to have that kind of impact on the scene. Personally, I usually always consider whatever our latest release is to be the best, since we all evolve and mature continuously. Looking back and listening to *Destroy Erase Improve* now, it's still cool and I'm still proud of it, but at the same time, some parts of the album feel and sound "adolescent" in some ways.

Nordin: I agree. It was released at a time when this was something new. If you compare it with a lot of other bands today, it's not that different. But Meshuggah has continued to break new grounds with their music.

Hagström: Like I said earlier, it wasn't like that when it came out. It's great that there is so much respect given to such an old album, but it's still something that was us in '95. For every album, you add something to the whole of a band. I think that with every album there is an aspect of Meshuggah that we explore, and that's why I like *Destroy Erase Improve* for some things and *Nothing* for some things and so on. We haven't made a "best" album, in my opinion; we've recorded a bunch of pretty OK albums, each one with its individual benefits and drawbacks. *Destroy Erase Improve* is, in my opinion, by far the most "commercial" of our albums so far and represents a fairly small portion of Meshuggah as we are today. But it's still a cool album. I think *Catch 33* is a more . . . complete album, but you can't compare '95 to '05.

What's your overall assessment of **Destroy Erase Improve**? *Have you ever stopped to consider how influential the album is/was, not just on extreme music as a whole, but for you as a band in the sense that your label seemed to finally be coming through on their end in terms of promo, support and regular tours after its release?*

Haake: I really don't think in those terms and even though I believe it had an impact on the scene at the time, there were so many other bands coming up and growing with the scene as well. Nuclear Blast definitely did a good promo job for the album, but I think that mainly it was just the right time for them and for us, with changes going on in the music industry as well as general acceptance and open-mindedness to new and different things.

Thordendal: For me, it's one of the three Meshuggah albums I felt most satisfied with as a whole when I heard it from start to finish for the first time; the other two being *I* and *Catch 33*.

Hagström: It's hard to say. I'm not sure we know how much or little it's influenced anything. It's not something I reflect over. We know it's been a really important album for some and that's really gratifying to know.

Kidman: "Future Breed Machine" must be the three most spoken words at our shows. What's the problem?

With hindsight being 20/20, is there anything that you'd go back and change about **DEI?**

Kidman: A lot! But that would be stupid.

Haake: My hairdo at that time!

Nordin: Ha! Yeah, your hairdo was very funny! If I could do it all over again, I would have taken more time off from work and been there for the entire recording.

Hagström: I don't know. On one hand, there is always stuff you'd like to change, but on the other, *Destroy Erase Improve* is what we were in '95, so I guess it's just the way it's supposed to be.

Thordendal: I don't think any songs off *Destroy Erase Improve* would end up on a new Meshuggah album if one of us wrote it today. But I wouldn't wanna go back and change anything either; I'm proud of what we accomplished.

CHAPTER 17

MASTERBURNER & THE INFINITE BADNESS

THE MAKING OF MONSTER MAGNET'S *DOPES TO INFINITY*

by J. Bennett

Release Date: 1995
Label: A&M
Summary: Dope-driven rock monolith
Induction Date: October 2006/Issue #24

After Nirvana's *Nevermind* tore the "alternative rock market" a seven-figure asshole, every major label with easy access to a couple of guitar-wielding longhairs was vying to shove its swollen corporate phallus into the proverbial money-ring of brown fire. The A&M roster—buoyed by the likes of Soundgarden, Paw (remember them?) and four dudes from Red Bank, NJ, who called themselves Monster Magnet—was cocked, locked and ready to move some serious units. When 1993's *Superjudge* saw some light *Headbangers Ball*

action with the Sabbath-inspired video for "Twin Earth," the label dumped even more cash on vocalist/guitarist Dave Wyndorf, bassist Joe Calandra, drummer Jon Kleiman and guitarist Ed Mundell for their 1995 follow-up. Recorded at the Magic Shop in Manhattan, *Dopes to Infinity* thrust Monster Magnet headfirst into the preliminary bright lights and big titties of international rock stardom via the soaring flanged riffery and psychedelic double-talk of "Negasonic Teenage Warhead." Too bad they kinda hated each other by the time they got there. With the status of the band still unknown as of press time (Kleiman and Calandra split after 2002's *God Says No*; Wyndorf is still recuperating from a February 2006 drug overdose), *Decibel* tracked down all four members—and lighting guru/atomic propagandist/original member Tim Cronin—to find out why *Dopes* will last forever, even if Monster Magnet doesn't.

PART I: LOOK TO YOUR ORB FOR THE WARNING

What do you remember most about the recording sessions for **Dopes***?*

Dave Wyndorf: We came off *Superjudge*, and I didn't do anything except play with my kid for at least a year. Then I actually got a visit from an A&R guy who was like, "Look, you gotta write something." I think the winter of early '94 is when I wrote the songs. I just dragged all my recording stuff into my room and wrote a song every day until I was done. Then we'd all get together and practice. We did a lot of work on that record—it was the first one I was completely anal about. I remember tuning the drums to the guitars with a guitar tuner. It was insane. I was hell-bent to make it the most in-tune record ever.

Ed Mundell: I was smoking a lot of pot and listening to a lot of Robin Trower. We had played a lot in Europe for *Superjudge*, but if you listen to that record, the production isn't all that great. The songs are good, but the production sounds like a good demo or something. So we definitely wanted *Dopes* to sound better than *Superjudge*. We worked really hard in pre-production, and we were really prepared by the time we got into the studio.

Joe Calandra: It was the most intense recording we ever did. Before *Dopes*, we'd just go into the studio and just knock 'em out in two or three takes. But in this situation, the engineer was a maniac. His name was Joe Warda, and he could hear anything—even if it was just a hair out of tune or a 30th of a second off-time. So the whole recording session was really slow because the guy had amazing ears. I'd be like, "How do you listen to music at home?" And he'd say, "Oh, I can shut it off if I have to." And I'd be like, "Then shut it off, already."

Jon Kleiman: Joe Warda had amazing ears, and he was just doing his job. This was before Pro Tools, so it was all done on two-inch tape. We used a click-track, too, which I didn't mind at all. So Joe Warda would roll the tape back, and you'd hear the click and then my bass drum, and he'd go, "Hear that? It's about a 64th note off." I was like, "No one fucking cares." But he was amazing—he had Pro Tools in his head. I feel like he must've cut his teeth recording jazz bands or something, because he was obviously used to achieving a way higher level of fidelity than was required with us.

What kind of preparation had you done beforehand?

Calandra: Dave would come up with riffs. Sometimes he'd come in with songs completely done—he'd bring in a tape, and there'd be a bass line, and a basic drum pattern worked out on a Casio. Like "Negasonic" and "Dead Christmas" came in completely done. But other songs, there'd just be a riff and we'd figure out the song. I'd go home, write like three different bass lines and then we'd pick which one we wanted. But it wasn't like Dave walked in like, "Here's the next golden hit."

Mundell: We were rehearsing for *Dopes*, and it was about a week before we were gonna go into the studio when Dave was like, "I got these songs." And they were "Dopes to Infinity" and "Ego, the Living Planet." We had just started tuning down to C, and Dave wanted to experiment more with that because it sounded like Sabbath, you know—heavy as shit. So "Dopes" and "Ego" are both in C. Before "Dopes" came along, the centerpiece of the album was supposed to be "King of Mars," because it's totally unlike any other song on the record. And out of that came "Vertigo," which is just part of "King of Mars" looped.

Calandra: We never played any of these songs live before we recorded them, and I always thought that sucked. We'd be on tour for one album, come home, write songs for another album, and then play those songs on tour mixed up with some other stuff. And by the time you get done touring, the songs are totally different. You come up with parts, things happen, and you finally click. You're not nervous anymore. For me, Monster Magnet was a constant state of being nervous about going into the studio. I never thought the songs were rehearsed enough—whereas if we had played the songs on tour for three months, I could just bust them out.

Mundell: With *Superjudge*, some of it was left to chance—we didn't know what we were gonna do here or there. But with *Dopes* and *Powertrip*, we knew exactly what we were gonna do. It was just a matter of getting the tones down. We worked our asses off—we'd rehearse like five-to-eight-hour days. By the time we got to the studio, we even had the drum fills worked out.

Monster Magnet always used vintage musical equipment. Was that just part of the band's late '60s/early '70s aesthetic?

Mundell: We'd listen to Sabbath and Zeppelin records and think, "What gear did they use?" 'Cause that stuff sounded great. So we naturally gravitated toward that stuff. We were fortunate that we were in New York City, and we knew people who were willing to lend us or rent us really old, really good gear. On this record, especially, we listened so closely to sounds. And the Magic Shop had this vintage Neve board that Zeppelin had recorded on.

Tim Cronin: At one point, they were trying to rent a Mellotron, and they figured out that Lenny Kravitz had bought every Mellotron in New York City, and they couldn't find one.

Mundell: The big rock bands in New York at that time were Raging Slab, Circus of Power and Blitzpear, which [current Monster Magnet guitarist] Phil Caivano was in. He was driving a cab at the time, and had been in a bunch of bands with Dave—they went to high school together. So Phil came in with all these cool old Les Pauls and Marshalls and Tube Screamers.

Dave, what kind of things were you thinking about when you were writing the lyrics?

Wyndorf: Oh, the usual [*laughs*], for me. There're a lot of secret messages going on that I couldn't really let out, so I tend to write in metaphors. The songs actually have very down-to-earth meanings, but when they come out, of course, they're as ambiguous as fuckin' possible. It's kind of an ersatz bullshit poetry routine that I have going on, but it works for me. I write with my heart, and if something sounds too boring or normal, I'll just change the metaphors around until it sounds cool. Songs last longer that way, I think—unless you're Burt Bacharach. For Monster Magnet, I thought it was best if I knew what was going on and everybody else kinda half-knew what was going on.

PART II: KING OF MARS

What was the Magic Shop like?

Mundell: The Magic Shop is a great place. Andrew Loog Oldham went there to re-master all the Stones records for CD. Lou Reed worked there a lot, too. You never knew who was gonna walk in there. The guy who ran it, Steve Rosenthal, knew *everybody*. We did *Superjudge* and *Dopes* there. It was in SoHo, but we were staying in Times Square, so we'd take the subway downtown to the studio every day and then we'd take it back again at night.

Wyndorf: People were dropping by all the time. Lenny Kaye, from Patti Smith's band, played on "Five Years Ahead of My Time," which was a B side. And what's-his-face from Guns N' Roses—Slash—wanted to record at the

Magic Shop while we were in there. I was like, "Damn, how can we get this guy on the record?" But he was too high and then he left.

Kleiman: The Magic Shop was a great studio, and they had tons of good gear. I remember wandering around and seeing that some shitty Ramones record was recorded there—maybe the Phil Spector one. That was kinda cool. I guess I didn't have the best relationship with Steve Rosenthal, though. He was the co-producer and main engineer, even though Dave got main production credit. I liked Steve at first, but to people outside the band, it really became apparent quickly that the only person they had to talk to and listen to was Dave. No one else really mattered. So Steve could be sort of dismissive of everyone else.

Tim Cronin is credited with "atomic propaganda" and "slave drum" on "Ego, the Living Planet."

Wyndorf: Tim has been a huge part of Monster Magnet from the very beginning. He started out as our drummer, and then the singer, and then things got pro and weird and of course I kicked him out. But you know, he really was uncomfortable at that point, being lead singer. But he's always been right there—he's like the guru—and he always played on the records in one way or another. The "slave drum" was this one big giant drum that he beats the living fucking out of. It ended up ridiculous, with us out in the street in SoHo at like four o'clock in the morning with a giant cord from the studio banging on garbage cans and Dumpsters. It was really cool.

Cronin: I went over there to hang out a few days while they were making the record, and Dave asked me to play drums on "Ego, the Living Planet," because when the band first started, I was the drummer. But my drumming style made Mo Tucker look like Carl Palmer. At best, it was like one of those wind-up monkeys that plays drums.

For all of the album's psychedelic qualities, it's not like you guys were dropping acid or eating mushrooms while you were recording.

Wyndorf: No—not at all. You know what happens when you take psychedelic drugs and you're making psychedelic music? You get the Grateful Dead. The best way to make psychedelic music is to have the memory of the experience and drag it out of the music, instead of laying back all lazy and experiencing it. That's the problem with drug use and creating music. It's great if you're blowing some Coltrane and you're super-talented and everybody wants jamming. But jamming gets boring—people wanna hear songs. I always thought it was better to remember the experience or—even better—invent the experience that you wanna have and fight like hell to try to get it.

Kleiman: By that point, I had definitely stopped taking psychedelics. I think I took acid for the last time during my first year of college. I was too much of an anxiety-ridden wreck to do that anymore. I think even Dave still drank at that point, so there was a lot of drinking, but never in the studio. I think the Magic Shop cost something like $750 or $1,000 a day, so if someone was fucked up, it wouldn't have been permissible. Dave was a super-alcoholic before that, and was definitely still drinking at that point, but then he went clean and eventually changed over to sleeping pills.

Mundell: Me and Jon were talking a lot of pills, like Xanax and time-release morphine pills and stuff. We'd scrape off the time-release coating and snort 'em. We'd get all fucked up, so our timing would always be a little slow. I remember we could never play "Blow 'Em Off," because I'd start off way too slow. Dave was still drinking at this point—I think it was on this tour, actually, that he got sick and quit. But the rest of us were mostly drinking beer and Jack Daniel's. I was still smoking pot; I don't think Joe was, and Jon wasn't a pot smoker, anyway.

Joe and Jon stuck around for two more albums, but there was tension in the band even back then.

Kleiman: Just to put this in perspective, the first two Monster Magnet releases, *Spine of God* and *Tab*—that was when [guitarist] John McBain was in the band. John and Dave would write together, and everyone was into the music. I was the youngest, and I was a fuck-up. I drank a lot, and did whatever I could, so I kinda defined my position in the band way back then. So I didn't really have a say later on, because I was still considered the fuck-up, even though that didn't really translate later. By *Superjudge*, Dave was writing the music all by himself, and that's when, for me, the band really took a turn for the worst. I hated *Superjudge*. I thought the music was really poorly written. It sounded like bad '70s cock rock. I liked *Dopes* better, but by then all the basic moods were set. There was animosity between Dave and pretty much everyone.

Wyndorf: A bunch of weird stuff went down on *Dopes*, just like all Monster Magnet records. Jon was playing great, but out of time, like all drummers do. We had to punch in a lot of his takes, and he was not digging it. I heaved a lot of songs on these guys at the last minute, as usual, so Jon was still getting used to them, because we had only rehearsed for about a month before. But Jon never liked anything in Monster Magnet. He lived his life in Monster Magnet constantly putting everything down and saying it was corny and stupid. But I have a hard time firing people. I didn't need to fire him, though—I could do everything myself. If people weren't into it, but served a function, all I'd need them there for was about four hours a day. I can do the rest myself. I was really into being a band, but Jon was the type of guy who would write two songs in five years and go, "How come you're not publishing my songs?" Meanwhile, I'm writing 50 songs a year, and 49 of them suck. So you gotta write a lot of shit, you know? And now that Jon is the leader of his own band, I think he realizes that. Jon's no dummy. He's a really smart guy, but man, lazy as a box of fuckin' hair.

Kleiman: I'll just be honest. Fuck it—I've got nothing to lose. What sticks out to me most about those sessions was the fact that Joe got kicked off the record. He played bass on some of it, but he was having major personal problems at that time. He's married now, but he's been with the same woman for, I don't know, 300 years, and at the time he thought they might be splitting up. *And* he thought he had cancer—he had some weird thing on his tongue. So he was really freaked out and distracted. I don't know that his playing was all that bad, but I remember a lot of arguing. And there was never any arguing except between someone and Dave. So I ended up playing bass on two songs, and Ed probably played on three or four. I guess Dave might've done one or two, and then Joe did the rest. That was a major thing. Even one record prior, I would've never imagined that happening.

Calandra: We were in the studio, and I was having some personal problems at home, plus I thought I had some kind of disease that I was freaking out about. I couldn't concentrate in the studio, and I was playing like shit. And like I said, that guy Joe Warda was on my case, and I was fucking up left and right. I went home for the weekend, just to take a break. On Sunday, Dave called me and goes, "You can stay home. I'm gonna take a couple passes at this, and Jon's gonna play some bass." I was like, "Shit." It wasn't a band anymore, you know? All of a sudden, we had to make this product, and I wasn't holding up my end, so I was out. It was like Dave had his sights set on bigger things and if you were in his way it was like, "Fuck you—get off." And that happened to Jon on the next record. Dave wanted him to hit really hard, and Jon was like, "Look, I don't play that way." So he got some douchebag to come in and play drums. And I had to play bass with this guy. It sucked.

Wyndorf: I make these calls all the time, man. Joe was choking, and he wasn't ready to play those parts. I love Joe, and he's a nice guy, but he didn't know how to play the songs. But I would never boot anybody out of the band for not being able to play on a record. That happens more times in more situations than anybody will ever admit. It happens all the fucking time. So we shared the bass credits on that record, and the real hero was Ed—he played bass like a motherfucker on that album. We'd go through the track five times, and he would have the part. Ed's like this laid-back Leslie West character, and I'm in his ear, chainsmoking and driving him nuts. He played most of the bass on the record.

Mundell: The hardest thing I ever did in my whole life was play bass on the song "Dopes to Infinity." It was the first time we had tuned down to C. It was such hell getting everything in tune and on time. I remember going to the bath-room after working on the bass line for like six hours. I was just leaning against the wall thinking, "Please, let me get through this."

PART III: SLUTS, COURAGE & AIRPLANES

Is it true that the album was originally going to be called Sluts to Infinity?

Wyndorf: Yes, but ultimately I didn't think it sounded as cool as *Dopes to In-finity*. For some reason, the word "dopes" sounded goofier and cooler to me—not to mention that it probably wouldn't get us into trouble with the record company. For Christ's sake, I wanted to call it *Cunt Circus* for a while. [*Laughs*] Can you imagine that?

Kleiman: We hated the name. It's just stupid and meaningless. His first idea for it was *Sluts to Infinity*. It just sounded really sophomoric and stupid. It was like, "Grow up." But Dave is a comic book guy, you know? I think he was fat when he was a kid or something. I don't think he ever got out of the high school thing—he wanted to relive it while he was thin and the lead singer of a semi-popular band. He was obsessed with the whole groupie scene. Jesus, I couldn't count how many women he slept with, but they were always idiot groupies.

Wyndorf: The more I lay off the booze and drugs, the more sex I had. Finally, I wasn't drinking or getting high at all—it was all sex. I was just picking my pri-orities. I'd get into arguments with Jon about it. He'd say, "This isn't right, fuck-ing around like this," and I'd say, "You want to—you're just too drunk and afraid." Look, there's precious few reasons—besides the love of music—that you get into a rock 'n' roll band, and I can't see getting high to the point of not being able to think as one of them. But getting as much pussy as you possibly wanted when you were 17? That's actually something to go for.

What did you do to entertain yourselves when you weren't in the studio?

Calandra: We were being spazzes in the hotel, because we were drinking a lot. We were up on the 10th or 11th floor, and I remember we were throwing water balloons out the window, and all of a sudden I hear Jon behind me going, "Look out!" I turn around, and he's got a garbage bag filled with water—I don't even know how he was carrying it—and he rolled it over the windowsill. When it hit the ground, it sounded like a bomb went off. All the car alarms started going off instantly. It was insane.

Kleiman: I think we were staying at the Gramercy Park Hotel. It was three of us in one suite. We never threw out any of the beer cans or alcohol bottles we consumed—we just stashed them in a closet to see how much we consumed.

Joe used to be really good at making paper airplanes—he'd throw them out the window, and they'd go for blocks. Of course, when Ed or I tried to make 'em, they'd just take a nosedive. Then I guess we started throwing water balloons. We missed a guy on a bicycle by maybe five feet. I don't think it would've have killed the guy, but it definitely wouldn't have felt good. And it would've absolutely been a lawsuit.

In addition to bass and backing vocals, Joe is credited with "courage" and "airplanes." What's the courage for?

Calandra: I had just woken up and went out for a cup of coffee, and I see Ed bouncing across the street toward me. He goes, "Joe, there's this dude right over there with a gun, and he says he's gonna shoot me if I don't give him money." I had just rolled out of bed and was like, "Ed, that's bullshit." I can see the guy has his hand under his shirt, and I tell him, "You're full of shit." The guy's like, "I'm not fuckin' full of shit!" And I didn't know if he had a gun or not, so we go into this Popeye's with this guy and I sit down with him at this two-seater booth. He goes, "OK, we need to see your money." So I took out a dollar. And he's like, "No, we need bigger currency than that—we need like 20s and 50s." I finally stood up and said, "Fuck you." I grabbed Ed and we took off. Ed is the only person I know who would get into a situation like that. He's like a big pink target. People see him on the street and they're like, "Let's get him." And then of course I come along and he sucks me into his drama. [*Laughs*]

Mundell: Well, you know, Times Square is kinda sketchy, and I was young back then, still smoking pot, and this guy comes up to me on 48th Street, where all the guitar shops are, and goes, "You better come in here—there's a guy with a gun trained on you out there." I was like, "What are you talking about?" All of a sudden, I saw Joe, and I was like, "Joe, I don't know what's going on, but I guess some guy has a gun on me." So this guy brought me and Joe into this restaurant, and he's trying to get us to give him 20 bucks to get us out of it. Joe was like, "Fuck you—shoot us, then." It was so retarded.

PART IV: NEGASONIC BREAKTHROUGH

"Negasonic Teenage Warhead" was Monster Magnet's breakthrough song, but it actually came out before Dopes to Infinity.

Wyndorf: Yeah, "Negasonic" was written in the spring of '93, I think. The business guys at A&M asked us to record a song for this lousy movie called *S.F.W.*, so I went up to my room with the purpose of writing a commercial rock song. I figured if I could stick it on our record, too, they'd push our record more.

To make up for it, I put in lyrics that nobody could understand—I figured that would get my integrity factor back into order. So we recorded it on a 16-track here in Jersey with my sound guy, and we fucked it up—we thought the studio was gonna be better than it was—and it was a shitty recording. I knew we had to do it over again.

Kleiman: The movie, I thought, was, like, abysmally bad. I remember going to see it with my girlfriend at the time, and we ended up walking out. But that was our first song that had any sort of national impact. And not to put down Dave or anything, but I think it was definitely written with the record company in mind, because they really did want us to be the next Nirvana.

How did things change for the band when "Negasonic" started getting radio play?

Wyndorf: That song kinda upped the ante. It also got me the chance to make a ridiculously huge video, which was really fun to do. They pretty much gave me the keys to the kingdom, because I had no manager on that record. And record companies *hate* that. When "Negasonic" became the single and started doing OK, the record company was like, "Oh, it's commercial!" So they wanted a video, which turned out to be this ridiculously overpriced thing, in total *Spinal Tap* fashion. The guy who directed it was Gore Verbinski, the guy who did *Pirates of the Caribbean*. He was doing commercials and rock videos back then, and he was a really nice guy. I was talking to him on the phone, explaining what I wanted, and then I faxed him a storyboard that explained all the meteors, the drugs, the stuff flying around. I had said that I wanted the meteors to be CGI, because it would be cheaper and easier to do. But he thought I wanted him to construct giant meteors. So we come back after a European tour and show up at the soundstage and he had these fucking life-size meteors built on 60-foot towers inside the biggest soundstage at Universal. The crazy thing is that nobody stopped me from spending the money. I forget exactly how much it cost, but I think it might've been like $250,000. It was typical Hollywood—and believe me, rock 'n' roll *is* Hollywood. Thank god it fucking worked. That video sold a lot of records—especially in Europe.

Kleiman: It definitely took us to the next level. All of a sudden, we were playing festivals and opening for bigger bands—but it wasn't like one day we were nothing and the next day we all had yachts. Nothing ever really changed that much. Promoters would hire limos to take us between the hotel and the venue, so that was pretty cool, but as soon as we got back from tour, we'd be off for two months and Joe and I would go back to painting houses.

Cronin: When "Negasonic" came out, that completely caught everybody by surprise. Everybody was psyched about it, and it made for more expectations when *Powertrip* came out. But that was back when record companies would still nurture a band along. They'd see a little bit of growth and stick with them. Now it's like, one record and out. I mean, nowadays, if *Superjudge* came out on a major label, I don't think there'd be a second major label record.

Calandra: That song was huge—it seemed like something was gonna happen. We were on MTV, we would even go *to* MTV and do stuff on the air with them. It was weird, because half the year, we'd be in the band, and the other half, I'd be flipping hamburgers in a restaurant, just working a regular job. But then you go on tour and there's like thousands of people screaming at you. And then you're on TV. And the next day, you gotta go back to work, flipping hamburgers. It's like, "What world am I living in?"

Kleiman: There was a picture disc for "Negasonic," and the picture is supposed to be an atom bomb, but it looks like an orange piece of broccoli. Every once in a while, when I'd get really poor, I'd go through my back catalogue of seemingly rare Monster Magnet stuff and check on eBay to see if they were getting any kind of good money. Inevitably, you'd go on and the opening bid would be, like, 99 cents. It was like, "OK, guess I'm not getting rich this way."

Calandra: The other "Negasonic" picture disc had Dave's face on it. I think at one point, me and Jon and Ed were gonna photocopy it and make Dave masks for us to wear onstage at this warm-up gig at a local bar. That way, when Dave walked onstage, it'd be like a whole band of Daves—which is the way he wanted it to be. I'm so sorry we never did that, because it would've been hilarious.

PART V: EGO, THE LIVING PLANET

In **Dopes'** *back cover photo, the only band member's face that is completely visible is Dave's. What were the circumstances there?*

Wyndorf: I had seen this ad around New York when we were making the record, and it was for the Sci-Fi Channel, when it was first stating out. It was this really cool photo of a room, like an old *Batman*-type thing. I was like, "That is so fucking cool—I'm gonna steal that." So I ripped it out of a magazine and showed it to the photographer, Michael Lavine, who was not into it. I finally talked him into it, and he came up with the set. Of course, it looked nothing like the Sci-Fi ad, but it still looked cool. We started taking pictures and I was like, "OK, everybody throw themselves down on the ground like you're dead."

Kleiman: That was stupid. It looked like a fucking *Romper Room* set, with bright red and yellow blocks. And that stupid engine in the middle of nowhere? I remember giving Dave shit about it and he was like, "Shut the fuck up! We only have to be here for 30 minutes, and I don't wanna hear you bitch the whole time." So that was that. I don't like what the photo implies—that Dave's the king or whatever—but I'm not gonna argue with not having my face on something. Every normal person hates seeing photographs of themselves.

Mundell: I just remember Dave going, "Pretend you're dead," and then some stylist ran over to fix my hair. I hate taking band photos. The girl in the photo on the inside, that's Tim's old girlfriend, Aryn, but people still come up to me and ask me to sign it because they think it's me in drag. Jon always busts my balls about that.

Calandra: If you look at it, you can see exactly what Dave's personality is. It's like, "This is my record, and these guys are my little puppets." I don't wanna sound like sour grapes, but it was fucked. I'm sure Dave will have another take on it, though.

The image definitely seems to suggest that Dave is the driving force of the band.

Wyndorf: Yeah, and I felt that way, too. I always feel like I'm on this supermission to finish something, and God bless 'em, everyone else is really cool, but nobody actually gets it but me. And sometimes I'm right. And then sometimes I'm not right, but who cares? Which makes you feel guilty. In the end, I felt like I had killed everybody. That was the vibe I got, so I ran with it. It probably pissed everybody off.

Did you ever feel like you were being a dictator?

Wyndorf: Sure. It didn't make me feel good, but it felt right. I had to finish the fuckin' thing, you know? Nobody else was coming up with the vision for it. I was what I would call a benevolent dictator. I never fired anyone, and I always gave everybody the chance to contribute whatever they wanted, but it had to be done within like two hours, you know? You couldn't say, "I'm gonna go home and mull over this part." If somebody didn't have their parts, I'd make 'em up for 'em. When you're making an album, you can't go back and forth and hope for the best, you really have to lay out a plan. As sucky as it is, there's not a lot of room for experimentation once you're paying the money to go in there.

PART VI: VERTIGO

What kind of influence do you think **Dopes** *had on the legions of stoner rock bands that came later?*

Wyndorf: I never really saw any Monster Magnet influence beyond the "drug rock" propaganda. I never saw it musically. I did see a lot of Kyuss influence show up, though—I think they were probably more influential on stoner rock than anybody else. I was totally flattered when anybody mentioned us, though.

There are always different camps, too, you know, as far as which record is the best. You know, like, "First two records, great, and everything else sucks!" Which I can totally get into because, being a record collector myself, I've been like that my whole life. But *Dopes* and *Spine of God* seem to be people's favorites.

Calandra: I'd notice little things here and there; some smaller bands would take this tiny riff of ours and write a whole song around it. Dave and Tim and Jon were all about, you know, "drug rock" and it was funny as hell in '88/'89. We'd hang up a big banner that said "Drug Rock" and we'd be playing in front of like 14 kids at a youth center. I guess. But then all of a sudden the whole stoner rock thing came, and all these bands started coming out of the woodwork. I could never figure out if we started something, or if it was a collective consciousness thing.

Kleiman: I think Monster Magnet was seminal in a way, but most of the time, when you read about that kind of stuff, all you really hear about is Kyuss. So, even though I think the Monster Magnet influence is genuine, I don't think it lasted as long in people's minds. I never really thought other bands were ripping us off, but I know we definitely influenced a handful of bands—like Nebula and Clutch. We actually toured with Clutch after they put out their first record, and they were pretty metal at that point. I think they smoked pot with us for the first time on that tour, and their next record was a lot more psychedelic.

In retrospect, is there anything you'd change about the album?

Kleiman: Well, I didn't have the power to change anything. I always thought that maybe "Negasonic" could've been a bigger hit if I didn't put that weird drumbeat to it. You know how it sorta skips a beat? Afterward, I thought it might've done better if I had played it straight and made the song, dare I say, danceable. But like I said, I didn't have the power to change anything. So I guess I would ask for renewed contract negotiations.

Calandra: It wasn't my place to change anything. If you asked Dave, I'm sure he'd go on for about half an hour about what he'd change, but I didn't really have a part to play in any decision making. Nobody did. It was all Dave. So would I change anything? Maybe I'd record it better. I don't know. I hate to say it, but I'm pretty disconnected from this one. I'm glad I did this record, though, because analog was about to die, and I got to see stuff like tape-splicing firsthand. Nobody's gonna see that anymore. Who's gonna sit there and cut tape when you can do it in three seconds on Pro Tools?

Wyndorf: The one thing that that record was missing for me—and is still missing—is emotive vocals. I don't think I sang my best on that record, because I was so into keeping everything in tune that when it came down to being an animal on vocals, I was too into being on key. So I think some of the songs lost their emotional edge because I didn't know how to separate my producer self from my performance self. That album was a lot of fun, but it was also a huge pain in the ass. The people who worked on it and played on it were excellent, though—they really were above and beyond—especially concerning me, because I tend to push people a lot.

Mundell: You know, I submitted so many songs to Dave for this record, and he didn't like any of them. But I listened back to them a couple of years ago, and everything sounded like stoned-out Robin Trower guitar jams. I was like, "Of course he didn't use any of my songs. What the hell was I thinking?" So I wish I would've written a song that didn't sound like Robin Trower. I always thought *Dopes* was a good record, though. I think this is my favorite record of ours, so I'm glad you picked this one.

CHAPTER 18

AT THE GATES OF IMMORTALITY

THE MAKING OF AT THE GATES' *SLAUGHTER OF THE SOUL*

by J. Bennett

Release Date: 1995
Label: Earache
Summary: The most influential death metal album of the past decade
Induction Date: March 2005/Issue #5

> We are blind to the worlds within us, waiting to be born.
> —TOMAS LINDBERG, "BLINDED BY FEAR"

In May of 1995, At the Gates entered Studio Fredman in Gothenburg, Sweden, to record what would be their fourth and final full-length, *Slaughter of the Soul*. Unbeknownst to the band's members—not to mention heshers, headbangers and mustache warriors worldwide—it would become the most influential death metal album of the next decade. In the States, the now-legendary "Blinded by Fear" video hit *Headbangers Ball* face-first, and Riki Rachtman's red-eyed disciples were stupefied. Milk shot from a veritable legion of hairy nipples on the way to the record store, but the fallout wasn't fully ascertainable until many years later, when Shadows Fall, Killswitch Engage and countless other metal/hardcore crossover bands began incorporating what became known as the "Gothenburg Sound" into their sonic templates. Vocalist Tomas Lindberg's immortal command—"Go!"—in the opening seconds of *Slaughter*'s title track had become the war cry for a generation of future hardcore heroes and metal mercenaries. Unfortunately, during the seven consecutive months of touring that followed *Slaughter of the Soul*'s release, At the Gates went tits up in a blaze of alcohol and bad blood. While Lindberg went on to front half the metal bands in Sweden (the Great Deceiver, Hide, Nightrage, the Crown, Lock Up, Disfear), brothers Anders (guitar) and Jonas Björler (bass) formed the Haunted with drummer Adrian Erlandsson (currently of Cradle of Filth); guitarist Martin Larsson faded into the private sector (he still plays music, but not professionally). For the first time since the band's demise, *Decibel* tracked down all five members of At the Gates to find out why *Slaughter of the Soul* is so fucking good.

Was Slaughter of the Soul *a revenge album?*

Adrian Erlandsson: Totally—it was written in pure desperation. Before we recorded it, this promoter tricked us into going on a tour that had no real financial backing, and we got stuck for four days without any food or drink or anything in this parking lot outside a gig in Norwich [England]. We didn't even have a record deal at the time. Peaceville Records, who released *Terminal Spirit Disease*, wouldn't help us because we obviously didn't have a deal with them. [Patrick] Jensen's band, Séance, managed to talk their record company [Black Mark] into doing a deal over the phone with us in order to lend us money. They faxed all the record contracts to a truck stop, and we had to sign the deal there and then, and fax it back to be able to get the money to get back home. It was absolutely horrible. We had to pay them back in 45 days or they would have the rights to the next album.

Anders Björler: It was a really fucked-up situation. We only played two gigs on that tour with Séance; it was supposed to be 40 dates. Two days in, the promoter just left with the money. When we got in touch with Earache, we were really sparked by that because back then it was a really good label. Of course, we had all the old albums—Morbid Angel, Carcass, Bolt Thrower. It was a legendary label, and we were really surprised that they were interested in At the Gates.

Was the band close to breaking up at that point?

Erlandsson: Oh yeah, totally. We were really insecure with what was going to happen with the band. When we came back from that tour, it could've gone either way. It didn't have to do with any friction in the band at that point—it was just the frustration with the business. But then we got the Earache deal—and some royalties from *Terminal Spirit Disease*—so we managed to buy our way out of the deal with Black Mark. Had that not happened, *Slaughter of the Soul* would've ended up on Black Mark. I'm sure there wouldn't have been the inspiration for the band to continue.

Tomas Lindberg: So many things had gone wrong for us, organization-wise. We pushed ourselves more than we would have if it hadn't been bad times. We felt it was now or never.

What's the story behind "Blinded by Fear"?

A. Björler: It was the last track we wrote for the album. [*Laughs*] I actually think it's the worst track on the album. Everybody thinks it's fantastic, I think it's boring. But we wrote it as an opening song—we had the whole album, but not a real opener. I wrote it in maybe two or three hours, literally—a complete stroke of luck. Sometimes you get the whole song in your head and just show the other guys, sometimes it takes months.

Lindberg: People always mention "Blinded by Fear," but it's just the opener for us. It was written that way, and it fills its purpose as the opener when it's followed by the title track. But alone, it's not as strong as the others. As a single, it's always seemed out of context to me. I mean, when you hear a song from *Reign in Blood* taken out of the context of the album, when it stops, you know what song is supposed to come next. And when something else follows it on the radio, you're disappointed. It's like, "Hey, where's 'Postmortem'?" I like that vibe, one natural flow, and [*Slaughter*] is one of those albums for me.

What was the atmosphere like in the studio?

Lindberg: It was the most creative atmosphere I've ever felt. That album was everything we lived and breathed for. You probably couldn't talk to us about anything else in those months. Adrian was so serious about getting his parts right from the very start. You have to consider that the album was recorded before digital. Nowadays, you can move around drumbeats, you can reproduce parts of songs. All the songs [on *Slaughter*] were recorded start to finish on every take. You also have to remember that Jonas and Anders are twins—they fight like brothers, but even more so. There were a lot of compromises, a lot of disputes over riffs, but everybody was focused on the final effort. We were all young—between 21 and 23, and maybe not the best diplomats ever. [*Laughs*] Nowadays, it'd probably go a bit smoother. I felt like I had the worst part in one way, because everyone else had pushed themselves so hard and done such great work—

but the singers are always [recorded] last. It was like, "OK, I'm gonna go in there and ruin this now." I hate that feeling. The expectations were already up there.

Martin Larsson: We were all pulling in the same direction. I wasn't really much part of the writing process, because I wasn't living in Gothenburg. I lived four hours away, near Stockholm. I had my whole life [there]—family, girlfriend, all that—except for the band. I think I was in the studio for maybe a week or a little bit more, but not the whole time.

Erlandsson: I went in on a Monday, and the following Monday, I was starting a new job. So I had to finish all the drum tracks in one week. On that Sunday night, I finished the title track, and I still had to do "Blinded by Fear." It was really fucking late, but I managed, somehow, to get it done. I didn't have any energy left. A few days later, when I got back to the studio and heard the guitars on it, it was like, "Yeah, cool."

What did Fredrik Nordström bring to the table for the recording sessions?

Erlandsson: We did some demo tracks with him prior to *With Fear I Kiss the Burning Darkness*. He'd just moved into new facilities, and was really keen to make an impact. He had tons of ideas of how he wanted stuff to go. I had this really, really crap drum kit that I recorded the album with, but he's really good at tuning—which at the time I had no clue about—and he mixed it with the top end of the kick drum from [Pantera's] *Far Beyond Driven*. It was just a tiny bit, you can't even tell. It's quite a common trick these days, but I think *Slaughter* was one of the first albums he attempted something like that on.

Lindberg: It's about 80 percent live drums, and then about 20 percent of the bass drum is from *Far Beyond Driven*; 20 percent of the snare drum is from *Reign in Blood*. So most of it's live, but we spiced it up a bit to get that extra "click."

A. Björler: *Slaughter of the Soul* was an experiment on the guitar sound. I think we tried different things for like two or three days before we were satisfied. We went through a lot of pedals and tried all the amps we could get our hands on. I think we mixed two distortion pedals, and I played [through] a home-built cabinet that me and my dad built. I was maybe 21 or 22 at the time, and we didn't have any money, so we couldn't afford to buy much equipment. The funny thing is that Jesper [Strömblad] from In Flames wanted to borrow my stack on their next record—he was impressed with the sound on *Slaughter*. [*Laughs*] I had a cheap-ass guitar, too—it cost like $200 or something. But we had a sponsorship to study music from the government, and we used that to buy some equipment—but in general, we didn't have money. You'd have to report when you had your meetings and what you were studying, but it's basically a scam. You'd just rehearse and write music. The economy is worse now, so it's not as easy to get government funds as it was in the middle '90s.

Were all the lyrics written in advance?

Lindberg: I usually have most of the lyrics ready [beforehand]. Parts of the first two At the Gates albums were written lyrics-first. I'd give them to Anders, and he'd actually write songs around the lyrics. So we'd worked both ways before. I think about 90 percent of the lyrics were written [in advance], but you always have one lyric here and there that ends up being a last-minute thing. There's actually a line in "Suicide Nation" that's stolen from the first Meathook Seed album. We had one line that wasn't really working rhythmically, and I always stress out about that—the vocal rhythms have to be perfect. We needed to get the song done that day, and the Meathook Seed album was lying around. I happened to flip through it, and found the line "brainwashed into submission." So Mitch Harris should probably have some copyright money from me.

Whose idea was it to bring in Andy LaRocque to play the solo on "Cold"?

A. Björler: I think it was my idea, actually. Fredrik knew Andy very well, so we asked if he'd be interested in playing a solo. We're all King Diamond fans—and Mercyful Fate, of course. The funny thing was that we had given him a tape of that track, and when he came to the studio, he had it transcribed all wrong. So he had to rearrange all the notes, and he still did the whole thing in one hour or something. It was impressive. He's a very good musician.

Erlandsson: There's this music shop in Gothenburg where Andy used to work—just to be able to play guitar, I guess—and we all picked our gear up from there. We actually tried to get him play on *Terminal Spirit Disease* and *With Fear I Kiss the Burning Darkness*, but he listened to those albums when they were in their final stages and said he had no idea what to do. So then we played him all the tracks from *Slaughter* and he said he'd do one for "Cold." He came in the next day, sat down—he was really humble about it—and just played us his idea for the solo. Luckily, Fredrik hit record. He played it back for Andy, who wanted to try it again. So he rolled again, and Andy put this harmony on top of it, so it's actually doubled. It was pretty fucking cool. We were all like, "Wow—Andy LaRocque's playing on our album."

Lindberg: This was before we knew him, so we were not allowed in the same room when he was actually laying down the solo. [*Laughs*] We had to hang out in the recreation area of the studio. He said goodbye, and then we went in and listened to it.

At what point did you realize the impact **Slaughter** *had?*

Erlandsson: That's just been the last few years, to be honest, that new bands will come out and cite us as an influence. It's kind of difficult to say. At the time the band broke up, I was bitter—I thought we did way better with the Haunted.

A. Björler: It's really hard to say because bands like In Flames were influenced by us, but we were influenced by them as well. Same with Dissection and the whole Gothenburg scene—we kind of inspired each other. But the outside influence? Maybe one or two years afterwards. We noticed that hardcore bands in the U.S. would mix the Gothenburg style with New York hardcore. That was around '97 or something. I can't remember all the bands, but we toured with Hatebreed in '96. It's pretty weird, because when Fredrik and I mixed it, I was pretty disappointed. I thought we'd made a very bad record. [*Laughs*]

Jonas Björler It was after the break-up—maybe late '96 or early '97—when we began to realize the impact. When the album came out, we didn't really get many good reviews. I remember we got some really bad reviews from the German magazines. They said it was too generic or something, but people are always suspicious of new stuff.

Larsson: It was a gradual process—it wasn't a particular point in time. Old albums seem to fade into oblivion and become cult favorites for a limited few, but people still talk about this album—even more so than when we were still around. I didn't think it would last this long, but I'm happy about it. Every once in a while, someone will mention it to me, but not many people recognize me. Not like Tomas—everybody recognizes Tomas. But there are a few guys at my job who didn't realize I was in At the Gates—when they did, it was awkward, you know?

Lindberg: I can't remember a particular day where it crossed my mind or where people were getting into it on a wider scale. But the statements from Earache probably helped to make it clear for us. [*Laughs*] It's funny when sales actually increase eight years after an album has been out. It allows you to concentrate on what you're doing today, because at least you're getting paid.

Slaughter is as influential in hardcore and emo circles as it is with the metal crowd. Even musicians who don't necessarily play heavy music are into it. Why do you think that is?

Erlandsson: On this Cradle [of Filth] tour I'm on right now, we're with Bleeding Through and Himsa, and they all swear by that album for some reason. They've been telling me stories about how they came to see At the Gates live when we toured with Morbid Angel and Napalm Death. I know when [*Slaughter*] came out, Tomas was really into hardcore and he kept talking about various bands during the interviews—so I'm not sure if that's got anything to do with it or not. It seems far-fetched actually, because that was like 10 years ago. Without trying to sound cocky, some albums withstand the test of time, I guess. And I think whatever genre of heavy music you're into, that will come through. I don't wanna draw any comparisons to *Reign in Blood*, but that was another album that hardcore kids, emo kids, anyone who's into heavy music will relate to it. So I'm really flattered that there are people from different genres who are into it.

Lindberg: It's amazing. Especially the hardcore kids getting into it means a lot to me. I've always been 50 percent hardcore, 50 percent metal—that's always been my direction. Adrian played with me in my hardcore band, Skitsystem, while we were still in At the Gates. Everyone in the band was into hardcore to one degree or another, but maybe I was most into it. My lyrics were getting more—I wouldn't say political, but more hardcore-oriented. Also, the song structures we probably fought over most back then—a lot of that was in the hardcore sense, you know, thousands of riffs versus, like, three or four. For me, it's rewarding that it came across that we actually had a hardcore influence in the band. We even had some gigs here in Gothenburg—parties and stuff—where we played some hardcore covers. If you had been in Gothenburg around '93 or '94, you could've actually seen At the Gates doing "Skins, Brains & Guts" by 7 Seconds.

How did you settle on the cover art?

A. Björler: I think Tomas had some ideas about the whole thing being about . . . well, not really suicide, but the lyrical content is very dark. We did some over-the-top things, too—we had a gun upside down as the Nike symbol on [an At the Gates] t-shirt that said, "Just Do It." We have that kind off stuff with the Haunted as well—it's a powerful image.

J. Björler: It's not the best cover I've ever seen, but it fits the music. It's pretty good, but maybe it's too brown. [*Laughs*] If you play metal music, guns are good symbols for violence—and it fit the concept and lyrics as well.

Erlandsson: I was a bit shocked, actually. I wasn't sure about having Jesus on the front, with guns and stuff. At the time, I was more conservative than I am now. We were really psyched about the music at the time, so just the fact that we actually got to choose the album cover ourselves was pretty cool.

Lindberg: It was really fun to get Kristian [Wåhlin] to do the artwork for what we felt was a big album for us. Kristian and me go back a long time—we're childhood friends. We had a band before At the Gates; he's also playing with me now in the Great Deceiver. I remember giving him mix tapes of songs that, for me, portrayed the same atmosphere we wanted for the album—I know he likes to paint with music in the background. Everything from hardcore to death metal to noise music was on those tapes. Then we went to magazine shops looking for copies of *Guns & Ammo*. [*Laughs*] We settled on guns and religious symbols—but most of the actual ideas come from him.

The drunken band photo in the CD booklet was staged, wasn't it?

Erlandsson: Yeah. We went to this friend's house to snap some pictures, and we had a few drinks. Pretty soon the night was over, and there were no pictures taken. We went back there the next day and thought it'd make a pretty cool shot, like *Master of Puppets* or something. We all grew up listening to that album, and we wanted to show it somehow.

J. Björler: It was half-staged, maybe. The picture was taken in the photographer's living room. We wanted a picture like *Reign in Blood*, you know?

Larsson: We put together all the empty bottles and brought out all the cool albums to make it look right. And it does.

In retrospect, is there anything you'd change about the album?

Lindberg: No, I don't think so. There are always details—some words on the album have a strong sound, but it's stupid to change stuff like that afterward. Yeah, there are misprints in the lyric sheet, but people already figured that out 10 years ago. It's one of those albums I wouldn't change too much on because of the impact it had. It must've been right.

A. Björler: I think it's very complete. I'm very satisfied with it, but my favorite is *Terminal Spirit Disease*.

Larsson: The songs are a bit samey to me. The ultimate album is a mixture of *Slaughter of the Soul* and *Terminal Spirit Disease*, with the production of *Slaughter*. I think the composition of songs is better on *Terminal Spirit Disease*—I think *Slaughter* could've been more varied.

J. Björler: If you'd asked me that directly after we did it, there were probably a lot of things I'd change. But now I'm pretty satisfied with it. I wouldn't change a thing.

Erlandsson: Had we done another album, I'm sure there would've been other ideas for it, but as far as being our last album, I couldn't wish for a better one. That was actually one of the twins' arguments for quitting the band—that we'd never be able to come up with anything better. Then again, they're really cynical. Had I gone with the feeling I had when Anders wanted to leave the band, I would've pushed to do another album, to be honest. I didn't want to let go at the time that it happened, but it wasn't really a choice for any of us. It had to be that way. I'm obviously really fucking happy that I was part of it, but it's kinda hard to try to re-create that feeling that was there when that album was being written. Everything surrounding it just had this aura about it, but we were sort of magically unaware. Had we known that we were doing something good, it would've been a bit more pretentious, I think.

CHAPTER 19

FLOWER POWER

THE MAKING OF OPETH'S *ORCHID*

by Chris Dick

Release Date: 1995
Label: Candlelight
Summary: Death metal gets its prog on
Induction Date: February 2008/Issue #40

O peth's *Orchid* existed, either as a partial or full album with the songs cut in random places, among tape-traders for almost a full year before Candlelight ceremoniously unfurled it upon an unsuspecting public in May 1995. The tapes—typically a Maxell XL-II 90 in most respectable circles—with "Opeth" scrawled in pen on both sides, were for all intents and purposes a mystery. Before the Internet, every road went uphill, so finding anything (who they were, where they were from, etc.) on "Opeth" wasn't as simple as Googling the name. So, why trouble through endless flyers, sift fact from rumor from like-minded metalheads at shows, or blindly send cold hard cash in the mail to some far-flung country for a zine, a demo or god knows what else? Quite honestly, it was the music. After ordering (yes, with cash) a copy of Dutch zine *Mortician* from an old flyer advertising coverage of the enigmatic outfit, "Opeth" became Opeth—they were Swedish, friends of Katatonia and were being courted by Candlelight. Opeth were like nothing I, or anyone else for that matter, had ever heard before. Sure, death metal, after its formative stages, wasn't averse to experimentation or the influence of other genres (like jazz, for example), but it never sounded as powerful, fearless or skilled as on *Orchid*.

In reality, *Orchid* wasn't death metal, for it was conceptually, structurally or sonically analogous to no other. Rather it was something more. With five songs traveling near and past the 10-minute mark, a piano piece (not an intro!), an acoustic guitar/tabla raga and an album cover with a pink flower—an orchid, obviously—on it, Opeth's debut was, to quote frontman Mikael Åkerfeldt in 1993, a masterful hybrid of "Wishbone Ash, Black Sabbath and Bathory." To put it another way, Opeth weren't too far from, say, Morbid Angel adapting "Moonchild." Songs like opener "In Mist She Was Standing," "The Twilight Is My Robe" and the anthemic closer "The Apostle in Triumph" destroyed the verse-chorus-verse construct, un-mapping death metal into a genre of tangents and limitless possibilities, whereas "Under the Weeping Moon" and "Forest of October" were unheard-of great. "Under the Weeping Moon"'s sprawling, psyche-satanic midsection is the blackest metal this side of *Under a Funeral Moon* and "Forest of October"'s incessant fireworks (check out 5:46–6:27) and riffing (everywhere) are countless reasons why the album is above and beyond awesome. Produced by Opeth and engineered by the ever-gifted Dan Swanö at Unisound in March 1994, *Orchid* also sounded different from albums produced there before and after. It was inviting, abrasive and full of subtlety. Despite *Symbolic*, *Slaughter of the Soul*, *Domination*, *The Gallery* and *Storm of the Light's Bane* blowing minds in 1995, it was Opeth's *Orchid* that changed death metal forever. But in the early '90s, nobody—not even Opeth themselves—knew that. Good thing hindsight is 20/20.

PART I: SLEEP, TO WISH IMPOSSIBLE THINGS . . .

What are your memories of Orchid*?*

Mikael Åkerfeldt: When I think of the album, I think of the recording, actually. We had been playing those songs for years. We were tight. We rehearsed the songs several times a week. We rehearsed in the dark, so we could play the songs without looking, which is fucking stupid. The rehearsal room we borrowed from a neighbor in Sörskogen, where me and Anders [Nordin, drummer] grew up. We had old Vox 8030 amplifiers with a Heavy Metal pedal through it. We blew up a few speakers doing that.

Peter Lindgren: We really just wanted to get these songs on tape. We had been rehearsing them for years. At the point when we recorded the album, the songs were mature enough to be recorded. We were pretty serious about rehearsing. We rehearsed five or six times a week for a year. We were a three-piece. We always recorded rehearsals. The idea wasn't to spread the band's music, but to use it to improve the songs. Even though we didn't do many gigs at the time, we had a plan in mind. So, we decided to rehearse in darkness. We thought if we could play the songs in total darkness, we could cope with anything onstage.

Anders Nordin: I remember I was quite anxious before the studio to hear the final results. *Orchid*, to me, was like a receipt of years of rehearsals. Sweat, blood and tears. Even though those sessions were fun, it's always nice when you get some kind of recognition for it. Being anxious, however, changed quickly into stress when we finally started the recordings. Twelve total studio days divided into four instruments isn't exactly a huge amount of time.

Johan DeFarfalla: My overall memories of *Orchid* are good memories. It's musically quite cool. I don't like the sound, 'cause it's too noisy. It's the wrong sound on the bass and the wrong sound on the guitars. It's full of errors as well. We didn't hear it at the time, so the engineer should've told us to do the retakes. I think we could've done better.

We had a lot of fun during the recording, though.

Åkerfeldt: I remember I was working in a guitar store when it was released. It was delayed like a year or something, and I went up to my local post office to ask them if they'd call me when I got a package from England. They called, so I took off work and picked up the little box from Candlelight. A 25 box. I thought, "Wow, this is my album!" It didn't take long to see the horror of everything that was wrong with it. It was pretty magical.

Do you remember what people thought of **Orchid** *when it came out?*
Åkerfeldt: It made a big impact, I remember. Most people, at least in the Swedish scene, were recording at Unisound, and Opeth, before the album came out, was considered a joke band. No one expected anything from us. The rumor wasn't great about us. Some of the early shows we did were awful and David [Isberg], our singer who formed that band, wasn't liked too much. We didn't have a good vibe going about the band. We didn't have any friends in the scene. I didn't know anyone. We were total outsiders. When the album came out, I remember I got a call from Dan. Unanimated was in the studio after us, and he's like, "I just recorded this band from Stockholm called Opeth. Do you know them?" They laughed and said we were a joke band. He's like, "No, it's pretty

good. I can play it." So, he played and they listened to a couple of songs, and, according to Dan, they had to have a band meeting. Like, "What the fuck should we do now?" I was a fan of Unanimated, so it's like "Whoa! That's great!" In the underground of undergrounds in Sweden, it made an impact. We got a good review from *Close-Up*, the big one in Sweden. I remember one bad review in a French magazine called *Metallian*. It's a free magazine, of course. The review just said, "Boring and uneventful. 1/10." Most people seemed to like it. My only friends in the scene at the time were in Katatonia. They loved the album. Before it was released, I was a session guitar player for Katatonia and I would play a tape of it in the dressing room hoping somebody would say, "What is this? This sounds good." Nobody really said anything.

Lindgren: We didn't know what to expect. We thought something big would happen, but it didn't. We thought we'd get instant success, but I think we were a little naïve. At the time, we were writing material for *Morningrise*, 'cause it was delayed for such a long time. People really seemed to like it. It's cool to have people you don't know tell you they like your music. People could tell we stood out.

DeFarfalla: There are two answers. From the death metal scene, they thought, "Wow! This is cool!" From the educated musicians I knew, they said, "This sucks. The sound is bad. You should re-record this." But I think people really liked it, apart from the sound.

Why didn't you ever record a demo?

Åkerfeldt: We didn't have any money. For us, to go into the studio to record a demo was as big a step as going in to record an album. We didn't have any money to spend on things like that. That would cost us, at least, a couple of hundred bucks. I was living with my mom at the time. I was working, obviously, but I didn't make that kind of money. The other guys weren't really rich or anything. We didn't know where to go to record a demo. We had planned it all along. Then, out of the blue, we got an offer from Lee [Barrett] to do an album. It was quite weird. I was sending out rehearsal tapes to all the usual labels, and I never had a reply. I'm not sure if anyone listened to them. Then Anders [Nyström] from Katatonia said Candlelight was interested based off a rumor from Emperor. Samoth, I think it was, sent out a tape of unsigned bands to Lee at Candlelight. It only had a couple of seconds of "The Apostle in Triumph." Lee liked it so much he wanted to sign the band. I never heard anything, though. One day when I was walking up to the apartment where me and my mother lived, there was a letter taped to the board with all the names of people who lived in the apartments. It said, "To Opeth . . ." He didn't know who the fuck we were. It asked us to record a three-song EP. I was like, "Yeah, fuck, yeah!" I couldn't believe it. So, I went upstairs to read the letter again, and the phone rings. It's

Lee! He's like, "Did you get my letter? I sent it weeks ago." He then said, "Forget what I said in the letter. I want to release a full-length album from you." And that was it.

Lindgren: Initially, we couldn't afford it. Maybe that's why we did rehearsal tapes instead. We always wanted to be great, so maybe we thought it would be better to keep practicing and rehearsing than to record a demo. Then we got a record deal, so we never had to record a demo. I liked the idea of us not having a demo. It was sort of a non-image image. Nobody knew who we were, so it was a little more mysterious to not have a demo.

Nordin: I guess we never came to that point, as Candlelight offered us a deal from a rehearsal tape. If we hadn't got that deal, I think we would've recorded a demo.

You signed a deal with Candlelight off a rehearsal song. Looking back on it, do you think Opeth were lucky to have found a label willing to believe in the band?

Åkerfeldt: Yeah, I guess. We struggled like every other band. We just didn't have any demos. If we'd done a proper demo, we would've been signed from that. We were a good band. Those rehearsal tapes were quite good, and there's no bass on them. We had been playing those songs forever. We were tighter than most bands in Stockholm. I mean, Katatonia were sloppy. They could barely play. It was only At the Gates we found to be our biggest competition.

Lindgren: Yeah, looking back it's awkward. It's cool, too. We got a record deal from 20 seconds of a song on a rehearsal tape.

Nordin: I think Candlelight were lucky to find us. Yes, a little lucky, but thanks to my mum's Dixi radio-recorder, we got the deal.

What was your relationship with Sörskogen like?

Åkerfeldt: It's a fake romance. It's a beautiful place, but it's a place for families with kids. Every house had kids my age. They were into metal, I think. But there were no bands. Maybe a couple. It was kind of isolated in a way. It was a suburb with three streets. It was almost like a little mountain. You have to drive up a little slope. We didn't really leave. We just hung out there. My dad was taking care of this house that people could rent for parties. I basically borrowed the key. That became our rehearsal place. I rehearsed there with my other band, Eruption, which was me, Anders and some other guys. I would say, in retrospect, it meant a lot. We never went into town. We just spent every day listening to music and, eventually, started playing in bands. Now, since we're a professional band, I always want to connect with that place.

Lindgren: Both me and Mike grew up in a suburb of Stockholm called Huddinge. Both Sörskogen and Visättra, where I grew up, were situated near this forest and a big lake. On the other side of the lake was Sörskogen. We didn't really hang out until we were about 14 or 16. We both grew up doing the same things, but on different sides of this lake. We started hanging out together 'cause we both had the same interests: basically, metal. I wouldn't consider moving back. Where I was from was a bad suburb. Where Mike was from, it's like this neat little suburb, with all these little nice houses.

Nordin: Sörskogen is the neighborhood where Mikael and I grew up. Sörskogen played a big role in how the music came to develop, as we used to rehearse here and we also got to know Charlie [a drummer], who later on helped us use his rehearsal pad and equipment.

DeFarfalla: I had a girlfriend in Sörskogen. I was from more downtown Stockholm. I met the guys in Crimson Cat in '88, and then I met Mikael and Anders. I didn't know Peter before we played together.

Wasn't the silhouette photo on the back of **Orchid** *taken in Sörskogen?*
Åkerfeldt: Yeah. The front cover of *My Arms, Your Hearse* is also from Sörskogen. The band pictures from *Deliverance* and *Damnation* were also taken there. The picture inside *Damnation* is from Sörskogen. Obviously, before we got signed there were a lot of photo sessions there.

PART II: IN THE WILDERNESS, EVEN FOES CLOSE THEIR EYES AND LEAVE . . .

How much time did you guys spend playing, rehearsing and writing back then?
Mikael Åkerfeldt: All the time. There are parts to *Orchid* that go all the way back to 1990. When I first joined the band, one of the first riffs I wrote was the solo riff in "Forest of October." It was the first riff I ever did for Opeth. It was just me and David. The idea for Opeth was for it to be evil—satanic lyrics and evil riffs. I chose my notes so they sounded evil. We eventually found a place to rehearse and a little PA. I had a 20-watt Marshall amp that I lined through the PA. The bass went right into the PA. Anders bought a drum kit later on, so we had drums. It was the same kind of gear we used up to *Morningrise*.

Lindgren: As soon as you start playing an instrument, you have plans to form a band. We had dreams. We tried to make plans out of those dreams. Writing and rehearsing was important to me and Mikael. We were teenagers, trying to find our identity. We took pride in writing our own material. We spent a lot of time writing and rehearsing, 'cause we wanted to achieve something.

Nordin: We rehearsed quite often, sometimes four to five times a week. But I never saw it as rehearsals. It was more time spent being with friends and to have fun.

DeFarfalla: I don't remember us rehearsing a lot, but during the time I was with them—maybe two months before we went in to record the album—things started to heat up. I really liked playing those songs with those guys. They were nice guys.

The playing style was a bit different for a death metal band. Were there specific sounds or things you were going for?

Åkerfeldt: I was never a big fan of the bands we might relate to. I had the first My Dying Bride EP [*Symphonaire Infernus Et Spera Empyrium*], and I didn't really like it. It was too slow. My favorite band was Morbid Angel. I couldn't play like Trey [Azagthoth] or write that stuff. I also liked '80s heavy metal, and during that time I started to listen to prog rock. I didn't have a preference, really. I just tried to come up with good riffs. I must say, At the Gates was a big influence on us. They were my favorite Swedish band. I didn't want to sound like them, but if there was one band I wanted to sound like, it would be At the Gates. I got a rehearsal tape from [ATG drummer] Adrian [Erlandsson] at a gig with them, and I was like, "Wow!" I worshipped them. I loved them. We became friends early on. On top of that, I was also influenced by a lot of prog rock.

Lindgren: It was due to our influences. We were all into metal, except Johan. He was more into glam rock. He knew different kinds of music we didn't know in the beginning. Both me and Mikael started to dig into other kinds of music, like '70s music. There's a lot of freedom in '70s music. You realized a song could be textural and 14 minutes long. We learned a lot from listening to '70s-style music, 'cause metal bands didn't really have those ideas or freedoms. We wanted to incorporate that into our music. When Mikael started using his clean voice, all hell broke loose. We realized not many other bands had clean vocals. Mikael was pretty brave at the time. We always wanted to enhance what made us different.

Nordin: We all had our influences. We always played and made music that suited our own music tastes. We made the music for ourselves. We didn't try to find any sound. The sound ended up the way it did.

DeFarfalla: Well, since I didn't know death metal too much, I didn't try to go for anything specific. I really just played in the best possible way. I think they liked that I was a bass player who knew the bass. I wasn't some guy who just showed up, hoping to play something. I don't think it mattered what kind of music I was into.

What role did Mefisto play in the formative years?

Åkerfeldt: Mefisto was the first death metal band I really liked. I tried to fool myself with bands like Celtic Frost, Venom and Bathory. They couldn't play, in my opinion. I was more into good guitar players from bands like Scorpions, Judas Priest and Iron Maiden. There's no comparison between Tom G. Warrior's guitar solos to Matthias Jabs' solos. I was interested in aggression, but I didn't like the fact they couldn't really play. Then David gave me a tape of Mefisto. The guitar player could play classical guitar, interludes and shit like that. Even though the solos were noisy, they had a ton of emotion in them. It was tight. I was like, "Fuck! This is what I want to hear!" Then, a year later, I got to hear Morbid Angel. That was it. I was lost. That's when I started to really get into death metal. With that, I came to realize Celtic Frost was actually quite musical. Like *To Mega Therion* and *Into the Pandemonium*. They were interesting. Mefisto was the stepping-stone for me. To this day, those two tapes they did are still very good. Very grim.

How did the band operate? Was the process democratic when it came down to finalizing the songs?

Åkerfeldt: It was me and Peter. Peter came up with a few riffs. I wrote most of them, but it was basically the two of us jamming. Anders also had a few riffs. He had the piano thing. We had never heard it until he recorded it. He was very musical. He could've done so much more. He helped with a couple of riffs on "In Mist She Was Standing." We were a democratic band, with me coming up with most of the riffs.

Lindgren: We tried to be democratic. We gathered at my place one time. It was me, Anders, Mikael and Johan. We had three acoustic guitars and Anders was playing drums on pillows. We tried to write together. It didn't really work. Some people write better on their own. Anders was like that. He came up with great stuff, but as soon as we were together, he'd not say anything.

DeFarfalla: In the beginning, it was democratic. There was lots of discussion about everything. Everything was arranged with all the members, and we talked a lot about how to do music. I really enjoyed that. But, I think, in the end, it ended up not being so democratic.

How old were you when you when **Orchid** *was recorded?*

Åkerfeldt: I was 19 when we recorded the album. I turned 20 during the recording. I was 21 by the time it was released.

Nordin: 22.

Lindgren: 21. Metallica were my heroes. Metallica were the same age when they recorded *Kill 'Em All*.

DeFarfalla: 23, I think. I was born in 1971.

Did your family support the idea of being in a band, touring and recording albums?

Åkerfeldt: I was convinced this is what I wanted to do. Peter was studying at the time and went into the Army. My parents supported my interest in music, but they didn't believe I would make a living off it. Every parent worries about that. A bum with a dream. It was only years later she said she was glad I went for it. Originally, my mom tried to get me into studying. She's like, "Look at Peter. He's studying. His hobby is second." I would say, "It's not a hobby for me, mom. It's what I want to do." She didn't believe in that, but she loved the fact I was interested in music. So did my dad, but he never said anything. Johan was the only other guy who was a musician. He was in other bands before. He worked at a place that had rehearsal rooms, where we also later rehearsed. He was in the scene in a way. He came from the sleaze rock scene. He was a proper musician, whereas myself and Anders were just dreamers. Peter, who loved music, was more realistic. He went for a strong education. Me and Anders, at the time, didn't have anything to fall back on if the band didn't work out. That's one of the reasons why Anders left eventually. I remember going up to Anders' house and ringing the bell. I just wanted to hang out. His dad answers and is firm with me. He's like, "No, Anders isn't interested in music anymore. He's going to concentrate on his studies." That kind of speech. I had a sour taste in my mouth after that. I liked Anders' dad. With him leaving the band, I was very disappointed. When you're young and friends, you say you're going to play together forever. We were really tight. I think eventually after the first tour, it was kind of fine. We still didn't have any money, but we started out with nothing and now we had an album, fans overseas, and we toured. But we didn't make any money. That was the issue. If we would've come home from tour with a hundred grand saying, "Look, mom!" they probably wouldn't complain at all. It was still a dream. The support from our parents was mixed, now that I think of it.

Lindgren: Yeah, my dad is a jazz enthusiast. He plays jazz guitar. On a Levin acoustic. He was really supportive. My mom and sister were supportive, too, but he was genuinely interested in what I was doing. He never told me to cut my hair or anything like that. Even nowadays, he'll buy magazines to get the reviews. He saves them in a little book. He was encouraging all the time.

Nordin: My family was always supporting me and the band. My parents often helped me transport drums when I didn't have a driver's license. And I think they were never worried about us being in the wrong company or [whatever] because they kind of knew where we were all the time. In the rehearsal pad!

DeFarfalla: Yes, absolutely. My family always supported my music. Music was, at the time, was first and foremost. I started playing when I was nine years old. I was playing in a punk band. It's all I ever thought about and wanted. I remember my mom said, "You can always study later. If you want to play music, then go play music." I appreciated that a lot. I met my wife during that time, so looking back I think it was great for me.

'60s and '70s progressive music was also important in defining Opeth. I remember you talking a great deal about Wishbone Ash, Camel, King Crimson and, to a lesser extent, Swedish artists like Bo Hansson, Kebnekajse and Huvva.

Åkerfeldt: We used to have parties on the weekend. There was one particular party by a classmate of mine where I got drunk and slept on the couch. The next day, he's like, "Here's a band. You might like it." It was Yes. I was blown away. The odd thing is he was in a punk band. He only listened to punk, and I didn't like that. But he played me Yes and, at the time, we were really a standard death metal band. When I heard Yes, I saw what we could do. To incorporate that into death metal. It wasn't long after I heard Dream Theater. They're also a big influence. I remember going to the secondhand store and picking everything that looked cool. You know, a cool sleeve, if they looked cool in the band photo. It was so cheap. Like a buck. I was working at the guitar store and I asked the guy there if he knew any bands in the style of Yes and Genesis. He was like, "Yeah, check out Camel, King Crimson and stuff like that." So I did. Basically every lunch break I'd go to the record store to buy secondhand vinyl. That became my obsession. It is to this day. I was always a collector, and this was perfect. It was a new scene. I felt special. I felt extra cool, 'cause none of my friends were into it. I was alone. Like, "Never heard of Wishbone Ash? What a tosser!" My oldest friend got me into Wishbone Ash. He was more into the Beatles. He played the *Argus* record. I was blown away by that. It made a big impact on me. It was the guy from Mellontronen who really sent me over the edge. He would recommend zillions of bands like Comus.

Lindgren: In the late '80s, it was only metal. I only bought metal vinyl. But after a while, you could hear a pretty good song that wasn't metal. I wouldn't buy the album. Why? It's not metal. Eventually, I bought something that wasn't metal, so once I crossed that line I realized I liked music that didn't have anything to do with Slayer or Metallica. We thought—and it was a pretty mature idea—that we'd actually create something out of music that wasn't metal. As soon as we started listening to '70s music, we realized there was so much to discover. Songs could be really long and have a lot of texture. A lot of those bands were heavy for the day, but if you compare Wishbone Ash to Slayer, it's hard to hear how they connect to one another. But Black Sabbath must've turned the world upside down when they started.

DeFarfalla: The cool thing about this was Mikael showed me bands I had never heard of. Like Wishbone Ash. I still like them now. I listened to Led Zeppelin and old Uriah Heep. Mikael is very musical, so when he hears good music, he'll listen to it. It doesn't have to be metal. Me and Mikael are similar in that way.

Did you know Orchid *was different from what was going on at the time? I remember everyone struggling to classify it. It was so new.*

Åkerfeldt: I was pretty sure it was different. I didn't know any bands that sounded like us. I mean, I knew where we came from with bands like At the Gates, Therion and Morbid Angel. I was the one who bought the most records. It was bound to be different. I have always loved ballads. Like ballads from Judas Priest and Scorpions. There's a lot of acoustic parts and clean singing, so yeah, it was different. The only thing we had in common, at the time, was that we were melodic metal.

Lindgren: We knew it was different. Not only because we had different influences, but also we had been working on the songs for so long that we could tell they weren't part of any trend.

Nordin: I had a feeling it was different, but I never thought of it that much. It never bothered me what other people thought, to be honest. Having said that, of course, it's nice if other people like it, too!

DeFarfalla: Yes, I think so. I didn't come from the death metal scene, but I knew it was different. It was musical. I think other death metal bands, at the time, weren't too musical. It was like noise. Opeth was different.

Didn't Jonas [Renkse] jokingly call it "forest metal"? Foolish as it sounds, it's fitting.

Åkerfeldt: Yeah, he had all sorts of ideas. I was into the new wave of black metal, like Darkthrone and Emperor. It was cool to come up with new descriptions for music, even if it didn't mean anything. We weren't black metal. We weren't death metal. So why not come up with something completely ridiculous? When I listen to it, I have an image or illusion that we wrote songs in the woods, which wasn't true, obviously.

Lindgren: I don't know why we were called that. We had a song with "forest" in the title. They were forest-like tunes. Having all these people trying to brand or tag you is kind of strange. It was a joke. We heard a rumor that In Flames heard that we had gone forest metal, so they felt that they had to make their music even more forest metal.

What is your favorite song from the album and why?

Åkerfeldt: There are parts in every song that are favorites. If there's one song, though, it's "Under the Weeping Moon." We've been playing it live and it's the one song that hasn't aged as much. It's got more in common with what we're doing today. At the time, it was "The Apostle in Triumph." It had the volume swells, which I stole from King Diamond.

Lindgren: I thought at the time "Twilight Is My Robe," but "The Apostle in Triumph" was also special. We played "The Apostle in Triumph" so much, it's actually quite boring. It's dreadful to play. Same with "The Night and the Silent Water" from the second album. Looking back, "Forest of October" is the best song on the album.

Nordin: My favorite song is "The Apostle in Triumph." It has many parts that bring back old memories from older songs.

DeFarfalla: "Requiem," for sure. I really like what we did on this song. It was short, but it was so different for the time. More like a jam. I played the acoustic bass.

The instrumental pieces "Silhouette" and "Requiem" were pretty different for a death metal band.

Åkerfeldt: Yeah, Anders was a piano player. He and the friend who introduced me to Wishbone Ash were piano players. They kind of showed each other stuff. Anders was leaning more into classical stuff, while my other friend was doing boogie-woogie. When we heard it, it was like "Wow!" That song made us feel really small as musicians. He's a fucking pro. Even Johan was like, "That's awesome!" I don't remember the aim with "Requiem," but we had no real plans with the sequencing of the album. It was recorded in a different studio. It was recorded by a guitar player who's now in a band called the Poodles.

Lindgren: "Silhouette" was a song Anders had written on his own. He came up with these things on his own. It's like, "Fuck! What is he doing?" Anders could only have three or four takes. He played on a synth-piano. The keys were totally different. The whole thing is one take, I think. There's a flaw, but it's great. I remember when Dan played it back, it was like, "Yes, this is great!" We always prided ourselves on doing all the music ourselves. As opposed to cheating. We never did overdubs on the albums, especially on the first one. Everything you hear, we can do it live. With "Requiem," we had to record it at another studio. Opeth's music has always been organized. There's a piece at the end of "Requiem" where the tension builds. We didn't really plan it. So that was cool. It's mastered wrong. At the time, we didn't know what mastering was. None of us attended the mastering session. The guy, Peter In de Betou, cut the song in the wrong place. It's cut in half. "The Apostle in Triumph" has an acoustic intro it was never supposed to have. I guess Peter thought it made sense. "Requiem" is divided into two parts, but he got it wrong.

Nordin: "Requiem" was meant as a prologue to "Apostle," so I think it really fits in where it is. If I'm not mistaken, the gap between those two is too long. It should've been one song. But both "Requiem" and "Silhouette" were supposed to calm down the other metal songs. Regarding "Silhouette," it's done. It's there. I'm trying to live on and forget about it.

DeFarfalla: Yes, I agree. They were not too death metal in concept. These songs were more like proper music. They weren't noise. "Requiem" was written at Unisound, I think, but we recorded it at a different studio due to time issues. I can't remember which studio. The music is quite good. Mike had some guitar parts and we basically jammed through them. Such good memories of that.

PART III: WHEN YOU ARE CALM INSIDE THE WILDERNESS, THE BROTHERS ARE STILL SEEKING . . .

Why didn't you change the band name after David left?

Åkerfeldt: First, I wanted to be in Opeth 'cause the name sounded cool. Second, I loved the logo. It's the reason I joined. It's perfect. We decided to keep it. We had done a few shows with the name, so some people recognized the name. I redid the logo, 'cause I didn't want us to be perceived as a satanic band. More like metal minstrels.

Lindgren: We just got used to it. I joined the band as a bass player. Mike joined the band as a bass player. Then, all of a sudden, the guy who came up with the name left. Both me and Mike were guitar players, so we had an opportunity to change the direction of the band and take over the guitar player roles. We did that. I remember when Mike joined the band, everyone else was fired by David. Mike showed up at an Opeth rehearsal with David, and David didn't tell the bass player there's another guy coming in. There was a big quarrel, so David fired everyone. He reformed the band with him and Mike. I joined a little later. This guitar player, his name was Kim [Pettersson], was quite cool. He had a lousy memory. He couldn't remember the songs. Mike and him were the guitar players and I was the bass player. So, as soon as he forgot the parts, he'd solo over the riffs. It sounded pretty good, but it wouldn't work in the long run with a guitar player with no memory. We didn't fire him, though, 'cause he was in Crimson Cat. He thought of Opeth as an experiment. When Kim left, I stepped up to guitars. When Mike and I started writing songs together, we found that David had a specific personality. He could cause problems for us. He was annoying people, basically. We thought David could fuck it—the dream—up for us, but we couldn't fire David from his own band. So, we thought of quitting and forming a new band. But then when David and Mike were in Austria on a skiing trip, he told Mike, "I quit the band." Mike was like, "Yeah!" We liked the name. It was mystical enough. It never occurred to us to get a new name.

At what point did the recording lineup for **Orchid** *solidify? Johan was still regarded as a session musician at the time, if I remember correctly.*

Åkerfeldt: He did a gig with us in '91 with At the Gates. The second guitar player, at the time, was also from Johan's band, Crimson Cat. We asked Kim if he knew a bass player, and he recommended Johan. When we went to record the album, we had fired our bass player Stefan [Guteklint], 'cause he was messing around with another band on the side. It's a classic dismissal of a band member. We had just gotten three-way calling in Sweden, so me and Peter planned how we were going to fire Stefan. So, I called Stefan, but Peter wasn't there when I hit the three-way button. It's like, "Uh, fuck, can I call you back in a moment?" So, we called him back and fired him. We asked Johan to play on the album, so when he did it was at the point he joined the band. During the photo session for it, he said, "From now on, I'm only going to work with professional musicians." Me and Peter were like, "Uh, does that mean us?" He was a terrific bass player. He was a strong character. He had a strong musical mind. I was extremely happy to have him in the band.

We had a proper bass player. Apart from Steve DiGiorgio, there were no proper bass players. Most were guitar players who weren't good enough, so they had to play bass.

Lindgren: Mike joined the band in 1990. I joined the band in late 1991 just for one show. Anders was in the band when I joined, so he must've joined sometime after Mike. We were a three-piece for a long time, rehearsing heavily. We recruited Johan for basically the recording of *Orchid*. He was two years older than us. It was cool to have Johan in the band, even for the album. We had a plan for him to stay with us. He was a funk/glam rock player. We had broader ideas than most metal bands. I think he liked that. We didn't want him to be Jason Newsted. We wanted him to play cool stuff—to be a bass player. He lifted us to a new level. He had a few cool ideas, and some weird ones. All those bands never had good bass players. They were just guitar players who were forced to play bass. They played with a pick and held it like a guitar. We wanted to take advantage of having a real bass player. He actually carried a cell phone on his belt, I remember. When he joined the band, the cell phone was a big thing for us.

DeFarfalla: That was during the recording. Well, I was never hired, so to speak. Hiring would mean I got paid for something. And I didn't. I remember the reason I joined the band is because of Mikael. I really liked him. He was a good musician, too. They were all good people, so I think that was the most important thing. I don't think I would've agreed if I didn't like them as people or I didn't like their music. I remember telling them I needed to continue developing my band and playing different kinds of music, and they were fine with it.

How did you meet Dan Swanö, and how did he end up engineering **Orchid?**

Åkerfeldt: Katatonia had recorded their album there. They were my friends and I didn't know anywhere else. He was cheap and had a place to stay. It was just two hours from Stockholm. He had done Dissection and Marduk. I knew about Edge of Sanity and I knew about Dan. I thought the Katatonia record sounded awesome. Now, it's like, "God, this is fucking awful!" But I called him up and that was it. We had never been in the studio before, so we figured it would be like the old days. You know, everybody standing in a room, playing it live. We could've done that. We were so well rehearsed. But we started with the drums in one room. He didn't really produce much, 'cause there wasn't much to produce. He coached me on the clean singing. I thought he was a great singer. He didn't come up with musical ideas, though. We were ready.

Lindgren: Mike came up with his name. He recorded Katatonia. Jonas and Anders were fans of Opeth and came to our rehearsal room. I didn't know them at the time. Mike and Jonas became good friends. That's how it went. Everyone was recording in Sunlight at the time, and we wanted to do something different. We also had the idea of leaving town with nothing and coming back with something. Cowboy style.

Do you remember much about your time at Unisound?

Åkerfeldt: It was done in 12 days on 16-track with quarter-inch tapes. It was really low-budget. For us, 16 was like, "Wow!" We had two before. I remember having shivers all over when I was doing the vocals. It was just me and Dan in the studio. Dan was screaming, "You're the fucking best!" I recorded a guide guitar with Anders drumming. We saved some of that. You can hear it on "Under the Weeping Moon."

Lindgren: The studio was in Finspång, a village in the middle of nowhere. Dan had his studio there. We rented this one bedroom flat. You could walk down to the studio. I remember when we mixed the album, we were really hung over. We went out the night before and got really wasted. Nothing was digital back then, so it was me, Dan and Mike trying to get this 14-minute song down on tape. We had to write everything down. It was really hard when you have a splitting headache. We had a great time during those two weeks.

Nordin: I remember a lot of good things from the studio and around the studio, but also, of course, the stress that when you wake up and are about to go to the studio, you know that when you come back to the apartment, almost half of your parts have to be recorded—no matter what happens—as we basically had two and a half days each to record.

DeFarfalla: I remember a lot about Unisound—some good and some bad. I remember saying, "This is the studio?" It was so small. It wasn't the most professional studio, if you know what I mean. I thought the sound, and I'm being honest here, was terrible.

How much input did Dan have on the recording process?

Åkerfeldt: I don't remember him having much, actually.

Lindgren: Not much, really. The songs were done. But Dan is a musical guy. It was easy for us to work with him. He was a mentor. He was stubborn, though. He would refuse to listen to arguments. Then he'd turn around and say, "Yeah, you're right." He's not diplomatic about things. It's no or yes. You can't manipulate him. Pretty often he's right about things with music. Maybe Johan had a little clash with him. Johan thought he was more musically experienced than the rest of us. And he was. But I don't think Dan liked him too much, 'cause he was the guy with the funky bass.

Nordin: Dan was extremely important to the final results in all possible ways, and he had huge input during the recordings. He made me relaxed, despite the pressure that we had due to the short studio time. That was very important. He's a funny guy, so he kind of broke the ice.

DeFarfalla: I don't remember that, but I do remember Dan being stubborn. I worked in a studio as well, and we didn't agree on [how to do] certain things. The way he recorded things basically would end up as noise. He wasn't diplomatic at all. I would say we didn't have a clash. More like many disagreements. Dan was not producing, so he had to listen to us. And this is important, we, the band, produced *Orchid*. He was the engineer.

PART IV: THE SKY WILL FALL, THE EARTH WILL PRAY . . .

"In Mist She Was Standing"

Åkerfeldt: It's the longest song on the album. The last one we completed. We were excited about it to begin with. It's still a good song, but I don't remember much about it. There's one part where Johan's playing bass over the acoustic guitar. I don't like that. Anders has a cool riff on it. Lyrically, it's about a nightmare. It's inspired by a film called *Lady in Black*. I remember I forgot the book with my lyrics, so we had to turn around and go get them. I ended up rewriting them anyway. I didn't have a clue about lyrics, though.

Lindgren: A great opening track. We probably should've rearranged the track order. I thought "In Mist She Was Standing" would be a great opening track for live shows. Never was, though.

Nordin: First song ever that I recorded in a real studio. I remember that for a short period of time—just moments before I started to record this song—I wanted to back out of all this and go home when I saw all the microphones. But as soon as Mike started to play and the recordings were under way, it proceeded quite well, despite major rhythm changes and errors that I made. Mike helped me a lot by showing up in the little window on the drum room door, which gave me a lot of inspiration. I think he knew that I was nervous and stressed, especially from all the swearing between the takes.

DeFarfalla: It was really long, with lots of changes. I don't remember much else of this song, to be honest.

"Under the Weeping Moon"

Åkerfeldt: It's my favorite song. It's our attempt at black metal, I guess. It has a simple riff. I really like it. The middle section is awesome. It was quite daring at the time. That's why I think it hasn't aged as much. It's quite fresh, to this day. Lyrically, it was some kind of satanic worship of the moon. It doesn't really deal with anything. We didn't record to a click-track, so it really goes out of tempo. It gets faster and faster.

Lindgren: It's the weirdest song in the middle. It's the most evil song on the album. We did this song a couple of times in 2006, and it's the only song where there's room for experimentation. We didn't experiment. Everything was figured out. It was really non-Opeth in that sense. Everything was worked out except that part. The riffs are great.

Nordin: I don't remember much of this song other than "In Mist She Was Standing" and this one were made during the first day, as it took a while to get going with the first song.

DeFarfalla: This is the song with the cool middle part. It was a bit different for us, I think. If you listen back to bands like Jethro Tull and Wishbone Ash, you could hear them doing stuff like this. Of course, it's not death metal, but I think that's where Mike got the idea. It's a cool song.

"Silhouette"

Åkerfeldt: Awesome! I'm still quite impressed. Some movements in that song are stellar. Well played. I don't like the sound. It's a keyboard, so the sample sound is dated.

Lindgren: Great! For Anders' sake, I think he wanted another take. Considering we're a metal band, it's kind of cool. I remember the look on Dan's face when we said, "Our drummer can play the piano." He didn't believe a word we were saying. Dan can play the piano. Most guys play like shit. When Anders started playing, Dan was actually impressed. Most people thought our dad or mom played it. At least that's what people thought back then.

Nordin: This was recorded hours just before we were leaving the studio. I didn't feel good about it before, during and after the recordings.

DeFarfalla: I like this piece, but I remember the sound was not so good. It was a keyboard with bad sample. I suggested we record this properly in a church with a real piano and a lot of microphones to get the right ambiance, but sadly, that never happened.

"Forest of October"

Åkerfeldt: Even though it goes in and out of all the movements, it's still quite coherent. The arrangements are quite cool. I still like the song. It's the most simple song to play, 'cause it's one of the earliest songs. Some of the riffs go back to 1990. Lyrically, I don't remember what it's about. Some cool lines. The lyrics had to sound like the music.

Lindgren: The best song on the album. When you put out more and more albums, especially with songs being 10 or 12 minutes, you have to pick certain songs to play live. Eventually, you leave albums out. We played this song the most until we abandoned it for "Under the Weeping Moon."

Nordin: Second day, I wasn't as nervous, but yet as stressed, even though the first part of the song went pretty well until I managed to lose the sticks in the middle of a drum roll. As I had covered a great part of it in one go, Dan didn't think we had time to waste to re-record all of that part, so it was decided that I should retake the recording from the drum roll, which isn't the easiest thing. I remember this as it was yesterday because after the third retake, I heard Dan in the headphones say, "We don't have time for this. Whatever you do now goes on the CD. Are you ready?" And I was like, "OK, no, I'm not ready, but who cares?"

DeFarfalla: This was the older song. I think it was too death metal for me. It was a bit simpler than the other songs. I didn't like the growling too much, but the music was great.

"The Twilight Is My Robe"

Åkerfeldt: It has calm parts with clean singing. You can hear how shy I was. I didn't dare sing more powerfully. You can tell it's a teenager singing. It has some of the strongest twin guitar leads on the album. But it doesn't sound powerful on the album. When we played it live, it's a powerhouse. One part was nicked from the Scorpions' "Fly to the Rainbow." A complete rip-off. It's a satanic song. Like an oath to Satan. It used to be called "Oath."

Lindgren: The start is kind of happy. There's a lot of twin guitars playing the different things to add heaviness. There's counterpoint, too. Two melodies added together make something cool. This song has a lot of that in it. I like the acoustic parts, too.

DeFarfalla: This song reminded me of Spinal Tap. You know, when the 18-inch Stonehenge comes down onstage and they're dancing around it. I think of Spinal Tap when I hear this song. It's a fantastic song, but the image of it now sort of makes me laugh. Actually, a lot of things in Opeth were like Spinal Tap.

"Requiem"

Åkerfeldt: The sound is OK. I borrowed an awesome acoustic guitar from the guitar store. A Spanish guitar called Trameleuc. I want to buy one, but you can't find them anywhere. The theme of the song is pretty good. Johan's solo at the end is fantastic. He had an acoustic bass. Anders was playing tablas. It's a song no death metal band would've done at the time. It was fucked up in the mastering. I was insane when I heard it.

Lindgren: It was mastered wrong. It's an acoustic epic. It builds tension for a while. It turned out pretty good, even though it was cut wrong. If you listen to the full album, you can't really notice it.

"The Apostle in Triumph"

Åkerfeldt: The flagship song for us in the early days. Not many people hailed it as the best song. It has a really nice melody. The guitar swells I was proud of. Lyrically, it was a combination of nature and satanic worship. Peter has a great solo in the end. Quite emotional. I kind of cringe when I hear the clean vocals. I sound so insecure. Johan did the higher harmony vocals. On Martin Mendez's first gig, we played it. It was the last time we played it.

Lindgren: It was like a hit song for us. We did it on the Cradle of Filth tour in '96. The beginning is trademark Opeth. We played it too much, so it got boring. Those 10 or 20 seconds that got us the record deal were from this song. It's magical in that sense.

Nordin: This song was no doubt the most emotional one to record. When I had the headphones on and Mikael—who played along with me for reference, as the drums were the first instrument to be caught on tape—got started with the recordings, it felt like my life was rewound and played for me right there in the drum room at Dan's studio. I don't remember much of the actual drumming other than Mikael was a great support for me during all the stress and pressure when there's no room for retakes. Once he was even inside the drum room just to be present. It inspired me.

DeFarfalla: I remember having more freedom on the bass for this song. It's a song where the bass and guitars are playing different things together. The bass doesn't push away the guitars. More like a complement. I think it's one of the better songs on the album. I like this song a lot. It's great.

PART V: HIDDEN IN THE FOG . . .

Did you have side projects at the time?

Åkerfeldt: Yeah, it had many names. Planet was a stoner thing. We had one riff and two lyrics. In those days, you were quick to announce that, even if you didn't have material. Jonas and me had hundreds of projects. We had a hip-hop band. El Triunfo de la Muerte. It was taken from the famous painting. Like Black Sabbath's *Greatest Hits* album. We had alias names. My name was Las Vegas. Jonas was Paco. We sang in broken Latin-Swedish. We did a demo tape. Jonas still has it. We did four or five demos with our country band. It was called Black Horse, then Black Horse Experience, and then Slow Train Company. It had many different names. We had a Meshuggah rip-off band called Erase. We had a Popul Vuh rip-off band called Bruder Der Schatten. We did one 15-minute song. It was like a mantra, but we got bored, deleted it and had coffee and smokes instead.

Lindgren: I had a synth project with a friend of mine. I was more into metal/industrial stuff. We needed a drummer, but he didn't see my point since the music he listened to didn't have real drummers. It also didn't help he lived in a different city. I didn't have many side projects. Most of it was for fun. Like Steel. I remember when we were recording *My Arms, Your Hearse* and Fredrik [Nordström] played us a band that sounded like Steel with a better production. We thought it was pretty funny. Turned out it was HammerFall.

DeFarfalla: I had a lot of side projects. I was in Crimson Cat as a main band, but I also had a jazz-fusion trio at the time. I was playing with a lot of other musicians that weren't from the death metal scene. I really liked playing in Opeth, though.

You've had some interesting photo sessions. The top hat photo is legendary.

Åkerfeldt: It was my idea. That was a bit of a fiasco. I wanted it to look like an early 20th century photo. I rented the costume with white gloves. All that shit. Johan didn't want a suit. He wanted to be bare-chested with sunglasses. It's like, "Ah, well, that kind of spoils it." Those pictures were taken for the Celtic Frost tribute album. I sent them to Raul [Caballero] at Dwell and they were meant to be in the booklet, but he ended up using a different picture. Now, I think it's awesome. We had lots of photos. We took a band picture outside the studio in Finspång. There was a park there with a big old oak tree. Being that we were nature romantics, we took some pictures of the band there. We did it on the way back from shopping. They came out great. They looked awesome. I was standing in the tree. It sounds stupid, but it looked cool. But something was wrong. As I looked closer, Anders was holding a big bag of apples. I was like, "Fuck, we can't use them now!"

Lindgren: We also had a photo session in Finspång, where we had a smoke grenade. It was supposed to look like fog. You can't see anything in the pictures. Just smoke. We were laughing, 'cause we couldn't see anything either. We had all these ideas, but we didn't know how to fulfill them. We were a little stupid.

Did you ever think Orchid *would be remembered as a pivotal release? I remember some of the labels I was in contact with said Opeth wouldn't amount to much. The songs were too long and nobody knew who you were.*

Åkerfeldt: We didn't have any commercial value whatsoever. To be honest, I expected once I got a record deal I'd be able to buy a Rolls-Royce. I expected to be wealthy like a rock star. It's the opposite. You're more worthless after getting a record deal. I never thought of *Orchid* being a classic. I never thought that of any of our albums. I'm too involved. I was confident in the band, and I knew it was a good album after it was finished. I had high expectations.

Lindgren: No, not really. The reason why we got somewhere is we matured musically pretty early on. It's a good thing we didn't get a record deal earlier. It took us a while to mature. We had to find a concept for our songwriting. If we would've recorded *Orchid* 18 months earlier, it wouldn't be good. It's important we had a year or so to rewrite the songs.

DeFarfalla: I don't think so. I knew it was different, but I didn't expect to be talking about this record 13 years later. Maybe five or six years, but definitely not 13. I think it's good that people remember this record now. It's a special record.

Q&A WITH DAVID ISBERG

The curious Opeth founder bitchez at Decibel

— Chris Dick

What were your impressions of Orchid at the time it was released?

David Isberg: I thought *Orchid* was a great album. I just thought that the cover and band's image was a bit wimpy. I'm the kind of guy who still adores Hellhammer and shit.

Opeth formed, at least theoretically, while you were on vacation in Thailand. Can't imagine Phuket being the birthplace for anything evil and menacing.

Isberg: Thailand's a good place for evil behavior. As the country itself suffers from a religion that does not count good or bad or evil, you have all the opportunities in the world to desecrate! Surrounded by sin, such as hookers and illegal gambling, you will get inspired.

How did you meet Mike, Anders and Peter?

Isberg: It must have been around 1986, as me and Mike played soccer for Sörskogens IF and were skateboarding. I thought he was a poser at the time. He was listening to Iron Maiden and, maybe, Metallica and Slayer, but had a hard time accepting Mercyful Fate, Possessed, Celtic Frost, Necrophagia, Sodom, Mayhem, Morbid and them bitchez who were around. But he was always curious about what bitchez were wrecking my ears in my walkman. One day I played the second Mefisto demo, and eventually lent him the tape, and that tape sort of convinced him to listen to the real extreme metal. Soon enough there was all new bitchez blowing out of his speakers at Taggsvampsvägen [a very important street in the early days of Opeth]. We started Opeth and we sounded really shit. I listened to a rehearsal tape from that lineup the other day with the two very first Opeth songs, "Servants of Satan" and "Depraved by Christianity," and damn we were bitchez. Me and Mike bitched at Taggsvampsvägen as a two-piece until we found Anders Nordin and started forming a real band. About a year and half after, this dude named Peter, who was someone's friend, started to play bass with us.

Why did you end up leaving the band? You cited "creative differences," I think.

Isberg: Well, I was ung and hällig. I wanted bitchez and Kristian Whålin wanted me in Liers in Wait. I felt like I had all this shit to bitch out, but Opeth was my band, yet the guys playing with us were Mike's bitchez. So, on a bus home from Austria, I told him the news. Me leaving was the best thing for Opeth. I have another project almost done nicknamed the Stockholm War Ensemble. You will soon have the opportunity to hear us again. Watch out for upcoming reissue by Procreation.

CHAPTER 20

PILLAR OF ETERNITY

THE MAKING OF DOWN'S *NOLA*

by J. Bennett

Release Date: 1995
Label: Elektra
Summary: Saintly sludge sometimes supergroup
Induction Date: July 2008/Issue #45

I f there's just one person in the world who'll never forget the exact date *NOLA* came out, it's Eyehategod guitarist/Down drummer Jimmy Bower. "September 19, 1995," he rattles off. "I remember because it was my 27th birthday." It was also the culmination of a four-year process in which the members of the South's biggest, baddest, heaviest bands formed the kind of hard rock/metal confederacy that would make later "supergroups" like Velvet Revolver and Audioslave look even more like the spoiled has-beens everyone knew they were to begin with. Back in 1991, Bower joined Crowbar mainman Kirk Windstein, newly christened Corrosion of Conformity vocalist/riff-master Pepper Keenan, then–Crowbar bassist Todd Strange and Pantera frontman Phil Anselmo in a friend's garage and almost instantly struck upon Down's bruising formula. Combining the towering doom of Saint Vitus (*NOLA* opener "Temptation's Wings" takes its name from a line in Vitus' "Ice Monkey") with thundering power grooves ("Lifer," "Bury Me in Smoke," "Underneath Everything") and Skynyrd's infectious swamp-swing ("Stone the Crow," "Rehab"), the band cranked out a trilogy of demo tapes that quickly became legend in the underground, thanks in no small part to Anselmo and Keenan's genius guerrilla-marketing tactics. By the time Down descended upon Ultrasonic Studios to record their full-length debut, the die had been cast. The record's title—now a well-worn acronym for New Orleans, LA—was a tribute to the band's flood-prone home base that extended to album artwork featuring ghostly John Clarence Laughlin photographs, an image of the members strolling through a potter's field and a picture of the Superdome emblazoned on the disc itself. But it was the unstoppable jams within that make *NOLA* our latest induction into the Hall of Fame.

How did Down first materialize?

Phil Anselmo: Jimmy and I had been talking on the phone. He was living in Atlanta at the time, but he was preparing to move back to New Orleans. Back in those days, everything in the underground was fast, fast, fast. It was the rule of the day. There was a lot of Slayer worship going on. But when the Melvins came out with their first record, *Gluey Porch Treatments*, it really broke the mold, especially in New Orleans. People began to appreciate playing slower. With that, all the old Black Sabbath came back around and then you start digging and you come to your Saint Vitus, your Witchfinder General, your Pentagram, etc. So Jimmy and me were trading tapes like that back in '88 and '89. I was still living in Texas while Jimmy and I were concocting this band idea, and we were thinking, "Who the hell could we get?"

Pepper Keenan: I was living in New York part-time when COC did *Blind*, and I would hang out with Phil whenever Pantera came through. They'd just done *Cowboys From Hell* and they were playing little bitty places, just starting off. Phil and I would hang out on his tour bus—which was a new thing for both of us—and we'd listen to Saint Vitus and the Obsessed. We didn't really know many other people who were into that shit besides Kirk and Jimmy back in New Orleans and Lee Dorrian over in England. Lee had sent us this fucking doom compilation called *Dark Passages* that he was putting out on his label. Phil and me were really into it. A couple weeks later, Phil had an idea for a band, and he wanted to call it Down. I came up with the logo and crap before we had even rehearsed.

What was the first rehearsal like?

Kirk Windstein: It was a long weekend in '91. [Then–Crowbar bassist] Big Todd [Strange] picked me up and then we went to pick up Phil and Pepper at the airport. We went to the store, picked up a bunch of beer, some weed or whatever, and went to my buddy Mike Savoie's house on the west bank of New Orleans. He was one of the few people we knew who had his own house, and he had his garage set up like a jam room. So we went out there, and in those first three days we actually recorded "Temptation's Wings," "Losing All" and "Bury Me in Smoke." We had a friend of mine come over with his little portable recording deal, which was pretty primitive even for back then, and made the demo. We actually filmed some of it—I've seen some of it pop up on YouTube, so someone obviously got a hold of it. We all look about 15 years old—it's ridiculous. Then we brought Pepper and Phil back to the airport on Sunday night, and that was it for a bit.

Keenan: I remember I spray-painted the word "Down" on a bed sheet and we hung it behind the drum riser. We were fucking into it, man. We wanted to do it New Orleans–style: super-laid-back, slippery, Graveyard Rodeo, Exhorder, way-behind-the-beat shit. The majority of that sound came from Jimmy. He was such a lazy, stoned-out drummer that he was almost falling off the drum stool, he was so far behind the beat. But it fucking worked. We were all from New Orleans, so we knew about the Meters and the whole nasty funk thing. I mean, you could tell we weren't from Berlin. We hadn't been away in our own bands long enough to really have our own identities in those bands. It wasn't quite clear at that point what COC or Crowbar or Pantera or Eyehategod would turn into. We were still huddled up in our own little world.

After we wrote those three songs, we just laughed our asses off. We had this little four-track recorder and a couple of outboard effects. I believe we did drums and all the basic tracks raw. I can't even remember if we overdubbed solos. And then Phil overdubbed vocals. But we had no way to do playback because it was a four-track, so whoever was overdubbing had to wear headphones and play to

---

it. We didn't have any speakers or anything. [*Laughs*] So we're sitting on the fucking couch while Phil's standing there with his shaved head singing "Temptation's Wings" and we can't even imagine what it sounds like. I remember when he played it back for me. He moved a coupla faders, put the headphones on my head and goes, "Dude?" [*Laughs*] I heard it and I was like, "Oh my fuckin' god." I knew we were onto it big time. Then he did "Bury Me in Smoke" and that was just ridiculous. We'd never heard anything like it, but it was exactly what we had all been hoping the band would sound like. It was a band we'd be into even if we weren't in it.

That first demo acquired legendary underground status years before NOLA was even recorded.

Jimmy Bower: I remember listening to the tape in my car after the first practice and thinking, "Damn, this could do something." It's crazy how fast the word spread about the band. There was no album; it was just a demo tape kinda floating around. Pepper and Phil would come back from tour and tell us that they played it for the guys in Soundgarden and Alice in Chains and they all liked it. I was just doing Eyehategod tours at that time, so I wasn't really meeting that caliber of successful musicians, you know? But I'd play it for my underground buddies, and they seemed to dig it. So it was really cool and flattering to be involved in something that was respected by people that were so successful.

Keenan: I made sure each of us had the three-song demo, and I made the case with the logo with the face and everything and put it on a TDK-90 cassette. Whenever we'd be on tour and people would ask us if we'd heard anything new, me and Phil would tell them about this band Down. People would be like, "Can I tape it?" And we'd always say, "Hell yeah, man." Phil was on tour with Skid Row or some shit and he wore that thing out. When COC went to Sweden, some kid turned up at the show with a homemade Down shirt asking me if I'd heard this band. So he played me this 12th generation copy that he had. [*Laughs*] You could barely hear what was going on, but you could get the general idea.

Anselmo: The demo ended up becoming legendary. The sound on it was just crushing, and we knew we had something. It was a catalyst to move forward.

Keenan: It worked perfect, man, so we did two more tapes like that: three three-song demos, for nine songs total. We kept handing 'em out, and I don't think anybody knew it was us until the third demo. One of the most genius things I ever did was spend some of my hard-earned cash to make a dozen Down shirts—just silver ink with the Down logo and a fleur-de-lis on the front and the Down face on the back. I don't think I ever paid the dude for the damn shirts, either, but I gave one to James Hetfield and he wore the motherfucker in a couple of photographs. Then it was really on, because Hetfield knew who

Down was and the record was just about to come out. That really set the whole thing up killer.

Looking at the credits, it seems like Pepper and Phil wrote the bulk of the material.

Windstein: Yeah, for the most part. But Pepper and me are a two-guitar band in the truest sense of the word: He doesn't know what I play and I don't know what he plays. He'll come up with the main riff and I'll do my thing on top of it that kinda complements it. We laugh about it sometimes, but it works well. For the fatness and heaviness of Crowbar, it makes sense to have two guys playing the same thing just to beef up the sound—even though I'll play some harmonies sometimes. But with a band like Down, where there's a lot more dynamics going on, the way we do it makes more sense. But ask me to play his parts on "Stone the Crow" or something, and I'll have no idea.

What else do you remember about the songwriting process?

Keenan: We were practicing at Phil's house all the time, because he'd made some cash from the Pantera thing and bought a house on Colbert Street in the city. It was like Snoop Dogg's house, but dirtbag, you know? He had this pool with a red light in it and a black tile pentagram at the bottom. We actually did a photo shoot in that pool for *NOLA*, but if we had used those photos, we would've ended up looking like Obituary or something. Phil had also sound-proofed the entire basement and painted a pentagram on the ceiling. This house got flooded under 12 feet of water during Katrina, but that's where we wrote 90 percent of the Down songs. That's where he kept all his cassettes, too, back when we were cassette freaks, trading tapes all the time. People knew me and Phil collected demo tapes—Phil more so than me. People throw demos onstage when we play to this day. He probably had 3,000 cassettes down there from bands all over the world.

Anselmo: For that first Down record, it was really off the cuff. Lyrically, I was thinking Wino all the way through guys like Ronnie Van Zant. But one of the biggest influences on that record was Trouble. I've said it before and I'll say it again: Without Trouble, there would be no Down. They were definitely influenced by Black Sabbath, but they have so much of their own sound that they're just another band—they're not a Sabbath rip-off band by any means. They're in a class all their own. Oh, and definitely Saint Vitus, especially the vibe that Vitus had on their fifth record. To me, that was the culmination of Vitus with Wino. "When Emotion Dies," etc. Really great.

Keenan: We were always on tour, so we'd mail riff tapes to each other. I remember Phil and Kirk would take Sabbath songs and just twist 'em a little bit and send them to me like that was their new riff tape. Motherfuckers must've spent hours doing that shit. [*Laughs*] Then they'd wait for me to call and put me on speakerphone.

Windstein: We really tried to get the Sabbath influences across—and bands that were influenced by Sabbath, like Vitus and Trouble and Witchfinder General and the Obsessed, along with the stuff we grew up on, like Led Zeppelin and Skynyrd. Obviously, a song like "Stone the Crow" has a pretty strong Skynyrd influence. And the rhythm to "Rehab" kinda reminds me of ZZ Top. In fact, I think that was the working title for that one. [*Laughs*]

Bower: We wrote "Rehab" at Phil's house, the one that got ruined in Katrina. That was one of the last songs we wrote for the record, I'm pretty sure. That song was really cool—it had a real Southern rock sound, like "Eyes of the South." Shauna [Reynolds, a.k.a. Sean Yseult] from White Zombie was on bass when we wrote "Eyes of the South," actually. She'd come to New Orleans a lot to hang out with us, so one day we were like, "Fuck it—let's go have a jam session." I was really into the Skynyrd thing at the time—like way too much. And I still am. I'm looking around my room right now and it's covered with Skynyrd shit. I could see the way our band could easily become a Southern rock band, and I really wanted to that happen.

The Southern/Skynyrd vibe really comes through on "Stone the Crow," especially.

Bower: Yeah, totally—I agree. I honestly thought that song was gonna get radio play, too. We did an awesome video for it out in the swamps, at this little bar about 20 minutes from my house. It's basically just a hole in the wall with Hank, Jr. posters and rebel flags all over the place. It's not necessarily a biker bar or nothing, but it was the perfect setup. It was fun, man—we had Pepper out on this sunken shrimp boat playing the lead—it's fuckin' killer. [*Laughs*] It's over-the-top stupid, but it looks cool. We actually re-recorded that song acoustically back in 2002—we just haven't done anything with it yet.

Anselmo: That was always the thing with Down. We want to be heavy, and we all have metal influences, but with a song like "Stone the Crow" or "Jail" or even something like "Swan Song," there were certain breakdowns within songs where we didn't wanna be absolutely stuck in that rut where every song has to be heavy and then heavier. We've all done that, so we wanted to leave that window open to be as diverse as possible without throwing people off. Not many bands have been able to do that. You think about a band like the Beatles or Queen, and they could get away with *anything* and be accepted because they wrote great songs.

Down played a handful of shows in the years leading up to NOLA—what were those like?

Bower: I think we did about two or three shows in the years before the album was recorded. Our first show was at the RC Bridge Lounge, which is an old club down here. That was with Eyehategod. The second show was with RAWG, which was GWAR without the costumes and makeup. We opened up for them and I remember it was packed when we went on—there were about 800 people there. When RAWG went on, there were about 50. Crowbar played that night, too. I remember watching Craig Nunenmacher play skins that night and I felt compelled to be competitive.

Keenan: For our first show, we just grabbed Eyehategod's equipment during Mardi Gras and played. We were fuckin' blasted, dude. I have a photo from that show somewhere. Kirk has on Everlast boxing shorts and white Reeboks or some shit. [*Laughs*] That's the early '90s for ya. When we opened up for RAWG in New Orleans, we did the nine songs from the demos, plus a Robin Trower song and "Ice Monkey" by Saint Vitus. Somebody videotaped the show, and I think that's when it got out to the label. They knew that it was us, so we did the record deal.

With four band members already signed to four separate labels, the negotiations must've been an insane hassle.

Keenan: Oh, yeah. I mean, imagine the publishing deals. I think the lawyers made more money off it than we did.

Bower: When we tried to do the record, Century Media really gave me a raw deal, and I'm not scared to mention it. They took all my publishing from the Down record—they took it all because they owned me through Eyehategod. That was their stipulation for letting me play on the record.

Windstein: It was no problem for Phil because he was the biggest star, the best-known musician in the band. And we put it out through Elektra, which was East West, which was the same label Pantera was on. In hindsight, that ended up being a conflict of interest I think. It would've been better to do it on a label that none of us were involved with. But you can't cry over spilled milk.

Anselmo: Yeah, everyone wanted a piece of this or that, and the first two Down records ended up being squashed by Elektra out of fear because in Pantera they had a steady platinum-selling band, and they wanted no threat to that. So instead of having two multi-platinum bands—which it could've been—they squashed the records. And as we speak, the first two records are out of print. No more sales, man. So we're attempting to get the rights back.

Keenan: The label thought it was just Phil's little side project. They figured they'd let him do it just to shut him up and then it was back to Pantera business. But that was understood. Shit, I was in love with Pantera. Who the fuck wasn't back then?

What do you remember about the recording sessions?

Keenan: I was with COC doing the *Deliverance* tour, and our last show was at Donington, opening for Metallica. I caught a flight back to New Orleans the very next day and started working on Down shit. I was pretty much on top of my game guitar-playing-wise, so we just went right to it. We had a decent little budget, so we went to Ultrasonic on Washington Avenue, which is a really popular studio in New Orleans for all the R&B and funk shit. The day we were loading our gear in, this killer old Louisiana guitar player, Clarence "Gatemouth" Brown, was loading his gear out. I was a big fan of his. Some friends of mine were in Desert Storm, and I'd sent them cassettes of his music. He was like this 80-year-old black dude in a cowboy hat playing a Jazzmaster or some crazy old fuckin' thing. So we were bringing all these piece-of-shit Randalls in, and he was bringing all this cool vintage gear out and throwing it in the back of a pickup truck. I remember that truck smelled like dope.

Windstein: We went into Ultrasonic in like late April of '95. Then the May 8 Flood hit. It was a Monday night and a buddy of ours was cooking a big pot of red beans in the studio kitchen when all of a sudden the power went out. So we decided to take a break and eat, but the rain was ridiculous. In no time, it started coming in under the door. Luckily, the control room was three or four steps up from ground level, so the console and all the expensive outboard gear were relatively safe. So we ran into the main recording room and picked up all the amps, guitar heads, pedals, cables, and just piled 'em up as high we could.

Anselmo: I remember the day exactly because I was at home and I was tired, tired, tired from working the night before. The plan was that the band was gonna go in and they were gonna call me when they were ready for me later in the afternoon. So I kept getting phone calls, like, "Let's push it back a little further" while the rain kept coming down steady and hard. Sure enough, I had water up to my ankles in the downstairs part of my house, and the entire studio flooded.

Keenan: It just rained and rained and didn't stop, man. We were drunk and high as kites and we were doing the song "Jail." Li'l Daddy [Joey LaCaze] from Eyehategod was with us and Sid [Montz, future Crowbar drummer] was with us and Big Ross [Karpelman, future Mystick Krewe of Clearlight organist] on this little rinky-dink Casio. The place had a glass ceiling, so you could see the clouds coming in and lightning from miles away. Li'l Daddy was hammering on two little plastic Halloween pumpkins that Phil brought—we duct-taped them together to make bongos. [*Laughs*] I had this nylon-string guitar that wouldn't stay in tune. We just sat there and smoked weed and recorded the whole thing in two or three takes while the rain just kept coming in. Then the canal across the street overflowed and it just came pouring in. Then the power went out and it was pitch black.

Bower: Within 15–20 minutes of the electricity going out, we were knee-deep in water. I was using an old 1970s Slingerland drum kit—it was a sweet kit, man—and I was just watching it sink. We spent the entire next day in there because we were pretty much stuck. The studio used to have a picture of all of us sitting in the water. That studio doesn't exist anymore, but I'd love to get that picture.

Windstein: Most of the damn city flooded that night. My mom's house got hit with a good three feet of water. But that's New Orleans, brah. There're a lot of great things about it, but the downfalls are that it's hot as hell and it's below sea level. So yeah, we were trapped in the studio all night that night. We finally got out, but we had to wait a good week for them to rip up all the carpets and dry the place out.

Todd Strange was in the band photo and played live with you, but didn't actually play on the record. Why is that?

Windstein: By the time we actually got around to doing the first Down record, I had already realized that Todd got nervous in the studio. He was fine live, and he played on the first Crowbar record, but on Crowbar *Crowbar*, he finally just handed me the bass and said, "Dude, just play the fuckin' thing for me." So I ended up playing the bass on *NOLA* even though I'm not a bass player. When you hear Rex [Brown] play those songs now, it's like night and day. But we'd do shows here and there when we had an opportunity, and Todd was good enough for that, but in hindsight, it would've been great to have Rex in the band back then.

Anselmo: Todd had a complex about being in the studio. He didn't have the best timing in the world, and in music that's a no-no. And when it came down to the precision of a studio situation, he froze up. And that's why he did not do his tracks. That's all I can say.

Keenan: Todd was just this ham-fisted dude who played in Crowbar with Kirk. He looked cool in the band because he weighed 800 pounds. It was Phil's idea to get him in the band because he was this big giant motherfucker. And he had a car. [*Laughs*] You know that drill. The bass player or the drummer always has the PA.

Bower: We did maybe 25 shows with Todd between '91 and 2002, and he did fine. He did fine with Crowbar live for years, too. He just got nervous in the studio. We've actually been talking about having Rex go in and re-record the bass lines, though. People don't understand what Rex has added to those songs. It makes a big difference. Some people are like, "Original or nothing," which is cool, too, but I'd like to see him have the opportunity. When we do "Temptation's Wings" live now, Rex does all this crazy shit during the break-down—it's a completely different part now, you know?

Phil, is there a particular set of lyrics from **NOLA** *that you're especially proud of?*

Anselmo: It might sound generic, but "Lifer" turned out cool. Being a lifer is what I am and exactly what every dude around me is. I mean, I wrote my first song when I was nine years old, man, and from there it grew. I'm still fucking doing it. This doesn't go away, you know? You're born with it, and once you recognize it, you follow that path. Look at the Rolling Stones. They're lifers. Look at Metallica. Lifers. And I dedicate that song each and every night to [Dimebag] Darrell. He was a lifer, man. He lived it—every second of every day, he made something of it.

In "Lifer," you mention the "brotherhood of eternal sleep," which was also the name of the Down fan club. Is that a specific reference to the dudes in Down?

Anselmo: Not just them—anyone who does what thou wilt. Aleister Crowley, you know? But he was plagiarized by Anton LaVey.

There's a picture of Anton LaVey in the **NOLA** *artwork.*

Anselmo: Well, I admit I had a giant gap in knowledge then. I was a young man, and I had not read *Diary of a Drug Fiend.* I was a late bloomer as far as that tome. I was always a reader, but fiction grew old fast. I wanted reality—and knowledge. Certain bits and pieces you get late. But if you look at Anton LaVey, he played the part until he was in the dirt and people fell for his carny act. That's a poor example of a lifer, though.

How did the rest of the album artwork come together?

Keenan: COC did a video for the song "Dance of the Dead" with the same company that had done the Soundgarden video for "Jesus Christ Pose." This girl who was working on the video took a photograph of me wearing the crown that Chris Cornell had worn. At the time I had stupidly long straight hair, and I was smoking a cigarette. This photographer chick was like, "Don't fuckin' move!" I was standing underneath this really strong light, and she took the photo. She asked if she could use it in her portfolio and I said, "Yeah—if you send me a copy of it, you can do whatever the fuck you want with it." So months later I get the photograph. I went to Kinko's and Xeroxed it a hundred times so it looked crude, like some Killing Joke thing, and then I made the logo by cutting and pasting Old English letters out. That was the back of the *NOLA* record. We had that image and the logo before we had even written a song.

A lot of the collage stuff came from a bunch of drug books I had borrowed from a friend. Me and Phil put a lot of that stuff together. "Pillars of Eternity" was about the shaft of a hallucinogenic mushroom that was called the Pillar of Eternity, so we used giant mushrooms on that page. And the picture for "Eyes of the South" came from one of those truck-stop paintings of a wolf looking over a mountain with snow coming and shit. If you look at some of the collages, there's photos of us interspersed in there. We've all got no shirts on and some of us are as big as whales. It was just one of those stupidly simple things to put together. The last thing was a postcard of the Superdome that Phil had—we put that on the CD itself. We were out of our fuckin' gourds.

Anselmo: Pepper and I really collaborated a lot with the then–art director at Elektra Records. His name escapes me, but he was an awesome guy to work with. We used so many different images from books that Pep and I had, and a lot of those photos came out of an old fanzine called *Answer Me!* by Jim Goad.

Author of **The Redneck Manifesto** *[who later went to prison for beating up his girlfriend] . . .*

Anselmo: Absolutely. And check who he thanks first in that book. He used to call me from jail constantly. I'd go on tour for a couple of months, come back, and he'd still be in the can. One time we were on the phone, and in the middle of our conversation the line went dead, and then I never heard from him again until he was out of jail. When I talked to him after he got out, he told me that he thought he'd hung up on me.

What about the Clarence John Laughlin photos?

Keenan: I think we had to buy the rights to [Laughlin's 1948 photo book] *Ghosts Along the Mississippi*. He's got another book, too, of these bizarre photos from the French Quarter, like him and his wife posing in a veil in these old creepy buildings. Some of those places are still there.

What do you remember about the album's graveyard photo shoot?

Bower: That photographer was nuts, man. He was getting on the ground and doing all this crazy shit. I've never met a photographer with that much passion. It was like he was surfing or something. He was like Jeff Spicoli on speed with a camera. But that graveyard is a poor people's graveyard, so you'll see headstones made out of shopping baskets and TVs and shit like that. Eyehategod had done pictures for *Take as Needed for Pain* there, too. But with Down, we just walked around out there, and of course New Orleans is hot as piss, so a couple of us had our shirts off.

Keenan: It was right next to Delgado College, across the street from a cemetery called Odd Fellows Rest. It's one of the poorer cemeteries in New Orleans, with wooden tombstones and shit like that.

Anselmo: It's a pauper's cemetery that's behind a school in New Orleans, and it closes at 2 p.m. so you have to get there early. And the thing about paupers' graves in New Orleans is that you don't get dug deep and you're not in a casket. And we're below sea level, so it's not uncommon after a heavy rain to see bones and body pieces washed up. [*Laughs*] But it is very picturesque and eerie—and beautiful in its own way.

How did you feel about the album when it was all said and done?

Bower: I knew when the record was finished that we definitely had something different. It's influenced by a bunch of bands that are lumped into a genre, but for some reason, ours sounds different. I just remember being real proud of it.

Windstein: I was blown away at how great the songs were and how different it was from what everyone else was doing at the time. I had no expectations, but I felt it most definitely had the potential to be a classic. But being that it was a side project and knowing that we weren't gonna be able to tour on it, I wasn't sure what level it would be accepted on.

Keenan: I always tell people, "You don't make that record twice." You can try for the rest of your fuckin' life, but it all came down to timing and energy and not giving a fuck. There was no pressure, so we took our time, you know? We wrote those songs over a three- or four-year period.

Anselmo: It was a good experience, man, a very positive experience. With the Down records, there's never been any real shape or form or rhyme or reason. When they come together, they come together and it's always just out of nowhere and it always makes sense in the end.

After the album came out, you played 13 shows and then pretty much disappeared for the next seven years. What happened?

Windstein: Well, we pretty much knew going in that it would probably be a while. I mean, Phil had just come off having the number one record in the country, playing arenas and shit like that. We knew he'd be busy with that for years and years. And we were busy with our projects as well.

Bower: We always knew we wanted to do another one, but at the time, Pantera was at their height. Eyehategod was busy; COC was busy; Crowbar was busy. I was in like five bands back then, too. A lot was going on.

Keenan: Time just flew, man. We didn't know it was that long. Whenever anyone would tell me that, I'd be like, "What?" But now that I look back, it seems like it was 10 years between records when I think about what everybody had accomplished and done in that time. It was like we were completely different people when we got together to do the second one.

Anselmo: Yeah, that whole thing was a total rip-off. We should've been out for eight weeks on that tour and then doing our own things with our own bands for six months and then doing it again with Down. But that's a wish. And if you have a wish in one hand and a pile of shit in the other, what do you have?

In retrospect, is there anything you'd change about the album?

Windstein: Well, I wish Rex would've been in the band. He would've been able to do what he does to those songs now. Some of the tones are maybe not as great as they could be, but in a way that kind of adds to the classic sound of it. I mean, it's real, it's organic and it's not *too* perfect, you know what I mean? It's like, for me, Iron Maiden's first record will always be my favorite one, even though the production is probably the worst that they have. And that's kind of how I feel about *NOLA*. The vibe was really magical and it still stands up today.

Bower: The snare sound bugs me a little bit, but other than that, we were just completely happy with what we did. As far as we were concerned, it couldn't be any better.

Anselmo: I always think about how I could've done things better. My performance is what it is, especially for the time, and the snare sounds like a tin can. Even with the new Down record, after six weeks of touring, I wish I could go back and sing that motherfucker again, you know?

Keenan: No, no. Not at all. I mean, what could you do? Every time you put it on, it gets the party started.

CHAPTER 21

TOTAL ECLIPSE: METAL, MAYHEM & MURDER

THE MAKING OF EMPEROR'S *IN THE NIGHTSIDE ECLIPSE*

by J. Bennett

Release Date: 1995
Label: Century Media
Summary: Notorious symphonic black metal classic
Induction Date: December 2005/Issue #14

I n the Norwegian summer of 1993, the second wave of black metal was still in its ultra-violent infancy, and only a handful of bands were actively exploring the parameters of what was then an obscure and distinctly Scandinavian art form. Upon its release in 1995, *In the Nightside Eclipse* established Emperor as the reigning masters of a more complex, atmospheric style of "symphonic black metal," but before the album was even mixed, half the band was in prison on charges ranging from arson to murder. The recording sessions at Grieghallen Studios in Bergen were completed in July 1993, just a month before black metal hysteria would seize Scandinavia in the grip of screaming newspaper headlines detailing the vicious murder of Mayhem founder/guitarist Øystein Aarseth (a.k.a. Euronymous) by Burzum mastermind and onetime Mayhem session bassist Varg Vikernes (a.k.a. Count Grishnackh). Suddenly, a Pandora's Box of criminal activity in the black metal underground was sprung wide open. Shortly after Vikernes' apprehension, Emperor guitarist Samoth was arrested for church-burning and Emperor drummer Bård Eithun (a.k.a. Faust) was arrested for killing a man in the Lillehammer Olympic Park—a deed he had committed almost a year prior to the recording of *In the Nightside Eclipse*. Released from prison in December 2002 after serving nine years and four months' time, Faust joins fellow ex-Emperors Samoth, Ihsahn (guitar/vocals/keys) and Tchort (bass) on the eve of a sudden Emperor reunion (featuring Samoth, Ihsahn and longtime Emperor drummer Trym) to recount the making of one of the most historically fascinating and sonically influential albums in the annals of extreme metal.

What are your most vivid memories of the recording sessions for In the Nightside Eclipse?

Faust: There were a lot of practical things we had to organize, because Bergen is like 500 kilometers from Oslo, and we were very young at the time, and we didn't really know how to organize ourselves. But we managed to get hold of a car and we managed to actually get an apartment in Bergen. The car we used was from Samoth's father, and I was the only one who had a driving license.

Ihsahn: For me personally, it was kind of a turning point. We had recorded demos before, and also the first Emperor EP, but that was in a very cheap studio. This time we went to Bergen and Grieghallen, and recorded in a big studio with an experienced sound engineer and everything. I was only 17 at the time, so I couldn't get into the pubs, and since I had to do the guitars and the vocals and all the keyboards, I spent a lot of time in that studio. When the other guys finished their parts, they could always go to the local rock pub and hang out. I'd generally been very interested in sound engineering, and because I couldn't get into the pubs, I'd spend my nights with Pytten, the engineer, learning about recording and studio technology.

Tchort: I remember Varg Vikernes walking around the studio in his chain mail eating ice cream. I had just turned 19 and was starting to drink coffee for the first time. Grieghallen was huge—the drums were set up in a big hall and that's where I recorded the bass as well. Before, I had only been inside a small basement studio, and this was a hall where big orchestras could be recorded live.

Samoth: I had just turned 19 that summer, and I remember Bård and I terrorizing the Bergen neighborhoods in my dad's old Ford Econovan. [*Laughs*] We had a lot of fun during those weeks, but also a lot of work. We were quite inexperienced as far as being in the studio, and this was really the first big recording for any of us. There were some magic musical moments in the studio, for sure, but I don't remember too many concrete incidents from the actual studio session. I remember more about the time, the atmosphere and the total rebellious freedom I felt back then.

Were all the songs completely written beforehand, or were parts improvised in the studio?

Ihsahn: Oh, yes, we've always had all the material ready before we go into the studio. I would say it was pretty well rehearsed. We never booked time before we were actually finished writing the songs.

Samoth: The song structures were all done, but a lot of the symphonic keyboard parts were actually made in the studio. We didn't have a keyboard player at the time, so we never rehearsed with keyboards prior to the recording. Of course, certain parts we already had planned the keyboard lines for, and some riffs were made with keyboard lines in mind to begin with, but the overall symphonic and atmospheric layering on *Nightside* was pretty much composed by Ihsahn during the recording session.

Tchort: As far as I remember, most of the material was written beforehand, but the intro for the song "Towards the Pantheon" was made during our stay in the apartment next to the studio.

The album was co-produced by Pytten, who also produced Mayhem's De Mysteriis Dom Sathanas *and the first Burzum albums. What was he like?*

Ihsahn: He was the sound engineer at Grieghallen Studios, and still is, as far as I know. He also recorded several Immortal and Enslaved albums. Grieghallen came to be the studio where everybody recorded their first black metal albums. But Pytten wasn't a metal guy at all—he was just a very good sound engineer. He used to work for Norwegian television, as a host on a youth program. He's a very nice guy and a very skilled guy, socially. He related very well to all these extreme types—all these young black metallers who were coming in. He took it very seriously.

Faust: I have only good memories about him. He was very well educated in his work, and very relaxed. In the past, Grieghallen wasn't one of my favorite studios, but I think he put a trademark sound on each recording—a very organic and dynamic sound. I think he was a part of getting the right sound for *In the Nightside Eclipse*. At the time, he was already famous in Norway as a musician—in the '80s he was in a band called Blind Date. His daughter is one of the most famous handball players in Norway now—she's a very known icon for sports, and I think she was voted most sexy female in a magazine back in 2002 or something. We met her, because she would always drop by the studio when bands were recording there. I think she was maybe a year or two younger than us.

Tchort: Everyone seemed to "know" Pytten from a TV show he used to be on, but I didn't recognize him. He was cool to work with, kinda relaxed. I remember he didn't like the bass I brought, so I borrowed one of his for the recording. I don't think his bisexual daughter was into handball—or at least not known—back then, as she was probably only 15 or 16 at the time.

Five of the songs on **Nightside** *actually have the word "Emperor" in the lyrics. Did you think of Emperor as a character, or was it purely self-referential?*

Ihsahn: [*Laughs*] I didn't realize that. You know, I can't really remember all that was put into the lyrics at that time, because some of them are mixed with stuff that Mortiis wrote before he left the band. He wrote lyrics for "I Am the Black Wizards" and "Cosmic Keys [to My Creations and Times]" and then me and Samoth wrote some lyrics together. I wrote the lyrics to "Inno a Satana" and "The Majesty of the Nightsky" on my own. So it's all a big mixture, but I think they were partly drawn out from some of the concepts that Mortiis was working on at the time. The rest was pure imagination. I think there was a lot of running through forests [*laughs*]—it's all very epic. I suspect we used the word "landscape" more than once as well.

Samoth: I think we saw "Emperor" as a sort of entity. We didn't really ever use the word "Satan" much in our lyrics. We've always used a lot of metaphors and symbolism. Emperor became a metaphor for our own entity, for the dark lord, for the devil, for the strong and the mighty. There could be several ways to see it, you know.

Tchort: I don't think I read the lyrics until I was holding the finished album in my hands. I came from a different part of Norway, so the few times we met were for rehearsals—I didn't witness the birth of the songs and the lyrics behind them.

There's an essay in the appendix to the book **Lords of Chaos** *that compared black metal as a Scandinavian youth phenomenon to the Norse legend of the* **Oskoreien,** *"the ride of the dead," which was also reflected in a Norse folk custom that involved groups of young males terrorizing villages on horseback while wearing masks, making noise, etc. Are you referring to* **Oskoreien** *in "Into the Infinity of Thoughts" when the lyrics go, "In the name of the almighty Emperor I will ride the Lands in pride, carrying the Blacksword at hand, in warfare"?*

Ihsahn: Until you say it now, I've never heard that comparison. To be honest, my only connection to *Oskoreien* is more or less the famous Norwegian painting—I've seen the original at the national museum here in Norway. It's also on the cover of the Bathory album *Blood Fire Death*, which is my favorite black metal album. But I never read *Lords of Chaos*. I know I did an interview with that guy, and I think I'm referenced in the book, but I never bothered to read it. I've never had any interest in that side of it—all the hysteria, and what everybody else wanted it to be. Of course, in the beginning, we knew all the people involved, but the whole idea of a unified black metal scene was just very unfamiliar to how I experienced it. I've always been detached from that and, how do you say? . . . kind of self-centered about my own work. I've never cared very much for the whole scene and its development.

Was there anything in particular that influenced the lyrics—books, films, etc.?

Samoth: Emperor expressed many things, both internal and external, during the years. The power of Norwegian nature was always a source of inspiration for us, especially in the earlier years. We found great motivation in the vast forests and mighty mountains, and would actively be a part of it and also use its visual strength in our artistic vision. We also had a strong fascination for anything ancient, such as the Viking era. Ihsahn and I would spend a lot of time brainstorming on concept ideas, and at one point we had this whole concept of a dark fantasy world going. It was all very visual, I think. We drew a lot of influences from artwork related to Tolkien's *Lord of the Rings*. And keep in mind, this was 10 years before you could buy a "Lord of the Rings burger" at Burger King—quite a different vibe, so to say. We also had a period where we had a strong fascination for the whole Dracula myth and everything related to Transylvania, the Carpathian Mountains, the dark corners of Eastern Europe and folklore. For example, a film like *Nosferatu*—both the 1979 one and the 1922 silent movie—was a big part of our ambiance and visual influences.

Ihsahn: The lyrics represent very much the imaginary world we were occupied with. I never really read *The Lord of the Rings* or any of the things that everybody in that scene was reading at the time. I steered away from that, but the words we used and the fantasy imagery were still part of the whole way we thought and played. It doesn't really mean much in particular on this album, but it does capture the essence of the atmosphere of that time.

There weren't that many black metal bands in existence at the time you recorded In the Nightside Eclipse. *Were you enjoying the freedom of what was essentially a new art form, or did you feel restricted in any way by an ideology you felt you had to adhere to?*

Samoth: I don't think we felt too restricted. When we first started Emperor, we stripped everything down from what we were used to with our death metal outfit, Thou Shalt Suffer. Our aim was to go back to basics and sound like Celtic Frost, Tormentor from Hungary and Bathory . . . lots of Bathory! But as we got more serious with Emperor, we started to develop a more personal sound in addition to the obvious black metal influences. It was based a lot around the use of keyboards and the whole atmospheric and symphonic aspects. It became our thing, and we just took that further and further, really. But at the same time, it was very important for us to make sure we still maintained a certain spirit in the sound.

Faust: Black metal had existed for many years, but this was the second wave, and ours was the more symphonic black metal. We knew—or we started to realize—that it would be something different, but I don't think we felt we were caught by any ideology because we pretty much did what we wanted.

Tchort: Black metal was still very new to me, and since I hadn't been in the scene—I came from a death metal band—I didn't know much about the ideology, so I certainly didn't feel any restrictions. I understood the passion for atmosphere and even melodies that was put into the music, but besides that, I tried to play my part well and not be concerned about anything else.

Ihsahn: We were so young, and we had no idea what kind of impact this whole thing was going to have. I suppose now black metal has become a worldrenowned phenomenon, but at the time, it was so small and so totally underground, we were just occupied with trying to do our best. I mean, I know Pytten used a lot of big reverbs, so it all sounded very majestic, which is maybe how he interpreted it. For *In the Nightside Eclipse,* we also kind of built further on the use of keyboards to try and give it more of an orchestral feel.

Not many other black metal bands were using keyboards very extensively back then.

Ihsahn: Yeah—I think that came from when me and Samoth played in several bands prior to Emperor. We used keyboards in [Thou Shalt Suffer], so that kind of developed into a more progressive death metal. At the time we did the first Emperor EP, we wanted to use some layers of keyboards, and that kind of evolved on *In the Nightside Eclipse*—but even on that record the keyboards are very simplified, compared to later releases. At the time, there were no bands using keyboards in the same fashion.

Faust: Emperor and Enslaved were the only bands with guys who could actually play the synth and the piano. Up 'til then, all the use of synth in black metal had been made out of very minor knowledge of the instrument—just making the easiest chords and stuff. But Ihsahn and Ivar from Enslaved were able to create good melodies on the synth and use it as an instrument along with the guitar and bass and drums. I remember people in other bands would see Ihsahn and say, "Shit, this guy really knows how to play the synth." It wasn't really that common back then, so I think we realized that we were a lot different from bands like Immortal and Burzum, who played a very primitive kind of black metal back then.

Tchort hadn't been in the band very long at that point.

Faust: Tchort replaced Mortiis, who was kicked out or asked to leave in the beginning of 1993, after the recording of the mini-album.

Samoth: After Mortiis left, we played without a bass player for a while, and then actually Ildjarn [who had been in Thou Shalt Suffer] played bass for us, but that didn't end up being anything permanent. I think we hooked up with Tchort during the winter of '93. We left for our first tour in June, which was the U.K. tour with Cradle of Filth, and by that time he had already been with us for a little bit.

Tchort: I felt comfortable with the band and its other members, especially since we had just spent two weeks together touring in the U.K., but recording the album and being in a professional studio was a new experience for me. I had only recorded a demo before that. I didn't have more than a handful of rehearsals before we went to the U.K. to play—and then we went straight to the studio.

Ihsahn: [*Laughs*] When we went to the U.K. to tour with Cradle of Filth, they were our support act!

The album was recorded in July of 1993, but wasn't mixed until the following year. Why the delay?

Faust: Well, basically because half of the band ended up in prison. I was arrested one month after the recording, as was Samoth, who was released not long afterwards. My charges were a bit more serious, so I stayed in prison and didn't take part in the mixing. I wrote down my point of view on a piece of paper for them to take into consideration during the mixing, but it was mostly about the drums and stuff.

Samoth: There was a lot of stress that fall with Bård and I being arrested and taken into custody. I was, however, let out again some few weeks later, but Bård didn't come out until nearly 10 years later. Fucking crazy, eh? There was a lot of turbulence within the scene around this time, and this pushed the whole thing back quite a bit. I believe that Grieghallen was also booked for a while, so we had to wait. Eventually we found the focus and got studio time booked for the mix. It was just Ihsahn and I who went for the mix; I remember us sleeping in a rehearsal room in Oslo, and taking the early morning train to Bergen. I believe we gave Candlelight all production parts by late fall of '94. They had it pressed in '94, but it didn't really reach most distributors and shops until early '95, so that's why many see it as a '95 release. It was a very frustrating time, as we lost our drummer, the stable lineup, and the whole Norwegian scene was in turmoil and we weren't really sure what lay ahead for us as band. But in retrospect, I actually think the whole delay of the album made it an even stronger release. We sent out advance tracks to a lot of friends, and the tracks spread around the world and created a great expectation for the release.

Tchort: I also remember Ihsahn was sick during the recording of his vocals and he was spitting blood during the sessions. He did some vocals that were replaced with new vocal recordings later on—when he got better—so I think that contributed to the delay as well. They had to go back to the other side of the country to redo the vocals and do some more keyboards. He probably couldn't do any clean vocals when he was sick, either.

Bård, were you nervous about getting caught by the police while you were recording the album?

Faust: Not really, because a lot of time had passed [since the murder], so I didn't really think that much about it. I think it was a bit of luck that we were able to finish the recording before both Samoth and I got caught.

Varg Vikernes killed Euronymous shortly after you finished recording **In the Nightside Eclipse.** *He also lived in Bergen. Did you see him often during the recording sessions?*

Tchort: He came by and we spent some time at his apartment, too. I think I took a shower there and used his bubble bath. [*Laughs*] The killing happened later on, but I can't recall exactly when Euronymous was murdered.

Samoth: It was just weeks after we returned from the studio that all hell broke loose in Norway. It's weird to think about, really. If all the controversy with the police had happened a little sooner, this album would have never been made and the future of Emperor would probably have taken a whole different turn. We went to see Varg several times during the recording sessions. Even though we knew there was some tension between him and Euronymous, we didn't really involve ourselves in that and didn't really think that it would come to such extremes only weeks later. I have a classic memory of Varg stopping by the studio in his chain mail and standing in the recording room enjoying a huge ice cream with a smirk on his face.

At what point did you decide to dedicate the album to Euronymous?

Samoth: Sometime during '94, I'm sure, when we pieced together the artwork for the album. It was natural for us to do so, as Euronymous had always been very supportive of what we were doing and he was also a friend of ours, especially to Bård. He wanted to sign us to his label, Deathlike Silence Productions, but we had already done the mini-album with Candlelight and made the decision to stick with them.

Ihsahn: I think it felt very natural at the time, since he was so recently deceased, and we were releasing an album at that time. Bård was working very much with Euronymous at [Euronymous' infamous record shop] Helvete, so it felt right at the time.

Faust: Yeah, I reckon that I was the one closest to Euronymous. I worked in his record shop and also at some point lived together with him. I think it was a consensus some time after the murder when things finally started coming down to ground again. No one thought about *not* dedicating the album to him. It was the most obvious thing in order to commemorate his memory.

Where did you pose for the photos on the back cover?

Faust: Apart from Tchort, I think they were all taken outside of Samoth's place—in the woods—but at different times.

Tchort: My photo was taken at a local cemetery. I was later arrested because I stole that stone angel with the blood covering it and placed it in my bedroom.

Ihsahn: I remember there was no Photoshop or anything like that at that time. If you look at my photo, there's this dark background, and that was a very manual cut and paste. I'm cut out with scissors and glued onto a different background. I think it was the same with the goat in Samoth's picture. We had to be very handy at that point—we didn't have all the technology that people have today. We took our own photos, too—we didn't have any contact with photographers or designers, you know? Things are almost too easy these days.

How did you decide on Necrolord's cover art?

Samoth: I'd seen some of his work, like Grotesque's *Incantation* mini-LP and Dissection's *The Somberlain*, and liked his style. This was before he took off as an artist, I guess, and before long, every black metal album had a blue-toned art piece as a front cover. [*Laughs*] Originally, an ex-girlfriend of mine had tried to draw something for us, and from that we had a sketch of the tower that can be seen on the cover. Later, Ihsahn and I pieced together a bunch of ideas, [including] the tower and incorporating the death rider from the first mini-album, and we sent that to Necrolord. He did an awesome job and totally got our ideas and the vibe we were looking for at the time. I think to this day it stands out as a classic black metal album cover.

Faust: I thought it was fantastic—the perfect visual for the music—even though today it might seem a bit cheesy. It's a little bit mysterious, and maybe a bit *Lord of the Rings*.

Which song holds up the best for you personally?

Ihsahn: I think both "Cosmic Keys" and "I Am the Black Wizards" hold up well still—especially "I Am the Black Wizards," which was popular from the beginning. But usually my favorites from the albums we've made have hardly ever been the same as everybody else's. I think my favorite from this album is probably "In the Majesty of the Nightsky" because it has some musical elements that I feel were very well thought out for the time.

Samoth: Actually, I think the whole album holds up still. Of course, songs like "I Am the Black Wizards" and "Inno a Satana" have both gone down as "classics," but the whole album has a very real and natural flow, I think.

Faust: I think "Inno a Satana" is the perfect black metal hymn. That track manifests itself as the personification of symphonic black metal. I think it's a really, really good track—it's what constitutes symphonic black metal for me.

In the Nightside Eclipse *is the record many people would consider the first fully realized symphonic black metal album.*

Faust: Yeah, I think it's the first album that consciously tried to make black metal symphonic. Ihsahn has always been very good at orchestrating music, and I think that everybody who has a relationship to symphonic black metal always points back to *In the Nightside Eclipse* as maybe the first album that inspired him or her to start making that kind of music. That's a huge compliment.

How long after its release did you realize the influence/impact it had?

Ihsahn: I remember the first time we went on a European tour with Bal-Sagoth. They were actually older than us, but they said they started playing more black metal–style music—with keyboards—because of the first Emperor EP. We felt that was a bit strange, but later on we were in England and we met the guys from Cradle of Filth, who claimed that *In the Nightside Eclipse* was the album that everybody had. But the impact Emperor, as a band, has had on this black metal scene—and to some extent extreme metal—has been most noticeable after we quit the band. But I haven't given much thought to how influential we were, or how influenced we were by others, or any of the more superficial aspects of it.

Tchort: I am still to this day overwhelmed by the impact the album seemed to have on the scene. I travel more than ever now, with my bands [Green Carnation, Carpathian Forest], and in the darkest and most uncommon places of the world, I meet with people who approach me and tell me how much that album means to them.

Samoth: It wasn't really until after [1997's] *Anthems* [*to the Welkin at Dusk*] was released that we started getting a lot of front covers and bigger media attention, and then Emperor really started to become larger and taken more seriously in general. Looking at *Nightside*, I think there was a lot of buzz and hype about the album even before it came out—with advance tracks spreading around the world, there was a lot of anticipation in the underground about the release. When it finally came out, it quickly became an album that led to a lot of influences in the growing black metal scene—or black metal boom, rather.

Faust: I corresponded with Samoth while I was in prison, and I had access to magazines and stuff, so I saw that black metal was growing bigger and bigger. The album sold very well, and I saw that people were inspired by it, but I'm not sure I realized how big Emperor were before I started to see the tours they did and things like that. I was a little bit hidden from all that attention when I was in prison, so I didn't really see or understand it before I started to come out again on weekends to meet people and go to gigs again. I think it was in 1998 that I had the possibility of actually going out, but it wasn't very often—maybe six times a year or something for 12 to 24 hours. I was given that opportunity because it's a part of the Norwegian prison rehabilitation program. I remember going to a Dimmu Borgir gig in Oslo in 1998, and it was packed with a lot of people and young girls who I wouldn't really imagine going to a black metal show.

That's when I saw how big it had become.

Do you feel differently about the album now than you did at the time you recorded it?

Ihsahn: At the time we recorded it, I was of course very proud of it. By the time we did a couple of more albums, it's always like you wanna go back and change things you think you could've done better. [*Laughs*] By now I feel like that about all our albums. But I see it as a product of that time, where we were musically, and how old we were. It makes me feel like an old man at times, because it's such a long time ago, and there are so many kids coming up these days that have the album, but were barely born when we recorded it. But I'll be 30 in October, so I guess I'm not that old.

Tchort: For a period of time, I didn't like it so much, mostly because of the production. But I've probably only heard it three or four times since it was recorded. The last time I heard it was earlier this year, after a show I had done with Carpathian Forest. There was an after-show party and I was lying on a couch when they played the whole album, and it struck me that I really got a kick out of the music. And I got that old vibe again . . .

Faust: Well, I do realize that if it was released today it would be a very cheesy album, but that's something you can't take into consideration, because it was recorded in 1993 and released one and a half years later. I don't really listen to the album anymore—it's been many years since I actually put it on, but I can appreciate the moods and atmospheres in the music and I can understand that a lot of people like it because it was a very good album at the time. But for me, today, there wouldn't be any point in trying to re-create that album or to establish a band to continue in that vein.

Samoth: The album was something totally fresh for us when we were in the middle of making it, but today I see it almost in a historical sense—as a part of my life that also had great impact on how my life has become today, actually. We didn't really know that we had made a groundbreaking album. We knew it was a good album that had something personal and unique to it in our genre, but we never really saw it becoming one of the classic black metal albums of all time. Even saying this now is weird, but it makes me really proud of what we managed to put together. We took our music and everything around it very seriously. Those times were very special. We were quite young and very active in a rather obscure underground movement. It almost seems like another life looking back at it now.

CHAPTER 22

HIGH TIMES

THE MAKING OF SLEEP'S *JERUSALEM*

by J. Bennett

SLEEP - JERUSALEM

Release Date: 1999
Label: Rise Above
Summary: The best 52-minute song of all time
Induction Date: March 2006/Issue #17

The words "stoner epic" don't even come close to describing the extreme riff-hypnosis that *Jerusalem* visited upon the red-eyed legions of heshers, grass pirates and acid casualties who genuflected at the altar of the legendary San Jose power-trio known as Sleep. In 1995, after two albums—'91's *Volume One* (Tupelo/Very Small) and '93's *Holy Mountain* (Earache)—Sleep bassist/vocalist Al Cisneros, guitarist Matt Pike and drummer Chris Hakius were ready to record their masterpiece: a one-song, 52-minute album, with financial assistance from their new corporate benefactors at London Records. *Jerusalem* was Sabbath in slow motion, *Earth 2* without track divisions and the soundtrack for an eternal bong-huffing caravan to the heart of the Holy Land rolled into a thick, hazy hour of thundering chords, booming vocals and terminal battery. Little did its architects know that the album (originally entitled *Dopesmoker*) would be shelved, and that Sleep would break up years before its first official release in 1998. The legends and rumors surrounding the album's creation are as numerous as they are fantastic. Tales of the band's staggering weed intake, master tapes delivered in skull bongs and drug-related budgetary indiscretion proliferated, despite (and probably due to) the fact that Pike (currently of High on Fire), Cisneros and Hakius (both currently of Om) never actually did promotional interviews when the album eventually came out. For our latest Hall of Fame induction, *Decibel* talked to all three former members of Sleep to find out what really happened on the road to *Jerusalem*.

PART I: SOME GRASS

What's your most vivid memory of the **Jerusalem** *recording sessions?*

Matt Pike: Well, none of it's vivid. I was smoking so much weed that everything was kinda surreal at the time. [*Laughs*] But I remember a lot of loud amps and trying to memorize all these crazy-ass combinations of parts. There was so much to memorize for that album, and we had to do it in like three different sections, because a reel-to-reel only holds something like 22 minutes. It was really cool, but it was one of the hardest things I've ever done in my life. I was also trying to make my bass player and my drummer get along, because they were having a hard time with each other in the studio. And at the same time, my mom was dying from cancer. It was tough.

Chris Hakius: I remember a lot of hard work and a lot of stress. We put in a lot of hours to create that album. We had just got onto London Records and we were all really broke, which made things difficult.

Al Cisneros: When we finished the tracking and all sat down together in the studio to finally hear the song straight through, it was pretty special. It's weird when your entire life is coming back through the speakers in the control room, and all three of you kind of mutually acknowledge that internally. But at the same time, it was like somebody hoisting a flag on a sinking ship.

The popular legend is that Sleep got a big advance for **Jerusalem** *from London Records, smoked it all and then ended up having to rush through the recording sessions. Is that what actually happened?*

Hakius: I've heard that before, and it's certainly not true, but you can't argue with a piece of paper when you read it, you know? Al was always kind of the band leader, so I think an A&R guy contacted him first. At the time, London said they'd give us full artistic freedom, so that's what we did. But when it got down to the final stages of things, we were all really stressed out—and broke—because the money we got from them initially pretty much covered how badly in debt we were at the time that we signed. It wasn't because of drugs or anything like that, either—it was because we were trying do to this for a living, and we had bills piled up from the time between *Holy Mountain* and *Jerusalem*. We never really had real jobs, either. Matt and I worked on a plastering crew for a while; Al worked in a bookstore—we all just did odd jobs so we could stay loose and go on tour whenever we wanted. But the story that we smoked our budget [*laughs*] is not true. I can't say we didn't spend a few dollars on it, but I mean, it would have almost been literally impossible to spend it all on that.

Was London aware, before you signed, that your plan was to record a one-song album?

Cisneros: Absolutely. We were actually talking to Elektra at the same time as London, and one of the reasons we decided to go with London is because they were OK with that idea. But within two or three weeks of signing with London, the A&R guy who had been coming out to California to negotiate with us got transferred and replaced. There was a new head of the A&R department, and a new representative for our band, both of whom didn't have any connection with the template that was laid down. So immediately—even before we began tracking—we were nervous and uncomfortable about what they could end up doing to the album, what they might demand in terms of a video, radio edits and all the rest of it. The conditions of the entire deal changed right underneath us. In a certain sense, all the horror stories we had heard from bands that had gotten onto a major label came true. They told us, "Don't do it; don't do it." And it was too good to be true. When reality set in, it was like, "We heard this story. We shouldn't have done this."

Pike: Yeah, that was weird because we let them know what we wanted to do before we even signed with them. Both London and Elektra were biting at us, and we went with London because they offered us more money for the recording. Plus they didn't have as many metal bands, so we thought they'd give us special attention.

You'd been working on the song itself for quite some time before the London offer came along.

Pike: Oh, fuck, we'd been working on it for like four years. We also had two other songs that we were working on that were really long, too—like 15 and 20 minutes. But we never recorded them.

Cisneros: We toured Europe and the United States on *Holy Mountain*, and we were really reaching the point where we had to have some new stuff. So the song formulated at sound checks, and then we'd work on it some more in motel rooms or at friends' houses. We'd just keep coming up with ideas, and the song just started to assemble itself. At our last show before we decided to settle down and make the record—it was here at Slim's in San Francisco sometime in early or mid '94, and I think we played with the Melvins—we played a shorter, much more up-tempo version of the song. But it was pretty much the same song that you hear on the record. And it was long—the intention was to just keep cycling. We had lots of riffs that kept answering each other in a series, so we said, "Shit, if it's a long song, it's a long song."

How crucial was your collective weed intake to the creative process?

Pike: We were smoking a lot. Between us all, we were probably smoking two ounces a day or more.

Cisneros: Back then—from the time of *Holy Mountain* through *Jerusalem*—it was definitely a ritual that got more and more frequent. Personally speaking, I was really dependent on the space I got into when I was using it, and some of the lyrics are about that. It was pretty integral to the scope of my life at the time. The line, "Drop out of life [with bong in hand]," was kind of a creed at that point.

Hakius: I'd say it was crucial. It helped a lot, but at the same time, everyone was having a rough time personally during and prior to the recording. There was a lot of growing up and learning. We were all in our early 20s, and after the Hawkwind tour we went on, everyone was pretty tore up. That's when we were really working on that song, and I can honestly say everyone wasn't really taking care of themselves that well—and that snowballed into the recording process. As far as the herb, that probably kept everyone more grounded, actually.

PART II: PROCEED THE WEEDIANS TO NAZARETH

When did you actually go into the studio?

Cisneros: We were ready to record it in '95—we just wanted to go into a studio somewhere and just fuckin' do it, but it didn't happen until '96. First we had to get free from Earache Records. They would not let us go—they would not budge for anything. [Earache Records owner] Digby [Pearson] was waiting . . . I mean, London bought the guy out, but he waited to make the most prime conditions for himself before he let our contract go. So there was about a year and a half of legal wrangling between our manager and lawyers with Earache, and then, once we signed to London, their team of lawyers and Earache. And it took forever. At one point, we even asked a friend of ours to give us a couple thousand bucks so we could put it out ourselves, but he feared that he'd get sued.

Pike: Earache sat on us forever, and London was trying to get us out of the Earache deal. And then we finally got out of it and London took a shit on us, too. It was tragic, man—I think it was a great album, and it was stupid that they didn't market it.

The waiting must've taken a toll on the band, mentally.
Cisneros: The waiting definitely affected all of us. The song demanded to be recorded, and we couldn't because of all these lawsuits. Comparing our collaborative creativity to having a child together or something, it was like we were forced to watch the kid suffer. It was killing us. The song was begging to be given food, and it was terrible. We worked from the time we had met—Chris and I in eighth grade, and Matt and us in ninth grade—tunnel-visioned on that moment, and we couldn't record it. I don't even know how to explain the way it felt.

Hakius: When we finally went into the studio, the song was starting to take on a different form for me personally than what we had originally envisioned. We recorded it one way, and then we wanted to try it another way, and it turned into a conflict. When you write a song that's 50 minutes long, you get used to playing it one way. We spent a couple of years working on the song, and then when we went to record it, it started turning out a little differently and creating a lot of anxiety. We could reasonably handle that, but as we were going along, the record label wanted to hear what we were doing, and they were scoffing at it from what I could tell. So that added more stress and anxiety, and it started piling up. Then we had some equipment failure at some point, and the whole thing just started to kind of feel like it was doomed. We're still good brothers to this day, but it made us fight about nothing.

Pike: Everyone was going insane from learning that song—it was really dramatic. The song was getting slower and slower and then it got weird. We started tripping out and second-guessing ourselves. And then it was like we didn't know what we were doing anymore.

What do you remember about Record Two, the studio you recorded in?
Cisneros: It was really nice—it was up near Mendocino. It was this old studio, and the guy had this really old Neve board. Billy [Anderson], our engineer, walked in there and was pretty impressed with the gear and the way it had been maintained over the years. So that combined with the environment made it seem like it was the place to do it. It was up in the mountains with this cabin vibe, and being embedded there with London hovering over our heads made me feel like I was in *The Shining* or something. But overall, the recording environment was pretty decent.

Hakius: It was awesome. I think either Al or Billy found the place. They had top-of-the-line equipment, but the rate for being there for a long time was really good. It was out in the woods on like 15 acres or something, and it was really secluded. We were in the middle of nowhere, so when something went wrong, we'd lose a day—or even two days. It started going by fast, even though we were there for like a month. We got down to the wire, and the more the pressure built, it got harder and harder. We tried to maintain the best quality control we could, but it was getting to the point where we just wanted to get it done and go on vacation. [*Laughs*] Not that anyone had any money to go anywhere.

Pike: We were in the studio for a month, and then went home and re-rehearsed it, and then we went in for another month. So it was about two months altogether, I think, and I believe we ended up with two or three different versions.

You originally wanted to call the song "Dopesmoker." How did it become "Jerusalem"?

Cisneros: When we played it live, it was announced as "Dopesmoker." After playing it live, and after lots of smoking and reflection, we started becoming interested in more of a Middle Eastern desert theme. I remember one practice the idea [of calling the song "Jerusalem"] came up, and we all started laughing really hard. I just put my bass down and walked out. It was such a fucking good idea, it was too much. But now there's a couple different versions out—I think *Dopesmoker* is the more up-tempo one, and *Jerusalem* is the slower one.

Was it difficult breaking the song up into sections to accommodate the reels?

Cisneros: Yeah, and part of that was inexperience. We were all around 23 or 24 at the time, I think, and being that it was only our third full-length—and not really knowing anything about studio techniques—we had to learn along the way. We'd always recorded live from day one, but we weren't just making a good live recording—we were in a studio making an album. But yeah, it was weird, because we'd only viewed the song as one continuous flowing piece.

Pike: We were rehearsing it one straight take, for the most part, but we also broke it into sections to make sure we got the parts tight and down. We'd just take one third of it, play it through, practice a little transfer part, play the second part, practice another transfer, and then play the last part.

Jerusalem is often regarded as a kind of stoner spiritual—it seems to have strong elements of transcendental meditation to it. Do you think of it that way?

Cisneros: Yeah, totally. There was a middle section in that song when we were still doing it live, and the vocal line I put down called for these long, windy, resonant notes over one continuous 12th fret note that just started to cycle. When we'd play back our live tapes, we'd be like, "Whoa." It definitely tapped something. Again, it wasn't intentional; it just started to happen, and we didn't fight it. Not knowing the formula that made that take place, but recognizing that it had shown up through the speakers, we figured something was going on. Then it became, "Keep your head down and your eyes shut." [*Laughs*]

Hakius: We definitely wanted it to be something where you'd sit down to listen to it and not want to get up for an hour. I think that spilled over from our tour with Hawkwind. A certain crowd of people who we began to associate with and play to liked to just sit and listen, you know? We didn't write the song for them so much—*we* were becoming that way, too.

Pike: It's not something we talked about all that much—it's something we just did. But you know, I just want people to enjoy it however they want to. It's definitely better loud and when you're alone so you can meditate on it, but that's probably true for listening to any music.

PART III: THE DOPESMOKER CHRONICLES

There's a story on Julian Cope's website that says Sleep delivered Jerusalem *to London on a DAT tape inside a skull bong wearing a military helmet.*

Cisneros: [*Laughs*] That's very, very untrue. The only thing I remember about marijuana at London Records was in Peter Koepke's office. He was the president of London Records, and one of the first times we went to the London building—which was in this big old high-rise in Manhattan—we went into his corner office overlooking Times Square. It was this totally surreal experience—three stoner friends from high school walking around this building like, "Whoa—look at that record on the wall!" And we asked if there was anyone there who had some pot or could get us some pot. So we had this pipe, and we're at Peter Koepke's desk, with our manager, and there's this lawyer on the speakerphone—like all official and business-like, right? And we put the whole quarter-ounce into the pipe, smoked it and put the pipe on his desk. But I have absolutely no idea about the military helmet and the skull.

Pike: We made something like that, but we didn't send it to the label. We had an aviator mask with a blower motor that you could hook up in your car. You'd put the mask on, and smoke would pour out the back—it was pretty cool.

What finally happened when you sent the album to London?

Cisneros: We were told by our manager that they weren't gonna release it as is—they were gonna remix it. When I heard that, I considered getting our master reels and destroying them myself. I would rather have faced a lawsuit than release something I wasn't behind. But that plan wouldn't work, because they had backup DATs. So then we were like, "Well, seeing as how we're the band and this is all last-minute—and not part of the deal we signed—can we be in the room when it's being remixed? Can we say yes or no if something doesn't sound right?" Keep in mind, this is *after* we all thought it was over, and now we were in this position where we were trying to keep it from getting worse. We spent 10 months going back and forth between studios in New York watching all these major-label engineer types walk in and completely mutate the sound of the album—it was bad.

Pike: They tried to make a bunch of radio edits out of it—which was nearly impossible with that song—and the one that they came up with was ridiculous. It didn't make any sense. The record label had that dude David Sardy come in and remix it, and we thought he lost a bunch of shit, and then he brought in my throwaway guitar tracks, and that kinda pissed me off. So it isn't exactly the way we intended it.

In addition to Billy Anderson, there are four assistant engineers listed in the credits. That seems like a lot.

Cisneros: That was all London—those were people we didn't know. It's like the patient being strapped down and then four people come in and just start fucking with veins and stuff.

Hakius: There's another thing that made us all fight: At that point, we didn't even wanna listen to it anymore, but we didn't wanna be in some kind of breach of contract, and we owed them so much money that we just agreed to the remix. At that point, Al and I weren't getting along too good anymore [*laughs*], because . . . well, no one was really living that well at that point. So we had to go in and tear the song apart, and they kept making us bring in more and more people. We had to get out the two-inch tape and splice another song out of the original—and then listen to it 5,000 times in a way we didn't want it. The thing is, if you listen to that song more than once, it kind of puts you in a trance, and you can't even remember what you were doing 10 minutes ago—especially if everybody in the room is a total head. Then it turns into, "Oh, did we catch that? We better listen to it again." I didn't even go to the last remix. I couldn't take it anymore.

Pike: We went to four different studios to finish "the product," you know? London kept wanting us to change it. They thought if we changed this and changed that, it'd make the record more marketable or something, but really they were just nitpicking. The thing is, it *was* a marketable thing—just not to mainstream people. But that's not the kind of band we were. But even if it came out, we would've broken up anyway.

Of the four CD versions that have surfaced—the rare London Records promo, the [almost as rare] bootleg with Arik Roper cover art, the Rise Above/Music Cartel version and the **Dopesmoker** *version—not a single one has the cover you guys wanted.*

Hakius: That was politics between people at the label—it had nothing to do with us—over the real cover that we wanted, which they originally said they were gonna give us. There're literally three or four versions out that I never OK'd; I didn't even know about half of them, and I think Al was the same way. Once we were done recording, there was a lot we didn't know about what happened with it. It went into limbo—it was really strange. We knew what we wanted for the cover, and we had already sent it to them. It was the picture on the inside of . . . I think it was the Music Cartel version. It's been licensed by like three different labels now, so I'm not sure, but it's a photo of a coconut chalice. It was supposed to be really simple, and it matched the time period for us personally. And it was originally supposed to be on green vinyl, like the amplifiers we use. But we pissed them off because they didn't like it and we said we weren't budging.

Pike: I think Tee Pee got sued over that first Roper bootleg. Then [the Music Cartel] wasn't doing anything to either sell it or promote it, and the guy wasn't paying us any royalties on it, because he wasn't selling any. It was like, "Dude, you gotta advertise it to sell it." So I went over the dude's head and told him he already had his chance.

Cisneros: From the time we sent London the band-approved mix—Billy's mix, produced by the band and Billy, engineered by Billy—we knew it was out of our hands, and nothing from that point until today, really, has gone according to the original plan. I remember seeing the London promos, and then the Roper edition and then the Music Cartel one you mentioned. And then I walked into a record store one day and saw the *Dopesmoker* version. I was like, "Oh, that's interesting."

Hakius: I didn't even know about the Arik Roper [bootleg] version until after it came out. I'll be straight up with you—Arik Roper is an extremely talented artist, but the cover he did has nothing to do with our vision. Let me put it this way: I meet people at shows who get all kinds of different messages out of that album. Some are completely satanic and evil, some are completely spiritual, and some are like they were sniffing glue at home. And that's what happens when other people decide what your album art is gonna be.

The **Dopesmoker** *version is about 11 minutes longer than the Rise Above/Music Cartel Jerusalem disc. Do you consider either one to be the definitive version?*

Cisneros: I don't think the *Dopesmoker* thing is the exact version that we submitted, but that's the closest one that's come out of the four. If I had to pick a favorite, that would be it. The reason that the song went from 45 minutes—which was the way we practiced it—to somewhere around 63 [the *Dopesmoker* version] was because after we stopped doing live stuff and just focused on recording, we kept slowing the song down in rehearsals. We'd A/B it against our live tapes and we'd be like, "You know what? This feels a little bit better." I think the original outtake was somewhere around 65 or 70 minutes—it was much longer. I think the differing musical temperaments between Matt and myself . . . I mean, we didn't have a strained friendship or collaboration in any sense, but it may have begun two different roads that may be more evident today.

Hakius: We all started to have a little bit of a different idea about what that song was about. The beef was pretty much between Al and I, because we were the rhythm section and we worked very closely together on everything—and we obviously still do in Om. But because of how the song radically changed and how the communication was so bad between us at the time, we didn't see eye to eye anymore. We both had to grow up and get over a few things. When we were done with that album, it was literally the end. I didn't talk to Al for a long time. Matt stayed pretty neutral the whole time, but he was like, "I can't wait around for you guys to make up, so I'm gonna start a new band." And we were like, "Do it, man. Don't work at a gas station—that'd be stupid."

Pike: I tried to stay neutral, but I was also trying to keep my band together. I wanted them to work things out—which they eventually did, and now they're playing together without me.

PART IV: NEBUCHADNEZZAR'S DREAM

Are you happy that the album finally came out, or is there part of you that wishes it had stayed buried?

Cisneros: I definitely wish that it hadn't. If you're involved in something creatively, to allow that to be exposed, you have to be emotionally supportive of it in itself. But I feel like somewhere along that formation, it was taken from us, painted with a different cover and just re-presented. It'd be like if you were writing a novel and you died before you finished the last two chapters and somebody tried to put it together as the book you really wanted to publish. Only they had no idea what was supposed to happen in those last two chapters, which could be imperative to the whole flow of the novel. You'd be rolling in your grave, and the outside world would have no idea.

Pike: I wanted it to come out anyway. We did all that work, so why leave it sitting around? It's taking its course the way it is, so I try not to second-guess it. I figure it's happening the way it's supposed to.

Hakius: Being on a major label is not something that everybody can do. It really depends on how much ass-kissing and giving in and changing things for other people you wanna do, because those are the things that kind of determine your success. That's why there's a lot of shitty music on the radio and TV. There were like five or six reasons why we broke up, but one of them was that we were on a major label and we owed them a lot of money. We couldn't go to another label or anything, so we were screwed. For a long time, I thought I couldn't even play music again without getting served papers or something. The funny thing is that London Records isn't even around anymore. I think Sony bought them and flushed them.

Cisneros: I've had to accept it having happened, but it took a long time. That's why personally, out of all of us, I couldn't play music for a while. I could physically, but I absolutely refused to do it from a disingenuous point. It has to be a necessity. And to get back to the healed point where my thoughts and feelings—in terms of lyrics and riffs—started to naturally fill me again, it took years. Honestly, it felt like I had died. I obviously was physically alive, but it felt like I was gone—and there's no reason to play music when you feel like that.

When did you start to realize Jerusalem's influence on other bands?

Pike: Well, I started noticing the band's influence right after the second album, even. People were dressing the same and playing Sleep riffs—that was going on for a while.

Cisneros: I didn't really notice so much because I really closed off from the whole thing. During that time I really kept my head down, and I wasn't observing the outside. But Chris and I get tons of people who wanna talk about the old band, and I wouldn't have it any other way. I know it's strange to say that after the horrible period that took place, but those guys are family, you know, and we did what we did. What didn't go right has to be accepted along with what did go right. Those were some of the best years of my life, so it's OK to talk about it.

Hakius: That's hard to explain, because when we finished the album, we all went in different directions. It was like a divorce, but we still cared about each other. We all took different jobs—I put my drums away for a couple of years and drove a big rig to pay some bills. Al put his stuff away, too, and even sold some of it—we both didn't wanna play music ever again. Matt continued with High on Fire, and we were stoked for him—we wanted him to run with his talent. But, to answer the question, I didn't listen to that type of music for a long time. But I did start to notice [the influence] within a couple of years. I never felt anyone was ripping us off, though. For me, *Jerusalem* was a low point in my life, and I'm not really satisfied with my playing on that record. But if it caused someone else to be creative and write music, then it was a success in my opinion.

In retrospect, is there anything you'd change about it?

Cisneros: I don't think I would. I've gotten to a place where I accept it for what it is. And you know, despite all these things I've told you, I don't regret it. It's really important, and we did our very best. That's its own reward in a sense. And that seven or eight years I took after our last band practice to just go forward and go to school was important. I needed to live life for a little while and just watch the world around me. It's helped me a lot.

Hakius: I have a two-way answer for that, I guess. I wouldn't change the parts we're playing or the length of it, but what I'd wanna change is how we were living up to that point, because it had everything to do with what happened in the studio. [*Laughs*] I don't even know if that's an answer. But I'll tell you something, and this is the truth for me: I believe that when a song is finished, that's the way it's supposed to be. When you capture something in time, that's the way it is. Whether you like it or not doesn't matter. It's like being dealt something in life. If you're in a car accident or end up with a disease, you have to deal with it. [*Laughs*] And that's kind of how I feel about that album. But if we were to play that song tomorrow, it'd probably be just a little bit faster.

Pike: It's been about a year since I've listened to it, but I'd probably change the tempo. It's so slow, but it's not *slow*, you know? It's weird. It might be the fuckin' weirdest song ever. I think it might've been better if we'd recorded it at a faster tempo and hadn't been so anal about it. We were just a bunch of massive stoners trying to do something that no one else had done—which I think we accomplished.

CHAPTER 23

100% CLASSIC

THE MAKING OF THE DILLINGER ESCAPE PLAN'S
CALCULATING INFINITY

by Kevin Stewart-Panko

Release Date: 1999
Label: Relapse
Summary: Soundtrack to the tech-metal revolution
Induction Date: December 2006/Issue #26

This one's a no-brainer. Regardless of what you think about *Calculating Infinity*, you can't deny that the 11 tracks on this album revolutionized extreme music and raised the bar in terms of technicality, musicianship, speed, dynamics—even visual presentation, album photography and design. What's also quite incredible is that this album was completed in any sort of timely fashion, considering the 15-month rollercoaster preceding its September 1999 release. After the northern New Jersey quintet's explosive three-song *Under the Running Board* EP, things started toppling around guitarist Ben Weinman, drummer Chris Pennie and vocalist Dimitri Minakakis like a losing game of Jenga. Guitarist John Fulton walked out right around the same time bassist and original member Adam Doll found himself paralyzed from the chest down with limited use of his hands after a seemingly minor fender-bender. Former Jesuit guitarist Brian Benoit was added to the mix, but so was an incalculable amount of pressure in the form of record company deadlines, financial constraints, bad business decisions, upcoming tours and a guitarist trying to play bass with "gay little fingers." With all of this piling ever-higher on their individual and collective plates, Dillinger still somehow created the groundbreaking metallic hardcore album they wanted to—one that has been often imitated, never duplicated and is about as obvious an induction to *Decibel*'s Hall of Fame as you could hope for.

Can you give a rundown of everything going at the time and where the band and your heads were at going into Calculating Infinity?

Ben Weinman: It was a really weird time because so many exciting things were happening, but so many challenges were also being presented. It was the start of "nothing's ever gonna be easy for the Dillinger Escape Plan." We had put out the *Under the Running Board* EP on Relapse and, in our small world, it was getting a lot of attention. At that time, there weren't a lot of middle-sized bands; you didn't have Shadows Fall or Lamb of God. Even the bands that were doing well—bands like Poison the Well, who people thought were huge—weren't that huge, and Neurosis and Today Is the Day, then, were probably half the size of what they are today. But that's what we knew. Deadguy was the biggest band in the world and Earth Crisis was huge and when I saw them play to 300 kids, it was like Madison Square Garden to me.

So, in that little world, we started to do well; we could actually play a show and people who knew our music would come. We got a few cool tours, and signing to Relapse was really exciting. We started to write this full-length that was highly anticipated because people were saying that *Running Board* was different and that we were on top of our game. At the same time, John Fulton, our other guitar player on *Running Board*, got freaked out and was like, "Well, I never expected this to go anywhere." To him, you didn't do this for real; you did it after school for fun, whereas I was very proactive and I had it all planned. I was like, "All right, we have this show and some guys from Relapse are going to be there. I'm going to tell them that Earache wants to sign us and piss them off and get them to take our demo. And once that happens, I'm going to get them to another show and we're going to kick ass and get signed." At that point, everything was going as planned until John decided to quit and become a computer programmer. He was the sickest guitar player ever; he really inspired my playing and introduced me to technical music. The writing situation at the time was one where he would come up with these crazy ideas and I would turn them into songs. When he announced he wasn't going to do this anymore, I shit myself because I didn't know how I was going to write a full-length that destroys *Running Board* without the guy who's been a big part of that progression.

On top of that, when we first started writing the record, Adam, who was also a big part of that progression, got into a car accident and was paralyzed. I wanted to do benefit shows to help him get the best health care and therapy and, at the same time, figure out how we were going to move forward. In my mind, we were going to get a fill-in until he got better, because there was no way this dude's not getting better and there's no way he's not going to walk. And even if he doesn't walk, he's still gonna play in our band. Chris took that I would even be thinking about this kind of stuff as almost insulting; he just wanted to almost grieve. He didn't even want to play or talk about the band. To me, we had to play shows [and] put out a sick record, and when Adam got back, the band would be this developed thing instead of something that fell apart because of his accident. There was definitely some tension because of that.

Chris Pennie: My head was in two places because of Adam's accident—I was really shaken up by that—and John quitting. Those were two people that I grew up playing with; they were close and important to me and now, musically, they were gone. On the other hand, I had all sorts of fire because things were starting to happen for the band; we were finding our own sound and I was just really motivated. I remember writing a lot in the basement at my house. Ben and I would get together, jam ideas and hammer them out. When we weren't playing, I was playing four or five hours a day, just working on my own to perfect the tunes. I remember arguing with my mother about it, constantly. She didn't understand that this is what I wanted to do, that I loved it so much and all I wanted to do was make this shit as awesome as possible. I had a lot of arguments with her; now she understands, but back then, getting her to understand was hard. We just wanted to make an awesome record, push the boundaries of what we could do.

Brian Benoit: Basically, I got in after the Jesuit/Botch/Dillinger tour. Ben called me saying that Fulton was giving the vibe that he didn't want to tour and that they were looking for a touring guitar player. A couple weeks after that, he got back to me saying that he didn't even think Fulton wanted to do the band at all. It worked out because I had just graduated college, Nate [Newton, also ex-Jesuit] had already joined Converge and I had the option: a career or the band.

Dimitri Minakakis: We'd always had a "backs to the wall" thing going on. I guess at the time we weren't too worried about writing a record because, at any time, Dillinger always has three songs written. I think we were really concerned about getting a solid lineup together. But because I never really contributed musically, I never knew what was or wasn't written until it was presented. For me, it wasn't that stressful—it just wasn't fun being impatient. In one sense, there was frustration because I wasn't able to map, or get help mapping out, my parts until the songs were totally completed, and what was the point of fitting vocals into something that might change tomorrow? In some ways, I felt like a slouch, but I was fine with that.

Adam, can you tell us about your accident?

Adam Doll: My accident was August 13, 1998. We had been home for two weeks or so from the Botch/Jesuit tour. I was driving home from picking my sister's car up, and I wound up rear-ending somebody on a road nearby. I was probably going 35, 40 miles an hour. I don't really remember exactly what happened, but an eyewitness report said that someone stopped in front of me to make a left, I went to go around them, missed someone in my blind spot, jerked the car back and rear-ended someone. I never lost consciousness or anything—I didn't even have a scratch on my body—but with the type of impact it was, I ended up dislocating the vertebrae right where my neck meets my shoulder. Right after, I'm sitting in the car and I try to get up to see what happened, and I basically couldn't stand up. I got to the hospital and they just thought I had severe whiplash. It wasn't until they did an MRI that they figured out what was wrong.

So, when all this was happening, how much of the album was written?

Weinman: Three songs and a couple of other parts. "4th Grade Dropout" was on a split with Nora and "Jim Fear" was done as well. The EP was getting great reviews, our peers liked it and all of a sudden we had to do this full-length that, I felt, fell on my shoulders. Me and Chris would write together, but we would also tour pretty actively while we were writing. That's when we got Brian in the band. There were a couple songs we started playing live that we taught him before we went into the studio. My main concern was that nobody could tell the difference and know that those other guys weren't in the band anymore. It was definitely a pressure situation; there were time restrictions because of everything that happened and Relapse wanting to capitalize on the *Running Board* buzz. All that pressure came out on the record.

Doll: We had recorded three of the songs that appeared on *Calculating* before we went on tour, but those were for splits with Drowningman and Nora, and the other was supposed to wind up on a compilation that never happened.

Was there any thought of putting off the writing or the recording until Brian was fully integrated into the band?

Weinman: We had so many deadlines and the idea was—and this is the way we continue to work—for us to progress and build on what we had done. We always used ourselves as a marker and our own competition. To me, there was no point in stopping our progression waiting for someone else to catch up. There's no point in having someone who's new in the band try and write a Dillinger-ish riff when I can write a Dillinger-ish riff. This isn't my first Dillinger riff; I did the first Dillinger riff a couple years ago [*laughs*]—let's do the next thing.

Benoit: Nah. I knew my role, which was getting up to par live. I moved up to Jersey right after Thanksgiving in '98, and our first tour was two and a half weeks later with Cave In and Converge, so I had to cram my ass off and prepare for that. I had just moved up to Jersey and it was a shock trying to adjust from a beach environment in Virginia Beach. I'd be wearing a winter coat and they'd be wearing t-shirts and laughing their asses off at me.

The credits say the album was recorded over three months in '99. How broken up over three months were the sessions?

Pennie: Ultimately, I think it was done in 13 or 14 days over the course of March, April and June. We only had seven or eight songs written in March. After that, we went back and wrote the three or four other songs. It was a complete whirlwind and, looking back, it's completely amazing to think we did that in that amount of time.

What was the recording process like?

Doll: None of us had ever recorded a full-length before, so I don't think anyone knew what we were getting into. We did *Running Board* in two and a half days; who were we kidding? [*Laughs*]

Weinman: It was awesome being able to spread it over time because Chris really worked hard on the parts. Even as were writing new songs, he'd be working on the other songs. My whole thing was that shit had to be ridiculously and inhumanly fast. To me, the only way to get energy from technical stuff was to make it like a machine gun hitting you in the chest. Whether you understood what was going on or not, you felt that shit smack you in the face like you were a little bitch. I came from the world of noisy rock and punk music, whereas Chris had a bit more of a technical metal background. I remember writing songs and it was like:

Me: "This has to be louder! No, don't play that on a bell; play that on a crash cymbal."

Chris: "But crash cymbals aren't supposed to be hit like a ride."

Me: "No, that crash cymbal is now a ride!"

Chris: "But I'll break it. They're only supposed to be hit a few times."

Me: "Fuck it, we'll buy another one. That china cymbal is now a ride."

Shit like that, to me, is what brought the energy. I remember sitting there with Chris saying, "This has to be faster, this has to be louder." He'd be like, "I can't. I'm getting tendonitis!" And I kept telling him it's gotta be faster, and by the next practice, he'd be playing it twice as fast. Then I'd tell him, "Faster!" He'd be, "It's not humanly possible!" but by next practice, it'd be faster. Then, by the time we played it in the studio, it'd be twice as fast, then twice as fast as that by the time we played live. Seeing Chris progress from being a light and precise hitter like he was in [previous band] Arcane, to being able to beat the shit out of his drum kit—play so fast, but also be so precise—was awesome. As far as me being pretty much the only guitar player, I really enjoyed having control over everything and having my whole vision realized with writing, but I was worried about not being able to pull off some of the technical, lead-y stuff, because I didn't know if I had the ability or confidence in my playing to pull it off in the studio. The idea was for me to step up to John's plate and for Brian to be the guy that I was initially in the band. So, I just started getting into a lot more jazz and fusion and taking a lot of the stuff that John had shown me to the next level. Anything that John had done on the EP, I wanted to do faster and crazier. It was really competitive for me. This record had to fucking slay, and that's all I cared about. In the studio it was really hard, because at the time we didn't use Pro Tools and did everything to tape. It was insane being in the studio because I was sitting with Chris doing scratch tracks while he did his drums, and he had to nail all that shit. So, I'd be sitting there all day playing along with Chris, making sure everything was right. After that, I was doing guitar tracks and [producer] Steve Evetts was so brutal; everything had to be perfect. We did multiple, multiple guitar tracks and I was just destroyed, and then, when it was time for the bass, it was like, "Oh my God . . . "

Pennie: It went smooth for me. We had rehearsed the songs so much that by the time we got in there, we just flew through the drum tracks. We didn't have a lot of time and I just wanted to be efficient and make them as best as possible. I wanted to get everything on the first take, and if I didn't I'd just throw my sticks across the room all pissed off and would be like, "Go! Again!"

Minakakis: For me, it depended on the day and how I was feeling. I'd have to wait until at least the drum track and one guitar was done. Some days, it'd be like, "Do you want to work on a song?" If we were working on something and my voice was starting to feel a little weird or I wasn't feeling confident about it, they could always go and work on something else. There wasn't really anything set in stone; it was more mix and match. It worked out because I was able to go back and do things over later on.

What were Brian's contributions to the recording?
Weinman: He played parts. He would do another track on something I already did to thicken it up or get another feel. In most cases, it made more sense

---

to just have me do it. There were one or two other parts where we needed a second guitar idea. In "Clip the Apex . . . Accept Instruction" he wrote a second guitar part with a different vibe that I would have never written. He also helped with vocal phrasing on "Variations on a Cocktail Dress." I was drained and Dimitri had no idea how to sing over it, but I couldn't do it. Everything was done on the whole record, I had been involved in every aspect of it, and we got to that song and we didn't have any phrasing for it—we just had a sheet of lyrics and a song. I just gave it to Brian, passed out, and they ended up doing some awesome vocal phrasings on it that probably were a little bit different than what I would have done.

Benoit: That was the first time I had recorded with a full-on serious producer. I was always used to recording with friends in punk rock situations. So, when I sat down with Steve, I'd think I nailed a part and Steve would be like, "No, that's not right, do it again." I'd be like, "What?! No way, I know I did it right." "No, this one note is slightly off." So I'd go through it again and he'd be, "It's still a little off, you need to do it again." Ben, Chris and Dimitri had worked with him before, so they knew what to expect, whereas I took it personally. I was like, "What, this dude doesn't like me?" But, after I heard everything coming together, what he was doing made sense. At the time, it was so intense. He would have Ben doing guitar parts and he wouldn't want anyone else in the control room. I took all that shit personally when I shouldn't have, and Ben and Chris were like, "Don't worry about it, that's just how he is." It was definitely an eye-opening experience.

As the story goes, Ben played bass on the record, but Adam coached him through the writing and performance of the bass lines.

Weinman: He came into the studio a few times, but a lot of what happened when I was writing the bass lines, he'd sit there and he'd yell at me saying, "No, you have to do it more like this!" I studied what he did on *Running Board*. I remembered how he would just go for it; sometimes he'd just hold his breath, you'd hear the [count in] clicks, he'd start wailing and nail it on the first take. In Adam, I saw the importance of putting feeling and attitude into your playing; you can hear him beating the shit out of his bass on *Running Board*, and he didn't have to do that. He was very proficient at playing delicately with his fingers. When he first started playing, Flea was his favorite dude; he was very good at jazz and funk, and when he played in a band with Chris previously, it was very tame. But when he started playing with us, it was like, "Nope, *this* is how it is."

But recording the bass sucked, man. I never realized how hard it was. I'd played around on a bass, but I was still a guitar player playing a bass. Steve Evetts is a bass player, and those two really worked me: "No, you have to hold your hand like this! You have to let things breathe! You can't play so staccato! Let the low end seep in." My gay little fingers were bloodied and it made me respect bass players a lot.

Doll: I was mostly involved in the first session, which were the songs I knew, and a little of what we had worked on before my accident. Ben had demos of those songs and we'd just kind of go through them to figure out what I would do or what he should do. When they went in to record, they used my gear. Basically, playing bass is a lot more different than guitar players realize, and it was the feel that Ben was struggling with. I was able to mentally approach it like a musician, but it was hard to explain to him how to physically play. The songs that I had already played, he basically did those note-for-note, because I remembered everything that I played.

Pennie: Ben played most of it, but Steve played some parts as well. There were parts where Steve would be like, "Let me try this or that; you guys punch me in and press record." I guess that was the introduction of Ben and I getting into the engineering side of things. [*Laughs*]

Keeping in mind that you guys were still working on the songs right up to going into the studio, that **Calculating Infinity** *was your first full-length, then John leaving and Adam's accident, were you at all nervous about the whole thing not coming together?*

Weinman: Absolutely! I mean, every record I'm like that, but *Calculating* was the first time of all the difficult times we've had. To this day, it seems like there's always an obstacle, but back then, it was like, "Whoa, we finally have this thing that people actually seem to give a shit about." We were so used to being in bands that no one cared about, and after *Under the Running Board* came out, suddenly there was this expectation within our small little subculture. We're on Relapse, in the *Resound* catalogue, we're doing all these metal fests, hearing that the dudes in Meshuggah think we're awesome—it's like, "Wow, what's going on?" Then, suddenly, there's no guitar player and no bass player. I was never the technical guy; I was like the hardcore punk, "let's make shit noisy and loud" guy, and Adam and Fulton were the musicians. I certainly wasn't the guy sitting at home shredding; I just wanted to break shit [*laughs*], but all of a sudden I had to step up to the plate. I could visualize the songs and style in my head, and I had to up my game. It was up to just Chris and I to come together, figure it out and make it work. It was back and forth between "I can't do this!" and "I have to do this!" It's always like that with me.

Was there any stumbling over recording the electronic parts in songs like "Weekend Sex Change" and "#..,*" such as how to incorporate them, where to place them or even how to do them?*

Weinman: Well, Chris and I were so into that sort of stuff and we wanted to do so much of it, but because there were time restraints, we ended up going to Steve Evetts' apartment, setting up a keyboard and just doing it there. It wasn't very planned out. Chris had this Roland keyboard with some cool stuff on it and we'd just call up sounds and record. We had a loose idea of what we wanted and Chris had a good idea of what was in his keyboard, so we'd just dial things up. It was much less realized than the way we do things now, where we're actually programming and doing electronic stuff on laptops.

What's the craziest thing that happened in the studio?

Doll: I almost single-handedly destroyed an entire day's worth of mixing. You get the bunch of us in a room together and it's like we're seven years old.

Weinman: We had one day to mix the whole record. Adam was hanging out in the studio with us and he didn't have much control over his hands at all at the time. He threw a packet of barbeque sauce from some fast food we ordered— it flew across the room at lightning speed and the corner of the packet hit the reset button on the computer. It shut down the entire computer, restarted it right in the middle of the mixdown, and Steve didn't know when he had saved last. Dude, I almost rolled him into traffic. It turned out he saved about 15 minutes before and we lost a little bit of work.

Minakakis: Yeah, it mysteriously made a right-angle turn in mid-air and restarted the computer. Everyone just got quiet and looked at each other because Steve couldn't remember when he saved last. Actually, it was me and Adam fucking around. I was facing where he was in his wheelchair. I said something smart to him, he threw it, some magnetic force took the packet and it made some sort of JFK mid-air bullet-turn, and it hit the computer. We both knew what happened and I was kinda like, "Uhhhh . . ." and Adam was just like, "Yeah, it was me." The coincidence was amazing, especially when you'd probably miss this button 999 times out of 1,000 if you were deliberately throwing at it.

Benoit: Seriously, that was insane! How, especially with Adam throwing it, did that thing hit a frickin' button a quarter of an inch in diameter?! Evetts, being Evetts, started freaking out: "What the fuck?! What the fuck was that?!" That seriously took the cake.

Actually, I also remember doing some feedback part for "Clip the Apex" and how serious I took it. I had just come out of Jesuit and being obnoxious with volume and feedback was what we were all about, so when the time came to do something like that, I was jumping for joy. We had three amps on full volume in this room and it looked like I was playing a show, throwing my guitar around and making an ass of myself while everyone looking at me through the glass was laughing their asses off.

Weinman: Also, at the end of "The Running Board" there's this little robot sound and we have no idea where it came from or what it was, so we just raised it in the mix and left it in there. We did a couple overdubs at Mike Romeo from Symphony X's home studio. We ran out of time and he has a little basement studio, so we did some overdubs and guitar leads there. That was really intimidating, because that dude is like the craziest shredder ever; he gives clinics, writes for guitar magazines, people in Japan hire him to play their bar mitzvahs and shit. [*Laughs*] It sucked having to do my leads in front of that guy.

Why? Did he hate the record?

Weinman: He was fucking *way* into it. He said he had never heard anything like it and that it was insane. But I had no confidence going in there. I was like, "Does this sound all right? Was it tight?" He'd be like, "Sounds good to me." I'm like, "No it's not, it's sloppy as fuck." He's like, "No, sounds all right." Then, I'm all, "I suck. I think I suck. I really suck, don't I? Fuck, I'm a jerk. I'm an idiot!" He's like, "Dude. Relax. It's awesome."

Is it true that you ran out of money and traded your publishing rights to Relapse for $2,000 to finish the record?

Weinman: Um, yeah. Pretty much. [*Laughs*] That's pretty unheard of, but we didn't care. We weren't thinking about the future, just the present and how this record had to rule. That publishing bought us maybe backing vocals and some keyboard sounds.

Benoit: [*Laughs*] Yep . . . that's like the ongoing theme of the band, man. Everything we do gets constantly put into the band; we don't want to release anything that we're not 110 percent satisfied with. That's probably still the reason why we haven't seen a royalty check for *Calculating Infinity*. Actually, I think I got one royalty check back in 2000 for something like $75.

Minakakis: At that point, we just wanted to put out a good record, but we had no money. So who comes swooping in with an offer to trade us our publishing? That decision wasn't made by just one person, and we were all cool with it at the time. We weren't focused on what the record could *possibly* do; we just wanted a record we were happy with.

Pennie: We were a bunch of kids who didn't care and didn't know any better. We just wanted to make something awesome. Obviously, that's a really, really stupid thing to do, but at the time, we didn't know the options. All we knew was making this fucking record as best as we can, and if it takes a couple more days and selling off our publishing, then that's what we gotta do. *Stupid!* [*Laughs*]

But even after that, you still wanted to remix the record?

Benoit: We weren't totally happy with it. I remember we got a copy of it the day we left for the Mr. Bungle tour. The tour started in California, so we had to drive out there. We got the finished copy and I remember us driving, listening to it and saying, "Holy shit, this doesn't sound like it needs to!" I remember we called Steve saying we had to remix it, but there was no money left.

Minakakis: It sounded horrible. It was mixed and mastered bad. At the time, we were comparing the sound quality to 108's *Threefold Misery* and the 108 recording just dwarfed *Calculating Infinity*. We drove out to California playing no shows, and that whole time we were listening to it and getting mad and then talking about it, then forgetting about it, then talking about it and getting mad again.

Pennie: That was really disheartening at first, especially since we were so passionate about wanting everything to be perfect. But we're not a major label band who has the budget to take three months and go into Andy Wallace's studio.

There's always been a misunderstanding about what the title refers to. It has to do with relationships, not mathematical metal, correct?

Minakakis: Yeah, whether it was with women or friends, any kind of human relationship, actually. Most of my Dillinger lyrics were predicated on myself, and people have no idea about that and always interpret them in weird ways. I just had stupid relationships with idiotic people, and I'd just write a song about it. Most of the lyrics on *Calculating Infinity* were based on human insecurity. That's where I got the best material.

Weinman: Brian came up with the title. There were a couple things that went into it. Dimitri is a real sensitive guy and he was going through some girl things. We kind of played on that; we'd always piss him off by putting pictures of ex-girlfriends in front of him to get him to scream louder and all that. But we all had relationship situations, and being that active in the band and being that into what we were doing had an impact on those relationships. It's just kind of a testament to the idea that nothing is forever and even things that you think you can calculate and be so sure of in life are never the case; life is really unpredictable.

Benoit: Since so much of the material lyrically was about failing relationships, I kind of took it as a "love not lasting forever" sort of thing. People are always like, "Oh, I'll love you forever," and that sort of thing. Obviously, forever—or infinity—isn't going to happen. Love isn't going to last forever, so let's see how long we can calculate before this blows up in our face. All the Relapse dudes were into it because it sounded "mathematical."

If all the songs are about relationships, I'm curious about what is probably the most recognizable lyric on the album: "I smell that whore / Bring me back / Bring me a brick" from "43% Burnt."

Minakakis: That song originally started out at the fast part, and once we started piecing the album together we discovered that they all started the same, so Ben wanted to add a slow part. I had lyrics already done for it, and now that they had the new part, I kind of had to add an intro. So, "I smell that whore" came from me, but the rest was collaboration around a misunderstanding. This sounds so stupid, but we were at a practice and I sang, "I smell that whore" and mumbled something else I can't remember. Ben's eyes lit up and he was like, "Did you just say, 'Bring me back, bring me a brick'?" I was like, "No, but that sounds awesome," and that was the immaculate conception of that line. I think the human sense of smell is the strongest sense we have and, for me, if I smell something, it can take me back to an exact memory, almost like déjà vu; that's where I got that from.

Was the vintage gear pictured throughout the CD booklet equipment you actually used to record the album?

Minakakis: We had an old shirt design with a radio tube on the back and we wanted to keep going with that old recording look. My mom had this old record player. It looks like a normal chest, but when you open the doors it's a radio with a record player. This guy who used to come on tour with us and do lights, Paul Delia, took the photos. I took the tubes out, we set up the lighting, laid the tubes out a certain way and he just took close-up photos of them.

Weinman: Some of it was stuff we used, some of it was an old radio or something. I don't really remember, but we definitely wanted that vibe. We were always about the irony of things. People always said it was ironic that we played this aggressive music and didn't look "metal." To us, having a really technical, precise record with pictures of vintage things on it made sense. We didn't like the whole metal look or the clichés that went along with heavy bands. We didn't feel like we were those people, and we wanted to make sure the record represented that.

What were the reactions like upon the album's release?

Weinman: The reviews were pretty good. Obviously, people who weren't used to what we were doing were pretty freaked out. It was always one of those things where people would talk trash on it, like, "This isn't real music. This is just noise." But certain people thought it was something different and the next step in extreme music. There were definitely things that were crazy, like how we got onto *Terrorizer*'s "Best Albums of the '90s" list, even though the album came out in [September] of '99. We never looked at the big picture; being in a magazine was something we could show our parents, but to me it was just a piece of work in the catalogue that we want to do as a whole.

Minakakis: It was shocking. I automatically think the worst in life, and if I think the worst and people liked it, it was a pleasant surprise and we were pleasantly surprised. I also think that made people who didn't like us from the beginning hate us even more, which was awesome! We started that band not giving a crap what people thought of us, so if you really hated us, we really liked that.

Pennie: It was really crazy. With Slipknot coming along with a heavier sound and two million kids buying their album, it seemed like our little world and scene was becoming an international thing, even if it wasn't us specifically. But I never really paid attention to that. People would say we did an awesome job with the record, and that was flattering, but I never really perceived it as more than that. I was like, "Cool, but what's the next step?" When we went on tour with Bungle, we played it for Mike Patton and he thought we were really onto something. That was awesome, but I just wanted to step up to the next level and just keep getting better.

Doll: It's always really great to hear something you've been working on start to come together, and in this case I got to hear on record a couple songs I had heard them play in practice and it was crazy. But I'm kind of a perfectionist when it comes to sound and I was actually kind of bummed that it didn't sound as good as I would have liked it to. But at the end of the day, I was pretty psyched, especially about the stuff I hadn't taken a part in. I thought it was pretty cool.

By your guess-timation, how many records has Calculating Infinity *sold?*

Weinman: I don't really know, but I think in North America it's at least 100,000. Worldwide? Who knows? There's no SoundScan-type system for Europe and the U.K.; they just keep track of it by the numbers that get shipped out. Still, selling 100,000 copies of anything was a big deal in our world; no bands we knew had really done that and it was so foreign to everyone involved.

Looking back on the whole experience, is there anything you would have changed about the recording, the recording process or the artwork?

Weinman: At the time, I had all kinds of ideas about how things could have been better. I remember listening to it and freaking out over every detail—about how there wasn't enough low end in the kick or whatever. I remember our friend Brian Montouri, who did *Miss Machine*'s artwork, was supposed to do the artwork for *Calculating*, but he had never really done a layout before. He was a painter and he couldn't get it together in time. He had this huge vision about how it was going to be a 40-panel booklet and how he was going to paint every picture, but that was kind of unrealistic and we didn't have the time, so we ended up using the pictures of the tubes and stuff and keeping the letterbox format of *Under the Running Board*. It came together, but it wasn't our initial vision of having our friend do paintings with this insane packaging. Still, it ended up being really cool and having its own kind of vibe, and now, you can't picture it sounding or looking or being any other way. The thing about *Calculating Infinity* is that when I listen to it, it's pretty clear that it's got its own sound. I remember people back then saying, almost disappointedly, that it didn't sound like this or that favorite record of theirs. Which is cool; it didn't sound like any other record back then and it still doesn't sound like any other record to this day.

What are your thoughts on CI's impact and influence on extreme music seven years down the line?

Weinman: I probably don't think it was important or as influential as most other people. Still, at the end of the day, we did something with this band that was never supposed to happen. We've always thought we've gone way farther than we ever could.

Minakakis: What's pretty cool is not how *Calculating* became the new "something" and spawned a whole genre of bands—because there were bands before us doing it great and a lot of terrible bands that followed—but that it motivated and drove someone. That's what's cool; that someone recognizes your work so much that they want to mimic it or be influenced by it.

Benoit: In the end, that we put out an awesome record we were all happy with and people still look at as a benchmark is what ultimately counts. I'd rather have something that stands the test of time rather than some gimmick, fly-by-night record. It's great to be able to look at that record and have it stand up; we never thought it would.

CHAPTER 24

FALLEN EMPIRE

THE MAKING OF BOTCH'S *WE ARE THE ROMANS*

by J. Bennett

Release Date: 1999
Label: Hydra Head
Summary: Math-metal bellwether
Induction Date: November 2005/Issue #13

999 was a transitional year for both underground music and America's
most iconic freestanding structures. Seattle's Space Needle was no longer
the world's tallest metaphor for heroin abuse, and Tacoma/Seattle quartet Botch were about to redefine a genre with the hyper-kinetic guitar squalls and
contortionist rhythms of *We Are the Romans*. On the other side of the country,
the Twin Towers were two years away from being annihilated in a terrorist
firestorm, but Botch guitarist Dave Knudson had already drawn a target over the
New York City skyline on the album's unforgettable cover. By 2002, both the
Towers and Botch were gone: Chronic tension between Knudson (currently of
Minus the Bear) and drummer Tim Latona forced the band tits up before it
ever really got its due. Bassist Brian Cook and vocalist Dave Verellen went on

to form Roy (Cook is also a member of These Arms Are Snakes; Verellen is also a Tacoma firefighter), and Botch released a posthumous EP, *An Anthology of Dead Ends*, in late 2002. But *We Are the Romans* lives on as one of the most influential "hardcore" records of the last decade, its jagged grace and terminal discord revered by the likes of future noisemongers Norma Jean, the Used and Every Time I Die—which is ironic when one considers that the album essentially called bullshit on the prevailing hardcore aesthetics of its time. Produced by Matt Bayles (who'd go on to record similarly lauded albums by the likes of Isis and Mastodon) at Pearl Jam guitarist Stone Gossard's Studio Litho, *We Are the Romans* is the electrifying epitaph of a band that quit while it was *way* ahead.

What do you remember best about the recording sessions for **We Are the Romans***?*

Dave Verellen: Recording *We Are the Romans* was probably the most serious we'd ever been in the studio. We'd worked with Matt [Bayles] before, and he can be kinda hard-nosed about doing stuff right, but this was different for us in terms of work ethic. We were always the kind of band that never really knew how things were gonna sound until it was done.

Dave Knudson: We had maybe had a week or six days to track it, which was way longer than the previous record [*American Nervoso*], but we still felt like we were rushing to get everything done and do it as well as we wanted to. I think Matt had heard most of the songs before, but we recorded some live demos with him about two months before we did the actual album. We played five or six songs, and then we did "Saint Matthew Returns to the Womb," which he hadn't heard yet. So we ripped through the song, and it's, you know, this thrasher that ends kind of abruptly. He's sitting in the control looking at us and goes, "Holy shit." I think he was kind of flabbergasted that that came out of us.

Brian Cook: I remember watching a lot of TV at the studio, and it was when Limp Bizkit's "Nookie" was on MTV every half hour. I was really intrigued by it because obviously it's a really terrible song, but it was this really terrible *heavy* song that was super-popular. It was inspiring in a way, because it was so moronic, so I thought that what we were doing could feasibly do really well.

Tim Latona: I was really proud of what we were doing, but I was also kind of concerned. Maybe I'd call it cautious optimism. I was so stoked on what we were writing and what we were doing, but I was really worried about how it was gonna come out.

Were you all getting along with each other at that point?

Knudson: I don't think there was that much fighting during the recording, but on tour, we'd definitely butt heads, so maybe there was some of that energy lingering when we were writing the songs for *Romans*. I don't remember any specific fights during the recording process; it was more of an underlying thing. It was Tim and I who would probably butt heads the most, but then again, I think that helped create the tension in the music. If Tim and I never fought, it would've made being in the band a lot easier, but I think it would've made the band a lot more boring musically.

Verellen: Recording was a lot different for me than the other guys because I didn't have a lot of input as far as guitar tone or whatever, so I wasn't the guy going, "Hey, we need more 3Khz here" or some insane technical term. [*Laughs*] So I just tried to keep a good attitude through the whole thing, 'cause it was pretty taxing. It's not like me to sit at a console and figure stuff out for hours and hours and hours. But Studio Litho had a nice outside deck, and I spent a lot of time out there so I wouldn't feel drained or annoyed.

Latona: All four of us have very strong personalities—some of us more than others. That said, Dave Knudson and I were the main writing force behind the band, but we were also the main force that broke up the band. I didn't really want that to happen, but I'm sure when we were in the studio there were arguments and pissing matches. We were all best friends, and who doesn't fight with their best friend? But as frustrating as the recording process was, we were really proud of what we had written.

Did you have all the songs finished beforehand?

Knudson: Pretty much the whole record was written already, except for the chanting part in "Man the Ramparts," which was improvised in the studio, and some of the guitar parts toward the end of "C. Thomas Howell [as the 'Soul Man.']." At that point, I was living in Seattle, and everyone else was living in Tacoma. I was going to school at the Art Institute and working at Kinko's, so I had my schedule arranged so I could go down to our crappy rehearsal space in Tacoma on Fridays and Sundays or something like that. Sometimes it would just be me and Tim, but for the most part, everybody was there. But a lot of the riffs on "Transitions From Persona to Object" and "To Our Friends in the Great White North" I actually wrote at Thanksgiving at my mom's house on an acoustic guitar. It was weird, 'cause I think I was watching like the Turkey Bowl football game or something, but all that shit kinda flowed out. I think that's kinda where the record started building steam and getting interesting, because those two songs helped us become a lot more focused, I think.

Latona: Throughout the course of recording, one of us would always go, "Oh, fuck, dude! What if . . ." and out would come these ideas that were retarded 80 percent of the time and amazing 20 percent of the time. Right up to the last minute, there was always discussion about how things should go. Even during mixing, we talked about changing things around.

Cook: We added "Frequency Ass Bandit" at the last minute, which was from a split we did with the Murder City Devils. We rewrote it slightly and rerecorded it, kind of as an afterthought.

Verellen: I'd usually go in with only a chorus or something ready, as far as lyrics. I was such a procrastinator—it was terrible. But when I was in the studio and forced to be in that mode, it was very productive for me.

You went into the studio without an album title, right?

Verellen: We had the song "Man the Ramparts," and I had just written the line, "We are the Romans." Brian thought it'd make a great title, but I thought it was a totally silly gladiator song. The riff is kinda huge, so I was thinking about chariots and fire and stuff like that. It sounds like I pulled the words out of *Conan the Barbarian*. But then we started talking about the social decline of Western civilization, and how Americans are the new Romans—it's all slaves and Caesars. So we made it work.

Cook: Now that I look back on it, it seems like there are a lot of themes on that record that I don't think were necessarily intentional. "Man the Ramparts" is a perfect example, because I don't think Dave was originally trying to make some grandiose statement—I think he was just singing about Romans and using all this cheesy, medieval imagery. At the time, it seemed like sort of a joke, but when we went into the studio and actually finalized everything, it actually kinda worked as a metaphor for America as an empire in decline.

It seems like the song titles don't have anything to do with the lyrics.

Verellen: That's because I wrote most of the lyrics, but Brian actually came up with most of the song titles. He's got this knack for just coming up with random, weird stuff that I'm not nearly clever enough to come up with. Most of them had these really drawn out meanings. But we'd always have these running jokes within the band that would turn up in the songs. "C. Thomas Howell as the 'Soul Man'" started because the song had all of those tapping parts Dave would do, so we started calling it "Taps." We thought C. Thomas Howell was in the movie *Taps*, so we started calling it "C. Thomas Howell." But then we realized he wasn't in *Taps*—he was in *Soul Man*. So it became "C. Thomas Howell as the 'Soul Man.'" We thought it was hilarious, so we went with it, but I think the kids who were used to a song being called "Lawnmower" because the chorus is "Lawnmower, lawnmower, lawnmower" were like, "What the fuck?"

Cook: It's funny, because some of the titles ended up having some relation to the subject matter, which is what happened with "C. Thomas Howell as the 'Soul Man.'" In the movie, that character takes a bunch of tanning pills so he can get a scholarship for black college students. And the song was inadvertently inspired by that band Race Traitor and other bands with these very lofty political ideals that seemed like more of a marketing tool for the genre of political hardcore rather than a sincere agenda. It was more about creating controversy so people would pay attention to them, as opposed to actually saying something. So the title worked out, because the movie was also about pretending to be something you're not. But I don't think we realized that until the record had been out for several months.

Do you remember where any of the other titles came from?

Cook: I was reading *The Atrocity Exhibition* by J.G. Ballard, and I was really into it. We came up with all the song titles in the studio, so I think I ended up borrowing pretty heavily from that book for inspiration. Especially the idea of the human body as a landscape, and the way that culture and environment sort of dictates the human body and vice versa—that came out in things like "I Wanna Be a Sex Symbol on My Own Terms" and "Transitions From Persona to Object." "Mondrian Was a Liar" was a reference to [Piet] Mondrian's idea that reducing art to its most simple elements—so that there's no cultural iconography or symbols involved in it whatsoever—would make it more universal, and it would therefore bring everyone together and create a culture where everything is art and everybody understands each other. It seemed really inflated and naïve and hopelessly idealistic. But I think any Botch song could be refuting an idea like that.

What were the lyrical influences?

Verellen: I don't really read a whole heck of a lot, so stuff that I witnessed was usually what had an impact on me. I'd look at a social situation or whatever was going on in the world, and then just try to be creative with it. A lot of guys can write songs about war or something like that, but I'd try to be a little less blatant. People laugh when I tell them I was a Joan of Arc fan, because that band is so weird and sounds nothing like Botch, but I totally loved them, and half the reason was because the guy [Tim Kinsella] had such weird lyrics. I've always been attracted to abstract stuff like that, so I think that's where I drew most of my lyrics from. The rest was just me, I guess. "C. Thomas Howell" probably had the strongest meaning behind it. Most of the songs had pretty abstract lyrics. I'm proud of them, but I don't think they're works of art or anything. The other guys are a lot better at their crafts. I think I just kinda got away with a lot of stuff, to tell you the truth.

I've always thought of "C. Thomas Howell as the 'Soul Man'" as your epic, like Botch's "War Pigs" or something.

Verellen: Yeah, it's such a big-sounding song, and there's the line "worst music I ever heard," so people would always ask what it was about. I don't think we told people at the time, but that band Race Traitor had a huge impact on us because we weren't accepted into the hardcore scene when we first started. We were playing catch-up with these kids we thought we had to impress so we could be a band. Then all of a sudden we realized we were a band anyway, and that half those kids were idiots and elitists. We thought bands like Race Traitor and Earth Crisis were over-the-top. It was like, "You guys need to relax." And that was definitely an inspiration for "C. Thomas Howell." We talked about that stuff all the time—we couldn't believe that these bands would have songs about hurting people because they didn't believe the same things as them. Let's see, who else did stuff like that? Hitler?

Latona: I don't think I ever recognized that song for what it was until we played it live and there would be like a hundred people up front screaming that line about "worst music I ever heard." I mean, I've read reviews of *We Are the Romans* where people singled out that song, and I can see the allure that draws people to it.

Knudson: Yeah, the ending—that big huge chord part—is just like triumph over everything. Brian came up with that chord progression—he's great at writing those things.

Cook: I guess that *is* a pretty big "fuck you" song. And it was definitely one of our more anthemic songs. I'm not usually one for writing riffs—my contributions tend to be thematic or dealing with song structure, but that's one of the few riffs I guess I brought to the table.

What's the story with the hidden electronic track at the end?

Latona: That's kind of a sore subject. It wasn't really my thing. I think the electronic thing was some of the members in Botch's way of showing that we had a whole lot more influencing us than metal. But when I listen to *We Are the Romans* now, I can fucking tell that there were more than metal influences. I mean, when we were on tour, people would come up to me and say they could tell that I'd played jazz before. So I didn't think that was a necessary addition to the record, and I don't like it, to be honest with you. I think it sucks.

Knudson: You know, I kinda forgot about that. I haven't listened to that song in forever, but it was a friend of ours, Derek, who does all this electronic stuff and he wanted to do a Botch remix. I think it had some riffs from "[Thank God for] Worker Bees" from *Nervoso*. We thought it came out pretty cool, and we put it on the record. On the vinyl, it's on its own side at 45 rpm.

Verellen: I loved it. That guy DuRoc—Derek was his name—was my roommate for a long time. He actually did some of the enhanced stuff on *An Anthology* *of Dead Ends*, too. And I think he's a roadie for Modest Mouse now. He was doing this thing called Logic Probe, and it was like the weirdest music I've ever heard in my life. They did like nine-hour songs, but it was fun to listen to. So I asked him to do a remix, and he spent like 20 hours in the basement with his computer system.

Cook: Honestly, I don't like electronic music. It's a whole genre that just doesn't appeal to me. But our friend was interested in doing a remix. I didn't really think about it being good or bad at the time. We just figured someone did it, so we'd put it on as a secret bonus track. I never really thought of it as part of the album. I don't wanna talk too much trash about it, but I never listen to it.

Dave's guitar-playing style makes the album instantly recognizable. Did you intend for it to be so different, or did it just come out that way?

Knudson: You know, it wasn't necessarily like, "Oh, man—people are gonna love this shit." It was more like, "This is pretty cool what I wrote—I really like this." It was excitement with where the music was going. I remember one point right after *Nervoso*, I was talking to [Aaron] Turner about how the songs for *Romans* were coming out, and at that point in hardcore, there was just a lot of dumb chugga-chugga open-E shit. I liked that stuff before, but it was getting kinda boring. So I was telling Turner how there was going to be hardly any palm-muting on the new record—it was going to be all notes and pull-offs. At that point I was listening to a lot of Angel Hair and [Drive Like] Jehu—stuff that was, for lack of a better term, just crazy and angular. That music, along with Sepultura and Meshuggah, combined to really influence my playing. After I wrote the acoustic parts for "Transitions," I was jamming down at the practice space with Tim, and I had this DOD sampler pedal that had like a second and a half of memory. So I just started sampling some of those parts and speeding them up, and that opened up a whole new world of possibilities.

The sound on **Romans** *really did turn the notion of "hardcore" on its ear. It was heavy and graceful at the same time.*

Knudson: Graceful—that's a nice thing to say, man. Thank you. I know what you mean, though—"C. Thomas" starts off all brutal and crazy and then towards the middle it breaks into that nice tapped melody part. I think that's probably what we were all subconsciously missing in hardcore, too. We loved hardcore because it was so visceral and in-your-face, but at the same time there were other bands that we liked that incorporated a lot more emotion and melody—and we wanted to bring that to *Romans* as well.

Cook: You know, I still like the idea of hardcore as something that's supposed to be independent and creative. I'm into the notion of it as a pure art form, but in reality it ends up being pretty simplistic and moronic—and to me, pretty uninspiring. I like the idea in a high-minded Fugazi respect. In fact, I feel bad talking shit on hardcore, but Fugazi is kind of the exception to the rule. I think hardcore should be constantly evolving, constantly challenging the notions of what music is, something that has a lot of artistic integrity and doesn't give a shit if people like it or not. We wanted to do something creative and daring, and maybe it was a "fuck you" to the Trustkill bands, but I never really considered them to be hardcore. They were just ruining my good time.

It seems like **Romans** *calls bullshit on hardcore, both philosophically and sonically. Looking back, do you think you were severing yourselves from that kind of ideology and aesthetic?*

Latona: When we all started out in Tacoma, some of the guys who were a couple years ahead of us in school would always go see Undertow and all these hardcore bands, so we started going. That was our weekend thing. When we finally started playing some of these shows, we got fucking shit on by, like, the cool Seattle kids. It was really disheartening, because we really thought we had something cool to share with people, and they were total assholes to us. To this day, I don't understand what their motivation was. So we were *always* distanced from the hardcore community. I don't think the lyrics in "C. Thomas Howell" or the fact that we pushed the limits of what most bands were doing was what did it. We were just four guys who liked playing metal and didn't give a shit.

Cook: By that point, we were all getting burnt out on stereotypical hardcore—especially because the metal/hardcore thing seemed so vacuous and uninteresting. You had the bad Trustkill hardcore—which was strictly about the mosh—or the really bad hardcore, where if you don't spend at least as much [time] talking about your songs as playing them, it's not really hardcore. It was just people preaching the same shit to the same choir, and it was sort of depressing.

Verellen: You know, reading the lyrics on a Floorpunch record, you're like, "What?" I never really paid attention to lyrics like that, but then again, to tell you the truth, I didn't listen to too many bands like that. The bands that were inspirational for me as far as lyrics were Deadguy and I'm Broken. The guy from Deadguy has one of the best voices ever, and his lyrics were insightful. You had to read it all and put it together. I'm Broken was a little darker and kind of depressing, but they weren't the kind of band that, you know, in trying to get point A across, they'd repeat point A like a hundred times. We just wanted to do something different, and I think I got away with that, for sure.

A lot of bands can change members and still sound the same because it's just one dude writing all the songs, but it seems like **We Are the Romans** *could only be the product of exactly you four guys.*

Latona: We all went to high school together, you know? Dave Knudson and I started out playing Helmet covers on my back deck. We were playing together when we were 14 or 15 years old. I've known Dave Verellen since fifth grade. So bringing someone else in was never even an option. It really did take the four of us to reach the end product.

Knudson: Oh, totally. Everyone brought something to the table that, if they were replaced, would've never allowed the songs to develop the way they did. But that's why Botch never had any other members—no one ever quit or anything like that. We always knew that whenever one person was gone, it'd be the end of the band. It was that tight-knit group of people that had gone through the experience of starting a band, not knowing what we wanted it to sound like, being a really shitty fuckin' band for a long time, and then really maturing and growing and then, toward the end of our career, writing stuff that we're actually proud of. So I don't think anyone could've come in and filled anyone else's shoes—either personality-wise or talent/musicianship-wise.

Cook: I think that's pretty true. Each person definitely had a specific role in the band, and because it was four very different people, there were a lot of checks and balances. It was really hard to get anything done, because it was difficult to come up with anything that everybody liked—which is also kind of what destroyed the band. But it also meant that if we did come up with something that everybody liked, it felt pretty incredible.

Verellen: I totally agree, and that's exactly why we broke up. A couple guys weren't happy, so it was time to end it. There was no way we'd replace somebody and try to pull it off. It had a lot of character that way. Outside of Tim and Dave, Brian is pretty much a self-taught musician, and I'm not really much of a musician at all—I just kinda know what I like and dislike. All those components gave us a uniqueness.

In retrospect, the title of the album and the cover art—a target over the New York City skyline—seem oddly prophetic.

Knudson: I was going to art school, so I was always looking through old books looking for random images and scanning every possible photo that would lend itself to the artwork. I remember I was at Kinko's operating the 1590 Xerox copier [*laughs*], and I didn't have anything to do while I was running some job, so I started sketching ideas for the cover. I just started drawing targets and went from there. I think the aerial photo was a picture of New York from the '30s. I remember after 9/11, we were like, "Man, I hope we don't get arrested."

Latona: It's funny—I used to work at an airline, and there were a couple of people there who were interested in what Botch was doing. After 9/11, I distinctly remember making an offhand joke about the record cover and how it was so interesting because of what had happened. He said we called it.

Cook: We tried—unsuccessfully—to start a rumor that the record was banned after 9/11. The fact that it hinted at things to come makes it all the more appropriate.

You'd worked with Matt Bayles before on **American Nervoso,** *but it wasn't until* **We Are the Romans** *came out that both Botch and Matt began getting the reputations they have today. You made your names together, pretty much.*

Knudson: I agree. I mean, listening to *Nervoso*, it sounds good, but in the time between *Nervoso* and *Romans*, his production and engineering skills definitely took a step up the same way our songwriting did. He played an integral role in getting the sounds and making sure the performances were really tight. Anyone who's worked with Matt will tell you that he doesn't let you get away with stupid shit. He'll never say, "That part's fine," when it's not. He'll make you do it again and again—which is why *Romans* came out so tight-sounding.

Latona: *American Nervoso* isn't a record I'm terribly proud of, but with *We Are the Romans*, I think we recognized we had written something that was great. Apparently, a few other people noticed, too, which is pretty rad. But I don't think that album would be what it is if we had recorded with anyone else. Matt was absolutely key to the way that record sounds.

Verellen: It's funny because everyone who worked on that record talks about the repercussions of it. My other band, Roy, just mastered our new record with Ed Brooks, who also mastered *We Are the Romans*, and he was telling us how much business they get because people like how that record sounded. And Matt's always saying how bands will want to get the guitar sound from some song off of *Romans*.

Which song holds up the best for you personally?

Cook: I really like "Transitions From Persona to Object," because it's epic and sort of all over the place, but there're these little guitar parts and progressions that keep resurfacing over the course of the song. So it's never boring or repetitious, but it also doesn't seem like it was slapped together. It was experimental, too, with the looping guitar parts that were sped up and slowed down. I don't think we ever played that song the same way twice.

Knudson: I feel like "Transitions" was the height of creativity in the band. I don't know why—I just feel like it has so many different parts and feels to it. It had this herky-jerky motion to it when it would drop a beat and add a beat. And then at the end it just sort of explodes in this way that was always really exciting to me when we'd play it. But I think a lot of the songs hold up really well. The only one that bums me out is "Mondrian Was a Liar," because it starts out with this kick-ass riff but by the end it loses all its energy. I don't know; I don't think that song was fully realized.

Latona: That's a tricky question for me, because on the last couple tours, we'd link up "Transitions" into "Great White North" and make them into one awesome 12-minute song. But if I had to pick one directly off the record, I guess I'd say "Transitions." Especially Dave's guitar playing and the polyrhythms on top—I think that song's well constructed, and it was fucking awesome to play live.

At what point did you realize the influence/impact the album had? These days, there are Botch rip-off bands.

Verellen: Honestly, I didn't have any idea people felt that way until right around the time of our last show. I mean, being in Seattle kinda separates us from the rest of the country geographically, and bands don't come here as often. So you have to keep up with the magazines and stuff, and I've always been horrible with that. But Bayles is like my meter, and he'd play me tapes that bands would send him and be like, "Dude, you gotta listen to this—this band is totally biting you guys." And then I'd be embarrassed because the band wouldn't be that good. So when I see bands on MTV2 or whatever, I get the feeling we broke up at the perfect time.

Knudson: I think a year ago was probably the height of that craze, which is kinda funny. I don't really think we realized it was gonna mean that much to people, until maybe right before we broke up. We would tour, and the tours would go well, but it was never anything big. At the end, we went out with the Murder City Devils and then did some West Coast dates with Dillinger [Escape Plan], and it wasn't until then that it seemed like people were picking up on it. When it first came out, people said they liked it, but it didn't feel that ground-breaking, I don't think.

Cook: Probably just in the last year more than anything. Everything that happened during the band's existence happened in such slow increments that it just seemed like the natural progression of things. The first time we ever actually played a show where people sang along, we thought it was crazy, but I'm pretty sure it didn't make any of us think it was this big important thing that people were gonna remember five years down the road. I never equated people buying t-shirts with the longevity of the band. Earlier this year, [These Arms Are] Snakes did a U.S. and European tour that started at the beginning in April and lasted through mid-June. There wasn't a single night on that tour when someone didn't come up to me to ask about Botch. It's crazy enough when that happens every night in America, but when you're in Europe on a day off and someone is randomly like, "You were in *that band*," it made me realize that this'll actually be one of those bands people talk about. But I think we knew it would be a short-term success. When you play music like we played, you eat a lot of shit and you don't make much money. It's hard, so you at least want to think that what you're doing is important; that it's not this fleeting thing. I mean, we could've easily written a Snapcase record in two weeks—we would've been way more popular and made way more money. But it was more rewarding to write songs that would be interesting to us. And it worked, I guess.

Do you feel like Botch gets more props now than you did when you were together?

Latona: Sometimes. [*Laughs*] Every once in a while, I'll look on eBay and see what kind of Botch stuff is up there, and I'm floored by what people are willing to pay for this shit. I don't mean to sound like a dick, but it's like, "Where were you in 2001?" But I don't really know, 'cause I don't go to shows anymore, and I don't hang out with hardcore kids anymore. On the other hand, it's flattering to hear that people even give a shit about what we did, because I fucking loved what we did.

Knudson: I never really sit around and think about that. But it's weird to watch *Headbangers Ball* and think, "Oh, man—I wrote that riff a couple years ago, dude. Can I get some royalties?" [*Laughs*] On the other hand, maybe it's because I don't go out and try to find it, but there's not really a whole lot of that style of music that I'm interested in these days, because I feel like I've heard it before or it's been done. Then again, I can't say that I didn't rip off Soundgarden or Sepultura—I ripped off a ton of bands, too, you know? That's how you progress as a musician—you play stuff you love. If it sounds like another band, that sucks, but sometimes you can make that into your own thing and then own it—which is how I feel we did it.

In retrospect, is there anything you'd change about it?

Latona: There are definitely a couple of spots in there where I could've played better, but we didn't have the budget or the desire to do a thousand takes of each song. Doing that strips away the being of the songs, you know? Part of what makes *We Are the Romans* good are the things that aren't quite perfect. I love that record, to be honest with you. People are so weird about pride and arrogance—they think it's the same thing. I don't listen to that record because I'm arrogant; I listen to it because I'm proud of what I did. The music you write should be something that you want to listen to all the fucking time because it should be the music that reflects you as a person. And *We Are the Romans* is something I can listen to today from start to almost finish.

Knudson: I wouldn't change anything. We'd probably just fuck it up, anyway. It marks a period in time, and it still sounds good now. And for all the fighting that we had on tour or in the studio—that's the kind of energy that drives you to make a record like that. That was our performance-enhancement drug—when you get pissed off at someone, and you take it out on the song. It provides the kind of energy you can't quantify, but it influences your playing and your writing.

Verellen: Whenever I hear something we did, I always think, "Aw, we shoulda done this" or "We shoulda done that." I'm happy with it, though. It's weird to think about it, because I'm not really in that game anymore. My musical tastes have changed since then. You know, my girlfriend had never heard of Botch, so I played her the *Romans* CD and she was like, "No *way* is that you. No *way* were you in a band like that."

CHAPTER 25

WHO'S THAT GIRL?

THE MAKING OF CONVERGE'S *JANE DOE*

by J. Bennett

Release Date: 2001
Label: Equal Vision
Summary: Freeform mathcore maelstrom
Induction Date: January 2008/Issue #39

C all it the face that launched a thousand metalcore graphic designers (into a rat-race of feverish mimicry). Call it the record that catapulted a certain Boston quartet (then quintet) into permanent cult status with a slew of face-ripping live staples ("Concubine," "The Broken Vow" and "Bitter and Then Some") and a soaring, epic title track. Call it Album of the Year, like our esteemed British colleagues at *Terrorizer* magazine did. Any way you break it down, *Jane Doe* was both a semi-melodic milestone ("Hell to Pay," "Thaw," the title track) and a discordant landmark (everything else), far and away the most crucial metallic hardcore record since fellow Massholes Cave In (who had since stepped bravely onto the major label playing field) unleashed *Until Your Heart Stops* three years earlier. Shit, it even had a song that was just drums and vocals (the 42-second apocalypse of "Phoenix in Flames"). It was feral, it was ferocious, it was fucking unstoppable. And it's still all those things today.

It was also 2001, and change was everywhere. Bassist Nate Newton, formerly of Jesuit, had joined the band three years earlier and recorded on two split releases—1999's *The Poacher Diaries* (with Agoraphobic Nosebleed) and 2000's *Deeper the Wound* (with Japan's Hellchild), the inaugural release from Converge vocalist Jake Bannon's label, Deathwish, Inc.—but had yet to track a full-length with them. The band had also recently recruited local drum dervish Ben Koller, formerly of grind outfit Force Fed Glass, to replace skinsman Jon DiGiorgio. By the time the *Jane Doe* recording sessions—a three-month marathon spread across as many studios and helmed by Converge guitarist/producer Kurt Ballou—were complete, the band had kicked longtime second guitarist Aaron Dalbec (also of Bane) to the curb. On September 1, Ballou was laid off from his job as a medical engineer at Boston Scientific ("It was like the adult version of playing with Legos"), thus freeing Converge to expand considerably upon their annual one-month touring schedule. On September 4, *Jane Doe* was released to considerable critical and popular acclaim. On September 11, the day the band was to embark upon a two-week tour with Playing Enemy, the Twin Towers fell and the world changed forever. Converge—now a sleek and furious four-piece—drove into New York City under a blanket of ash, on the road to a silver future.

PART I: PHOENIX IN FLIGHT

What do you remember about the songwriting process for **Jane Doe***?*

Kurt Ballou: It was the first batch of songs we wrote after Ben joined the band, so we definitely had a new perspective and a new energy and a new means of working. And Nate was also finally living in Boston—prior to that he was commuting up from Virginia. And we were all on the same page musically. We all had a lot of respect for each other as musicians and friends, so that was the first record we wrote that was really a collaborative process. I'd always been a control freak prior to that—in a way it was because of who I am, but in another way, it was also because I'd had to because I didn't have people in the band who could contribute well until *Jane Doe*. Aaron was doing a lot of Bane stuff—they were really busy that year. They were doing a record and a ton of touring, so he wasn't really around for much of the songwriting. It was pretty much just the four of us hacking through the songs together.

Aaron Dalbec: I was on the road a lot with Bane at the time, so I would come back to work on new songs with everyone, and when I would leave for a Bane tour, I would be writing while I was on the road.

Nate Newton: I remember a lot of butting heads, between me and Kurt especially. That was the first record where I was really part of the songwriting process. I played on *The Poacher Diaries* and the split with Hellchild, and I had written a little bit on *The Poacher Diaries*, but that was a weird time, because Jon [DiGiorgio] was only in the band for a really short time on drums and we never really got acclimated to playing with him. I felt like a lot of those songs were just kinda hammered together really quickly. So *Jane Doe* was the first time I wrote full songs for Converge. And it was the first time Kurt had someone telling him, "Hey—I don't like what you're playing." I don't think there was much of a filter before, mostly because Converge wasn't as busy of a band. One of my focuses was that I wanted to write songs—I didn't want just a shitload of riffs piled on top of each other. I was really critical of what Kurt was writing, and ultimately I think that was a good thing for us—it taught all of us to be more critical of ourselves.

Ballou: The other big shift that happened with that record is that for "Minnesota," the last song on *The Poacher Diaries*, I had invented a new tuning that I had used for all the lead guitar parts. I ended up being really inspired by that tuning and used a lot of it to write a lot of the *Jane Doe* stuff. It gave me a totally new perspective and new harmonic structures. All the happy accidents you have on guitar when you're tuned one way—even though they might be physically similar—they sound completely different when you start tuning a different way.

Ben Koller: I remember being very impressed by Kurt's demoing skills. He demoed all the music himself for the song "Jane Doe." It's just such an epic, memorable song and we didn't deviate too much from that demo when we recorded it. I remember being very impressed by that demo. "Phoenix in Flames" was fun, too. I was half-joking one day at the studio, like, "We should just do a song that's drums and vocals only." I can't believe we actually put that on the record. I love that song.

Jake Bannon: I can only speak for my own experiences with the album. Life wasn't going all that well for me and I saw writing and rehearsals as an escape of sorts. I looked forward to that few hours a week more than anything at that time in my life. It was also an odd time for the band. Getting to practice wasn't easy. It was a half-hour to an hour commute each way for all of us. Because of that physical distance, it didn't feel like there was all that much communication between members. When we did get together to write, it felt like three of us—Ben, Kurt and myself—bonded a bit more than we did with Aaron. That growth between us as friends/family foreshadowed a great deal for all of us. As a band and as people, we were evolving.

How did you meet Ben?

Ballou: I recorded two of his previous bands. The first one was called Bastion—not too many people knew about them—and the second one was Force Fed Glass, and they were somewhat known. He and I started playing together in a thing called Blue/Green Heart that was kind of a short-lived side project. When Jon DiGiorgio, the previous Converge drummer, quit, it happened really suddenly. I think I actually found out about it at Blue/Green Heart practice. I was talking to Ben about it and we just started jamming some Converge songs. At the time, we weren't really sure if he could do it because he couldn't play double-bass, and at that time Converge had a lot of double-bass stuff. So originally he played as a fill-in and we tried out some other drummers, but it became pretty clear pretty quickly that Ben was the guy.

Newton: Ben joining the band made Converge who we are now. I have no doubt in my mind that we would've broken up if he hadn't joined the band. His drumming is such a big part of the direction that we went with this band, because songwriting-wise, we were never able to do what we wanted to do. He's got his own style, and it's punk as fuck. We were so excited about him joining, and you can hear it in the record. There's such a huge difference between that record and the ones that came before it. Sometimes when we're onstage, I'll turn around to watch him play and just think, "Fuck—you are so much better at your instrument than I am at mine."

Jane Doe *was your first recording with Ben on drums and your first full-length with Nate on bass. Did you feel invigorated by the relatively new lineup? Were you nervous about the potential results?*

Bannon: Both of them brought a new energy to everything, and I am still grateful to them for that. For Converge, it was the first time that there was a "whole" band—or at least four of us—participating in the writing process. In the past, it was Kurt as the chief songwriter, and I handled everything else for the band. Though Kurt still was at the helm musically, with *Jane Doe*, Nate and Ben played significant roles in shaping the music to the album. I also contributed rough versions of the riffs in "Homewrecker" and "Phoenix in Flight" to the album. Though I am a terrible guitarist, Kurt managed to make sense of my mess and turn both of them into great songs. I know that all of us playing equal roles was an reinvigorating experience for me. I felt excited and I had a second wind of sorts creatively because of that.

Dalbec: I was not nervous about the lineup at all. We had been playing for a while, and Ben was the first drummer since Damon [Bellorado] that really fit with us. As far as Nate, I loved playing with him. He is a great dude, and a great guitar/bass player. It added so much new energy to the band.

What were the recording sessions like?

Ballou: We did them at Q Division in Boston with Matt Ellard engineering. I guess I was producing—you don't really have producers when you're doing hardcore records. But I was the one who was there all the time presiding over stuff. Q Division has two studios and we booked our time in Studio A at a certain rate that was below their advertised rate. And then James Taylor came along and decided that he wanted Studio A during our time period. He was willing to pay the full rate, so they bumped us over to Studio B—which ended up being a blessing in disguise because even though Studio B is a little smaller, the room is a little brighter and the console is a lot more crisp-sounding. It's a Trident ATB, which I actually have in my studio now—and part of the reason I have it is because of the drums we tracked on *Jane Doe*. But we went back over to Studio A after James Taylor left, and then we did the guitars, bass and some vocals at my studio in Norwood. We mixed it and did the rest of the vocals at Fort Apache in Cambridge.

Koller: I remember it being very laid-back. It was a comfortable environment and there wasn't a lot of pressure. I also remember James Taylor recording in one of the other studios and him being escorted in and out by his entourage. Why did he need to be escorted? Who cares about James Taylor anyway?

Newton: James Taylor was across the hall from us and he kept sending his engineer over to tell us to be quiet. "Mr. Taylor is trying to record vocal tracks and you guys are goofing off and being way too loud over here." [*Laughs*] He had already knocked us into the smaller room, too—but that's fine. I don't really care.

Bannon: For me, it was the first time that we were in a more formal studio setting. Aside from the occasional weekend recording sessions at outside studios, we usually recorded on our own in some way. Even though the *When Forever Comes Crashing* album had Steve Austin at the helm, it was in a no-frills studio in a basement in Allston. At Q Division we had engineers and assistants helping during the initial tracking. We had an English engineer who worked with Motörhead and George Michael giving us assistance and guidance. It all felt "important" and "special" to me. We were all working together and I really appreciated that.

Dalbec: I just remember it being the most well-organized recording we had ever done. We made sure all the songs were 100 percent before we recorded them. We had recorded the drums at Q Division, and we did most of the guitars and vocals at Kurt's old studio in Norwood. That way we had more time to work on everything.

Newton: You know, I've never been a great bass player, and I'm well aware of that. But this was the first time that I was in a studio for a long period of time and someone was extremely critical of what I was doing. And I had a hell of a time recording some of those songs—like "Thaw." That song is fuckin' hard to play, and I would get really frustrated. But Kurt really pushed me, and I'm thankful for that, because I've learned a lot from playing with Kurt. He's a great guitarist. And I'm not taking credit for anything because I'm just some douchebag who plays bass, but I will say that Kurt is so much better now than he was then. I've never really said this to him, and maybe it'll make it to print and he'll tear up a little bit, but I'm honored to play with him. I'm constantly blown away by the things he does. But I don't say that when we're writing songs, because I gotta show him who's in charge. [*Laughs*] Which usually turns out to not be me.

Ballou: I did most of the guitars at my studio, which was in Norwood, MA, back then. It was really tough because I was recording myself and there was no one else in the studio, and everything for that record was done on two-inch [tape]. I sat with my shoes off and my feet up near the tape machine so every time I screwed up and had to punch in, I could work the tape machine with my toes while I played. And that machine would punch in, but it wouldn't punch out—or when it did punch out, it made a click. So you had to wait for some silence to punch out or you had to play all the way to the end of the song. It was really, really laborious. I think Matt Ellard actually came down for a day or two to help me out with some of the more challenging punch-ins so I could be free to just play. Between starting recording and mastering, the whole process probably spanned three months. But it's not like we were working the whole time. Jake lost his voice at one point and we had to wait a month to get another mix session. I remember I couldn't stay for all the mix sessions because I was doing some Cave In recording—I think they were demos for RCA or something. After that we went to West West Side to master it with Alan Douches, and I think we actually banged that out in a day. Alan pushed it really hard. To this day when I see him, he still talks about how loud that record is and how people always come into his studio commenting on it or asking him to use it as a reference when mastering their record. So that's cool to hear.

Bannon: Recording vocals was a surreal experience. Most of my tracking was done in the live room at Fort Apache. The studio used to host live recording sessions with audiences in the room, [so] it's set up much like a venue. I was recording on an actual stage with no band behind me—I felt really exposed and isolated by that. I also recorded most of the vocals in the dark. Not sure why, really—I think I was just feeling shy, in a way. By doing that, I was able to just lose control and get all my negative emotion out of me on that stage, and on tape. I listen back now and I sound like a rabid animal in a lot of places. It's definitely vicious. You can hear that real anger and emotion in there for sure.

PART II: FAULT AND FRACTURE

What was Aaron Dalbec's involvement in **Jane Doe** *and what were the circumstances surrounding his departure?*

Newton: Ah, the big question . . . Well, Aaron was around for some of the writing process, but at that time, Bane was really taking off. They were way busier than Converge at that point. It got to the point where he was gone so much and we would have to turn down tours and show offers because he wasn't around. Basically, if we wanted to continue as a band and do the things we wanted to do . . . Aaron just didn't have time to be in Converge. To this day, I'm still not happy about the way everything went down, because I love Aaron and I think he's a great dude.

Bannon: Aaron's role in *Jane Doe* was quite minimal, as it was in all records. In retrospect, he was primarily a live guitarist more than anything. Though he would track on albums, his style of playing wasn't that precise and didn't come off well in a recorded setting. My memory isn't the best, but the only song I remember him ever bringing to the table for Converge was "High Cost of Playing God," which was released on the *When Forever . . .* album. He concentrated his writing for his band, Bane, which was much more fitting for him.

Koller: He wrote a couple riffs here and there, but he was pretty disconnected from the rest of us. We would have rehearsal without him from time to time— then he would come back from a Bane tour and he would have to relearn certain riffs. It really dragged us down. He just couldn't devote his full attention to the band, and we wanted to push it to the next level.

Ballou: I'll let him answer that however he wants to answer it. I mean, he had talked about leaving Converge before, and it was always Bane-related. Bane was his band and suits his taste in music. When he joined Converge, we were a different band and a much less active band. We didn't really have the talents or tools to express ourselves how we wanted to. As we all progressed as musicians and songwriters, we progressed in different directions. I think Aaron was a little too stubborn to leave the band even though he knew it was right, so we kinda told him, "We're gonna do this now, and we just don't think you're able to do this on the level that the rest of us wanna do it, and we don't think you're into this

---

on the level the rest of us are into it, so it's probably time for you to just focus on the band that you're into."

Dalbec: Well, pretty much the way it happened was I had just come back from recording Bane's *Give Blood* record, and we got together to "talk" about our upcoming two-week tour when the record came out. At this point, it was about two or three weeks away. I got there and [was told] pretty much that I had to choose between Bane and Converge. Now, just for the record, Bane had *never* gotten in the way of Converge. It was always Converge first, then Bane. If Converge had a tour, Bane would not book anything—we would even wait for Converge to make plans before we would decide what to do.

As far as when I left the band, it was about two weeks before *Jane Doe* got released. So all the recording for *Jane Doe* had been long done.

Bannon: Matt Ellard, our engineer at the time, had Kurt play most—if not all—of the guitar tracks on the entire *Jane Doe* album. With that said, it was evident to the band and others around us, that [Aaron's] role was becoming a larger issue that couldn't be ignored. After playing an unannounced show with Isis in Cambridge, we called a meeting without Aaron and decided that it was best for him to step down from the band. The next day, the five of us, along with [Deathwish co-owner] Tre [McCarthy] and [former Converge roadie and current booking agent] Matt Pike, sat down and broke the news to him. After that, we did our first tour as a four-piece and loved it. We never had any drive to become a five-piece again.

Newton: Oh, man . . . the way we did this was so shitty. It was the night before we were leaving for tour and we had a band meeting. Everybody kinda sat down and explained stuff, and I think Kurt was the one who said, "Bane's going this way, Converge is going that way. Bane is busy—it's obvious that Bane is your band. A choice has gotta be made here, and we're gonna make the choice for you. You're in Bane." We all knew that it had to be done—and I'm sure Aaron in his heart knew it, too—but it was really fuckin' harsh. The whole situation fuckin' sucked and I'm not happy about the way it went down, but it had to happen sooner or later. We could've waited, and maybe he would've made the same decision himself. Or maybe we could have posed the question to him. But it had to happen eventually. I'd say it worked out better for everyone in the long run.

Dalbec: I was not happy at all about leaving Converge. I had dedicated over eight years of my life to the band and gave as much as I could for that eight years, and helped build the band up to where it was at that point. I had worked through the thick and thin, through the times in the beginning when nobody gave a shit about us, but we still worked our asses off. So I was not too happy about it. Now looking back at it, though, for things to end the way they did, I am happier to not be a part of that. I mean, I was ready to leave for tour and kill it with *Jane Doe* coming out, and at the last minute before the record comes out, they tell me I have to choose between Bane or Converge—and to quote Kurt, "You need to choose between Bane and Converge, and I think you should pick Bane." For someone to say that, there would be no way I would want to continue with them. Some people think I was stupid to say Bane, but when you are in that position, there is no other choice. I felt totally betrayed and let down.

Ballou: Dalbec only played one show on *Jane Doe*, but it was about a week before the album came out. We played a record release show upstairs at the Worcester Palladium—I think we had about 20 copies of the record. I remember because the record came out on September 4 of 2001 and we were supposed to start a tour with Playing Enemy on September 11, but we had a few shows cancelled because of the attacks. We drove through New York when it was still covered in dust. We were comfortable playing all the *Jane Doe* songs as a four-piece because we had pretty much practiced them all as a four-piece. But I remember we weren't sure if we were going to continue as a four-piece or get another guitar player. After that tour, the benefits of the simplified lineup outweighed the benefits of a second guitar player. There's more space onstage, more space in the van, more money to go around, and even though the stage sound might be a little less thick, a four-piece just seems more balanced. Live music can sound like shit, so you can hear the guitar more clearly if there's just one. Some of the older songs ended up suffering, but when you're the only guitar player, you can be a lot more expressive in your guitar playing without worrying about conflicting with someone else.

PART III: THAW

"Hell to Pay" stands out as very different from the rest of the record and very different for Converge at that time in general.

Newton: I guess it kinda was. I remember when I was learning that song—Kurt had written in it—it's basically his Hoover "Warship" right there. I wasn't that into it at the time, but in retrospect, it *is* pretty good. I did four bass tracks for that song. I had two amps and two basses and I played each amp with each bass.

Ballou: It was out of character for Converge, but not for our taste in music. You can hear in a lot of Converge records—going back to at least *Petitioning the Empty Sky* era, maybe even earlier—you can hear the Hoover influence, the Fugazi influence. You can hear me taking their ideas and trying to make them sound more metal. "Hell to Pay," for example, is a combination of that and . . . I think I got into Jesus Lizard a few years before we did that record. So it was our way of doing that, but not trying so hard to make it metal. It gets a little doomy at the end. I think that song is one of the best vocal collaborations we've ever done, actually—definitely the best vocals I've ever done on a Converge song. Especially at the end, when it's me, Nate and Jake switching off—it's pretty cool.

It's hard to imagine "Jane Doe" being anything other than the last song on that record. Did you know that it'd be the closer right away?

Newton: Yeah. It was like, "This is the one." We were all really excited about it.

Dalbec: Yeah, when you listen to the record in all one piece it is very hard to imagine that song anywhere else on the record. When we were writing it, I knew it was going to be slow and brutal, but I was not too sure where on the record it would go. At the time, I had no idea what the lyrics would be like.

Ballou: I think we knew before we recorded it that it would be the closer. I can never remember how songs come to me. To me, songs are just gifts. I mean, I know they're not given to me, but after I'm done writing them I usually have a hard time remembering how it came to me. I'm actually better at remembering what happened with stuff that other people write. With that song, I think I demoed it with a drum machine and showed it to the guys. It was much shorter at the time, and it didn't have the ending. I remember thinking it might not even be a Converge song but they heard it and were like, "Oh, that's awesome—we should use that." So we did.

Do you have a favorite song on the album?

Ballou: I don't know . . . "Hell to Pay" might be my favorite, actually. Or "Distance and Meaning"—two songs we never play. [*Laughs*] Stuff that sounds good live is not always what sounds good on record and stuff that's fun to play live isn't as much fun to listen to on a CD, unfortunately. I've kind of learned that throughout my entire musical experience, going back to playing jazz and classical on saxophone and clarinet when I was a kid.

Bannon: "Phoenix in Flight" gives me goose bumps. "Jane Doe" as well.

Dalbec: I really like "Fault and Fracture" and "Jane Doe." [Those songs] just showed where the band was going, and it was totally new for us. I also really like "Homewrecker."

Koller: Listening back to the record, I really like the song "Distance and Meaning." It sounds very different than anything Converge had done previously. Some of the riffs were Huguenots riffs [a defunct Kurt Ballou side project] and I was a big fan of the Huguenots/SevenPercentSolution 10-inch . . . well, I liked the Huguenots side, at least.

Newton: I love "Jane Doe." As far as the faster, more hardcore songs, I like "The Broken Vow"—and not just because I wrote it. [*Laughs*] It's just a live staple, and it's fun to play. I still really like "Thaw," too.

Tre McCarthy, Kevin Baker from the Hope Conspiracy and "Secret C" have backing vocal credits. I'm assuming the last one is Caleb Scofield from Cave In.
Ballou: Yeah. He was under contract with RCA at the time. He didn't think there would be any problem, but we thought it would be better not to take any chances. Isn't his publishing company called Secret C? I think it might be. All those guys were on "The Broken Vow"—I think that was the only song they were on. On the last line, "I'll take my love to the grave," with each repetition of the riff, we'd add another person. So it's Jake, me, Nate and then those guys, one at a time.

PART IV: UNIDENTIFIED FEMALE VICTIM

There's obviously a distinctly female theme dominating the album artwork. What inspired it, and how does it tie into some of the lyrical concepts?
Bannon: At the time I was going through a great deal of negativity in my life. When I was refining the lyrics, it was apparent that the album thematically dealt with that relationship disintegrating. The album was my lyrical purging of that experience. The artwork visually encapsulates that lyrical theme. The visuals attempted to capture the feeling of disintegration and rebirth. I spent a great deal of time on that—building figures out of texture and acrylic, scanning multiple layers of imagery, etc. I spent close to a month creating large mixed media pieces for each song on the album. I used a high-contrast approach to the artwork, as it was a style I was growing towards at the time. I felt that the cold iconographic feel was extremely fitting for the subject matter.

Was it your intention to obscure some of the lyrics in the layout, or did it just work out best that way, visually speaking?
Bannon: I wanted to incorporate them into the pieces themselves, so yes, it was intentional. I remember Equal Vision not being happy about it, as it broke from the standard that was set for the time. I don't care much for rules.

Did Jake discuss the lyrical themes with the rest of you?
Newton: Not really. On every record, we just let Jake do his thing. We had a general idea, though. I actually thought of the name *Jane Doe* when we were on

our first European tour—I think I may have seen a pamphlet or a billboard about violence against women or some shit. I just thought it was a cool name. If I remember correctly, we talked a little bit about the idea of a nameless, faceless victim. Jake sorta took the ball and ran with it.

Dalbec: Jake never really discussed any of the artwork or lyrics with any of us. It was kind of always a surprise when the record was done.

Koller: Nate and Jake came up with the whole concept for the record, I guess. I don't tend to get too involved with the art concepts. I just focus on the skins.

Ballou: He's pretty private about that, and we don't pry too much. He's become more open with that over time, and at least with me, he's gotten me more involved with phrasing and stuff. But circa *Jane Doe*, we just recorded his ideas the way he had it in his head and that's just the way it was. There's definitely a lot of mutual trust and admiration between us as songwriters. And whenever you have too many cooks in the kitchen, it tends to dilute the food. That's how it is with a lot of modern metallic hardcore, too—there's just too many ingredients in the mix. You've got your guy who screams, your guy who growls, and then you've got your melodic, Dashboard Confessional–style vocals here and there. I've always been opposed to that—I like to have a cohesive direction and a cohesive vision. So I don't really get in Jake's way too much and, in turn, he doesn't get in our way, either.

About a year after the record came out, I was walking down Cahuenga Boulevard in Los Angeles with Juan Perez and saw a huge oil painting that someone had done of the Jane Doe *cover. At first we thought it was Jake's original, but we later found out that it wasn't.*

Bannon: Yeah, I heard about that. That painting was also a few blocks from our lawyer's office in L.A. It was definitely a rendition of our cover, but it was meant to be an homage, not a lift, I guess. There have also been some other incidents. One high-end clothing company chose to use the image on a variety of t-shirts. They actually solicited my girlfriend's old store to carry their items and she brought it to my attention. When our lawyer contacted them, they claimed they got the image from a poster they saw on a wall in Italy, to which I responded, "Yeah, our tour poster." They later sent us their stock of apparel and I destroyed it. I've had that happen with other images I've made for other bands as well. The world is full of thieves. Since the release of the album, there have also been countless attempts at emulating that style of artwork. The attempts are both flattering and insulting. I feel that if you are putting that much effort into creating something to represent your band visually, you should do something original. Use your own artistic voice, not ours.

Newton: It's interesting to me how the cover of that record—the *Jane Doe* face—has become almost iconic in the hardcore scene. It's almost like the new Misfits skull or something—not that I'd compare us to that, but it blows my mind that we still sell a shitload of *Jane Doe* shirts. Go to a hardcore show and there's a good chance you'll see a kid wearing a Converge shirt, and there's a good chance it'll be a *Jane Doe* shirt. The face doesn't call to mind anything specific, but at the same time, it's a strong image that you can put meaning into. I think that's what makes certain pieces of art powerful—you can look at it and put your own meaning into it. It seemed like during that time period, Jake and Aaron Turner really put the focus on fine art back into album artwork—at least in this scene. It wasn't just, "Here's a picture of the band, here's our lyrics, here's our logo."

PART V: PHOENIX IN FLAMES

Do you remember reading any reviews of the album when it came out?

Ballou: I remember we got Album of the Year in *Terrorizer*. I was pretty blown away that it was being received that way, actually. At that point in time, we were a band that had had some moderate success—people liked us, and we never really did support tours—we had been able to tour the U.S. a few times on our own as headliners. But I didn't really feel like we had done a record that was a milestone in our genre. People consider *Petitioning the Empty Sky* that, but in general, the people who revered that record highly, I didn't revere their taste in music all that highly, so it didn't mean a lot to me. And it's not even an album, really—that originally came out on seven-inch. And then we recorded extra songs and put it out on CD. There's live tracks, too—it's really just a collection of stuff.

Newton: I remember the *Terrorizer* review that came out before they gave us Album of the Year. I felt pretty good about the record, but when I read that I was like, "Whoa!" Not that *Terrorizer* is the be-all, end-all musical judgment, but I remember thinking of it as a magazine that tears everything to shreds. I think they gave us a 9.5—it was a pretty big compliment.

How did things change for Converge after **Jane Doe** *came out?*

Ballou: *Jane Doe* was the first record where people I really respected responded positively to it—people my age and older than us actually started to respect Converge. That meant a lot to me, because prior to that, I felt like we hadn't really come into our own yet. People definitely treat you differently when you do something that they enjoy or respect musically. We got a lot of opportunities from the record label, booking agents were more interested in us, other bands were more interested in getting us to tour with them and other bands were interested in touring with us. And a lot more bands were interested in coming into my studio to record with me and getting Jake to design their records. On a personal level, doing something that resonated with people greatly affected my life outside of Converge in addition to inside Converge. Looking back on it, it was a major turning point in my professional life.

Newton: Definitely more people started coming to shows. It was definitely a gradual process, but it was happening. We suddenly got more attention from the metal community, too, and I think that had to do with the *Terrorizer* review. All of a sudden we were validated. People who had wanted nothing to do with us before all of a sudden thought we were great and wanted to go on tour with us. And because *Terrorizer* is based in the U.K., we noticed a vast difference when we went back to Europe. But honestly, I think *Petitioning* and *When Forever Comes Crashing* are more metal than *Jane Doe*—at least as far as blatantly playing metal riffs. The influence is certainly there on *Jane Doe*, but I feel like it's a much more punk record.

Bannon: I try not to pay attention to outside opinion to our band, so I'm not really sure. My goal with the album was the same as any other—to create something that our band could collectively be moved by, challenged by and proud of. *Jane Doe* was that for all of us, so that's the only real success that matters for me.

Jane Doe *was your last album on Equal Vision. Were you already planning on moving to Epitaph at that point?*

Ballou: No, we were planning on doing one more with EVR. They definitely ride a lot of fences between being a hardcore label and a rock label, and we couldn't really get behind any of the stuff they had on the label. We did a few Equal Vision showcase kinda shows, and we just wanted to align ourselves with something that fit the spirit of Converge—not necessarily the sound of Converge, but what we were about. We still like the EVR guys and we get along, but we just felt like we didn't have a lot in common with [their roster]. There were assorted tensions with them, but Epitaph approached us—we didn't approach them. So we got this opportunity to work with a label that's run by really good people who come from a DIY punk background and who still have those ideals. They run a successful business, but they still have that punk ethic that they had when they were younger—they still put art ahead of profit. Their basic philosophy is to work with established artists that are credible and have long-lasting success rather than seeking out the next big thing and jumping on it. I mean, they've made a few of those kinds of signings in recent history, but in general, I mean . . . they're working with Nick Cave and Tom Waits—they've got a classic catalogue.

Bannon: We were under the assumption that it was our last album for the label, but we didn't pay much attention to that. Our goal was just to write and record the best album that we could at the time. The creative end of what we are takes precedent over any business nonsense. After the album was released and we did our first world touring in support of the album, we started discussing what we wanted to do next as a band. That is when we first started experiencing turbulence with Equal Vision. Our experience with Equal Vision was certainly not all negative. In hindsight, I feel that we simply grew apart from one another. Their direction and our own didn't follow the same road of understanding. It was best that it ended when it did.

Newton: To be honest with you, a lot of it I don't even know. I sort of treated it like, "Hey—whatever, man. I just play bass." But I do remember thinking at that point that EVR was kind of getting away from hardcore. But it's kinda weird, I guess. If we had stayed on EVR, I probably would've been fine with it. I mean, it's a record label—who cares? But when the idea of signing to Epitaph came up, we were definitely really excited about it. They put out Tom Waits and Solomon Burke, all this cool shit. Obviously, Epitaph has put out some duds that I don't want to have anything to do with, but for every record they put out that I hate, they put out two that it's obvious they put out because they think it's good.

Do you think of Jane Doe *any differently now than you did when you recorded it?*

Newton: Yes and no—no in the sense that I don't really dwell on stuff that we've already done. We did a record, we toured on it and I'm on to the next shit. I'm proud of everything I've done, but I don't sit around thinking, "Yeah—I wrote *Jane Doe!*" In that respect, it feels like it's just something else we did. It's history to me. But at the same time, I feel differently about it now that I'm able to step back and see how that record might've affected the hardcore scene in general.

Bannon: Not really. Each new album you write and release becomes the most relevant, so it's not on my immediate radar—*No Heroes* is. But I am still excited by what the album accomplished creatively.

Koller: I like our new record *No Heroes* more than *Jane Doe* now. Maybe it's because the songs are fresher and more energetic live, or I'm just older and my tastes have changed. I like how salty and heavy *No Heroes* is. It gets me pumped up and makes me want to punch concrete walls.

Dalbec: I still think it's a great record, but after what happened I cannot look at it the same way.

Ballou: Every time we do a record now, I always have to prepare myself for kids and reviewers to say it's not as good as *Jane Doe*. Whenever any band does a landmark kinda thing, they'll never get past it. Metallica's never gonna do another *Master of Puppets*, you know? Slayer's never gonna do another *Reign in Blood*—or Pantera and *Vulgar Display of Power*. So I don't let that stuff affect me too much. Every once in a while I'll read something or someone will say something to me that will make me feel like I've peaked, but when we were doing *Jane Doe*, we definitely weren't of the mindset that we'd peaked. We weren't chasing our own shadow. Which is pretty much how we work now, but it's always in the back of your head. Not "Are we still good enough?" But "Are people gonna think we're still good enough?" I don't want my music to ever be driven by people's opinion of it, but, you know, it's hard to go about life completely independent of other people's opinions of you. So it was nice to be in a situation, with *Jane Doe*, where I didn't have to think about that at all.

In retrospect, is there anything you'd change about the album?

Bannon: No, nothing.

Koller: No, because the imperfections and rough edges are what gives the record so much character. A lot of my playing was really spur-of-the-moment and improvisational, and what I play live for those songs now is so much different than what's on the record.

Newton: Oh, yeah. I'd rewrite a couple of the songs, for sure—like "Fault and Fracture," definitely. It has parts that don't need to be there and parts that are too long—same with "Heaven in Her Arms." And I don't like how the record sounds overall—it's so compressed and metal. It sounds like it's cutting into your ears. I guess that's what some people love about it, but to me it sounds robotic. I like records with dynamics, where it goes from quiet to loud, where you can hear the guy breathing in the background when it gets quiet. But this record seems like it's one volume—really loud and in your face—all the way across the board. At the time, I thought it was pretty cool, because there wasn't another hardcore record that sounded like it. But in retrospect, I'm not very happy with how it sounds. And you can really hardly hear the bass on most of the songs—which is OK, I guess, 'cause I wasn't happy with my bass tone. Overall, I think the songs on *You Fail Me* and *No Heroes* are much better, and I love the recordings on those records. Pound for pound, I think both of those records are better than *Jane Doe*.

It's the time-and-place syndrome, though. People heard this record at a certain point in their lives and equate it with certain memories, so it holds a special place for them. For us, it's the record where we really started to change as a band. We came out of our shells and said, "This is what we're capable of." With certain bands, it's always one record that sticks with people. Like Entombed's *Wolverine Blues*—that was the record where Entombed started to change, and it grabbed people's attention. And there's no other record like that record. So I can understand why people say that about *Jane Doe*, but it's not my favorite record, personally.

Ballou: I wouldn't make it so loud. [*Laughs*] No, I don't know if I really would. But from an engineering perspective, I had to listen to *Jane Doe* while I was engineering and mixing *No Heroes*, because I had to make sure the new record sounded as least as good as that. And in the minds of some of the people in my band and some of our listeners, sounding as good also means that it needs to be as loud. Every stereo I've seen has a volume knob, but for some reason, people seem to demand that their records be obscenely loud. There's not really much more space on a CD to make it louder than *Jane Doe*, so it's getting challenging to make records that have as much or more impact from a sonic perspective. Other than that, I don't particularly care for the chorus of "Fault and Fracture," but there's really nothing on the record that gives me idiot shivers. Prior to *Jane Doe*, there's stuff in every song that we did that gave me idiot shivers.

PHOTO CREDITS

Black Sabbath © Fin Costello
Diamond Head © Simon Fowler
Celtic Frost, photographer unknown
Slayer © Joe Giron
Napalm Death reproduced courtesy of Earache Records
Repulsion reproduced courtesy of Relapse Records
Morbid Angel reproduced courtesy of Earache Records
Obituary © Tim Hubbard (both images)
Entombed, photographer unknown
Paradise Lost reproduced courtesy of Peaceville Records
Carcass reproduced courtesy of Earache Records
Cannibal Corpse reproduced courtesy of Metal Blade Records
Eyehategod reproduced courtesy of Century Media Records (both images)
Darkthrone, photographer unknown
Kyuss © Mike Anderson
Meshuggah reproduced courtesy of Nuclear Blast Records
Monster Magnet © Joe Giron
At the Gates reproduced courtesy of Earache Records (both images)
Opeth, photographer unknown
Down reproduced courtesy of East/West Records
Emperor, photographer unknown
Sleep, photographer unknown (all images)
The Dillinger Escape Plan © Paul D'elia
Botch © Jason Hellmann
Converge © Jason Hellmann (both images)

Every effort has been made to contact all copyright holders. If notified, the publisher will be pleased to rectify any errors or omissions at the earliest opportunity.

INDEX